Good
ARABIC-ENGLISH
Dictionary

Mohd Harun Rashid

Goodword Books

First published 2007
Reprinted 2014
© Goodword Books 2014

Goodword Books
1, Nizamuddin West Market, New Delhi-110 013
Tel. +9111-4182-7083, Mob. +91-8588822672
email: info@goodwordbooks.com
www.goodwordbooks.com

Goodword Books, Chennai
324, Triplicane High Road,
Triplicane, Chennai-600005
Tel. +9144-4352-4599
Mob. +91-9790853944, 9600105558
email: chennaigoodword@gmail.com

Islamic Vision Ltd.
426-434 Coventry Road, Small Heath
Birmingham B10 0UG, U.K.
Tel. 121-773-0137
Fax: 121-766-8577
e-mail: info@ipci-iv.co.uk
www.islamicvision.co.uk

IB Publisher Inc.
81 Bloomingdale Rd, Hicksville, NY 11801, USA
Tel. 516-933-1000
Fax: 516-933-1200
Toll Free: 1-888-560-3222
email: info@ibpublisher.com
www.ibpublisher.com

Printed in India

Preface

Arabic, one of the most widely used languages, occupies a prominent place among the major languages of the world. It is spoken by 170 million people in more than twenty different countries, from Morocco in the west to Iraq in the east, and as far south as Somalia and Sudan. Many languages, including English, Turkish, Persian, Spanish, Portuguese, Pashto and Urdu, have been enriched by words of Arabic origin. Studies show that English alone possesses nearly 1000 such words.

As the language of the Quran, the holy book of Islam, it is taught as a second language in Muslim countries across the globe. With its roots in pre-Islamic Arabia, it spread far and wide in the wake of Arab conquests from the seventh century onwards. The importance of this language should not, however, be gauged in the limited context of its religious significance, but in the broader terms of its international acceptance and relevance. It is noteworthy that the United Nations has included it among the selected languages of communication.

Economic, social, religious and political developments have recently created global interest in Arabic. It is to satisfy this newly awakened popular urge to become acquainted with the language that we have compiled this Arabic-English dictionary. This new, medium-sized volume, containing more than twenty thousand words and phrases, presents the entire range of vocabulary and phraseology in a clear and straightforward manner.

All the words and phrases have been completely vowelized. Unlike in English, diacritical signs (حَرَكات)play an important role in the pronunciation of Arabic words. Without them, it is very difficult for learners to achieve any level of accuracy. Keeping this in view, we have put them in for each and every character. Another striking characteristic of the dictionary is that, as well as all of the words having been etymologically arranged, they have been alphabetically listed to make it as easily approachable for beginners as it is for advanced learners. This pattern of arranging words will, no doubt, make it easier for users to cross check references. In particular, it will be more helpful to those who have not made a close study of Arabic morphology.

The dictionary includes not only classical words and phrases, but also words borrowed from foreign languages which have become current in modern texts. However, we have made every effort to select only those words and expressions which are in regular use. All slang and obsolete words have been deliberately discarded in order to avoid unnecessary enlargement of the dictionary.

All these features make it one of the most useful and reliable dictionaries for average as well as advanced learners. As will be attested to by usage, it is an accurate record of the language, and we hope it will meet the needs of all those who have felt the need to possess just such a dictionary.

M. Harun Rashid
March. 2007

originality, creation, uniqueness	إبْدَاع
change, alteration, replacement	إبْدال
monster, unusual thing	آبِدة
everlasting, eternal, perpetual	أَبَدي
eternity, endlessness, perpetuity	أَبَديّة
acquittal, absolution, discharge	إبْراء
displaying, production, presentation	إبْراز
confirmation, ratification, settlement	إبْرام
needle, tip, pin, stamen	إبْرَة (إبَر)
magnetic needle	إبْرَة مَغْناطيسيّة
speckled, spotted	أَبْرَش
parish, bishopric	أَبْرَشيّة
leper, leprous	أَبْرَص
pure gold	إبْريز
silk	إبْريسَم/إبْريْسم
water-jug, pitcher	إبْريق (أَباريق)
tea-pot	إبْريق الشاي

particle of interrogation	أ
August	آب
reluctant, unwilling	آب
father, male, parent	أَب (آباء)
rejection, refusal, dislike	إباء/إباءة
permissiveness, permission, justification	إباحَة
permissive, nihilist, licentious	إباحي
extermination, extirpation, eradication, demolition	إبادة
bale, large bundle	إبّالَة
time, season	إبّان
during	إبّانَ
tailless, curtailed, issueless	أَبْتَر
alphabetic-al	أَبْجَدي
wild, untamed	آبد
perpetuity, eternity	أَبَد (آباد)
always, forever, ever, never	أَبَدًا
expression, disclosure, displaying	إبْداء

bastard, natural son	إِبْن حَرَام	jug, ewer	إِبْرِيق الغَسِيل
knot	أَبْنَة	coffee-pot	إِبْرِيق القَهْوَة
ebony	أَبْنُوس	April	أَبْرِيل
ambiguity, obscurity, uncertainty	إِبْهام	wash-basin	أَبْزَن (أَبَازن)
thumb	إِبْهام (أَباهِيم)	clasp, buckle	إِبْزِيم (أَبَازِيم)
pomp, ostentation, grandeur	أَبَّهَة	armpit, axil	إِبْط (آباط)
Adam, progenitor of human race	أَبُو البَشَر	tarrying, slowing down, retardation	إِبْطاء
robin	أَبُو الحِناء	abolition, suppression, cancellation	إِبْطَال
poppy	أَبُو التَّوم	removal, elimination, separation	إِبْعاد
the Sphinx	أَبُو الْهَوْل	farther, more distant	أَبْعَد
rooster, cock	أَبُو اليَقْظَان	fugitive, runaway	آبق
stork	أَبُو حُدَيْج	flax, a kind of hemp	أَبَق
fatherhood, paternity	أُبُوَّة	dumb, mute	أَبْكَم
fatherly, paternal	أَبُوي	camel	إِبِل
disdainful, haughty, supercilious	أَبِيّ	conveyance, delivery, transmission	إِبْلاغ
white, clean, fair	أَبْيَض	serene, nice, fair, bright	أَبْلَح
following, coming, arriving	آتٍ	intenser, deeper, graver	أَبْلَغ
she ass	أَتَان	foolish, silly, stupid	أَبْلَه
tax, royalty, tribute	إِتَاوَة	devil, satan	إِبْلِيس (أَبَالِسَة)
fees, honorarium	أَتْعَاب	human being	إِبْن آدَم

affirmative, assertive, confirmatory	إِثْبَاتي	precision, perfection, proficiency	إِتْقان
selfish, egoistic	أَثِر	more perfect, more thorough	أَتْقَن
impression, trace, mark, monument	أَثَر (آثار)	reclining, leaning	إِتِّكَاء
bad impression	أَثر سَيِّئ	injury destruction, ruination, harm	إِتْلاف
antiquity, ancient monument	أَثَر قَدِيم	more perfect, more complete	أَتَمّ
selfishness, egoism	أَثَرَة	completion, perfection, fulfilment	إِتْمام
monumental, rudimentary, archeologist	أَثَري	autobus, bus	أُتُوبِيس
sinner, sinful, criminal, evildoer	آثِم	automatic	أُتُوماتِيكي
sin, crime, offense, evil	إِثْم (آثام)	automobile, motor car	أُتُوموبِيل
fruitage, produce	إِثْمار	oven, furnace	أَتُون/أَتُّون
antimony	أُثْمُد/إِثْمِد	abundant, pump, luxuriant	أَثّ/أَثِيث
during, in the course of	أَثْناء	furnitures, furnishings	أَثَاث
ether, preferred	أَثِير	monument, traces, relics	آثار
sinful, criminal, evil, culpable	أَثِيم	remnant, vestige	أَثَارة
Ethiopia	أَثِيوبِيا	stirring up, arousing, excitation, agitation, stimulation	إِثارة
replying, responding, response	إِجَابة	evidence, affirmation, confirmation, establishment	إِثْبات
poignant, pungent, bitter	أُجَاج		

procedure, proceeding	إِجْرَاء قَانُونِي
proceedings, measures	إِجْرَاءات
precautionary measures	إِجْرَاءات تَحَفُّظِيّة
preliminary proceedings	إِجْرَاءَات تَمْهِيْدِيَّة
drastic measures	إِجْرَاءات عَنِيْفة
legal proceedings	إِجْرَاءات قَانُونِيّة
wages, charge, rent, hire, price	أُجْرَة
postage, mailing charges	أُجْرة البَرِيد
tuition fees	أُجْرَة التَّعْلِيم
cartage, freight, transport, charges, carriage	أُجْرة النَّقْل
bald, bleak, shabby	أَجْرَد
druggist, pharmacist	أَجْزَائِي
drugstore, pharmacy	أَجْزَائِيّة
husky, hoarse, hollow	أَجَشّ
delayed, future, later	آجِل
yes, certainly	أَجَل
period, term, appointed time	أَجَل (آجال)

burning, blazing, fervent	أَجَّاج
annihilation, damage, destruction	إِجَاحَة
letting, leasing, hiring out	إِجَارَة
permission, leave, permit, licence	إِجَازَة (إِجَازات)
driving license	إِجَازَة السَّوْق
sick leave	إِجَازَة مَرَضِيّة
pear, plum	إِجَّاص
compulsion, coercion	إِجْبَار
obligatory, compulsory	إِجْبَارِي
injustice, bias, unfairness	إِجْحَاف
barren, sterile	أَجْدَب
worthier, more appropriate	أَجْدَر
mutilated, maimed	أَجْدَع
more useful	أَجْدَى
leprous, leper	أَجْذَم
baked brick	آجُرّ
wages, pay, reward, recompense	أَجْر (أُجُور)
execution, performance	إِجْرَاء

labourer, worker, employee	أَجِير (أَجَراء)	honour, respect, reverence	إجْلال
units, digits	آحَاد	the hereafter	آجِلة
encompassment, enclosure, encirclement	إحَاطة	bald-headed, hairless	أَجْلَح
referring, transferring, remittance	إحَالة	unanimity, general consent, agreement	إجْمَاع
dearer, more lovable	أَحَبّ	unanimous resolution	إجْماع الرَّأْي
foiling, thwarting, baffling	إحْباط	unanimous, based on general consent	إجْماعي
snare, noose, net	أُحْبُولة	summing up, totalling	إجْمَال
retreat, restraint, abstention	إحْجام	general, over-all, collective	إجْمالي
hooked, crooked, bent	أَحْجَن	thicket, jungle	أَجَمة (أَجَمات/أُجُم)
riddle, puzzle, conundrum	أُحْجِيّة (أَحَاجِي)	whole, entire, all	أَجْمَع
one, someone, unit	أَحَد	more beautiful, prettier	أَجْمَل
eleven	أَحَدَ عَشَر/إحْدَى عشرة	brackish water	آجِن
encompassment, encirclement	إحْدَاق	stranger, foreigner, alien	أَجْنَبِي
newer, more recent	أَحْدَث	exertion, straining	إجْهاد
someone, somebody	أَحَدما	abortion, miscarriage	إجْهاض
gossip, topic of conversation	أُحْدُوثة (أَحَاديث)	better	أَجْوَد
unity, oneness	أَحَديّة	empty, hollow, concave	أَجْوَف

lower, baser, poorer	أحْقَر	إحْراز	attainment, acquirement, achievement
precision, perfection, exactitude	إحْكام	إحْراق	burning, setting a fire, incineration
bons vivants, playboys	أخْلاَس اللَّهْو	إحْرام	ihram
more thankful, more laudable	أحْمَد	أحْرَى	more proper, more appropriate
red, ruddy, rosy	أحْمَر	إحْساس	feeling, sense, sensitivity
lipstick	أحْمَر الشفاه	إحْساس (احساسات)	feelings, sentiments
blood-red	أحْمَر قَانٍ	إحْساس الانْحطاط	sense of inferiority
enthusiastic, strenuous, zealous	أحْمَس	إحْساس مُشْتَرَك	concord, harmony
stupid, silly, foolish	أحْمَق	إحْسان	benevolence, charity, beneficence
club-footed	أحْنَف	أحْسَن	better, more beautiful
squint-eyed, wall-eyed	أحْوَل	إحْصَاء	counting, reckoning, calculating
livelier, more vigorous	أحْيَ	إحْصاء السُّكّان	census
revival, revitalization, animation	إحْياء	إحْصاء النُّفُوس	census
commemoration	إحْياء الذِّكْر	إحْصائي	statistical, statistician
biological, biologist	أحْيائي	إحْصائيّة	statistics
sometimes, occasionally	أحْيانًا	إحْضَار	bringing, fetching
brother, friend	أخ (إخْوان/إخْوة)	أحَقّ	more deserving, worthier
brother-in-law	أخ الزَّوْج/الزَّوْجة		

in the end, finally	آخِر الأمْر	full brother	أخ شَقيق
terminus	آخِر الطَّريق	foster brother	أخ في الرِّضاعة
the hereafter, the future life	آخِر/آخِرة	fraternity, brotherhood	إخاء/إخاوة
last but not least	آخِرًا وليس أخيراً	captivating, alluring, attractive	أخّاذ
taking out, dismissal, producing, evacuation	إخْراج	information, notification	إخْبار
dumb, mute, silent	أخْرَس	sports news	أخْبار رياضيّة
awkward, stupid, clumsy	أخْرَق	evening news	أخْبار مَسائيّة
relating to the future life	أخْرَوي	sister, counterpart	أُخْت (أخَوات)
the hereafter	أُخْرَى	sister-in-law	أُخْت الزَّوْج/الزَّوْجة
other, another (fem. of آخَر)	أُخْرَى	full sister	أُخْت شَقيقة
more fearful	أخْشَى	foster sister	أُخْت في الرِّضاعة
more specific	أخَصّ	groove, rut, trench	أُخْدُود
fertility	إخْصاب	taking, receiving, acceptance	أخْذ
subjugation, subjection, vanquishing	إخْضاع	argument, dispute, discussion	أخْذ ورَدّ
green, green coloured	أخْضَر	give and take, dealings	أخْذ وعَطاء
notification, warning, advice	إخْطار	other, another, the latter	آخَر (أُخَر)
lighter, weaker, slighter	أخَفّ	end, last, utmost, extreme, limit	آخِر (آخِرون/ أواخِر)
lesser of the two evils	أخَفّ الضَّرَرَيْن		

etiquette, rules of decorum	آدَاب السُّلُوك	hiding, concealment	إخْفَاء
tool, instrument, device, particle	أداة (أَدَوَات)	day blind, bat blind	أخْفَش
definite article	أداة التَّعْرِيف	ejecting, evacuating, emptying, release	إخْلاَء
indefinite article	أداة التَّنْكِير	sincerity, loyalty, frankness, fidelity	إخْلاَص
management, office, administration, reversion, turning	إدَارة	moral, manners, character	أخْلاق
mandatory administration	إدَارَة انْتِدَابِيّة	moral, ethical	أخْلاقِي
administrative, departmental	إدَارِي	infringement, violation, breach	إخْلال
condiment, fat, grease	إدَام	breach of the peace	إخْلال بالأمْن
conviction	إدَائة	breach of promise	إخْلال بالْعَهْد
host, entertainer	آدب	extinction, quelling, extinguishing	إخْماد
good manners, politeness, decorum, decency, refinement	أدَب (آداب)	brotherliness, fraternity	أُخُوّة/أخَوِيّة
retreat, flight, turning the back	إدْبار	fraternal, brotherly	أخَوِي
moral, ethical, literary	أدَبِي	the last, latest	أخِير
dark, obscure	أدْجَن	better, more excellent	أخْيَر
taking in, bringing in, insertion	إدْخال	finally, at last	أخِيراً
entry, insertion, registration	إدْرَاج	performance, rendition, payment, execution	أدَاء
		morals, decency	آداب

أدَوات البنَاء	building materials	إدْرَاك	attainment, obtaining, reaching, realization, understanding, reason, consciousness
أدَوات الكتابة	writing materials, stationery	أدْرَد	toothless
أدَوات المَائدة	tableware	أدْرَى	more knowledgeable
أدَوات المَطْبَخ	kitchen utensils	إدْغَام	insertion, incorporation
أدَوات حَرْبيّة	war materials	أدَقّ	more delicate, more accurate
أدَوات مَنْزليّة	household materials	أدْكَن	dark, blackish
أديب (أُدَباء)	man of letters, writer, well-mannered	آدَم	Adam
أديم	skin, hide, leather, surface	أُدْم	seasoning, condiment
أديم الأرض	surface of the earth	أدَم/أدَمة	skin, dern
إذْ	then, at that time	إدْماج	insertion, interpolation
إذْ ذاك	then, therefore, consequently	إدْمَان	addiction, dipsomania
إذا	then, in that case, if, when	آدَمي	human, humane
		أدْنَأ	inferior to, lower than
إذَابَة	dissolving, melting	أدْناه	hereunder
آذار	March	أدْنَى	lower, inferior, closer
إذَاعَة	announcement, propagation, promulgation	أدْهَم	jet-black, pitch-black
		أدْهَى	shrewder, craftier, subtler
إذَاعَة (إذَاعات)	radio broadcast	أدَوات احْتيَاطيّة	stand-by equipment

manufacturers, industrialists	أَرْبَاب المَصَانِع	broadcast, news cast	إِذَاعَة الأَخْبَار
skill, cleverness, intelligence	إِرْبَة	television broadcast	إِذَاعَة تِلْفِزْيُونِيّة
fourteen	أَرْبَع عشرة/ أَرْبَعَة عشر	radio broadcast	إِذَاعَة لاسِلْكِيّة
four	أَرْبَع/أَرْبَعَة	call to prayer	أَذان
Wednesday	أَرْبِعاء	compliance, obedience, submission	إِذْعان
forty	أَرْبَعُون	humiliation, debasement	إِذْلَال
inheritance, legacy, heritage	إِرْث	then, it that case	إِذَنْ
fragrant, sweet-smelling	أَرِج	permission, leave, license	إِذْن
fragrance, scent, sweet smell	أَرَج/أَرِيج	ear, handle	أُذُن/أُذْن (آذان)
adjournment, postponement	إِرْجَاء	aural, pertaining to the ear	أُذُنِي
return, refundment	إِرْجَاع	injury, harm, damage, offence	أَذًى/أَذِيّة
preferable, preponderant	أَرْجَح	will, desire, volition, intention	إِرَادَة
prevalence, probability, preponderance	أَرْجَحِيّة	voluntary, intentional	إِرَادِي
purple	أُرْجُوان	shedding, spilling	إِرَاقَة
purple coloured	أُرْجُوانِي	bloodshed	إِرَاقَة الدَّم
seasaw, swing	أُرْجُوحة	need, want, desire, skill	أَرَب (آراب)
Jordan	أُرْدُن	artists	أَرْباب الفُنُون
rice	أُرُزّ		

thinner, finer	أَرَقّ	sending, dispatch	إِرْسَال
spotted, variegated	أَرْقَش	guidance, instruction, direction	إِرْشاد
spotted, speckled	أَرْقَط	earth, ground, land	أَرْض (أَرَاضٍ)
more progressed	أَرْقَى	barren land, wasteland	أَرْض بُور
sore-eyed	أَرْمَد	agricultural or arable land	أَرْض زِرَاعِيّة
widower	أَرْمَل (أَرَامل)	wasteland, deserted land	أَرْض قَفْر
widow	أَرْمَلَة (أَرَامل/أَرَاملَة)	satisfying, fulfilment	إِرْضاء
rabbit, hare	أَرْنَب (أَرَانب)	suckling, lactation	إِرْضَاع
frightening, terrorism, threatening	إِرْهَاب	earthly, terrestrial	أَرْضِي
terrorist, terroristic	إِرْهَابي	floor, ground	أَرْضِيّة
Europe	أُوروبا	background	أَرْضِيّة الصُّورَة
European	أُوروبي	battalion	أُرْطَة/أُورطة
root, stump of a tree	أُرُومة/أُرُومة	frightening, terrifying	إِرْعَاب
skilful, clever, ingenious	أَرِيب	coercion, compulsion	إِرْغام
sofa, throne, raised coach	أَرِيكة (أَرَائك)	organ (in music)	أَرْغُن
opposite to, in the face of	إِزاء	flute, clarionet	أُرْغُول
elimination, abolition, removal	إِزَاحَة	higher, loftier, more sublime	أَرْفَع
wrapper, veil, cover, loincloth	إِزار (أُزُر)	sleeplessness, insomnia	أَرَق
removal, elimination, obliteration	إِزَالَة		

basic, fundamental, chief	أَساسي	hairy, shaggy	أَزَبّ
documents, records	أَسَانيد	dumpy, short and fat	إزْب
luxuries, ease and comfort	أَسْبَاب الرَّاحَة	strength, might, back	أَزْر
means of communication	أَسْبَاب المُوَاصَلَة	blue	أَزْرَق
spinach	إسْبَانخ	disturbance, trouble	إزْعَاج
previous, former, preceding	أَسْبَق	purer, better	أَزْكَى
seniority, priority	أَسْبَقيّة	eternity, sempiternity	أَزَل
week	أُسْبُوع (أَسَابيع)	eternal, everlasting	أَزَلي
next week	أُسْبُوع آتي	crisis, turning point	أَزمة (أَزَمات)
Passion Week	أُسْبُوع الآلام	chisel	إزْميْل (أَزَاميل)
weekly	أُسْبُوعي	florescence, bloom	إزْهَار
teacher, professor	أُسْتاذ (أَساتذة)	bright, shining, luminous	أَزْهَر
visiting professor	أُستاذ زائر	more flourishing, more brilliant	أَزْهَى
assistant professor	أُستاذ مُسَاعِد	whiz, whizzing, buzzing, fizzing	أَزيز
black	أَسْحَم	myrtle	آس
more relevant, more appropriate	أَسَدّ	basis, foundation	أُسّ
lion, leo	أَسَد (أُسُد)	offence, sin, insult	إساءَة
captivating, fascinating	آسِر	ill-treatment, mistreatment	إساءَة المُعَامَلَة
capture, captivity	أَسْر	enthralment, strap, captivity	إسَار
		foundation, origin, base, basis	أَساس (أُسُس)

إِسْكان housing, settling, settlement	إِسْرَاء night journey
إِسْلَام submission, yielding, religion of Islam	إِسْرَاف lavish expenditure, extravagance, prodigality
إِسْلاَمِي Islamic	أُسْرة (أُسَر) family, relatives
أَسَلة thorn, spike, tip	أَسْرَع quicker, faster
أَسْلِحَة نَارِيّة fire arms	أَسْطَع brighter, more luminous
أَسْلِحَة نَوَوِيّة nuclear weapons	أُسْطُورة (أَسَاطير) legend, fable, fiction, myth
أَسْلَم safer, sounder, healthier	أُسْطُوري fabulous, legendary, mythical
أُسْلوب (أَسَالِيْب) style, method, manner, way	إِسْعَاف (إِسْعَافَات) aid, help, relief
أُسْلُوب فَصِيْح pure style	أسْعَد happier, more fortunate
أُسْلُوب كِتَابِي literary style	آسِف sorry, regretful, sad
أَسْمَر brown, dark	أَسَف grief, sorrow, regret
أَسْمَى higher, more sublime	أَسْفَل lower part, bottom
آسِن brackish, stagnant	إِسْقَاط dropping, abortion, subtraction
أَسَنّ older	إِسْقَاط الجَنِيْن miscarriage, abortion
إِسْنَاد (أَسَانِيد) ascription, attribution	أُسْقُفْ (أَسَاقِفة) bishop
إِسْهاب expatiation, elaboration	أُسْقُفى episcopal
إِسْهال diarrhea	أَسَكّ stone-deaf
أَسْهَل easier, more convenient	إِسْكَاف shoemaker, cobbler
أُسْوة/إِسْوَة model, example	

courageous, valiant, brave	أَشْجَع	black, dark-coloured	أَسْوَد
stronger, harder, more powerful	أَشَدّ	jet-black, pitch black	أَسْوَد فَاحِم
maturity, virility	أَشُدّ	pitch dark	أَسْوَد قَاتِم
large-mouthed	أَشْدَق	grief, sorrow, mourning	أَسًى
liveliness, exuberance	أَشَر	Asia	آسيا
lively, exuberant, impertinent	أَشِر	Asia minor	آسيا الصغرى
superintendence, supervision, patronage	إشْرَاف	prisoner of war, captive	أَسِير (أَسْرَى)
radiance, shining	إشْرَاق	Asian	آسيوي
notification, information	إشْعَار (إشْعَارَات)	ill-omened, sinister	أَشْأَم
radiation, eradiation	إشْعَاع	commendation, extolment	إشَادَة
radiational, radiative	إشْعَاعِي	sign, signal, indication, suggestion, command	إشَارَة
inflaming, lighting, kindling	إشْعَال	sign of the cross	إشَارَة الصَّلِيب
cosmic rays	أَشِعَّة كَوْنِيَّة	wire, telegram	إشَارَة بَرْقِيّة
dishevelled, unkempt, matted	أَشْعَث	wireless message, radio méssage	إشَارَة لاسِلْكِيّة
hard labour	أَشْغَال شَاقَّة	signal man	إشَارِي (إشَارْجِي)
public works	أَشْغال عَامَّة	circulation, publication, news, rumour	إشَاعَة
public works	أَشْغال عُمُومِيّة		
pity, compassion, apprehension, care	إشْفَاق	satisfaction, satiation, repletion	إشْبَاع

exportation, issuance, edition	إصْدَار	more difficult	أَشَقّ
truer, more faithful	أَصْدَق	obscurity, dubiosity	إشْكَال
load, burden, compact	إصْر (آصار)	paralyzed, stunted	أَشَلّ
insistence, persistence	إصْرَار	haughty, supercilious, disdainful	أَشَمّ
bond, tie, obligation	آصِرة (أَوَاصِر)	gray-haired	أَشْمَط
smaller, younger	أَصْغَر	more general, more comprehensive	أَشْمَل
the lesser of two evils	أَصْغَر الشَّرَّيْن	hideous, ignominious, horrid, repulsive	أَشْنَع
yellow, pale, wan	أَصْفَر	written certification	إشْهاد
root, origin, basis, cause, lineage	أَصْل (أُصُول)	declaration, advertising, announcement	إشْهار
originally, primarily, in the beginning	أَصْلاً	gray, gray-coloured	أَشْهَب
mending, settlement, reformation, restoration	إصْلاح	blue-eyed	أَشْهَل
social reformation	إصْلاح اجْتِمَاعِي	malformed, ugly, misshapen, marred	أَشْوَه
correction	إصْلاَح الخَطَأ	grey-haired, aged, old	أَشْيَب
reformatory, reformer	إصْلاَحِي	score, injury, affliction, goal	إصَابة (إصَابَات)
bald-headed	أَصْلَح	bonds, ties	آصار
original, pure, genuine, main	أَصْلِي	finger	إصْبَع (أَصَابِع)
		finger, toe	أُصْبُوع (أَصَابِيع)
		more correct, healthier	أَصَحّ
		the seven sleepers	أَصْحَاب الكَهْف

deaf	أَصَمّ
stone-deaf	أَصَمّ أَصْلَخ
reddish	أَصْهَب
more proper, more apposite	أَصْوَب
principles, rules, assets	أُصُول
manuscript	أُصُول الكِتاب
according to the rules	أُصُولِي
flowerpot	أَصِيص (أُصُص)
genuine, indigenous, real, of noble origin	أَصِيل
time before sunset	أَصِيل (آصال)
lightening, lighting, illumination	إِضَاءَة
waste, dissipation, omission	إِضَاعَة
waste of time	إِضَاعَة الوَقْت
additional, secondary, supplementary	إِضَافِي
laughing stock, object of ridicule	أُضْحُوكَة (أَضَاحِيك)
blood sacrifice, immolation	أَضْحَى

sacrifice, slaughter animal	أُضْحِيّة (أَضَاحِي)
strike	إِضْرَاب (إِضْرَابات)
weakening, impairment, attenuation	إِضْعَاف
misguiding, misleading, deception	إِضْلال
frame, rim	إِطار (أُطُر)
hoop, ring	إِطار البِرْميل
tyre	إِطار العَجَلة
obedience, submission	إِطَاعَة
ability, capability, capacity	إِطَاقَة
lengthening, stretching, elongation	إِطَالَة
commendation, extolment, high praise	إِطْرَاء
delight, delectation, charm	إِطْرَاب
fingertips	أَطْرَاف الأَصَابِع
outskirts of the city	أَطْرَاف المَدِينَة
deaf	أَطْرَش
stone deaf	أَطْرَش أَسَكّ
feeding, nourishing	إِطْعَام

reconstruction	إِعَادَة البِنَاء	extinguishing, putting out, extinction	إِطْفَاء
rearmament	إِعَادَة التَّسَلُّح	fireman	إِطْفَائِي
reorganization	إِعَادَة التَّنْظِيم	fire-brigade, fire department	إِطْفَائِيّة
reprint	إِعَادَة الطَّبْع	release, releasing, freeing, application	إِطْلَاق
reconsideration, revision,	إِعَادَة النَّظَر	shooting, firing	إِطْلَاق الرَّصَاص
lending	إِعَارَة	release	إِطْلَاق السَّرَاح
retardation, deferment, impeding	إِعَاقَة	opening on fire	إِطْلَاق التَّار
sustenance, support, maintenance	إِعَالَة	absolutely, unrestrictedly	إِطْلَاقًا
aid, assistance, support	إِعَانَة	prolixity, exaggeration	إِطْنَاب
family charges	أَعْبَاء عَائِلِيّة	taller, longer, bigger	أَطْوَل
emancipation, liberation	إِعْتَاق	better, best, more fragrant	أَطْيَب
admiration, acclaim, delight	إِعْجَاب	fingernail, claw, nail	أُظْفُور (أَظَافِير)
conceit, self-admiration	إِعْجَاب بالذَّات	manifestation, exposition, demonstration	إِظْهَار
miracle, miraculous nature	إِعْجَاز	more obvious, more clearer	أَظْهَر
slim, emaciated	أَعْجَف	visiting, a visit, call on	إِعَادَة
faster, quicker	أَعْجَل	returning, restoration, repetition	إِعَادَة
speechless, dumb, irrational	أَعْجَم		

أَعْضَاء دَقِيقَة sexual organs, genitals	أَعْجَمِي non-Arab, foreigner
أَعْضَاء رَئِيسِيّة vitals	أُعْجُوبَة (أَعَاجِيب) wonder, miracle
إعْطَاء granting, presenting	إعْدَاد preparing, arranging
أَعْظَم greater, greatest, paramount	إعْدَادي preparatory
إعْفَاء remission, discharge, exemption	إعْدَام execution, annihilation
أَعْفَر dust coloured	أَعْدَل more upright, fairer
أَعْقَد knotty, more complicated	إعْرَاب parsing, expression, pronouncement
أَعْقَف crooked, hooked, curved	أَعْرَابِي (أَعْرَاب) Bedouin, Arab
إعْلَاء raising, elevating, exaltation	إعْرَاض avoidance, evasion
إعْلَام notification, information, notice	أَعْرَج lame, limping
إعْلَان (إعْلَانَات) announcement, declaration, notice	أَعْرَق deep-rooted, inveterate
إعْلَان الْحَرْب declaration of war	أَعَزّ stronger, more powerful
إعْلَان حُضُور summons, subpoena	إعْزَاز strengthening, consolidation, reinforcement
أَعْلَاه above	أَعْزَل defenseless, unarmed
أَعْلَى higher, highest, upper	أَعْشَارِي decimal
أَعْمَال حَرْبِيَّة military operations	إعْصَار tornado, hurricane, cyclone
	أَعْضَاء التَّنَاسُل sexual organs, genitals

إِغْرَاق drowning, flooding, scuttling	أَعْمَال مَنْزِليّة household work, home work
أَغُسْطُس August	أَعْمَال يَدَويّة handiworks
إِغْضَاب infuriation, irritation, vexation	أَعْمَر more populous, more flourishing
إِغْفَال neglecting, ignoring, omitting	أَغْمَش blear-eyed
إِغْلَاء extolment, admiration	أَعْمَى blind, ignorant
إِغْلَاق locking, closing, shutting off	إِعْنَات harassment, distress, torment
أَغْلَب most of, the majority of	أَعْنَف severer, harsher, more violent
أَغْلَبِيّة majority, greater number	إِعْوَاز want, necessity, need, destitution
أَغْلَبِيّة مُطْلَقَة absolute majority	أَعْوَج crooked, curved, bent
أَغْلَظ thicker, cruder, coarser, grosser	أَعْوَر one-eyed, blind of one eye
أَغْلَف uncircumcised, uncivilized	أَعْوَز needy, poor, destitute
أُغْلُوطَة (أَغَالِيْط) captious question	إِعْيَاء exhaustion, weariness, lassitude
أَغْلَى more costly, more expensive	إِغَاثَة help, succour, aid
إِغْمَاء swoon, faint, unconsciousness	إِغَارَة (إِغَارَات) attack, invasion
أَغْمَص blear-eyed	أَغْبَر dusty, dust-covered
	أَغَرّ magnanimous, beautiful
	إِغْرَاء instigation, incitement, inducement

exaggeration, extravagance	إِفْرَاط	obscurer, more ambiguous	أَغْمَض
evacuation, emptying	إِفْرَاغ	song, tune	أُغْنِيّة (أَغَان)
edge, curb, cornice	إِفْرِيز	temptation, seduction, enticement	إِغْوَاء
corrupting, spoiling, sabotaging	إِفْسَاد	oh! tush!	أُفٌّ
more eloquent, purer	أَفْصَح	fie on you!	أُفّ لك
better, more excellent, desirable, preferable	أَفْضَل	utility, bestowal of benefit	إِفَادَة
preference, priority	أَفْضَلِيّة	information, notice	إِفَادَة (إِفَادَات)
fast-breaking	إِفْطَار	إِفَادَة الاستلاَم	
broad-nosed	أَفْطَح	acknowledgement of receipt	
flat-nosed, snub-nosed	أَفْطَس	detailedness, profusion, elaborateness	إِفَاضَة
more effective	أَفْعَل	remote regions	آفاق
viper, snake	أَفْعَى	wanderer, vagabond	أَفَّاق
grumble, displeasure	أَفَف	recuperation, revival, recovering of senses	إِفَاقَة
horizon, range of vision	أُفْق/أُفُق (آفاق)	liar, slanderer	أَفَّاك
horizontal	أُفُقي	epidemic, pest, evil, damage, disease	آفَة (آفات)
lie, falsehood	إِفْك	deliverance of legal opinions	إِفْتَاء
jokes, jests, humour	أُفْكُوهَة		
setting, sinking, transitory	آفِل	liberation, release	إِفْرَاج
escape, release	إِفْلَات	exudation, secretion, discharge	إِفْرَاز

smaller, shorter أَقْصَر	bankruptcy, إِفْلَاس insolvency
tale, short story أُقْصُوصَة (أَقَاصِيْص)	Plato أَفْلَاطُون
remote, farther, farthest, ultimate or extreme end أَقْصَى	Platonic أَفْلَاطُونِي
	extirpation, destruction, إِفْنَاء annihilation
feudal state إِقْطَاع	in crowds, in shoals أَفْوَاجًا
feudal, feudatory إِقْطَاعِي	
more convincing أَقْطَع	setting, declination أُفُول
locking, closing, shutting إِقْفَال	cancellation, dismissal, إِقَالَة discharge
fewer, smaller, inferior أَقَلّ	raising, establishment, إِقَامَة erecting, setting up, dwelling
sailing, take off إِقْلَاع	
disturbance, troubling, إِقْلَاق restlessness	back and forth إِقْبَالاً وَإِدْبَارًا
minority, the small number أَقَلِّيَّة (أَقَلِّيَات)	blackish, dark أَقْتَم
	intrepidity, audacity, إِقْدَام valour
key إِقْلِيد (أَقَالِيد)	
region, country, district, climate إِقْلِيم (أَقَالِيم)	more ancient, older, senior أَقْدَم
territorial, regional, climatic إِقْلِيمِي	seniority أَقْدَمِيَّة
satisfying, contenting إِقْنَاع	establishing, setting, إِقْرَار confession, confirmation
stronger, more powerful أَقْوَى	nearer, more probable أَقْرَب
leading personalities أَكَابِر القَوْم	relatives, relations أَقْرَب (أَقَارِب)
	bald, baldheaded أَقْرَع

إِكْلِيل	wreath, garland, crown
إِكْلِيل الزَّوَاج	nuptial corona
إِكْلِيلِي	coronary, coronal
إِكْمَال	perfection, completing, concluding
أَكَمَة (أَكَمات)	hill, hillock, heap
أَكْمَل	more perfect, more complete
أَكْمَه	born blind
أَكْوَس	better, more handsome
أَكُول	glutton, gourmand
أَكِيد	sure, certain
أَكِيداً	surely, certainly
أَكْيَس	more intelligent, more skilful
آل	family, kinsfolk, mirage
آلُ خِبْرة	expert, authority
إلاَّ	unless, if not, except
إلْبَاس	dressing, clothing
أَلْبِسَة جَاهِزَة	ready-made clothes
آلَة (آلات)	tool, instrument, organ, implement, machine

أكّال	glutton, gourmand
أكْبَر (أَكَابِر)	greater, bigger
إكْثَار	increase, multiplication, augmentation
أكْثَر	more, most, majority
أكْثَرِيّة	majority, the greater number
أُكْذُوبَة (أَكَاذِيب)	lie, deceit
إكْرَاء	renting, leasing
إكْرَام	honour, respect, regard
إكْرَامِيّة	honorarium, bonus
إكْرَاه	compulsion, constraint, coercion
إكْرَاهِي	coercive, enforced
آكِل	eater, eating
أَكْل	food, taking food, nourishment
آكِل الحَشَرَات	insectivorous
آكِل اللُّحُوم	carnivorous
آكِل النّبَاتات	herbivorous
أُكْل/أُكُل	food, fruit
آكِلَة	gangrenous sore
أَكْلَة (أَكَلات)	meal, repast

long-bearded	ألْحَى	camera	آلَة التَّصْوير
bitter, grim, fierce	أَلَدّ	incubator	آلَة التَّفْريخ
compulsion, obligation, coercion	إلْزَام	incubator	آلَة التَّفْقيص
		safety razor	آلَة الحلَاقة
compulsory, obligatory	إلْزَامي	power loom	آلَة الحيَاكَة
poster, bill	إلْصَاق	sewing machine	آلَة الخيَاطة
more delicate	أَلْطَف	printing press	آلَة الطّباعة
gymnastic exercises	ألْعَاب جُمْبَازيّة	washing machine	آلَة الغَسْل
		typewriter	آلَة الكتَابة
sports, athletics, gymnastics	ألْعَاب ريَاضيّة	instrument of war	آلَة حَرْبيّة
fireworks	ألْعَاب نَارية	crane, winch, pump	آلَة رَافعَة
plaything, toy, fun	أُلْعُوبَة (ألَاعيْب)	steam boiler	آلَة غَلّايّة
cancellation, abolition, annulment	إلْغَاء	compressor	آلَة كَابسَة
		typewriter	آلَة كاتبَة
amalgamation	إلْغَام	engine, motor	آلَة مُحَرّكة
intimate, associate, companion	إلْف (أُلّاف)	vacuum pump	آلَة مُفَرّغَة
thousand	أَلْف (أُلُوف)	musical instrument	آلَة مَوْسيقية
familiarity, friendship, intimacy, agreement	أُلْفَة	insistence, obstinacy, stubbornness	إلْحَاح
brightness, glitter, glow, brilliance	أَلَق	apostasy, heresy, godlessness	إلْحَاد
throwing, casting away, delivery	إلْقَاء	attaching, joining, annexation	إلْحَاق

riddle, conundrum	أُلْقِيَة	good-by	إلى اللِّقَاء
pain, suffering, ache (آلام)	أَلَم	backward	إلَى الوَرَاء
acute pain	أَلَم مُبَرِّح	to a considerable degree	إلى حَدّ كَبير
acquaintance, congnizance	إلْمَام	to a certain degree	إلى حَدٍّ ما
shinier, more lustrous	أَلْمَع	to a certain extent	إلى حَدّ معلوم
god, deity (آلهة)	إله	how long, till when	إلَى مَتَى
Neptune	إله البَحْر	familiar, friendly, intimate, amicable	أَليف
Cupid	إله الحُبّ	intimate, close friend (أَلائف)	أَليْف
inflaming, kindling, ignition	إلْهَاب	more suitable, more proper	أَلْيَق
inspiration, instinct	إلْهَام	painful, distressing, grievous	أَليم
Venus	إلَهة العشْق	or	أَمْ
divine, theological	إلهِي	mother, origin, essence	أُمّ
affable, tame, familiar	أَلُوف	but, only, as far as	أَمَّا
mechanical, organic	آلِي	killing, putting to death	إمَاتَة
to, upto, toward, till, until	إلى	inciting, urging	أَمَار
blessing, boon, benefit (آلاء)	إلَى	inciting, instigating	أَمَّارة
and so forth, etcetera	إلى آخِرِه	sign, mark, indication, token	أَمَارَة
where, whither	إلى أَيْنَ	emirate, power, authority	إمَارة
for ever	إلى الأَبَد		
forward, ahead, onward	إلى الأَمَام		

praise, أُمْدُوْحَة (أَمَادِيْح) eulogy, laudation	liquefaction, melting إمَاعَة
commander, orderer, آمِر imperative	places of أَمَاكِن اللّهُو amusement
affair, matter, أَمْر (أُمُور) concern	recreation أَمَاكِن المُتْعَة centers
order, command, أَمْر (أَوَامِر) instruction, power authority, influence	in front of, before, in أَمَام the presence of
matter of course أَمْر بَدِيهي	leader, imam, chief إمَام
royal decree أَمْر سَامٍ	leadership, imamate إمَامة
royal decree, edict أَمْر عالٍ	front, anterior أُمَامي
something, certain أَمْر ما thing	security, safety, أَمَان protection
accomplished fact أَمْر وَاقِع	faithfulness, loyalty, أَمَانة honesty, trust
man, person إمْرَأ/إمْرَء	bond-maid, bond أَمَة (إمَاء) woman
woman, wife إمْرَأة	nation, people, أُمَّة (أُمَم) community
mental diseases أَمْرَاض عَقْلِيَّة	
contagious أَمْرَاض مُعْدِية diseases	personal أَمْتِعَة شَخْصِيَّة belongings
gastric diseases أَمْرَاض مَعِدِيَّة	example, أُمْثُولَة (أَمَاثِيْل) proverb, lesson
hereditary أَمْرَاض ورَاثِيَّة diseases	more glorious أَمْجَد
authority, influence, إمْرَة power	period, time, أَمَد (آماد) limit, extent
beardless, leafless أَمْرَد	aip, support, إمْدَاد assistance
America أَمْريكا	

the United Nations	أُمَم مُتَّحِدَة	American	أمْريكي
peaceful, secure	آمِن	yesterday, recently	أمْس
safety, peace, security, protection	أمْن	detention, restraint, abstinence	إمْسَاك
public security	أمْن عامّ	accomplishment, signature	إمْضَاء
collective security	أمْن مُشْتَرك	time server, trimmer, opportunist	إمَّع/إمَّعَة
wish, desire, longing	أُمْنِيّة (أَمَانٍ/أَمَاني)	care, attention, assiduity	إمْعَان
important events	أُمَّهات الحَوَادِث	faculty, capacity, ability, possibility	إمْكَان
the main problems	أُمَّهات المَسَائِل	possibility, potential, probability	إمْكَانِيّة
concession of a delay	إمْهَال	hopeful, full of hope	آمِل
movable property, real estate	أمْوَال ثَابِتة	hope, expectation, confidence	أَمَل (آمال)
immense fortunes	أمْوال طَائِلَة	fallacious hope, fancy	أمَل كاذب
motherhood, maternity	أُمُومة	filling, filling out, dictation	إمْلَاء
motherly, maternal, illiterate	أُمِّي	mineral salts	أمْلَاح مَعْدنِيّة
illiteracy, ignorance	أُمِّيَّة	movable property, real estate	أمْلَاك ثَابتة
prince, chief, commander	أَمِير (أُمَرَاء)	tender, soft, flexible	أمْلَد
major general	أَمِير الأُمَرَاء	smooth, glossy, sleek	أمْلَس
		hairless	أمْلَط

substitution, delegation, deputation	إنَابَة	admiral	أَمير البَحْر
endurance, patience, perseverance	أناة	brigadier general	أَمير اللِّوَاء
people	أُنَاس	commander of the faithful	أَمير المُؤْمنين
elegance, beauty, charm	أناقة	admiral	أَميرال
mankind, creatures	أَنَام	princess	أَميرة
pineapple	أَنَاناس	queen bee	أَميرة النَّحْل
egoist, selfish	أَنانى	government, governmental	أَميري
selfishness, egoism, egotism	أَنَانيَّة	trustworthy, chief, custodian, guardian	أَمين (أُمَناء)
storehouse, storeroom	أَبَار	treasurer, cashier	أَمين الصُّنْدوق
tube, pipe, duct (أَنَابِيْب)	أُنْبُوب	treasurer	أَمين المَال
vaccum pipe	أُنْبُوب مُفَرَّغ	store-keeper	أَمين المَخْزَن
tubular, tupeshaped	أُنْبُوبِي	librarian	أَمين المَكْتَبة
excavation, excavated thing	أُنْبُوش/أُنْبُوشَة	secretary general	أَمين عامّ
you, thou (f)	أَنْتِ	time, hour	آن
you, thou (m)	أَنْتَ	now, at prersent	الآن
producing, breeding, creation	إنْتَاج	that, even though	أَنْ/أَنَّ
domestic production	إنْتَاج أَهْلِي	at that time	آئذ
you (pl. m.)	أَنْتُم	I	أَنَا
		by and by, gradually	آنًا فآنًا
		vessles, utensils (آنية/أَوَانٍ)	إناء

creating, originating, إِنْشَاء construction, composition	you, both of you (du. أَنْتُما m. & f.)
creative, إِنْشَائِي constructive	you (pl. f.) أَنْتُنَّ
song, anthem (أَنَاشِيْد) أُنْشُوْدَة	feminine, womanly أُنْثَوِي
justice, equity, إِنْصَاف fairness, fairplay	female, feminine (إناث) أُنْثَى
reviving, animating, إِنْعَاش restoration to life	implementation, إِنْجَاز accomplishment, execution
gift, grant, favour, إِنْعَام bestowal	pear إِنْجاص
preceding, above آنِف	having large beautiful أَنْجَل eye
nose, spur of a (آناف) أَنْف mountain	warning, alarm, إِنْذَار notification
above, previously آنِفًا	ultimatum إِنْذار نِهَائِي
carrying out, إِنْفَاذ execution, dispatching	bringing down, إِنْزَال emission, disembarkation, discharge
spending, expenditure إِنْفَاق	familiarity, intimacy, أُنْس sociability
pride, self-esteem, أَنَفَة disdain	mankind, the human إِنْس race
nasal أَنْفِي	man, humankind إِنْسان
rescue, deliverance, إِنْقَاذ saving	human, humanitarian إِنْسَانِي
decrease, diminution, إِنْقَاص lessening	humanity, human إِنْسَانِيّة race
denial, refusal إِنْكَار	young lady, miss آنِسَة
self-denial إِنْكَارُ الذَّات	human, human being إِنْسِي

moan, groan	أَنِين	unfortunate, troublesome	أَنْكَد
oh! ah!	آه	more harmful, more grievous	أَنْكَى
skin, hide	إِهاب	only, but, however	إِنَّما
insult, affront, contempt	إِهَانَة	increase, promotion, furtherance	إِنْمَاء
preparedness, readiness	أُهْبَة	freckled	أَنْمَش
dolt, imbecilic, dunce	أَهْبَل	fingertip	أُنْمُلَة (أَنامِل)
satie, lampoon	أُهْجِيّة/أُهْجُوَّة (أَهَاجِي)	model, example, specimen, sample	أُنْمُوذَج
bestowal, conferment, presentation	إِهْدَاء	completion, termination, suspension	إِنْهَاء
having long eyelashes	أَهْدَب	arousing, awakening, stirring	إِنْهَاض
better guided	أَهْدَى	exhaustion, consumption	إِنْهَاك
shedding, spilling	إِهْرَاق	feminity, womanliness	أُنُوثة
bloodshed	إِهْرَاق الدِّمَاء	haughty, proud, disdainful, contemptuous	أَنُوف
taunt, sarcasm, mockery	أُهْكُومَة	time, period	أَنًى (آناء)
populated, inhabited	آهِل	chinaware, porcelain-ware	آنِيَة خَزَفِيَّة
family, relation, skin	أَهْل	intimate, affable, sociable, polite	أَنِيس
the prophet's family	أَهْل البيت	elegant, fastidious, dainty, spruce	أَنِيق
the wealthy, the rich	أَهْل الثَّرْوَة		
experts, authority	أَهْل الخِبْرة		

easier, simpler, more worthless	أَهْوَن	inmates of the house	أَهْل الدَّار
the lesser evil	أَهْوَن الشَّرَّيْن	wife	أَهْل الرَّجُل
more desirable	أَهْوَى	the adherents of the sunnah	أَهْل السُّنَّة
or, unless	أَوْ	the people of the Book	أَهْلُ الكِتَاب
wonders of the world	أَوَابِدُ الدُّنْيا	the nomads	أَهْل الوَبَر
end of the month	أَوَاخِر الشَّهْر	notables	أَهْل الوَجَاهَة
bonds of friendship	أَوَاصِر الصَّدَاقة	worthy of, deserving, fit	أَهْل لكذا
bonds of friendship	أَوَاصِر الوَلَاء	welcome to you	أَهْلاً بك
time, hour	أَوَان	welcome	أَهْلاً وَسَهْلاً
glass-wares	أَوَان زُجَاجِيّة	hairy, shaggy	أَهْلَب
earthenware, utensils	أَوَان فَخَّارِية	domestic, indigenous, national	أَهْلِي
opera-house, opera	أُوْبِرا	qualification, fitness, suitableness	أَهْلِيَّة
autobus, bus	أُوْتُوبِيس	more important	أَهَمّ
stronger, more solid	أَوْثَق	negligence, carelessness, inattention	إهْمَال
climax, acme, peak, zenith	أَوْج	importance, significance	أَهَمِّيَّة
burden, load	أَوْد/أَوْدة	thoughtless, reckless, rash	أَهْوَج
business papers	أَوْرَاق الأَشْغَال	crazy, blind, infatuated	أَهْوَس
credentials	أَوْرَاق الاعْتِماد		

possessor, owner (pl. of ذو)	أُولُو	credentials, identification papers	أَوْرَاق الهُوِيَّة
rulers, leaders	أُولو الأَمْر	banknotes, paper money	أَوْرَاق مَالِيَّة
men of responsibilities	أُولو الشَّأْن	Europe	أُورُبّا
priority	أَوْلَوِيَّة	European	أُورُبِي
more suitable, more deserving	أَوْلَى	goose	إِوَزّ
primary, original, elemental, initial, basic	أَوَّلِي	the middle classes	أَوْسَاط النَّاس
first, formar (fem. of أَوّل)	أُولَى	middle, central, medium	أَوْسَط
precedence, priority, axion	أَوَّلِيّة	more spacious, wider, larger	أَوْسَع
mildness, serenity, gentleness	أَوْن	clearer, more obvious	أَوْضَح
that is (i.e.), namely	أَيْ	mountains	أَوْطَاد
any, which, what	أَيّ	more abundant, more plentiful	أَوْفَر
yes, yea	إِيْ	more faithful, more complete	أَوْفَى
anything, whatever	أَيّ شَيْء	ounce	أُوقِية
return	إِيَاب	first, former, chief important, beginning	أَوّل
despair, hopelessness	إِيَاس	first, in the beginning	أَوّل الأَمْر
province, regency	إِيَالة	those	أُولئك
when	أَيَّانَ		
sign, mark, miracle, verse	آيَة (آيَات)	at first, in the beginning, primarily	أَوّلاً
preference, predilection	إِيثار		

إيْضَاح making elucidation, clarification, explanation	إيْجَاب affirmation, confirmation, consent
إيْضَاحي explanatory, illustrative, elucidative	إيْجَابي affirmative, positive
إيْعَاز recommendation, counsel	إيْجَاد creation, origination, procurement
إيْفَاء fulfilment, payment, accomplishment	إيْجَار lease, rent, letting
	إيْجَاز brevity, shortness, terseness
إيْقَاد kindling, setting on fire	إيْجَازًا in short, in brief
إيْقَاظ awaking, raising	إيْحَاء suggestion, inspiration
إيْقَاف stopping, detention, impending, stay	إيْدَاع depositing, consigning
إيْقَاف التَّنْفِيذ stay of execution	إيدروجين hydrogen
إيْقَاف الحُكْم arrest of judgment	إيذاء hurt, harm, offense, damage
إيْقَاف الدَّعْوَى stay of proceedings	إيذان announcement, declaration
إيْقَاف الدَّفْع delay of payment	إيرَاد production, introduction, bringing up, citation
إيْقَاف العَمَل suspension of work	إيْرَاد (إيْرَادَات) receipts, returns, revenues
إيْقَاف المُوَظَّف suspension of an official	أيْسَر easier, left-sided
أيَّل stag	إيْصَال conveying, connecting, connection, joining, transportation
إيلاء oath	
إيلَاج insertion, interpolation	أيْضاً also, as well, too

beginning, start	ابْتِداء	September	أَيْلُول
primary, initial, preliminary, preparatory	ابْتِدائي	title deed	أَيْلُولة
creation, innovation	ابْتِداع	widower, widow	أَيِّم
triteness banality, degradation	ابْتِذال	whatever, whatsoever	أَيَّما
embezzlement, robbing, fleecing	ابْتِزاز	gesture, nod, indication	إيمَاء/إيماءَة
smile, smiling	ابْتِسام	faith, belief	إيمان
smile	ابْتِسامة	widowhood	أَيِّمَة
forced smile	ابْتِسامَة قَهْرِيّة	right, right hand	أَيْمَن
wish, desire	ابْتِغاء	where	أَيْنَ
invention, creation, innovation, origination	ابْتِكار	wherever	أَيْنَما
affliction, tribulation, distress, visitation	ابْتِلاء	o...! (cocative particle)	أَيُّها
delight, pleasure, joy	ابْتِهاج	granting, giving donation	إيهاب
supplication, prayer	ابْتِهال	delusion, misleading, deceit	إيهام
clasp, buckle	ابْزِيم (أبازيم)	sheltering, accommodating	إيواء
son, off spring	ابْن (أَبْناء/بَنُون)	lobby, hall, mansion, palace	إيوان
son of Adam, man, human being	ابْن آدم	concord, harmony, coalition, union	ائْتِلاف
jackal	ابن آوَى	counsel, conspiracy, deliberation	ائْتِمار
nephew	ابْن الأخ	confidence, trust, credit	ائْتِمان
niece	ابْن الأخْت		

good order, harmony اتِّسَاق	ابن البَلَد native, local inhabitant
connection, contact, اتِّصَال junction, union, continuation	ابن الزَّوج/الزَّوجة step-son
consanguinity, اتِّصَال الدَّم kinship	ابنُ السَّبِيل wayfarer, foot traveller
telephone اتِّصَال تِلفُونِي connection	ابن العَمّ/الخال cousin
close contact اتِّصَال وثِيق	ابنُ حَلال legitimate son, good fellow
clearness, clarity, اتِّضَاح manifestness	ابن زِنا bastard, natural son
coincidence, contract, اتِّفَاق agreement, treaty, accident	ابْنَة = بنْت
unanimity اتِّفَاق الآرَاء	أبُو الهَوْل Sphinx
naval agreement اتِّفَاق بَحْرِي	اتِّبَاع following, adherence, pursuit, observance
commercial or اتِّفَاق تِجَارِي trade agreement	اتِّجار trade, business
اتِّفَاق عَدَم الاعْتِدَاء nonagression pact	اتِّجَاه (اتِّجَاهات) direction, tendency, inclination
accidentally, by chance اتِّفَاقًا	اتِّحَاد union, unity, oneness, alliance, combination federation
accidental, اتِّفَاقِي conventional	اتِّحَاد الآرَاء unanimity
agreement, treaty, اتِّفَاقِيَّة convention	اتِّحاد سُوفْيَاتِي/ سُوفْيِتِي Soviet Union
burning, combustion اتِّقَاد	اتِّحَادِي unionist, unionistic
reliance, confidence, اتِّكَال dependability	اتِّزَان balance, equilibrium
	اتِّسَاع vastness, extension, spaciousness, expanse

precaution, care	احْتراس	accusation, charge, indictment	اتِّهَام
adoption of a profession	احْتراف	twelve	اثْنَا عَشر/اثْنَتَا عَشْرَة
burning, combustion	احْتراق	two	اثْنَان/اثْنَتان
respect, reverence, honour	احْترام	Monday	الاثْنَيْن
self-respect	احْترَام الذَّات	gathering, meeting, assembly, convention, conference	اجْتماع
calculation, valuation, consideration	احْتسَاب	social, sociological	اجْتماعي
crowd, gathering, concentration	احْتشاد	avoidance	اجْتناب
shame, shyness, modesty, decorum	احْتشام	diligence, assiduity, endeavour, effort	اجْتهاد
embracing, hugging	احْتضان	destruction, eradication, suppression	اجْتيَاح
celebration, reception	احْتفاء	crossing, passing over, transit	اجْتيَاز
safekeeping, safeguarding, preservation	احْتفَاظ	obstruction, retention, inhibition	احْتباس
ceremony, festival, procession	احْتفال	retention of urine	احْتبَاس البَوْل
disdain, contempt	احْتقار	veiledness, hiddenness	احْتجاب
congestion	احْتقان	argumentation, protestation, objection	احْتجاج
monopoly, hegemony	احْتكار	paroxysm	احْتدام
sugar monopoly	احْتكار السُّكَّر		
friction, rubbing	احْتكاك		
occupation	احْتلال	caution, reservation	احْترَاز

اخْتِصَاصِي specialist	احْتِمَال bearing, suffering, toleration
اخْتِطَاف kidnapping, snatching, grabbing	اِحْتِيَاج need, want, necessity
اخْتِفَاء disappearance	اِحْتِيَاط precaution, care, prudence
اخْتِلَاس embezzlement, defalcation, malversation	اِحْتِيَاطِي prudential, preventive, precautionary
اخْتِلَاط mixing, mingling, association, disorder, confusion	اِحْتِيَال trickery, craft, deceit, fraud
اخْتِلَاف diversity, difference, dissimilarity, disagreement	احْلِيْل urethra
اخْتِلَال disturbance, disorder	اِحْمِرار redness, red colouration
اخْتِمار fermentation, leavening	اخْتِبَار test, examination, exploration, experiment
اخْتِنَاق suffocation, smothering	اخْتِبَارِي experimental, experiential
اخْتِيار choice, selection	اخْتِتَام conclusion, close, end
اخْتِيَاراً voluntarily, spontaneously	اخْتِرَاع invention, contrivance
اخْتِيَارِي voluntary, optional, elective	اخْتِراق piercing, penetration
اخْصَائِي specialist, expert	اخْتِزَال shorthand, stenography, shortening
ادِّخَار saving, storing, storage	اخْتِصَار abridgment, brevity, abbreviation
ادِّعَاء claim, allegation, charge, pretension	اخْتِصَاص special domain, jurisdiction
ارْتِبَاط connection, relation, lie, engagement	

exploration, visit	ارْتِيَاد	confusion, muddle, entanglement	ارْتِبَاك
pleasure, delight, satisfaction	ارْتِيَاه	shock, tremour, concussion	ارْتِجَاج
rice	أَرُزّ	reaction, return	ارْتِجاع
aristocrat, aristocratic	أَرِسْتُقَرَاطِي	reactionary	ارْتِجَاعي
aristocracy	أَرِسْتُقَرَاطِيَّة	extemporization, improvisation	ارْتِجَال
crowd, throng, jam	ازْدِحام	extempore, off-hand	ارْتِجَالي
disdain, contempt	ازْدِراء	retrogression, apostasy, withdrawal	ارْتِدَاد
splendour, flourishing, blooms	ازْدِهَاء	bribery, corruption	ارْتِشاء
flourishing, bloom	ازْدِهار	infiltration	ارْتِشَاح
doubleness, pairedness	ازْدِوَاج	shivering, shaking, trembling	ارْتِعَاش
increase, rise, growth	ازْدِياد	rise, increase, height, elevation	ارْتِفَاع
Spanish	اسْباني	ascension, progress, development, rise	ارْتِقَاء
Spain	اسْبانيا	expectation, anticipation	ارْتِقَاب
weekly	أَسْبُوعيًّا		
buttocks, backside	اسْت	perpetration, commitment	ارْتِكَاب
monopolization, presumptuousness	اسْتِئْثار	support, prop	ارْتِكَاز
lease, rent	اسْتِئْجار		
leave-taking	اسْتِئْذان	suspicion, doubt, misgiving	ارْتِيَاب
elimination, extirpation	اسْتِئْصال		

bath, bathing	اسْتِحْمام	renewal, appeal, resumption	اسْتِئْناف
enquiry	اسْتِخْبار	appellate	اسْتِئْنافِي
utilization, employment	اسْتِخْدام	static	اسْتاتيكى
submissiveness, servility, subservience	اسْتِخْذاء	Constantinople	اسْتانبول/اسْطانبول
extraction, taking out, removal	اسْتِخْراج	tyranny, obstinacy, arbitrariness, despotism	اسْتِبْداد
levity, triviality, disdain, contempt	اسْتِخْفاف	tyrannical, despotic, arbitrary	اسْتِبْدادي
roundness, circularity	اسْتِدارة	brocade	اسْتَبْرق
correction, conception	اسْتِدْراك	utilization, exploitation, investment	اسْتِثْمار
sending for, summons, summoning	اسْتِدْعاء	exceptional	اسْتِثْنائي
argumentation, inference	اسْتِدْلال	recreation, relaxation	اسْتِجْمام
strategic	اسْتَراتيجي	interrogation, questioning, interpellation	اسْتِجْواب
rest, recess, repose, relaxation	اسْتِراحة	transformation, impossibility, alteration transmutation	اسْتِحَالة
Australian	أُسْتُرالى	bringing, making, preparing	اسْتِحْضار
Australia	أُسْتُراليا	merit, worth, worthiness, maturity	اسْتِحْقاق
restoration, retraction, retrieval	اسْتِرْجاع	consolidation, stabilization, strengthening	اسْتِحْكام
plea for mercy	اسْتِرْحام		

recovery, regaining استِعَادَة	looseness, استِرْخَاء limpness, lassitude
borrowing, استِعَارَة metaphor	recovery, استِرْدَاد restoration, retraction
metaphorical, استِعَارِي figurative	conciliation, استِرْضَاء conciliatoriness
enslavement, استِعْبَاد enthralment	Austria أُسْتِريا/أُوسْتِريا
preparedness, استِعْدَاد readiness	dropsy استِسْقَاء
aptitude, (استِعْدَادَات) استِعْدَاد tendency, disposition	dropsical, استِسْقَائِي hydropic
preparatory استِعْدَادِي	surrender, استِسْلام submission, resignation
parade, show, استِعْرَاض survey	advisory, استِشَارِي consultative
begging, mendicity استِعْطَاء	cure, treatment استِشْفَاء
apology, request for استِعْفَاء pardon	quotation, استِشْهَاد martyrdom
superiority استِعْلاَء	illumination, استِصْبَاح lighting
enquiry, information استِعْلام	approval استِصْوَاب
colonization, استِعْمَار imperialism	ability, capability, استِطَاعَة power
colonial, استِعْمَارِي imperialistic	investigation, استِطْلاَع study, exploration, probing
colonialism, استِعْمَارِيّة imperialism	exploratory, استِطْلاعِي explorational
use, usage, استِعْمَال application, utilization	

settlement, steadiness, stabilization, sedentation	اسْتِقْرَار	appeal for aid or help	اسْتِغَاثَة
enquiry, investigation	اسْتِقْصَاء	wonder, surprise, amazement	اسْتِغْرَاب
independence, freedom	اسْتِقْلَال	exploitation, utilization, investment	اسْتِغْلال
discovery, scouting, observation, exploration	اسْتِكْشَاف	use, utilization	اسْتِفَادَة
exploratory, scout	اسْتِكْشَافِي	consultation, consulting	اسْتِفْتَاء
receipt, acceptance	اسْتِلام	plebiscite	اسْتِفْتَاء عَامّ
blank form	اسْتمارة/اسْتِثْمارة	vacating, discharge, evacuation	اسْتِفْرَاغ
listening, hearing	اسْتِماع	instigation, inticement, excitement	اسْتِفْزَاز
enjoyment, pleasure, gratification	اسْتِمْتَاع	provocative, instigative	اسْتِفْزَازِي
continuation, continuity	اسْتِمْرَار	enquiry, question	اسْتِفْسَار
continuously, constantly	اسْتِمْرَاراً	question, enquiry	اسْتِفْهَام
masturbation, onanism	اسْتِمْنَاء	interrogative	اسْتِفْهَامِي
dependence, leaning	اسْتِنَاد	resignation, retirement	اسْتِقَالَة
discovery, drawing out, contrivance	اسْتِنْبَاط	uprightness, straightness, correctness	اسْتِقَامَة
inhaling, inhalation	اسْتِنْشَاق	reception, opposition	اسْتِقْبَال
		investigation, examination	اسْتِقْرَاء

astrolabe	اسْطُرْلاب	desdain, scorn, contempt	اسْتِهَانَة
pillar, column, cylinder, record	أُسْطُوانة	rashness, recklessness, wantonness	اسْتِهْتَار
fable, myth, legend	أُسْطُورة (أَسَاطِير)	disapprobation, dislike	اسْتِهْجَان
mythical, legendary	أُسْطُوري	ridicule, derision, mockery	اسْتِهْزَاء
fleet, squadron	أُسْطُول	consumption, attrition, waste	اسْتِهْلاك
air fleet	أُسْطُول جَوِّي	beginning, introduction, commencement	اسْتِهْلال
sponge	اسْفَنْج/اسْفُنْج		
spongy, porous	اسْفَنْجي		
threshold, doorstep	أَسْكُفَّة	straightness, equality, evenness, sameness	اسْتِواء
name, fame, reputation	اسْم (أَسْمَاء)		
demonstrative pronoun	اسْم الإشارة	equatorial, tropical	اسْتِوَائي
pet name	اسْم التَّدْلِيل/الدَّلْع	studio	اسْتُودِيو
appellation	اسْم الشُّهْرَة	displeasure, vexation, resentment	اسْتِيَاء
family name, sir name	اسْم العَائِلَة	import, importation	اسْتِيرَاد
title, name	اسْم الكِتَاب	comprehension, full grasp	اسْتِيعَاب
firm name	اسْم تِجَاري		
nickname	اسْم تَهَكّمي	capture, seizure, possessing	اسْتِيلاء
proper name	اسْم عَلَم	Israel	اسْرائيل
pseudonym	اسْم مُسْتَعَار	stable, barn	اسْطَبْل

selection, choice	اصْطِفَاء	pseudonym, pen name	اِسْم مُنْتَحَل
usage, idiom, term, convention	اصْطِلَاح	cement	اِسْمَنْت/أَسْمَنْت
conventional, idiomatic, technical	اصْطِلَاحي	nominal, titular	اِسْمي
making, production	اصْطِنَاع	godfather, sponsor	أَشْبين
synthetic, artificial	اصْطِنَاعي	godmother, bridesmaid	أَشْبينَة
yellowness, paleness	اصْفِرَار	dubiousness, misgiving, doubtfulness	اشْتِبَاه
confusion, unrest, embarrassment, disturbance	اضْطِرَاب	purchasing, buying	اشْتِرَاء
compulsion, exigency, emergency	اضْطِرَار	condition, provision	اشْتِرَاط
compulsory, Inevitable, obligatory	اضْطِرَاري	participation, sharing, partnership	اشْتِرَاك
blaze, flare, ignition	اضْطِرَام	monthly subscription	اشْتِرَاك شَهْري
oppression, suppression, persecution	اضْطِهَاد	socialist, socialistic	اشْتِرَاكي
fading, evanescence	اضْمِحْلال	socialism	اشْتِرَاكِيّة
cognizance, information, acquaintance	اطِّلَاع (اطِّلَاعات)	inflammation, ignition	اشْتِعَال
calmness, peace, tranquillity, serenity	اطْمِئْنَان	yearning, longing, passion, appetite	اشْتِهَاء
respect, regard, esteem, consideration	اعْتِبَار	renown, fame, celebrity, notoriety	اشْتِهَار
		craving, longing, desire	اشْتِيَاق
		disgust, repugnance, aversion	اشْمِئْزَاز

dependence, reliance اعْتِمَاد confidence	aggression, assault, اعْتِدَاء attack
credit, loan, (اعْتِمَادَات) اعْتِماد sanction	moderation, اعْتِدَال evenness, straightness
supplementary اعْتِماد اضَافِي loan	apology, excuse اعْتِذَار
self- اعْتِماد على الذَّات confidence	objection, اعْتِرَاض opposition, rebuttal
self- اعْتِماد عَلَى النَّفْس confidence, self-reliance	acknowledgement, اعْتِرَاف confession, recognition
care, concern, اعْتِنَاء attention	gratitude, اعْتِرَاف بالْجَمِيْل thankfulness
adoption, اعْتِنَاق embracement	pride, power اعْتِزَاز
contraction of a habit اعْتِيَاد	retreat, privacy, اعْتِزَال retirement
habitual, normal, اعْتِيَادي usual	deviation, اعْتِسَاف aberration, arbitrariness
sweeter أَعْذَب	safeguarding, اعْتِصَام preservation, adherence
blind, night blind أَعْشَى	faith, belief, dogma, اعْتِقَاد conviction
bend, crookedness, اعْوِجَاج curvature	dogmatic, dogmatist اعْتِقَادي
delight, rejoicing, اغْتِبَاط exultation, happiness	detention, (اعْتِقَالَات) اعْتِقَال arrest
emigration, being اغْتِرَاب away from home	ascention اعْتِلَاء
vanity, self- اغْتِرَار بالذَّات conceit	sickness, illness, اعْتِلَال weakness

multifariousness, multiplicity	اقْتِنَان	usurpation, illegal seizure, extortion, forcing	اغْتِصَاب
European	افْرَنْجِي	ravishment, rape	اغْتِصَاب النِّسَاء
Africa	أَفْرِيقا/أَفْرِيقيا	anger, ire, irage, wrath	اغْتِيَاظ
African	أَفْرِيقِي		
opium	أَفْيُون	assassination	اغْتِيَال
advent, arrival, approach, attention	اقْبَال	opening, introduction, inauguration	افْتِتَاح
quotation, citation, adoption	اقْتِبَاس	opening, inaugural, introductory	افْتِتَاحِي
invasion, inrush, rushing upon	اقْتِحَام	editorial, leading article	افْتِتَاحِيّة
following, copying, imitation	اقْتِدَاء	bragging, boasting, vanity	افْتِخَار
power, might, aptitude, capability	اقْتِدَار	falsehood, lie, slander	افْتِرَاء
approximation, approach	اقْتِرَاب	supposition, presumption	افْتِرَاض
improvisation, origination	اقْتِرَاح	inactment of laws	افْتِرَاض الأَحْكَام
suggestion, proposal	اقْتِرَاح (اقْتِرَاحَات)	suppositional, hypothetic	افْتِرَاضِي
vote, election	اقْتِرَاع	separation, disunion, dispersal	افْتِرَاق
connection, conjunction, link	اقْتِرَان	need, want, poverty	افْتِقَار
economy, frugality, thrift	اقْتِصاد	affliction, trial, sedition, temptation	افْتِنان

October	اكْتُوبر
eczema	اكْزِيما
oxygen	أَكْسِجِين/أَكْسِيجِين
oxide, rust	أُكْسِيد
elixir	اكْسِيْر
elixir of life	اكْسِير الحياة
cleric-al	اكْلِيرِكي
clergy	اكْلِيروس
dusky, swarthy	أَكْمَد
Albania	أَلْبانيا
intricacy, ambiguity, obscurity	الْتِباس
seeking refuge, recourse	الْتِجَاء
joining, entry, affiliation	الْتِحَاق
connection, adhesion, sticking	الْتِحَام
liability, obligation, commitment, engagement	الْتِزام (الْتِزامَات)
adhesion, coherence	الْتِصَاق
inclination, care, consideration, attention	الْتِفَاف
reunion, meeting	الْتِقَاء

economic, frugal, economist	اقْتِصَادي
need, necessity, exigency, requirement	اقْتِضَاء
abridgement, brevity, improvising	اقْتِضَاب
picking, gathering	اقْتِطَاف
acquisition, purchase	اقْتِنَاء
content, satisfaction	اقْتِنَاع
icon	أَقْوِنة
academic	أَكَادِيمي
academy	أَكَادِيمِية
depression, sorrow, grief, distress	اكْتِئاب
hiring, taking on lease	اكْتِرَاء
care, concern, heed	اكْتِرَاث
gaining, earning, acquisition	اكْتِسَاب
sweeping off, washing away	اكْتِسَاح
disclosure, discovery	اكْتِشاف
satisfaction, content	اكْتِفَاء
sturdiness, compactness	اكْتِنَاز

emperor	اِمْبَرَاطور	gleaning, picking up, gathering	الْتِقَاط
empress	اِمْبَرَاطورة	request, petition, solicitation	الْتِمَاس
emperialist, emperialistic	اِمْبَرَاطوري	inflammation, burning	الْتِهَاب
emperialism, empire	اِمْبَرَاطورية	tonsillitis	الْتِهَاب اللّوزَتَان
obedience, compliance	اِمْتِثَال	nephritis, bright's disease	الْتِهَاب كُلْوي
examination, (امْتِحَانَات) test, experiment	اِمْتِحَان	inflammatory, inflammable	الْتِهَابي
entrance examination	اِمْتِحَان الدُّخُول	curve, curvedness	الْتِوَاء
final examination	اِمْتِحَان نَهَائي	unevenness of the terrain	اِلْتِوَاء الأَرْض
extent, length, longevity, expansibility	اِمْتِدَاد	who, which, that, whom (fem. of الذي)	الَّتي
blend, mixture	اِمْتِزَاج	Tuesday	اَلثُّلاثَاء
suction, soakage, absorption	اِمْتِصَاص	who, which, that, whom	اَلَّذي
resentment, indignation	اِمْتِعَاض	electronic	الكْتُرُوني
fullness, repletion, plumpness	اِمْتِلاء	diamond	اَلْمَاس
possession, control, occupancy, acquisition	اِمْتِلاك	German	اَلْمَاني
		Germany	اَلْمَانيا
self-control	اِمْتِلاك النَّفْس	o god! good god!	اَللّهُمَّ
impossibility, refusal, rejection	اِمْتِنَاع	aluminium	اَلُومنيُوم
		divinity, divine power	اَلُوهيّة

mandate	انْتِدَاب سِيَاسِي	gratitude, indebtedness	امْتِنَان
withdrawal, removal	انْتِزَاع	distinction, previlege, advantage, concesson	امْتِيَاز
affiliation, membership	انْتِسَاب	extermination, obliteration	امِّحَاء
spread, diffusion	انْتِشَار	international, pagan	أُمَمِي
erection, raising	انْتِصَاب	omnibus, bus	أُمْنِيْبوس
erectile	انْتِصَابِي	fartherer, remoter	أَنْأَى
victory, triumph	انْتِصَار	lighting, illumination	انَارَة
order, regularity	انْتِظَام	effusion, outburst, emanation	انْبِثَاق
revival, animation, stimulation	انْتِعَاش	expansion, dilation, extension, delight	انْبِسَاط
swelling, inflation	انْتِفَاخ	emanation, resurgence	انْبِعَاث
shiver, shudder, tremble	انْتِفَاض/انْتِفَاضَة	alertness, wakefulness, caution	انْتِبَاه
utilization, exploitation, profit	انْتِفَاع	suicide, self murder	انْتِحَار
selection, choice	انْتِقَاء	plagiarism, literary theft	انْتِحَال
objection, criticism, disapprobation	انْتِقَاد	selection, choice, election	انْتِخَاب
biting remark, sarcasm	انْتِقَاد جَارِح	by-election	انْتِخَاب تَكْمِيْلِي
breakdown, collapse	انْتِقَاض	elective, electoral	انْتِخَابِي
transfer, removal, change of position, transition	انْتِقَال	delegation, deputation, authorization	انْتِدَاب

deviation, declination, obliquity	الانْحراف	transitory	الانْتقَالي
confinement, limitation	الانْحصَار	revenge, vengeance	الانْتقَام
decay, decline, fall, inferiority	الانْحطَاط	membership	الانْتمَاء
decomposition, dissolution, debility	الانْحلاَل	end, termination, conclusion	الانْتهَاء
curve, curvature, bend, bow, inclination	الانْحنَاء	rebuke, reprimand, repulsion	الانْتهَار
isolation, inclination, partiality	الانْحياز	seizing the opportunity	الانْتهَاز الفُرْصَة
subsidence, reduction, diminution, decrease	الانْخفاض	time server, opportunist	الانْتهَازي
outburst, outbreak, rashness, spontaneity	الانْدفاع	exhaustion, violation, profanation	الانْتهَاك
spontaneously, rashly	الانْدفَاعاً	profanation, sacrilege	الانْتهَاك الحُرْمَة
Spain	الأنْدَلُس	anthropology	اَنْثُرُوبُولُوجيا
amalgamation, insertion, assimilation	الانْدمَاج	pliability, flexibility	الانْثناء
bafflement, surprise, amazement	الانْدهاش	attraction, suction, endency	الانْجذَاب
uneasiness, disturbance, inconvenience	الانْزعَاج	England	انْجلْتَرا
		English	انْجليْزي
slipping, sliding	الانْزلاَق	icing, freezing up	انْجماد
		Gospel	انْجيل
		slope, declivity, decay, decline	الانْحدار

separation, segregation, isolation	اِنْعِزَال	separation, isolation, seclusion	اَلْزِوَاء
curving, twisting, inclination, sympathy	اِنْعِطَاف	harmony, fluency	اِنْسِجَام
conventing, meeting, holding	اِنْعِقَاد	retirement, retreat, withdrawal	اِنْسِحَاب
reflection, reflexion	اِنْعِكَاس	effusion, pouring forth	اِنْسِكَاب
reflexive, reflectional	اِنْعِكَاسِي	infiltration, slipping away	اِنْسِلَال
explosion, (اِنْفِجَارات) blast, outburst, eruption	اِنْفِجَار	inch	اِنْش
explosive, blasting	اِنْفِجَارِي	relaxation, delight	اِنْشِرَاح
relaxation, wildness	اِنْفِرَاج	branching, disruption, ramification	اِنْشِعَاب
solitude, loneliness, seclusion	اِنْفِرَاد	segregation, split, dissension, discord	اِنْشِقَاق
individualistic, tending to isolation	اِنْفِرَادِي	departure, going away	اِنْصِرَاف
ampleness, wideness, expansion	اِنْفِسَاح	discipline	اِنْضِباط
disengagement, detachment, separation	اِنْفِصَال	joining, connecting, affiliation, annexation	اِنْضِمام
separatist, separatistic	اِنْفِصَالِي	release, outburst, outbreak	اِنْطِلَاق
separatism	اِنْفِصَالِيّة	introversion	اِنْطِوَاء
breaking of, dispersal	اِنْفِضَاض	introverted	اِنْطِوَائِي
passivity, irritation	اِنْفِعَال	absence, non-existence	اِنْعِدَام

prostration, pursuit, bending اِنْكِبَاب	affective, irritable اِنْفِعَالِي
brokenness, defeat dejection اِنْكِسَار	disintegration, disengagement اِنْفِكَاك
despondency, dejection, broken-heartedness اِنْكِسَار القَلْب	influenza, flue اِنْفُلُوِنْزَا
occultation, solar eclipse اِنْكِسَاف	shrinking, shrinkage اِنْقِبَاض
withdrawal, retreat اِنْكِفَاء	constipation اِنْقِبَاض البَطْن
England اِنْكِلْتَرا	depression, gloom اِنْقِبَاضُ الصَّدْر
English اِنْكِليزِي	despondency, depression اِنْقِبَاض القَلْب
wrinkling, absorption اِنْكِمَاش	division, disruption اِنْقِسَام
retractive اِنْكِمَاشِي	expiration, passing away, termination اِنْقِضَاء
digestibility, state of being digested اِنْهِضَام	extinction of obligations اِنْقِضَاء التَعَهُّدَات
absorption, entire engrossment اِنْهِمَاك	dive, swooping down اِنْقِضَاض
downfall, collapse, falling اِنْهِيَار	cessation, break, separation, discontinuation, interruption اِنْقِطَاع
anemia أنيميا	power shutdown اِنْقِطَاع التَّيَّار
shaking, trembling, quivering, tremour اِهْتِزَاز	change, alteration, overthrow اِنْقِلَاب
concern, care, anxiety, heed اِهْتِمَام	overthrow, revolution اِنْقِلَاب اِجْتِمَاعِي
	obedience, compliance اِنْقِيَاد

how bad!	بِئسَ	autocratic	أُوتوقراطي
wretchedness, misery	بَأْساء	automatic	أُوتوماتيكي
miserable, wreched	بَئيْس	automobile	أُوتوموبيل
stale, old	بائت	hotel	اوتيل
temporal, passing, extinct	بائد	lower, more depressed	أَوْطَأ
fallow, barren	بائر	ocean	أُوقيانس/أُوقيانوس
wretched, miserable, unfortunate	بائس	Atlantic Ocean	أُوقيانس اَطْلَنْطى
seller, salesman	بائع	Pacific Ocean	أُوقيانس باسيفيكي
hawker, peddler	بائع دَوّار	Indian Ocean	أُوقيانس هندي
saleswoman	بائعة	orchestra	أُوكِستَر
calamity, disaster, misfortune	بائقة (بَوَائق)	Italian	ايطالي
clear, evident, apparent, obvious, patent	بائِن	Italy	ايطاليا

dower, dowry, dot	بائنة	origin, source, core	بُؤْبُؤْ
door, gate, section, entrance, chapter	باب (أَبْواب)	pupil of the eye	بُؤْبُؤ العَيْن
front door	باب الصَّدْر	well, spring, pit	بِئر (آبار)
revolving door	باب دَوّار	focal	بُؤْري
revolving door	باب لَفَّاف	power, strength, courage, valour, detriment	بَأْس
sliding door	باب مُنْزَلِق		
Pope, papa, daddy	بَابَا	misery, wretchedness	بُؤْس

بَارّ (أبْرار/بَرَرَة) godly, pious, righteous, obedient	باباوى/بابوى papal
بار (بارات) bar, taproom, tavern	بَابَة category, class
بارئ creator, maker	بابور engine, locomotive, steamer
باراشوت parachute	بات decisive, definitive, categorical
بَارجة warship, battleship	بَاتر sharp, cutting, trenchant
بَارحة last night, yesterday	باثولوجي pathologic-al
بَارد cold, cool, chilly, dull, blunt, stupid	باثولوجيا pathology
بَارد الطَّبْع cool, calm, composed	بَاحة (باحات) open space, courtyard
بَارع skilful, brilliant, efficient, outstanding, proficient	باحث (بُحَّاث) research worker, investigator
بَارق thundercloud	بَاخرة (بَوَاخر) steamship, steamer
بَارق الأَمَل glimpse of rays	باد apparent, obvious, evident
بارُود gunpowder	بَادئ beginner, beginning, starting
بَاز/بَأْز falcon, hawk	بَادرة (بَوَادر) harbinger, intuitive idea
بَاسق high, lofty, elevated	بَادية desert, wild
بَاسق الأَخْلاق noble, high-born	بَادية (بَوَادي) bedouins, nomad
باسل (بَوَاسل/بُسَلاء) brave, intrepid, courageous	بَادَية قَفْراء arid desert
باسور (بواسير) hemorrhoids, piles	باذنْجَان aubergine, eggplant

premature, precocious	باكور	bus, autobus	باص (باصات)
beginning, first, initial, firstlings, first fruits, first indications	باكورة (بَوَاكِير)	eye	بَاصِرة (بَوَاصِر)
first fruit	باكورة الفَوَاكِه	false, vain, unreal, untruth, absurd	بَاطِل
hired moarner	بَاكِيَة	hidden, inner, interior	بَاطِن (بَوَاطِن)
worn out, shabby, ragged, deteriorated, rotten	بَال	internal, inner, secret	بَاطِني
mind, memory, attention, condition	بال	internally	بَاطِنيًّا
adult, mature, major, extensive, profound	بَالِغ	length of outstretched arms	بَاع
ball, dance	بالو	motive, reason, inducement	بَاعِث (بَوَاعِث)
sink, drain, sewer	بَالُوعة (بَوَالِيع)	unjust, tyrant, inequitable, oppressor	بَاغٍ (بُغَاة)
balloon, aerostat	بالون	celluloid	بَاغَة
ballet	بَالِيه	remainder, remaining, lasting, eternal, unending	بَاقٍ
okra, gumb	بامية/باميا	bunch, tuft, bouquet	بَاقة
builder	بَان (بُنَاة)	good works	بَاقِيات صَالِحات
sexual potency	بَاه	weeping, weeper, wailer	بَاكٍ (بُكَاة)
pale, faded	بَاهت	early, premature	باكِر
dazzling, splendid, brilliant	بَاهِر	early, in the morning	باكِراً
exorbitant, extortionate, excessive	بَاهظ	early produce or fruits	باكِرة (بَوَاكِر)

بَحَّارَة السَّفينة	the crew of a ship	بَاهِل	unemployed, free
بَحْبُوح	lively, merry, gay, unconstrained	بَبْر (بُبُور)	tiger
بُحْبُوحة	comfort, ease, prosperity	بَبْغاء	parrot
بُحّة	hoarseness, raucity	بَتّ	settlement, adjustment
بَحْت	pure, unmixed, mere, sheer	بَتًّا/بَتَّةً	definitely, decidedly
بَحْث (بُحُوث)	search, research, investigation	بَتَاتًا	finally, decidedly, absolutely
بَحْثَرة	waste, dissipation, scattering	بَتّار	sharp, cutting, trenchant
بَحْر (بُحُور/ بِحار)	sea, ocean, metre	بَتَّة	final decision, adjudication
بَحْر أَحْمَر	the Red Sea	بَتْر	amputation, cutting off
بَحْر أَسْوَد	the Black Sea	بِتْرُول	petroleum
بَحْر الأَبْيَض المُتَوَسِّط	the mediterranean	بَتُول	virgin, maiden
بَحْر الظُّلُمَات	the Atlantic Ocean	بَتُولي	virginal, maiden
		بَتُوليّة	virginity, maidenhood
بَحْرُ القُلْزُم	the Caspian Sea	بَثّ	spreading, diffusion, propagation
بَحْر مَيِّت	the Dead Sea	بَثْر (بُثور)	pimples, pustules
بُحْران	delirium, crisis, climax	بَثِر/بَثِير	pustulous, pimpled
		بَثْرة (بَثَرات)	pustules, pimples
بَحْرة	pool, pond	بَحَّاث	investigator, researcher
		بَحّار	seaman, sailor, mariner

intuition, insight, impulse, immediate spontaneity	بَدَاهة/بَديهة
bedouinism, roaming, nomadism	بَدَاوة
full moon	بَدْر (بُدُور)
creation, invention, contrivance	بَدْع
new, novel, original	بِدْع (أَبْداع)
innovation, heresy, novelty, new doctrine	بِدْعَة (بِدَع)
substitute, alternate, recompense	بَدَل (أَبْدال)
subscription rate	بَدَل الاشْتِراك
suit, costume	بَدْلة (بَدَلات)
bathing suit	بَدْلة الحَمَّام
uniform	بَدْلة رَسْمِيّة
body, trunk	بَدَن (أَبْدان)
physical, bodily, corporal	بَدَني
corpulence, obesity	بُدُونة
bedouin, nomadic	بَدَوي

naval, marine, nautical	بَحْرِي
navy	بَحْرِيّة
lake, truck garden	بُحَيْرة
bravo! well done!	بَخْ بَخْ
vapour, steam, fume	بُخَار
vaporous, steam-driven	بُخَارِي
luck, fortune	بَخْت
very low, cheap	بَخْس
stinginess, avarice, greed	بُخْل
fortunate, lucky	بَخِيت
miser, stingy, avaricious, greedy	بَخِيل
escape, way out	بُدّ
beginning, start, starting point	بَدْء/بَدْأة/بَدَاءة/بِداية
primitive, original	بُدَائي
whim, caprice	بَدَاة
money changer, grocer	بَدّال
corpulence, obesity, fleshiness	بَدَانة
spontaneously, intuitively	بَدَاهةً

uniform, formal dress بَذلة رَسْميّة	maker, creator, unique, wonderful بَدِيع
obscene, foul, bawdy بَذيء	of wonderful workmanship بَدِيع الصُّنْع
foul-mouthed بَذيء اللّسَان	substitute, alternate بَدِيل (بُدَلاء)
piety, righteousness, godliness, benevolence بِرّ	corpulent, fat, fleshy بَدِين (بُدُن)
land, ground بَرّ	intuitive, self-evident بَدِيهي
wheat بُرّ	axiom, self-evident truth بَدِيهيّة
pious, godly, devoted, righteous بَرّ (أَبْرار/ بَرَرَة)	shabby, sloven, unclean بَذّ
creation, making بَرْء	obscenity, foulness, ribaldry بَذَاءة
recovery, restoration to health بُرْء	foul-mouthedness, ribaldry بَذَاءة اللّسَان
guiltless, free, innocent, recovered بَرِئ (أَبْرِياء)	filthiness, slovenliness, shabbiness بَذَاذة
overland, by land, outside بَرًّا	pomp, sumptuousness, luxury بَذَخ
by land and sea بَرًّا وبَحْرًا	seed, pits بَذْر (بُذُور)
innocence, acquittal, guiltlessness, discharge بَرَاءة	seed, pit, pip بَذْرة
licence بَرَاءة (بَرَاءات)	cotton seed بَذْرة القُطْن
empty or vast space, wideness بَرَاحة	spending, expending, surrender بَذْل
refrigerator, icebox بَرّادة	suit of clothes بَذْلة
filings, shavings بُرَادة	

hailstone	بَرَدَة	water cooler	بَرَّادِيّة
isthmus, gap, partition	بَرْزَخ	excrement, ordure, contest, duel	بِراز
pleurisy	بِرْسام		
clover, berseem, trefoil	بِرْسِيم	proficiency, skill, capability	بَرَاعة
mat, door-mat	بُرْش (أَبْراش)	shining, glittering, lustrous	بَرَّاق
rivet	بُرْشَامة	sharpener, penknife	بَرَّاية
leprosy	بَرَص	pencil sharpener	بَرَّاية الأَقْلام
stock exchange	بُرْصة	barbaric, savage, uncivilized, barbarian	بَرْبَري
trunk of the elephant	بُرْطُوم		
bud, blossom, burgeon, sprout	بُرْعُم (بَرَاعم)	barbarity, savagery, brutality	بَرْبَرِيّة
blossom, bud, burgeon	بُرْعُوم (بَرَاعِيْم)	orange	بُرْتُقال
		talon, claw	بُرْثُن
gnats, midges	بَرْغَش	constellation, tower, castle, fortress	بُرْج (بُرُوج)
flea	بُرْغُوث (بَرَاغِيث)		
screw	بُرْغِي (بَرَاغِي)	leo	بُرْج الأَسَد
lightning, telegraph	بَرْق (بُرُوق)	dovecot	بُرْج الحَمَّام
		water tower	بُرْج المِيَاه
veil	بُرْقُع (بَرَاقِع)	libra (balance)	بُرْج المِيْزان
plum	بَرْقُوق	knuckle, finger joint	بُرْجُمة (بَرَاجم)
telegraphic	بَرْقِي		
telegram, wire	بَرْقِيّة (بَرْقِيّات)	cold, coldness, coolness	بَرْد
volcano	بُرْكان (بَرَاكِين)	hail	بَرَد

cold-bloodedness	بُرُودة الدَّم	active volcano	بُرْكان ثَائِر
projection, protrusion, prominence	بُرُوز	extinct volcano	بُرْكان خَامِد
bronze	بُرُونز	dormant volcano	بُرْكان سَاكِن
dust, earth	بَرَى	volcanic	بُرْكاني
terrestrial, wild	بَرِّي	blessing, benediction	بَرَكَة
wild, widerness, desert	بَرِّيَّة	pond, pool, puddle	بِرْكَة (بِرَك)
creation, creature, universe	بَرِيَّة (بَرَايا)	swimming pool	بِرْكَة السِّبَاحة
post, mail, mailman	بَرِيد	parliament	بَرْلَمان
air mail	بَرِيد الجَوّ	parliamentary	بَرْلَماني
air mail	بَرِيد جَوِّي	twisting, winding	بَرْم
surface mail	بَرِيد عَادِي	bored, weary, discontented	بَرِم
postal, mailman, courier	بَرِيدي	barrel, coop, keg	بَرْميل (بَرَاميل)
British	بَرِيطاني/بِرِيْطاني	schedule, programme, catalogue	بَرْنَامَج/برناماج (بَرَامج)
Britain	بَرِيطانيا	curriculum	بَرْنَامَج الدِّرَاسَة
shine, glitter, gloss	بَرِيق (بَرَائِق)	proof, evidence	بُرْهَان (بَرَاهِين)
rope, lace, cord, twine	بَرِيم	a little while	بُرْهَة (بُرَه)
nipple, teat, udder	بُزّ/بِزّ	protocol	بُرُوتُوكول
draper, cloth merchant	بَزَّاز	signs of the zodiac	بُرُوج الأَفْلاك
spit, spittle	بُزَاق	coolness, coldness, frigidity	بُرُود/بُرُودة
tapping cock, faucet	بُزَال		

biscuit	بَسْكُوت/بَسْكُوِيت	clothes, attire, appearance	بِزّة
smile	بَسْمَة	uniform	بِزّة رَسْمِيّة
simple, plain, artless, trivial	بَسِيط (بُسَطاء)	seed	بِزْر (بُزُور)
open-handed, generous	بَسِيط الكَفّ	seed, grain, pip, kernel	بِزْرَة
good news, good omen, prophecy	بَشارة	tapping, puncture	بَزْل
cheerful, happy	بَشّاش	emergence, rising, appearance	بُزُوغ
smile, cheerfulness, happiness	بَشاشَة	sunrise	بُزُوغ الشَّمْس
ugliness, unsightliness	بَشاعة	carpet, rug	بِساط (بُسُط/أَبْسِطَة)
joy, cheerfulness, gaiety	بِشْر	pall	بِساط الرَّحْمَة
glad tidings	بُشْر	simplicity, plainness, artlessness	بَساطة
man, mankind, human being	بَشَر	courage, brevity, intrepidity	بَسالة
epidermis, skin	بَشَرَة	garden, orchard	بُسْتان (بَساتين)
glad tidings, good news	بُشْرَى	gardener	بُسْتاني
human, epidermal	بَشَري	gardening, horticulture	بَسْتَنَة
mankind, human race	بَشَرِيّة	piston	بِسْتُون
ugly, unpleasant, disgusting	بَشِع/بَشِيع	unripe dates	بُسْر
towel	بَشْكِير (بَشَاكِير)	spreading, stretching, dilating, delight	بَسْط
		extent, extension, capability	بَسْطَة

insight, discernment, penetration بَصِيرة	bath towel بَشْكِير الحَمَّام
glow, shine, glitter بَصِيص	satiation, surfeit بَشَم
ray of hope بَصِيص من الأَمَل	wimple بَشْنُوقة
tender-skinned بَضّ	cheerful, happy بَشُوش
goods, wares, (بَضَائع) بِضَاعة commodities	announcer of (بُشَراء) بَشِير good news, forerunner
a few, some بِضْع	discernment, insight, بَصَارة perception
meat, piece of (بِضَع) بِضْعة meat	glittering, shining, بَصّاص detective
duck (بَطّة) بَطّ	spittle, saliva بُصَاق
slowness, tardiness, بُطْء delay	look, embers بَصّة
battery بَطّارِيّة	brand, fire brand بَصّة نار
potato بَطَاطا/بَطَاطس	sight, eyesight, (أَبْصار) بَصَر glance
fried potatoes بَطَاطس مُحَمَّر	optic, ocular, visual بَصَري
card, ticket (بَطَائق) بِطَاقة	spit, saliva بَصْقة
deposit slip بِطَاقة الإِيْدَاع	onions (بَصَلة) بَصَل
ration card بِطَاقة التَّمْوين	stamp, (بَصَمات) بَصْمة imprint, impression
visiting card بِطَاقة الزِّيَارة	fingerprint بَصْمة الإِصْبَع
identity card بِطَاقة الهُوِيَّة	stamp imprint بَصْمة الْخَتْم
identity card بِطَاقة شَخْصِيّة	discerning, (بُصَراء) بَصِير discriminate, well-versed, acquinted
greeting card بِطَاقة مُعَايَدة	
heroism, bravery بَطَالة	

sole of the foot بَطْن القَدَم	unemployment, بطَالة/بَطَالة
palm of the hand بَطْن الكَفّ	vacation, inactivity
paunchy, stout, بَطِن/بَطِين glutton	innerside, inside بطَانة
	retinue, suite بطَانة الأمير
gluttony, epicurism بِطْنَة	lining of a بطَانة الثَّوْب garment
abdominal, ventral بَطْني	
heroism, bravery, بُطُولة intrepidity	blanket, rug, cover بَطَّانِيّة
	quacking (of a duck) بَطْبَطَة
world بُطُولة عَالَمِيّة championship	basin-shaped valley بَطْحاء
slow, sluggish, tardy بَطِيْء	arrogance, wantonness, بَطَر vanity, dissatisfaction
slothful, بَطِيء الحَرَكة sluggish	patrician, بِطْريق (بَطَارِقة) penguin
wide bed of a stream, بَطِيحة steppe	prowess, power, بَطْش strength, violence
melon, water melon بِطِّيخ	nullity, uselessness, بُطْل nothingness, falsity
clitoris بَظْر (بُظُور)	
bogey, bugbear بُعْبُع	brave, valiant, بَطَل (أَبْطال) intrepid, hero, champion
sending, dispatching, بَعْث resurrection	world champion بَطَل العَالَم
delegation, بَعْث (بُعُوث) mission	uselessness, nullity, بُطْلان invalidity, falsity
mission, بَعْثة (بَعَثَات) delegation, expedition	heroine, woman بَطَلة champion
archaeological بَعْثة أَثَرِيَّة expedition	abdomen, بَطْن (بُطُون/أَبْطُن) belly, interior

beyond reach, unattainable	بعيْد المَنَال	diplomatic mission	بَعْثة دِبْلُوماسِيّة
far-sighted, farseeing	بعيد النَّظَر	military mission	بَعْثة عَسْكَرِيّة
camel	بَعير	scattering, strewing	بَعْثَرة
prostitution, adultery	بِغَاء	remoteness, farness	بُعْد
surprise, sudden	بَغْتَة	after, afterwards, later	بَعْدُ
suddenly, surprisingly	بَغْتَةً	after, beside	بَعْدَ
drizzle, light rain	بَغْشَة	distance, space	بُعْد (أَبْعاد)
hate, hatred, detestation	بُغْض/بَغْضَاء	from now on, in the future	بَعْد الآن
mule	بَغْل (بِغال)	after that, later on	بَعْدَ ذَلِك
injustice, iniquity, adultery, prostitution	بَغْي	after that, thereafter, then	بَعْدَئِذٍ
prostitute, whore, adultress	بَغِيّ	dung, droppings	بَعْر/بَعَر
desire, wish, desideratum	بُغْيَة	scattering, dissipation	بَعْزَقَة
hateful, detestable, abominable	بَغِيض	part, portion	بَعْض
staying, remaining, continuation, existence, permanence, eternity	بَقَاء	husband, lord	بَعْل (بُعُول)
		wife	بَعْلَة
prattler, chatterbox, very talkative	بَقَّاق	mosquitoes, gnats	بَعُوض/بَعُوضة
		far, distant, remote	بَعِيْد (بُعَداء)
greengrocer, grocer	بَقَّال/بَقّالة	unfathomable, deep	بَعيد الغَوْر
		long-range, long-distance	بَعيد المَدَى

dumbness, muteness بَكَم	grocery بِقَالة
premature, precocious بَكُور	remains, leavings بَقَايا
prematureness, بُكُور earliness, precociousness	babbler, prattler, بَقْباق chatterbox
premogeniture بُكُورة	prattling, chattering بَقْبَقَة
early, premature بَكِير	oxen, bovine cattle بَقَر
but, however, even بَلْ	cow (بَقَرات) بَقَرة
wetness, saturation, بَلَّ moisture	stain, spot, lot, (بُقَع) بُقْعَة locality
recovery, recuperation بِلّ	vegetables, (بُقُول) بَقْل herbs, greens
tribulation, affliction, بَلاء misfortune	remainder, (بَقَايا) بَقِيّة remnant, rest, rudiment
anxieties, بَلاَبِل apprehensions	weeping, crying, بُكَاء bewailing
foreign countries بِلاَد أَجْنَبِيّة	virginity, maidenhood بَكَارة
stupidity, dullness, بَلاَدة silliness	bachelor's degree بَكَالُوريا
flagstone, tiles, palace بَلاط	bacteria بَكْتيريا
royal court or بَلاط المَلِك palace	young camel بَكْر
tile, flag, slab, paving بَلاطة stone	virgin, maiden, (أَبْكار) بِكْر new, first, firstling
tombstone, بَلاطة الضَّريح gravestone	early morning بُكْرة
	tomorrow, next day بُكْرةً
information, message, بَلاغ notification, announcement	bucle, clasp (بُكَل) بُكْلة
	bachelor's degree بَكَلُوريوس

pharynx بُلْعُوم (بَلاعيم)	ultimatum بَلاغ أخير
sufficiency, adequacy بُلْغَة	eloquence بَلاغة
phlegm, expectoration بَلْغَم	idiocy, stupidity, imbecility بَلاهة
phlegmatic, phlegmy بَلْغَمي	
bluff, imposition بَلَف/بَلْفة	concern, anxiety, perplexity, confusion بَلْبَال
wasteland, barren land بَلْقَع/بَلْقَعة	confusion, muddle, disorder, anxiety, perplexity بَلْبَلة
balcony بَلْكون	
moisture, wetness, dampness بَلَل	dates بَلَح/ بَلَحة
	country, town, city بَلَد (بلاد)
idiocy, imbecility, foolishness بَلَه	countries بَلَد (بُلْدان)
	capital city بَلَد رأس
crystal, crystal glass بَلُّور/بِلَّور	underdeveloped countries بُلْدان مُتَأَخِّرة
crystallization بَلْوَرة	town, city, village, community بَلْدة
crystal, crystalline بَلُّوري/بِلَّوري	
	native, countryman بَلَدي
blouse بَلُوز/بَلُوزة	local authority, municipality بَلَدِيّة
oak, acron بَلُّوط	
sink, cesspool, sewer بَلُّوعة	balsam, balm بَلْسان
attainment, maturity, arrival, majority, adolescence بُلُوغ	balsam, balm بَلْسَم
	extortion, exaction, blackmail بَلْص
balloon بَلُّون	big swallow, big gulp بَلْعة
calamity, misfortune, tribulation, affliction بَلْوَى	pharynx بُلْعُم (بَلاعم)

building, edifice	بِنَايَة	shabbiness, decay, decline	بِلىً
daughter, girl	بِنْت (بَنات)	yes, aye, certainly	بَلىً
cousin	بِنْتُ العَمّ/الخَال	worn, old, decomposed	بَلِيّ
cockroach	بِنْت وَرَدَان	billiards	بِلْيَارْدُو
beet root	بَنْجَر	trial, tribulation, misfortune, calamity	بَلِيَّة (بَلايا)
banner, flag, article, term	بَنْد (بُنُود)	stupid, dull, doltish	بَلِيد
emporium, commercial centre, central town	بَنْدَر	eloquent, profound, tense, serious	بَلِيغ
hazel, hazel nuts	بُنْدُق (بَنَادق)	cool and moist wind	بَلِيل
gun, musket, rifle	بُنْدُقِيّة (بَنَادق)	billion	بَلْيُون (بَلايِين)
shot gun	بُنْدُقِيّة رَشّ	coffee, coffee beans	بُنّ
rifle	بُنْدُقِيّة رَصَاص	mason, builder	بَنّاء
airgun	بُنْدُقِيّة هَوَاء	structure, building	بِنَاء (أَبْنِيَة)
petrol, gasoline, benzine	بَنْزِين/بِنْزِين	freemason	بَنّاء حُرّ
pence	بِنْس	building, construction	بِنَاء/بُنْيَان
boarding-house, boarding school	بَنْسِيُون	structural, constructional	بِنَائي
ring finger	بِنْصِر (بَنَاصِر)	adversities, misfortunes	بَنَات الدَّهْر
point	بُنْط (بُنُوط)	worries, cares	بَنَات الصَّدْر
pants, trousers	بَنْطَلُون(بَنْطَلُونات)	calamities, misfortunes	بَنَاتُ بِئْس
drawer,knickers	بَنْطَلُون تَحْتَاني	finger tips	بَنَان

splendid, pleasant, delightful بَهِج/بَهِيج	shorts بَنْطَلُون قصير
splendour, brilliance, resplendence, delight بَهْجَة	violet بَنَفْسَج
breathlessness, laboured breathing بُهْر	violetish بَنَفْسَجِي
dazzlement, deception بَهْر/بَهْرة	origin, core, heart, prince بُنْك
tinsel, gold thread بَهْرَجان	bank, bench (بُنُوك) بَنْك
vain show, hollow pomp بَهْرَجَة	national bank بَنْك أَهْلِي
acrobat, equilibrist بَهْلَوان	credit bank بَنْك التَّسْلِيف
acrobatic بَهْلَوانِي	blood bank بَنْك الدَّم
buffoon, clown, jester بَهْلُول/بُهْلُول	world bank بَنْك دُوَلِي
saloon, parlour, hall (أَبْهاء) بَهْو	Israelites, Jews بَنُو اسرائيل
splendid, brilliant, magnificent, bright بَهِيّ	sonship, filiation بُنُوّة
jet-black, pitch dark (بُهُم) بَهِيم	filial بَنَوِيّ
beast, animal, brute (بَهائم) بَهِيمة	structure, constitution بُنْيَة الجِسْم
bestial, brutal, brutish بَهِيمِي	structure, setup, physique بِنْيَة/بُنْيَة (بُنًى/بِنًى)
brutality, bestiality بَهِيمِيّة	splendour, beauty, brilliancy, radiance بَهاء
gatekeeper, porter بَوّاب	spice, condiment (بَهارات) بَهار
gate, portal (بَوّابات) بَوّابة	falsehood, lie, slander, calumny بُهْت
	falsehood, lie, calumny, slander بُهْتان
	amazement, bewilderment بَهْتة

police, policeman	بُولِيس	perdition, destruction, ruin	بَوَار
traffic police	بُولِيس المُرُور	bugler, trumpeter	بَوّاق
military police	بُولِيس حَرْبِي	melting pot, crucible	بُوتَقَة/بُودَقَة
detective, sleuth	بُولِيس سِرِّي	disclosing, revealing	بَوْح
policy	بُولِيسة	fallow, barren, uncultivated	بُور
insurance policy	بُولِيسة التَّأْمِين	exchange, stock exchange	بُورصَة
bill of lading	بُولِيسَة الشَّحْن	nozzle, spout	بُوز (أَبْواز)
owl	بُوْم (أَبْوام)	ice-cream	بُوزَة
environment, position, surroundings, residence	بِيئَة (بِيئات)	bus	بُوس
infantry	بِيادة	kiss	بُوسَة/بَوْسَة
whiteness, blank space	بَيَاض	mob, rabble	بَوْش (أَوْباش)
white of the eye	بَيَاضُ العَيْن	reed, inch	بُوصَة
day light	بَيَاضُ النَّهَار	melting pot, crucible	بُوطة
tradesman, merchant, seller, salesman	بَيّاع	ice-cream	بُوظَة
hawker, pedlar	بَيّاع مُتَجَوِّل	strait, port, sea-port	بُوغاز
statement, declaration, account, description manifestation	بَيَان	buffet, bar, refreshment room	بُوفِيه
proclamation	بَيَان رَسْمِي	trumpet, bugle	بُوق (أَبْواق)
piano, pianoforte	بِيَانُو	urine	بَوْل
explanatory, illustrative, demonstrative	بَيَانِي	steel	بُولاد
		urinary, uric	بَوْلِي

standard, banner, flag	بَيْرَق	verse	بَيْت (أَبْيَات)
bureaucratic	بِيْروقراطي	house, home, residence, family compartment	بَيْت (بُيُوت)
bureaucracy	بِيْروقراطية		
eggs	بَيْض (بُيُوض)	toile, water closet, privy	بَيْتُ الْخَلَاء
boiled eggs	بَيْض مَسْلوق		
fried eggs	بَيْض مَقْلي	brothel, bawdy-house	بَيْت الدِّعَارة
egg, testicle, helmet	بَيْضَة	treasure house, treasure	بَيْتُ الْمَال
oval, egg-shaped	بَيْضَوي		
oval, egg-shaped	بَيْضي	Jerusalem	بَيْت المَقْدس
veterinarian, farrier	بَيْطار (بَيَاطِرة)	commercial house, business house	بَيْتَ تجَاري
veterinary	بَيْطَري	country house	بَيْت خَلَوي
sale, selling	بَيْع	country house	بَيْت رِيْفي
forced sale	بَيْع جَبْري	call house	بَيْت سِرِّي
agreement, selling transaction	بَيْعَة	tent	بَيْتُ شَعْر
synagogue, churck	بِيْعَة	building, edifice	بَيْتُ مَدَر
separation, disunion, division	بَيْن	Jerusalem	بَيْت مُقَدَّس
between, among	بَيْنَ	domestic, private, home made, of the house	بَيْتي
clear, obvious, evident, plain, apparent	بَيِّن	pajama, trousers	بِيْجَامَة/بِيْجاما
before him, in his presence	بَيْنَ يَدَيْه	pawn	بَيْدَق
		beer, beer house	بِيْرا/بِيْرة

education, discipline, تَأْديب disciplinary punishment	whereas, while, بَيْنا/بَيْنَما whilst
corporal تَأْديب جُسْمَاني punishment	evidence, clear proof بَيِّنَة
disciplinary, punitive, تَأْديبي educational	circumstantial بَيِّنَة ظَرْفِيّة evidence
execution, payment, تَأْدية accomplishment, performance,	ovum, egg-cell بُبَيْضَة/ بُوَيْضَة

ت

swinging, rocking تَأْرْجَحَة	commemoration, تَأْبين funeral, oration
mutual support, تَآزُر assistance	stammering تَأْتَأَة
aggravation, critical تَأَزُّم situation	feeling, emotion, تَأَثُّر sensibility
aggravation of تَأَزُّم (الحَالَة) the situation	furnishing, providing تَأْثيث with furnitures
regret, sorrow, تَأَسُّف sadness	effect, impression, تَأْثير influence
consolation, comfort تَأْسِية	leasing, letting on تَأْجير lease, lease
establishment, تَأْسيس laying, foundation	delay, postponment, تَأْجيل deferment
fundamental, تَأْسيسي foundational	fraternity, تَآخٍ fraternization
official endorsement تَأْشير	delay, slowness, تَأَخُّر tardiness
visa تَأْشِيرة	
transit visa تَأْشِيرة اجْتِياز	delay, postponement, تَأْخير deferment, putting off
transit visa تَأْشِيرة مُرُور	

feminine, effemination	تَأْنِيث	grumbling, murmuring	تَأَفَّف
preparation, alertness, readiness	تَأَهُّب	assurance, reassurance	تَأَكُّد
interpretation, explanation	تَأْوِيل	confirmation, emphasis, assurance	تَأْكِيد
support, confirmation, maintenance	تَأْيِيد	familiarity, intimacy, harmony, concord	تَآلُف
repentant, penitent	تَائِب	shine, glitter, glow, radiance	تَأَلُّق
yearning, longing, desirous	تَائِق	feeling of pain, pain	تَأَلُّم
stray, straying, errant	تَائِه	composition, compiling, taming	تَأْلِيف
follower, adherent, subordinate	تَابِع (أَتْبَاع)	deification, apotheosis	تَأْلِيه
following, subordinate, subsidiary	تَابِع (تُبَّاع/تَبَعَة)	conspiracy, conference, deliberation	تَآمُر
consequence, result, dependency	تَابِعَة (تَوَابِع)	consideration, meditation, contemplation	تَأَمُّل
spice, condiment	تَابِل (تَوَابِل)	nationalization	تَأْمِيم
coffer, box, casket	تَابُوت	assurance, insurance, surety, security	تَأْمِين
crown, diadem	تَاج (تِيْجان)	fire insurance	تَأْمِين ضِدَّ الحَرِيق
tradesman, merchant, businessman	تَاجِر (تُجَّار)	life insurance	تَأْمِين عَلى الحَيَاة
retailer, retail merchant	تَاجِر التَّجْزِئَة	slowness, carefulness, deliberateness	تَأَنٍّ
wholesaler	تَاجِر الجُمْلَة	fastidiousness, nicety, elegance	تَأَنُّق
ironmonger	تَاجِر الحَدَائِد	reprimand, reproach, blame	تَأْنِيب

retardation, slowness	تَبَاطُؤ	retailer	تَاجِر القطاعي
successively, in succession	تِبَاعاً	once, sometimes	تَارَةً
racial hatred	تَبَاغُض عُنْصُري	sometimes, at other times	تَارَةً أُخْرَى
straw seller	تَبّان	date, time, history	تَاريخ
vainglory, self-exaltation, pride	تَبَاهٍ	biography	تَاريخ الحَيَاة
contradiction, difference, dissimilarity	تَبَايُن	historic-al	تَاريخِي
braggery, boasting	تَبَجُّح	ninth	تاسِع
reverence, honour, veneration	تَبْجيل	insignificant, trivial, paltry, insipid	تَافِه
profoundness, deep penetration	تَبَحُّر	following, succeeding, subsequent	تَالٍ
evaporation, exhalation	تَبَخُّر	spoiled, damaged, deteriorated	تَالِف
fumigation, evaporation	تَبْخير	astonished, bewildered	تَالِه
change, conversion	تَبَدُّل	complete, perfect, accomplished	تَامّ
scattering, dispersion, waste	تَبْديد	ruin, destruction	تَبّ/تَبَب
alternation, change, substitution	تَبْديل	exchanging, bartering	تَبَادُل
squandering, wasting, extravagance	تَبْذير	exchange of views	تَبَادُل الآرَاء
		exchange of greetings	تَبَادُل السَّلام
acquittal, discharge, exemption	تَبْرِئة	ruin, destruction	تَبَار
		first indications, foretokens	تَبَاشير

moistness, wetness, dampness, humidity	تَبَلُّل	contribution, donation subscription	تَبَرُّع
crystallization	تَبَلْوُر	weariness, boredom, discontent, restlessness	تَبَرُّم
tile-laying, paving with flagstones	تَبْليط	dandruff	تبْرِيَّة
conveyance, delivery, announcement, information	تَبْليغ	cooling, refrigeration	تَبْرِيد
adoption, affiliation	تَبَنٍّ	exculpation, justification	تَبْرِير
chopped straw	تِبْن	blessing, benediction	تَبْرِيك
accession, succession	تَبَوُّء	simplification	تَبْسِيط
accession to the throne	تَبَوُّء العَرْش	proclamation of good news	تَبْشِير
classification, categorization	تَبْوِيب	penetration, deliberation, consideration	تَبَصُّر
explanation, exposition, illustration	تِبْيَان	following, pursuing	تَبَع
whitening, timing, whitewashing	تَبْيِيض	follower, adherent (أَتْباع)	تَبَع
clean copy	تَبْيِيضة	portioning, dividing, division	تَبْعِيض
exposition, explanation, demonstration	تَبْيِين	tobacco (تُبُوغ)	تِبْغ
succession, relay	تَتَابُع	mild tobacco	تِبْغ بَارِد
pursuing, chasing, pursuance	تَتَبُّع	remorse, reproach	تَبْكِيت
one after another, in succession	تَتْرَى	confusion, perplexity, muddle	تَبَلْبُل
		silliness, obtuseness, idiocy, dullness	تَبَلُّد

commercial, mercantile	تِجَارِي	complement, supplement	تَتِمّة
similarity, resemblance, homogeneity	تَجَانُس	finishing, completing, completion	تَتْمِيم
facing, opposite of, in front of	تُجَاه	tetanus	تَتَنُوس
ignoring, avoiding	تَجَاهُل	crowning, coronation	تَتْوِيج
exceeding, going beyond, crossing	تَجَاوُز	yawn, yawning	تَثَاؤُب
trespassing	تَجَاوُز الحُدُور	sluggishness, dotishness	تَثَاقُل
bonesetting	تَجْبِير	verification, making sure, ascertainment	تَثَبُّت
orthopaedics	تَجْبِير العِظَام	consolidation, stabilization, affirmation, confirmation	تَثْبِيت
renewal, revival, restoration	تَجَدُّد	blame, reproach, censure	تَثْرِيب
renewal, renovation, regeneration	تَجْدِيد	cultivation of mind, refinement	تَثْقِيف
rowing, blasphemy	تَجْدِيف	weighting, burdening	تَثْقِيل
blasphemous	تَجْدِيفِي	trinity, tripling	تَثْلِيث
experiment, test, trial, experience, attempt	تَجْرِبة (تَجَارِب)	assessment, valuation, estimation	تَثْمِين
dismantlement, isolation, abstractness	تَجَرُّد	doubling, plaiting	تَثْنِية
testing, trial, attempt, temptation	تَجْرِيب	nuclear tests	تَجَارِب نَوَوِيّة
experimental, trial	تَجْرِيبِي	trade, merchandise, commerce	تِجَارة

beautification, cosmetics	تَجْمِيل	stripping, divesting, denudation, dismantlement, disarmament,	تَجْرِيد
avoidance	تَجَنُّب	military expedition	تَجْرِيدة
recruitment, enlistment	تَجْنِيد	division, partition, dessociation	تَجْزِئَة
military conscription	تَجْنِيد إِجْبارِي	reward, recompense	تَجْزية
gathering of people	تَجَهْمُر	materialization, incarnation	تَجَسُّد
equipment, preparation	تَجْهِيز (تَجْهِيزات)	spying, espionage	تَجَسُّس
preparatory	تَجْهِيزِي	corporification, embodiment	تَجْسِيم
wandering, rambling, roaming, roving	تَجْوال	drying, dehydration, desiccation	تَجْفِيف
roving, travelling, wandering round	تَجَوُّل	manifestation, revelation	تَجَلٍّ
betterment, intonation, improvement	تَجْوِيد	honour, respect, esteem	تَجِلّة
hole, cavity, hollow	تَجْوِيف (تَجَاوِيف)	freezing, icing, bookbinding	تَجْلِيد
avoidance	تَحاش	frozenness, coagulation, solidification	تَجَمُّد
alliance	تَحَالُف	gathering, meeting, crowd, mob	تَجَمُّع
discussion, debate	تَحَاوُر		
courtship, wooing	تَحَبُّب	solidification, consolidation, hardening	تَجْمِيد
under, underneath, below	تَحْتَ		
under the patronage of	تَحْتَ إِشْرَاف	freezing of assets	تَجْمِيد الأَمْوال

movement, motion, departure	تَحَرُّك	on probation or trial	تَحْت الاخْتِبار
liberating, liberation, emancipation, editing	تَحْرِير	on probation	تَحْت التَّجْرِبة
in writing, written	تَحْرِيرِي	in training, apprentice, probationer	تَحْتَ التَّمْرِين
provocation, instigation, incitement	تَحْرِيش	in press	تَحْتَ الطَّبْع
instigation, incitement, provocation	تَحْرِيض	under consideration	تَحْت النَّظَر
misconstruction, distortion, alteration, perversion	تَحْرِيف	available, at hand	تَحْتَ الْيَد
stirring, moving	تَحْرِيك	under his control	تَحْت يَده
prohibition, interdiction	تَحْرِيم	lower, placed below	تَحْتَانِي
partiality, factionalism	تَحَزُّب	petrifaction	تَحَجُّر
improvement, betterment	تَحَسُّن	prohibition, interdiction	تَحْجِير
beautification, betterment, improvement	تَحْسِين	challenge, provocation	تَحَدٍّ (تَحَدِّيات)
gathering, concentration	تَحَشُّد	slope, slant, declivity	تَحَدُّر
insertion, interpolation	تَحْشِيَة	limitation, restriction, determination	تَحْدِيد
protection, safeguarding	تَحَصُّن	cautioning, warning	تَحْذِير
		investigation, enquiry	تَحَرٍّ (تَحَرِّيات)
		meddling, tampering with	تَحَرُّش
		combustion, burning	تَحَرُّق

تَحَكُّم arbitrariness, despotism	تَحْصيص apportionment, allotment
تَحَكُّمي despotic, arbitrary	تَحْصيل acquisition, receipts, obtainment, summary, collection
تَحْكيم arbitration, arbitral decision	
تَحَلُّل decomposition, disassociation, dissolution	تَحْصين fortification, fortifying, strengthening
تَحْلِيَة ornamentation, decoration	تَحْضير preparing, preparation
تَحْليف swearing in	تَحْضيري preparatory
تَحْليق flying, hovering	تَحَطُّم crash, breakdown, collapse
تَحْليل dissolution, analysis, decomposition, absolution	تَحْطيم breaking, smashing, shattering
تَحْليل طَيْفي spectrum analysis	تُحْفَة (تُحَف) gift, present, rarity
تَحْليل نَفْسي psycho-analysis	تَحَفُّظ caution, precaution, reticence, reserve
تَحْليل وَصْفي qualitative analysis	تَحَفُّظي precautionary, preventive
تَحْليلي analytic-al	
تَحَمُّس zeal, enthusiasm, ardour	تَحَقُّق ascertainment, certitude, verification
تَحَمُّل bearing, toleration, endurance, durability	تَحْقير humiliation, disdain degradation
تَحْميض acidification, souring	تَحْقيق execution, realization, examination, investigation, substantiation
تَحْميل loading, burdening, shipment	

graduation from a college or university	تَخَرُّج
destruction, sabotage, demolition	تَخْرِيب
extraction, elimination, interpretation	تَخْرِيج
piercing, boring, punching	تَخْرِيم
storing, warehousing, accumulation	تَخْزِين
stiffness, rigidity	تَخَشُّب
specialization, particularization	تَخَصُّص
specification, specialization, allotment	تَخْصِيص
planning, designing, plan, design	تَخْطِيط
disguise, concealment	تَخَفٍّ
lowering, lessening, reduction	تَخْفِيض
lightening, lessening, reducing, alleviation	تَخْفِيف
reduction of taxes	تَخْفِيف الضَّرَائِب
commutation of punishment	تَخْفِيف العُقُوبة
renunciation, relinquishment	تَخَلٍّ

mummification	تَحَنُّط
precaution, care, carefulness	تَحَوُّط
transformation, change, turning, alteration	تَحَوُّل
modification, change, alteration	تَحْوِير
encirclement, walling in	تَحْوِيط
change, alteration, transformation, conversion	تَحْوِيل
endorsement	تَحْوِيل الصُّكُوك
remittance	تَحْوِيل النُّقُود
greeting, salutation	تَحِيَّة (تَحِيَّات/تَحايا)
compliments, regards	تَحِيَّات
confusion, perplexity, embarrassment	تَحَيُّر
partiality, prepossession	تَحَيُّز
conversation, talk, speech	تَخَاطُب
bed, bedstead, seat, bench, throne	تَخْت
blackboard, desk	تَخْتَة
anaesthetizing, narcotizing	تَخْدِير

interference, intervention	تَدَاخُل
threatening to fall or breakdown	تَدَاعٍ
cure, treatment	تَدَاوٍ
alternation, circulation	تَدَاوُل
contemplation, meditation	تَدَبُّر
embellishment, adornment	تَدْبِيج
measures, steps (تَدَابِير)	تَدْبِير
planning, disposal, management, economy	تَدْبِير (تَدْبِيرَات)
household management	تَدْبِير المَنْزِل
swindling, imposture, humbug	تَدْجِيل
intervention, entry, interference	تَدَخُّل
smoking, fumigation	تَدْخِين
graduation, gradual advance	تَدَرُّج
tuberculosis	تَدَرُّن
pulmonary tuberculosis	تَدَرُّن رِئَوِي

تَخَلُّص	release, liberation, escape
تَخَلُّف	staying or remaining behind
تَخْلِيَة	evacuating, evacuation, vacating
تَخْلِيد	immortalization, perpetuation
تَخْلِيص	liberation, salvation, clarification, purification
تَخْم/تُخْم	border, boundary, limit
تُخْمَة (تُخَم)	indigestion, dyspepsia
تَخْمِير	leavening, fermenting
تَخْمِين	guess, conjecture, assessment
تَخَنُّث	effeminacy
تَخْوِيف	frightening, intimidation
تَخَيُّل	imagination, fancy, phantacy
تَخَيُّلِي	imaginary, fanciful, fantastic
تَدَابِير احْتِيَاطِيَّة	precautionary measures

demolition, ruination, destruction	تَدْمِير	training, drilling, practice	تَدْرِيب
pollution, defilement, contamination	تَدْنِيس	military training	تَدْرِيب عَسْكَرِي
slump, fall	تَدَهْوُر	gradation, classification	تَدْرِيج
subjugating, vanquishing	تَدْوِيخ	gradual, progressive	تَدْرِيجِي
internationalization	تَدْوِيل	gradually, by degrees	تَدْرِيجِيًّا
recording, noting down, registering	تَدْوِين	teaching, instruction	تَدْرِيس
pendulation, oscillation	تَذَبْذُب	inauguration, consecration	تَدْشِين
remembrance, reminder, souvenir	تَذْكَار/تِذْكار	supporting, consolidation	تَدْعِيم
commemorative, memorial	تَذْكَارِي	warming, heating	تَدْفِئَة
remembrance, recollection	تَذَكُّر	effusion, influx, outpour, outburst	تَدَفُّق
momento, reminder	تَذْكِرَة	exactitude, accuracy, precision	تَدْقِيق
ticket, card, note	تَذْكِرَة (تَذَاكِر)	coddling, coquetry	تَدَلُّل
platform ticket	تَذْكِرَة الرَّصِيف	fraud, deceit, imposture	تَدْلِيس
pass, permit	تَذْكِرَة المُرُور	fraudulent, deceitful	تَدْلِيسِي
identity card	تَذْكِرَة الهُوِيَّة	massage, embrocation	تَدْلِيك
post card	تَذْكِرَة بَرِيد	proving, fondling, substantiation, petting	تَدْلِيل

mutual consent	تَرَاضٍ	return ticket	تَذْكِرَة ذَهَاب وإِيَاب
accumulation	تَرَاكُم	medical prescription	تَذْكِرَة طِبِّيَّة
dusty, earthy, dust-covered	تَرِب	reminder, reminding, impregnation	تَذْكِير
contemporary, match, colleague, equal	تِرْب (أَتْراب)	self-abasement, obsequiousness	تَذَلُّل
soil, dust, dirt, ground, grave	تُرْبَة (تُرَب)	degradation, debasement, surmounting	تَذْلِيل
probationary term	تَرَبُّص	grumbling, complaint, murmuring	تَذَمُّر
pedagogic, educational	تَرْبَوِي	melting, dissolving	تَذْوِيب
upbringing, education	تَرْبِيَة	chairmanship, presidency	تَرَؤُّس
childcare, upbringing	تَرْبِيَةُ الأَطْفَال	dust, soil, earth, ground	تُرَاب (أَتْرِبة)
cattle-farming, breeding	تَرْبِيَةُ الْحَيَوَان	dusty, dust-covered, earthy	تُرَابِي
chicken-farming	تَرْبِيَةُ الدَّجَاج	inheritance, legacy	تُرَاث
physical training	تَرْبِيَة بَدَنِيَّة	retreat, withdrawal, retrogradation	تَرَاجُع
square, plaza	تَرْبِيع/تَرْبِيعَة	looseness, slackness, relaxation	تَرَاخٍ
quadratic, square	تَرْبِيعِي	succession, synonymity	تَرَادُف
arrangement, order, sequence, regularity	تَرْتِيب	terrace	تِرَاس
ordinal	تَرْتِيبِي		
singing, reciting	تَرْتِيل		
hymn, song	تَرْتِيلَة (تَرَاتِيل)		

تَرْصِيع	decoration, ornamentation
تَرْضِيَة	compensation, satisfaction, gratification
تُرْعَة (تُرَع)	canal, channel
تَرْغِيب	exciting, alluring, invitation
تَرَف	luxury, ease, comfort
تَرِف	luxurious, opulent, at ease
تُرْفَة	luxury, affluence, ease, comfort
تَرَفُّض	bigotry, fanaticism
تَرَفُّع	haughtiness, aloofness, disdain
تَرْفِيع	promotion, raising, increasing
تَرْفِيه	recreation, relaxation
تَرَقٍّ (تَرَقِّيَات)	advancement, progress, rise
تَرَقُّب	anticipation, expectation
تَرْقِيَة	improvement, promotion, development
تَرْقِيع	patching
تَرْقِيع الجِلْد	skin grafting

تُرْجُمان (تَرَاجِمة)	interpreter, translator
تَرْجَمة	interpretation, translation
تَرْجَمة الحَيَاة	introduction, biography
تَرَح (أَتْرَاح)	grief, sorrow, distress
تَرْحَاب	welcome, greeting
تَرْحِيب	welcoming, greeting
تَرْخِيص (تَرَاخِيص)	permission, license, discount
تَرْخِيم	apocopation, elision
تَرْدَاد	frequenting, frequent repetition
تَرَدُّد	hesitation, reluctance, frequentation
تَرْدِيد	reiteration, repetition
تُرْس (أَتْرَاس/تُرُوس)	shield, armour
تَرَسُّل	art of letter writing
تَرَسُّم	design, planning
تَرْسِيب	precipitation, sedimentation
تَرَشُّح	infiltration
تَرْشِيح	nomination, candidature

تَرْوِيج	circulation, promotion, propagation	تَرْقِيم	numbering, numeration
تَرْوِيح	recreation, diversion, airing, fanning	تَرْك	leaving, omission, abandonment
تَرْوِيحَة	walk, stroll	تَرِكة (تَرِكات)	legacy, heritage
تَرْوِيسَة	caption, heading	تُرْكيا	Turkey
تَرْوِيق	filtration, purification	تَرْكِيب	fitting, setting, assembling
تَرْوِيقَة	breakfast		
تِرْياق	counter-prison, antidote, theriaca	تَرْكِيب (تَرَاكِيب /تَرْكِيبَات) composition, construction, structure	
تَرِيبَة (تَرَائِب)	chest, thorax	تَرْكِيز	fixation, establishment, concentration
تَزَاوُج	intermarriage		
تَزَحْلُق	skiing, skating	تَرْمُومِتر	thermometer
تَزْكِيَة	purification, sanctification	تَرْمِيد	cremation, incineration
تَزَمُّت	gravity, sedateness, puritanism	تَرْمِيم (تَرْمِيمات)	reparation, repair
تَزَهُّد	abstemiousness, asceticism	تَرْنِيمَة (تَرَانِيم)	song, hymn, anthem
تَزْهِير	flowering, florescence	تَرَهُّب	monastic life, monasticism
تَزَوُّج	marriage	تُرَّهَة	trifle, lie, mockery
تَزْوِيد	supply, providing, purveyance	تَرَوٍّ	consideration, deliberation
تَزْوِير	falsification, forgery	تَرْوِيَة	deliberation, meditation, consideration
تَزْيِيف	forging, counterfeiting		

release, discharge	تَسْرِيح	ornamentation, decorating	تَزْيِين
hairdo, dressing table	تَسْرِيحَة	competition, emulation	تَسَابُق
recording, noting down	تَسْطِير	falling down, collopsing	تَسَاقُط
one ninth	تُسْع (أَتْساع)	snowfall	تَساقُط الثُّلُوج
nine	تِسْع/تِسْعَة	loss of hair	تَساقُط الشَّعْر
nineteen	تِسْعة عشر/تسع عشرة	tolerance, forbearance	تَسَامُح
quote, quotation	تَسْعَرَة	carelessness, leniency, indulgence	تَسَاهُل
ninety, nineteenth	تِسْعُون	equality, sameness, evenness	تَسَاوٍ
appraisal, price-fixing	تَسْعِير	glorification of God	تَسْبِيح
roofing	تَسْقِيف	hymn, anthem	تَسْبِيحة
tranquillization, soothing, alleviation	تَسْكِين	covering, hiding	تَسَتُّر
armament, rearmament	تَسَلُّح	registration, record, entry	تَسْجِيل
chafing	تَسَلُّخ	subjugation, oppression	تَسْخِير
sequence, succession	تَسَلْسُل	settlement, defrayment, aiming	تَسْدِيد
predominance, control, rule, authority	تَسَلُّط	hurry, hastiness	تَسَرُّع
climbing, ascending	تَسَلُّق	amusement, pastime, distraction	تَسْرِيَة
infiltration	تَسَلُّل		
amusement	تَسْلِيَة		

similarity, likeness, resemblance	تَشَابُه	armament, equipment	تَسْلِيح
similarity, resemblance	تَشَاكُل	advance, credit	تَسْلِيف
haughtiness, pride, superciliousness	تَشَامُخ	credit, loan	تَسْلِيفَة
consultation, deliberation	تَشَاوُر	submission, assent, surrender, delivery, saluting	تَسْلِيم
tenacity, obstinacy	تَشَبُّث	poisoning, toxication	تَسَمُّم
imitation	تَشَبُّه	blood poisoning, toxemia	تَسَمُّم دَمَوِي
comparing, simile comparison	تَشْبِيه	naming, nomenclature	تَسْمِية
dissolution, splitting, scattering	تَشْتِيت	accession to the throne	تَسَنُّم
afforestation	تَشْجِير	facilitation, facilities	تَسْهِيل (تَسْهِيلات)
encouragement, heartening	تَشْجِيع	beggary, begging	تَسَوُّل
fatness, obesity	تَشَحُّم	settlement, levelling, adjustment	تَسْوِية
greasing, oiling	تَشْحِيم	leasing, hiring out	تَسْوِيغ
personification, designation, diagnosis	تَشْخِيص	deferment, procrastination	تَسْوِيف (تَسْوِيفات)
dramatic, diagnostic	تَشْخِيصِي	marketing	تَسْوِيق
strengthening, stress, intensification	تَشْدِيد	bargain	تَسْوِيقة
		pessimism	تَشَاؤُم
vagrancy, vagabondage	تَشَرُّد	intricacy, abstruseness	تَشَابُك

تَشْريح	anatomization, dissection
تَشْريحي	anatomical, dessective
تَشْريد	vagabondage, vagrancy, banishment
تَشْريع	legislation, enactment of laws
تَشْريعي	legislative
تَشْريفة (تَشْريفات)	ceremony, protocol, etiquette
تشرين الأوّل	October
تشرين الثّاني	November
تَشْطيب	slicing, finishing off
تَشْطيب الحسَابات	posting of the accounts
تَشَعُّب	ramification, branching, splitting
تَشَعُّع	radiation, eradiation
تَشَعُّع شَمْسِي	solar radiation
تَشْغيل	employment, occupation
تَشَفٌّ	satisfaction, gratification
تَشَكُّك	doubt, skepticism
تَشْكيل (تَشْكيلات)	shaping, forming, fashioning, formation
تَشْكيلات	organizations, formations
تَشْكيلَة	formation, variety, assortment
تَشْليح	plundering, looting, robbing
تَشَنُّج	shrinking, convulsion, spasm
تَشَنُّج رَعْشي	clonic spasm
تَشَنُّج كُرَازي	tonic spasm
تَشَنُّجي	convulsive, spastic
تَشَوُّق	yearning, craving, desire
تَشَوُّه	distortion, ugliness, malformation, disfigurement
تَشْويش	confusion, disturbance, derangement
تَشْويه	disfigurement, deformation, defacement
تَشَيُّع	partiality, partisanship
تَشْييد	construction, erection, building

purification, clearance, settlement, clarification,	تَصْفِيَة	collision, clash, conflict	تَصَادُم
settlement of accounts	تَصْفِيَة الحِسَابَات	conflict of opinions	تَصَادُم الآراء
plating	تَصْفِيح	vicissitudes of time	تَصَارِيف الدَّهْر
hand-clapping, acclaim	تَصْفِيق	vicissitudes of time	تَصَارِيف الزَّمان
applause, acclaim	تَصْفِيق الاستِحْسَان	snack, light meal	تَصْبِيرَة
hardness, rigidity, callousness	تَصَلُّب	rectification, proof-reading, correction	تَصْحِيح
amending, fixing, repairing	تَصْلِيح	distortion, stereotype	تَصْحِيف
decision, resolution, determination	تَصْمِيم	exportation, issuance, foreward	تَصْدِير
designs, plans, projects	تَصْمِيمَات	exportation of goods	تَصْدِير البَضَائِع
affectation, artificiality, pretence	تَصَنُّع	attestation, consent, approval, belief	تَصْدِيق
assorting, compilation, classification, composition	تَصْنِيف	disposal, behaviour, conduct	تَصَرُّف (تَصَرُّفات)
literary work, compilation	تَصْنِيف (تَصَانِيف)	declaration, licence, permission	تَصْرِيح
selection, assortment	تَصْنِيفَة	disposal, inflection, alteration	تصْرِيف
imagination, fantasy, conception	تَصَوُّر	diminution, decrease	تَصْغِير

تَضْيِيع squandering, wasting, waste	تَصَوُّري idealistic, fancied
تَضْيِيق tightening, constraint, restriction	تَصَوُّف Sufism, mysticism
تَضْيِيق الخَِنَاق oppression, suppression	تَصْوِيب (تَصْوِيات) rectification, correction
تَطَابُق congruence, agreement	تَصْوِيت voting, polling, shouting
تَطْبِيق accommodation, adaptation, application	تَصْوِير illustration, portrayal, description, photography
تَطْبِيقي practical, applied	تَصْوِير شَمْسِي photography
تَطَرُّف execessiveness, extremism, radicalism	تَصْوِيرَة (تَصَاوِير) picture, illustration
تَطْرِيز embroidering, embroidery	تَصْيِير transfer, rendering
تَطْعِيم vaccination, grafting, inlay work	تَضَادّ contradiction, contrast
تَطْفِيف scrimping, stinting, parsimony	تَضَاعُف multiplying, doubling
تَطَلُّع inquisitiveness, aspiration	تَضَاغُط compressure
تَطْهِير purging, purification, cleansing	تَضَامُن reciprocity, joint liability
تَطْوَاف roving, touring, itineration	تَضْحِية sacrificing, immolation
تَطَوُّر (تَطَوُّرات) evolution, development	تَضْحِية (تَضْحِيات) sacrifice
	تَضَخُّم dilation, inflation, distention
	تَضْلِيل misguiding, delusion, misleading

cooperation, contribution	تَعَاوُن	organic evolution	تَطَوُّر عُضْوِي
cooperative	تَعَاوُني	evolutional, evolutionary	تَطَوُّري
coexistence	تَعَايُش		
tired, fatigued, weary	تَعِب	voluntary service, voluntariness	تَطَوُّع
fatigue, tiredness, trouble, toil	تَعَب (أَتْعَاب)	encompassment, encirclement	تَطْوِيق
mobilization, conscription	تَعْبِئَة	prolongation, elongation, lengthening	تَطْوِيل
tired, weary, fatigued	تَعْبَان	pretension, hypocrisy	تَظَاهُر
devotion, act of worship	تَعَبُّد	charm, elegance, gracefulness	تَظَرُّف
expression, declaration, interpretation	تَعْبِير	endorsement	تَظْهِير
expressive, emotive, declarative	تَعْبِيري	proportion, equality, equilibrium	تَعَادُل
darkening, obscuring	تَعْتِيم	tie vote	تَعَادُل الأَصْوَات
amazement, astonishment	تَعَجُّب	contradiction, clash	تَعَارُض
hastening, expediting, acceleration,	تَعْجِيل	twists, turns	تَعَارِيج
transgression, trespassing, beach, violation,	تَعَدٍّ (تَعَدِّيات)	wretchedness, misery	تَعَاسَة
		practice, pursuit	تَعَاطٍ
		succession, in course of	تَعَاقُب
enumeration, counting	تَعْدَاد	dealings, trade relations, transactions	تَعَامُل
census	تَعْدَاد الأَنْفُس		

consolidation, strengthening, confirming	تَعْزِيز
wretchedness, misery	تَعْس
wretched, miserable, unhappy	تَعِس
difficulty, hardship	تَعَسُّر
arbitrariness, tyranny	تَعَسُّف
arbitrary, tyrannical	تَعَسُّفِي
enthusiasm, bigotry, partisanship, racialism	تَعَصُّب
supporting, backing	تَعْضِيد
breakdown, inactivity	تَعَطُّل
unemployment, joblessness	تَعَطُّل عَنِ العَمَل
destructing, injuring, damaging	تَعْطِيب
impairment, closure, prorogation, interruption	تَعْطِيل
magnifying, glorifying, glorification	تَعْظِيم
rottenness, putridity, decay, mouldiness	تَعَفُّن
pursuit, chase	تَعَقُّب
complexity, intricacy complication	تَعَقُّد
understanding, intelligence, discernment	تَعَقُّل

plurality, multiplicity	تَعَدُّد
polygamy	تَعَدُّد الأَزْوَاج
polygamy	تَعَدُّد الزَّوْجَات
ferry service	تَعْدِيَة
alteration, modification, adjustment	تَعْدِيل (تَعْدِيلات)
cabinet reshuffle	تَعْدِيل وِزَارِي
mining	تَعْدِين
torturing, agonizing, tormenting	تَعْذِيب
zigzag	تَعَرُّج
realization, knowledge, exploration	تَعَرُّف
Arabicizing, rendering	تَعْرِيب
bower, arbour, trellis	تَعْرِيشَة (تَعَارِيش)
indication, allusion	تَعْرِيض
notification, definition, introduction	تَعْرِيف
tariff, price list	تَعْرِيفَة (تَعَارِيف)
condolence, solace, consolation	تَعْزِيَة
reprimand, reproof, censure	تَعْزِير

intention, purpose, determination	تَعَمُّد	pursuing, chasing	تَعْقِيب
intentional, wilful	تَعَمُّدي	complication, intricacy, entanglement	تَعْقِيد
baptism	تَعْمِيد	sterilization, disinfection	تَعْقِيم
construction, building	تَعْمِير		
generalization, universalization	تَعْمِيم	muddying, troubling	تَعْكِير
pains, drudgery, toil	تَعَنٍّ	attachment, relationship, linkage	تَعَلُّق
embarrassment, obstinacy	تَعَنُّت	learning, studying	تَعَلُّم
reprimand, severe reproof	تَعْنِيف	elevation, exaltation	تَعْلِيَة
		suspension, hanging	تَعْلِيق
custody, support, charge, upkeep	تَعَهُّد	annotations, comments	تَعْلِيق (تَعَالِيق)
pledge, contract promise	تَعَهُّد (تَعَهُّدات)	marginal note, note	تَعْلِيقَة (تَعْلِيقات)
habituation	تَعَوُّد	explanation, account, justification	تَعْلِيل
habituation, accustoming	تَعْوِيد	education, teaching, training, instruction	تَعْلِيم (تَعَالِيم)
amulet, spell, charm	تَعْوِيذ		
replacement, recompense, substitution	تَعْوِيض	primary education	تَعْلِيم ابْتِدائي
civil remedy	تَعْوِيض مَدَني	higher education	تَعْلِيم عَال
compensatory, substitutional	تَعْوِيضي	co-education	تَعْلِيم مُخْتَلِط
specification, designation, appointment	تَعْيِين	educational, instructional	تَعْلِيمي

تَفَاعُل	interaction, interplay
تَفَاقُم	aggrevation, seriousness
تُفَال	spit, spittle
تَفَاهة	insignificance, stupidity, insipidity, paltriness
تَفَاهُم	mutual understanding, understanding
تَفَاوُت	difference, disharmony, dissimilarity
تَفْتَا	taffeta
تَفْتِيْش (تَفَاتِيْش)	investigation, inspection, examination, exploration
تَفْتِيْشِي	investigational, examinatory
تَفَجُّر	outbreak, eruption
تَفَجُّع	grief, distress, affliction, agony
تَفَرُّج	watching, viewing, observation
تَفَرُّق	separation, division, dispersal
تَفْرِقَة	dispersion, partition, separation, discrimination
تَفْرِيح	amusement, exhilaration

تَغَابُن	mutual cheating, defraudation
تَغَاضٍ	connivance, winking at, overlooking
تَغَافُل	neglect, negligence, inadvertence
تَغْذِيَة	nutrition, alimentation, nourishment,
تَغَرُّب	westernism, emigration
تَغْرِيْب	expatriation, banishment
تَغْرِيْد	singing, twittering
تَغْرِيْق	inundation, drowning
تَغْطِيَة	covering, coverage
تَغْطِيْس	plunging, immersion, submersion
تَغَلُّب	overcoming, surmounting
تَغَيُّر	change, alteration, variation
تَغْيِير	changing, alteration, modification
تَفَاؤُل	optimism
تُفّاح/تُفّاحة	apple
تَفَاخُر	boasting, bragging, vainglory

consideration, thinking, contemplation تَفَكُّر	hatching, incubation تَفْرِيخ
disintegration, split, fragmentation تَفَكُّك	neglect, negligence, remission تَفْرِيط
enjoyment, amusement, merry making تَفَكُّه	vacating, emptying, evacuating تَفْرِيغ
thinking, meditation, contemplation تَفْكِير	partition, distinction, differentiation, dispersion تَفْرِيق
decomposition, fragmentation تَفْكِيك	explanation, commentary, interpretation تَفْسِير (تَفَاسِير)
spit, spittle تُفْل	explanatory, explicatory تَفْسِيرِي
bankruptcy, insolvency تَفْلِيس	spreading out, breaking out تَفَشٍّ
multiplicity, diversity, versatility تَفَنُّن	تَفْصِيل (تَفَاصِيل/تَفْصِيلات) details, particulars
triviality, worthlessness, insignificance تَفَه	detailing, detailed statement تَفْصِيل
trivial, insignificant, worthless تَفِه	in detail, minutely تَفْصِيلاً
understanding, grasping تَفَهُّم	detailed, collaborate تَفْصِيلِي
instruction, orientation تَفْهِيم	courteousness, grace, condescension تَفَضُّل
superiority, excellence, proficiency تَفَوُّق	preference, choosing, preferment تَفْضِيل
authorization, charging, empowerment تَفْوِيض	investigation, checking, inspection تَفَقُّد
	hatching, incubation تَفْقِيص

advancing, offering, تَقْدِيم presentation, introduction	full power, تَفْوِيض مُطْلَق unlimited authority
oaring, rowing تَقْذِيف	rapprochement, تَقَارُب mutual approximation
approximation, تَقَرُّب approach	restraint, retirement تَقَاعُد
ulceration تَقَرُّح	negligence, تَقَاعُس carelessness
approximation, close تَقْرِيب approach	perfection, exactitude, تَقَانة solidity
approximately, nearly تَقْرِيبًا	kissing تَقْبِيل
approximative, تَقْرِيبِي approximate	stinginess, تَقْتِير niggardliness
settlement, fixation تَقْرِير arrangement	slaughter, butchery تَقْتِيل
report, account (تَقَارِير) تَقْرِير	advancement, تَقَدُّم advance, progress, precedence
overall report تَقْرِير إِجْمَالِي	
police report تَقْرِير الشُّرْطَة	introduction, تَقْدِمَة presentation, offer
self-determination تَقْرِير المَصِير	
eulogy, commendation تَقْرِيظ	present, gift (تَقَادِم) تَقْدِمَة
review of new تَقْرِيظ الكُتُب books	progressive, تَقَدُّمِي progressionist
scolding, chiding, تَقْرِيع reprimanding	estimate, (تَقَادِير) تَقْدِير assessment, supposition, discretion
division, distribution, تَقْسِيم partition	assessent of تَقْدِير الضَّرَائِب taxes
proportion, (تَقَاسِيم) تَقْسِيم structure	sanctification, تَقْدِيس purification, consecration

retractive تَقَلُّصِي	تَقْشِير paring, scaling, shelling
blind faith, covention تَقْلِيد (تَقَالِيد)	thorough examination, تَقَصٍّ investigation
conventional, customary تَقْلِيدِي	shortening, تَقْصِير abridgement, insufficiency
decrease, diminution تَقْلِيل	interruption, تَقَطُّع detachment, separation
birth control تَقْلِيل النَّسْل	distilling, filtering تَقْطِير
paring, trimming تَقْلِيم	dismemberment, تَقْطِيع cutting
manicure تَقْلِيم الأَظَافِر	shape, form, تَقْطِيع (تَقَاطِيع) stature
skilful, adroit, skilled تَقِن	poultry coop تَقْفِيصَة
law-making, legislation تَقْنِين	change, alteration, تَقَلُّب transformation, inconstancy
retrogression, recession, retreat تَقَهْقُر	fluctuation of تَقَلُّب الأَسْعَار prices
piety, devoutness, godliness تَقْوَى	change of تَقَلُّب الظُّرُوف circumstances
strengthening, تَقْوِيَة fortifying, encouragement, reinforcement	change of تَقَلُّب جَوِّي weather
destruction, demolition تَقْوِيض	vicissitudes of تَقَلُّبَات الدَّهْر times
erecting, edification, تَقْوِيم correction, appraisal	
piety, godliness, devoutness ثُقَّى	contraction, تَقَلُّص retraction, shrinkage
devout, pious, godfearing تَقِي (أَتْقِيَاء)	

suppuration, purulence تَقْيِح	condensation, solidification تَكْثِيْف
bond, tie, restriction تَقَيُّد	piling up, accumulation تَكْدِيْس
registration, binding, shackling, restriction (تَقَايِيْد) تَقْيِيْد	denial, refutation تَكْذِيْب
birth control تَقْيِيْد النَّسْل	repetition, reiteration تَكْرَار
restrictive تَقْيِيْدِي	repeatedly, again and again, frequently تَكْرَارًا
support, prop تُكَأَة	reiteration, repetition, refinement تَكْرِيْر
increase in number, multiplicity تَكَاثُر	dedication, initiation, consecration تَكْرِيْس
laziness, sluggishness تَكَاسُل	honouring, respecting تَكْرِيْم
sameness, equivalence تَكَافُؤ	dressing, clothing تَكْسِيَة
reciprocal responsibility تَكَافُل	fragmentation, breaking تَكْسِيْر
integration تَكَامُل	shaping, forming تَكْسِيْم
integrative, integral تَكَامُلِي	cubing, dicing تَكْعِيْب
arrogance, pride, haughtiness تَكَبُّر	inlay, plating تَكْفِيْت
enlargement, glorification, magnifying تَكْبِيْر	charge of disbelief, expiation تَكْفِيْر
formation of blocs تَكَتُّل	affectation, affected behaviour تَكَلُّف
secrecy, reticence, discretion تَكَتُّم	conversation, talking تَكَلُّم
tactics تَكْتِيك	formality, expenses, inconvenience, discomfort (تَكَالِيْف) تَكْلِيْف
increasing, multiplication تَكْثِيْر	

clothing, dressing, coating, deceiving	تَلْبِيس	complement, supplement	تَكْمِلَة
summarizing, abstract, abridgement	تَلْخِيص	completing, completion, perfection	تَكْمِيل
telescope	تلسْكُوب	complementary, supplementary	تَكْمِيلِي
amiability, friendliness, civility	تَلَطُّف	prophecy, prediction	تَكَهُّن
stammering, stuttering, hesitation	تَلَعْثُم	formation, genesis, origin	تَكُوُّن
telegraph, telegram	تلغَراف	creation, formation, shaping	تَكْوِين
telegraphic	تلغَرافِي	adaptation, formation, conditioning	تَكْيِيف
ruin, waste, damage	تَلَف	air conditioning	تَكْيِيف الهَوَاء
television set	تلْفَاز	hill, mound, elevation	تَلّ (تلال/أَتْلال)
television	تَلْفَزة		
television	تلْفِزْيُون/تليفزيون	shining, glittering, brilliancy	تَلَأْلُؤ
pronunciation, articulation	تَلَفُّظ	annihilation, evanescence	تَلَاش
telephone	تلفون/تليفون	adhesion, contiguity	تَلَاصُق
telephonic	تَلَفُونِي/تَليفوني	reparation, redress, removal	تَلَافٍ
convolution, winding	تَلْفِيف	reading, recitation	تلاوة
falsification, fabrication	تَلْفِيق	collar	تَلْبِيب (تَلَابِيب)
receipt, acquisition	تَلَقٍّ	response, answer, saying labbaik (at your service)	تَلْبِيَة
in front of, opposite of	تلْقَاء		
spontaneous, automatic	تلْقَائِي		

similarity, likeness, resemblance تَمَاثُل	automatically, spontaneously تِلْقَائِيًّا
gymnastic exercises تَمَارِين رِيَاضِيَّة	fecundation, vaccination, grafting تَلْقِيح
military exercises تَمَارِين عَسْكَرِيَّة	instruction, dictation, inspiration تَلْقِين
intermixing, intermingling تَمَازُج	that (fem. of ذَلِك) تِلْك
attachment, tenacity, cohesiveness تَمَاسُك	apprenticeship, schooling تَلْمَذة
completeness, perfection, complete, perfect تَمَام	allusion, hint, intimation تَلْمِيح (تَلَامِيح)
completely, perfectly, wholly تَمَامًا	pupil, disciple, apprentice تِلْمِيذ (تَلَامذة/تَلَامِيذ)
enjoyment, recreation تَمَتُّع	pupil, student (fem. of تلميذ) تِلْمِيذة
stammering, mumbling تَمْتَمَة	shining, polishing تَلْمِيع
statue, image تِمْثَال (تَمَاثِيل)	amusement, distraction, pastime تَلْهِيَة
exemplification, assimilation, representation تَمْثِيل	sign, signal, wave تَلْوِيح (تَلْوِيحات)
theatrical, dramatic تَمْثِيلي	annotations, remarks تَلْوِيحات
glorification, exaltation تَمْجِيد	reprehension, reprimand تَلْوِيم
stretching, spreading, distention تَمَدُّد	colouring, dyeing تَلْوِين
	inherited, long-possessed تَلِيد

stamp, mark	تَمْغة	تَمَدُّن	sophistication, civilization
power, capability, ability	تَمَكُّن	تَمَدُّني	civilizational, refined
strengthening, consolidation	تَمْكِين	تَمْدِيد	extending, stretching, lengthening, prolongation
slipping away, escaping	تَمَلُّص	تَمْدِين	civilizing, refining
flattery, adulation	تَمَلُّق	تَمْر هِنْدي	tamarind
possession, domination, control	تَمَلُّك	تَمْر/تَمْرة	dried dates
restlessness, fidgetiness	تَمَلْمُل	تَمَرُّد	uprising, rebellion, disobedience
salting, corning	تَمْلِيح	تَمَرُّن	training, exercise
flattery, adulation	تَمْلِيق	تَمْرِيض	sick-nursing
desire, wish, demand	تَمَنٍّ	تَمْرِين (تَمْرِينات/تَمَارِين) exercise, drill, practice	
refusal, denial, rejection	تَمَنُّع	تَمْرِين ابْتِدائي	basic training
ejaculation of sperm	تَمْنِية	تَمْرِين جَسَدي	physical training
slowness, leisureliness	تَمَهُّل	تَمْزِيق	tearing, fragmentation
introduction, preface, foreword	تَمْهِيد	تِمْساح (تَمَاسِيح)	crocodile
levelling, smoothing, paving	تَمْهِيد	تَمَسُّك	adherence, sticking, attachment
introductory, preliminary	تَمْهِيدي	تَمْسِيد	massage, rubbing
		تَمْشِيط	combing, carding
undulation, vibration	تَمَوُّج	تَمَعُّن	carefulness, scrutiny, careful examination

genital, sexual, procreative	تَنَاسُلِي	undulation, swaying	تَمَوُّر
symphony, harmony of sounds	تَنَاغُم	to and fro	تَمَوُّرًا
dissension, disagreement, incongruity	تَنَافُر	July	تَمُّوز
mutual competition, rivalry	تَنَافُس	financing, funding	تَمْوِيْل
struggle for existence	تَنَافُس حَيَوِي	provisions, ration, supply	تَمْوِيْن
contradiction, contrast, incompatibility	تَنَاقُض	coating, clothing, overlaying	تَمْوِيْه
paradox	تَنَاقُض ظَاهِرِي	mock, feigned	تَمْوِيْهِي
rotation, alteration	تَنَاوُب	discrimination, partiality, distinction, discernment, preference	تَمْيِيْز
eating, taking food	تَنَاوُل	scattering, dispersal	تَنَاثُر
prediction, prophecy	تَنَبُّؤ	fight, struggle, controversy	تَنَازُع
planting, cultivation	تَنْبِيْت	struggle for existence	تَنَازُع البَقَاء
warning, alerting, awakening, notice	تَنْبِيْه	resignation, surrender, foregoing	تَنَازُل
rescue, salvation	تَنْجِيَة	proportion, balance, comparative relation, harmony	تَنَاسُب
implementation, accomplishment, execution	تَنْجِيْز	transmigration of souls	تَنَاسُخ
defilement, pollution, contamination	تَنْجِيْس	order, symmetry	تَنَاسُق
carping criticism, disparagement	تَنْدِيد	reproduction, propagation	تَنَاسُل

arrangement, control, adjustment, organization	تَنْظيِم	stroll, walk, outing	تَنَزُّه
traffic control	تَنْظيِم المُرُور	reduction, lessening, revealing, sending down	تَنْزيِل
coddling, pampering	تَنْعيِم	discount, deduction	تَنْزيِل (تَنْزيِلات)
respiration	تَنَفُّس		
respiratory	تَنَفُّسي	reduction in rank	تَنْزيِل الرُّتْبَة
implementation, execution	تَنْفيِذ	tennis	تِنِس/تِنيِس
executive, executory	تَنْفيِذي	table tennis	تِنِس الطَّاوِلَة
alienation, estrangement	تَنْفيِر	uniformity	تَنَسُّق
change of residence, migration, transfer	تَنَقُّل	arranging, putting in order, arraying, decoration	تَنْسيِق
exploration, excavation	تَنْقيِب	upbringing, education	تَنْشِئَة
purification, cleaning	تَنْقِيَة	inhaling, inhalation	تَنَشُّق
revision, rechecking, rectification	تَنْقيِح	activation, animation, stimulation	تَنْشيِط
lessening, reducing, diminution	تَنْقيِص	drying, wiping	تَنْشيِف
disguise, masquerade	تَنَكُّر	appointment, setting up, installation	تَنْصيِب
degeneration, decadence	تَنَكُّس	baptism, christianisation	تَنْصيِر
promotion, progress, augmentation	تَنْمِيَة	quotation	تَنْصيِص
embellishment, ornamentation, decoration	تَنْميِق	halving, bisection	تَنْصيِف
		typesetting, composition	تَنْضيِد
		cleaning, cleansing	تَنْظيِف

sigh, sighing	تَنَهُّد
furnace, oven (تَنَانِير)	تَنُّور
skirt, petticoat	تَنُّورة
diversity, variety, multiplicity	تَنُوُّع
lighting, illumination, enlightenment	تَنْوِير
putting to sleep	تَنْوِيم
nunation, N-ing	تَنْوِين
laudation, praise, raising	تَنْوِيه
breakdown, collapse	تَهَافُت
negligence, carelessness, indifference	تَهَاوُن
adaptation, adjustment	تَهَايُؤ
shamelessness, impudence	تَهَتُّك
spelling	تَهَجٍّ/تَهْجِيَة
quieting, calming, tranquillizing	تَهْدِنَة
intimidation, threat	تَهَدُّد
fall down, breakdown	تَهَدُّم
threat, threatening, frightening	تَهْدِيد (تَهْدِيدَات)
threatening, meanacing	تَهْدِيدِي

demolition, destruction, ruining	تَهْدِيم
rectification, culture, revision, emendation, education, refinement	تَهْذِيب
educational, cultural, instructive	تَهْذِيبِي
smuggling, trafficking, putting to flight	تَهْرِيب
taunt, irony, sarcasm, derision	تَهَكُّم
sarcastic, derisive, mocking	تَهَكُّمِي
danger, peril, jeopardy, ruin	تَهْلُكَة
jubilation, rejoicing, exultation	تَهَلُّل
acclamation, jubilation	تَهْلِيل (تَهَالِيل)
accusation, charge, indictment	تُهَمَة
accusation, charge, blame	تُهْمَة (تُهَم)
congratulation, felicitation	تَهْنِئَة (تَهَانِئ)
hastiness, rashness, thoughtlessness	تَهَوُّر

parallelism, equivalence	تَوَازٍ	ventilation, airing, airification	تَهْوِيَة
balance, equilibrium, equipoise	تَوَازُن	commotion, agitation, excitation	تَهْوِيْش
balance of power	تَوَازُن القِوَى،	intimidation, frightening, terrifying	تَهْوِيْل
continuity, continuance	تَوَاصُل	preparations, adjustment	تَهَيُّؤ
humility, humbleness, modesty, lowliness	تَوَاضُع	preparation, disposition, adjustment	تَهْيِئَة
collusion, secret understanding	تَوَاطُؤ	commotion, agitation, excitement	تَهَيُّج
conformity, coincidence, agreement	تَوَافُق	agitation, excitement, provocation, instigation	تَهْيِيْج
craving, yearning, desirous, eager	تَوَّاق	twin	تَوْأَم (تَوَائِم)
succession, continuation, uninterruption	تَوَالٍ	twins	تَوْأَمان
		at once, immediately	تَوًّا
delay, slowness, tardiness, remission	تَوَانٍ	curve, curvature, twist, bend	الْتِوَاء
repentance, penitence	تَوْبَة	forgiving, repentant, contrite	تَوّاب
reprimand, rebuke, reproach	تَوْبِيْخ	succession, continuance, incessancy	تَوَاثُر
mulberry	تُوْت	good terms, friendly relations	تَوَادّ
raspberry	تُوْت العُلَّيْق	successive arrival	تَوَارُد

providing, supplying, supply	تَوْرِيد	tension, strain, stretch	تَوَتُّر
supply of goods	تَوْرِيد البَضَائِع	guarantee, surety	تَوَثُّقَة
distribution, division, dispensation	تَوْزِيع	consolidation, documentation, attestation	تَوْثِيق
distribution of wealth	تَوْزِيع الثَّرْوَة	pain, ache, suffering	تَوَجُّع
distribution of prizes	تَوْزِيع الجَوَائِز	attention, care	تَوَجُّه
mediation, intervention	تَوَسُّط	directing, guiding, orientation, steering	تَوْجِيه
extension, expansion, enlargement	تَوَسُّع	directives, instructions	تَوْجِيه (تَوْجِيهَات)
expansionist	تَوَسُّعِي	solitariness, soleness, seclusion	تَوَحُّد
plea, petition, solicitation	تَوَسُّل	barbarity, brutality, wildness	تَوَحُّش
widening, extending, expansion	تَوْسِيع	unification, belief in unity of God, monotheism, consolidation	تَوْحِيد
overture, prelude	تَوْشِيح	valediction, saying farewell, leave-taking	تَوْدِيع
achievement, arrival, attainment	تَوَصُّل	red colouration	تَوَرُّد
recommendation, advice, admonition	تَوْصِيَة	entanglement, involvement	تَوَرُّط
connecting, joining, conveyance, delivery	تَوْصِيل	swelling, rising	تَوَرُّم
ritual ablution	تَوَضُّؤ	dissimulation, allusion, hiding, concealing	تَوْرِيَة

yearning, ardent desire, craving	تَوْق/ تَوَقان	arrangement, putting in order, preparation	تَوْضِيب
burning, combustion	تَوَقُّد	explanation, elucidation, clarification	تَوْضِيح
expectation, anticipation	تَوَقُّع	lowering, preparation, preliminary step	تَوْطِئَة
pausing, stopping, stopover, cessation, hesitation	تَوَقُّف	lowering of the voice	تَوْطِئَة الصَّوْت
time, timing	تَوْقِيت	consolidation, strengthening	تَوْطِيد
local time	تَوْقِيت مَحَلِّي	employment, appointment	تَوْظِيف
signing, recording, execution	تَوْقِيع	investment	تَوْظِيف المَال
signature	تَوْقِيع (تَوْقِيعَات)	threat, menace	تَوَعُّد
detention, seizing, raising	تَوْقِيف	indisposition, ailment	تَوَعُّك
trust, confidence	تَوَكُّل	penetration, intrusion, preoccupation	تَوَغُّل
emphasis, stress, affirmation	تَوْكِيد	profusion, abundance, increase	تَوَفُّر
agent, representative, appointment as a representative	تَوْكِيل	fulfilment, satisfaction	تَوْفِيَة
administration, taking over an office	تَوَلٍّ	increasing, saving, multiplying	تَوْفِير
procreation, generation, production	تَوَلُّد	success, good fortune, compromise, adjustment, conformation	تَوْفِيق
giddiness, confusion, distraction	تَوَلُّه		

ثَأْرِي revengeful, vindicative	تَوْلِيَة investitue
ثَائِر avenger, agitated, excited, furious	تَوْلِيد procreation, producing, generation, midwifery
ثَائِر (ثُوَّار) rebel, insurgent	تَوَهُّم suspicion, illusion, imagination
ثَابِت firm, steady, constant, permanent, confirmed, established	تَيَّار current, tide, course
	تَيَّار كَهْرَبَائِي electric current
ثَابِت الْجَأْش steadfast, cool, fearless, staunch, undismayed	تَيَّار مُبَاشِر direct current
	تَيَّار مُتَقَطِّع alternating current
ثَابِت الْعَزْم determined, resolute	تَيَّاه wandering, straying, errant, stray
ثَابِت الْقَدَم firm-footed	تِيتَانوس tetanus
ثَاقِب sharp, piercing, penetrating	تَيْسِير facilitation, easiness
	تَيَقُّظ alertness, vigilance, watchfulness
ثَاقِب الفِكْر sharp-witted, acute of mind, shrewd	تِين fig
ثَاقِب النَّظَر sharp-eyed	تَيْه wild, desert, labyrinth, superciliousness, haughtiness
ثَالِب calumnious, slanderous	
ثَالِث third	تَيْهان stray, straying, errant
ثَالِثًا thirdly	
ثَالُوث trinity, triplet	
ثَامِن eighth	ثُوَبَاء yawn, yawning
ثَانَوِي secondary, minor	ثَأْر revenge, retaliation, vengeance
ثَانِي second, next, another	

wealthy, rich	ثَرِيّ (أَثْرِياء)	secondly, for the second time	ثانِياً
luster, chandelier	ثُرَيّا	secondly, for the second time	ثانِيَةً
dish of sopped bread	ثَرِيد	second	ثانِيَة (ثَوانٍ)
snake, serpent	ثُعْبان (ثَعَابِين)	persistence, constancy, firmness, stability, perseverance	ثَبَات
fox	ثَعْلَب (ثَعَالِب)		
bleating, bleat	ثُغَاء	fixed, firm, steadfast	ثَبْت
mouth, front teeth, port	ثَغْر (ثُغُور)	proof, evidence, index, list	ثَبَت (أَثْبات)
opening, breach, cavity, crack	ثُغْرَة (ثُغَر)	firmness, steadiness, permanence, constancy	ثُبُوت
sediment, dregs	ثُفْل	grief, destruction, ruin	ثُبُور
culture, civilization, education	ثَقَافة	density, thickness, consistency	ثُخُونة
cultural, educational	ثَقَافي	dense, thick	ثَخِين
heaviness, dullness	ثَقَالة	breast, udder, dug	ثَدْي
perforating, boring	ثَقْب		
hole, drill hole	ثَقْب (ثُقُوب)	fortune, wealth, riches	ثَرَاء
keyhole	ثَقْب المِفْتَاح	prattler, chatterer, chatterbox	ثَرْثَار
hole, puncture	ثُقْبَة (ثُقَب)	chattering, prattle	ثَرْثَرَة
confidence, trust, reliance	ثِقَة	wealth, riches, affluence	ثَرْوَة
self-confidence	ثِقَة بِالذَّات		
self-confidence, self-reliance	ثِقَة بِالنَّفْس	ground, rich soil	ثَرىً

threefold, consisting of ثلاثي three	ثِقَل heaviness, weight, sluggishness
three ثُلاثي الأبْعاد dimensional	ثِقْل (أَثْقال) weight, burden, gravity
trilateral ثُلاثي الأضْلاع	ثِقْل نَوْعي specific gravity, density
tricoloured ثُلاثي الألْوَان	
triliteral ثُلاثي الحُرُوف	ثَقَلان the human and the jinn
triangular ثُلاثي الزَّوَايا	ثَقْلَة trouble, hardship, inconvenience
trilingual ثُلاثي اللُّغَات	ثَقِيْل (ثُقَلاء/ثِقَال) weighty,
trisyllable ثُلاثي المَقاطع	grave, heavy, ponderous, burdensome
icebox, refrigerator ثَلاّجة	
defamation, slandering ثَلْب	ثَقيل الحَرَكة slow of motion, dull, sluggish
group, troop, ثُلَّة (ثُلَل) company	ثَقيل الرُّوْح dull, unpleasant
one third ثُلْث (أَثْلاث)	ثَقيل الهَضْم indigestible, heavy
icy, iced, frozen ثَلِج	ثَكْلان bereft of a child
snow, ice ثَلْج (ثُلوج)	ثَكْلَى fem. of ثَكْلان
icy, snowy, glacial ثَلْجي	ثُكْنَة (ثُكَن) barracks
breach, cleft, rift, gap ثَلْم	
gap, cleft, breach ثُلْمَة (ثُلَم)	ثَلاث/ثَلاثة three
there, thence ثَمَّ	ثَلاثاً three times, thrice
then, thereupon, ثُمَّ afterwards	ثَلاثة عشر/ثلاث عشرة thirteen
	ثَلاثُون thrity

fold, pleat, wrinkle (أَثْناء) ثَنْي	ثُمَالة sediment, dregs, residue
ثَنْيَة fold, plait, crease	ثُمَام grass
ثَنِيّة (ثَنَايا) mountain trail, front teeth	ثَمَانُون eighty
ثَوَاب reward, requital, recompense	ثَمَاني/ثَمَانية eight
ثَوْب (ثِيَاب) dress, garment, garb, clothes	ثمانية عشر/ثماني عشرة eighteen
ثَوْب الحِداد mourning band	ثَمَر (أَثْمار/ ثِمار) fruits, produce, profit, result
ثُوَة (ثُوَى) sign-post	ثَمَرَة fruit, result, produce, advantage
ثَوْر (ثِيران) bull, ox	ثَمَل intoxication, inebriation
ثَوَرَان outburst, agitation, disturbance, outbreak	ثَمِل intoxicated, inebriate, drunk
ثَوْرَة rising, uprising, revolt, revolution, agitation	ثَمَن (أَثْمان) price, cost
ثَوْري revolutionary, revolutionist	ثُمْن (أَثْمان) one eighth
	ثَمَن أَصْلي prime cost
ثُوْم/ثُوْمة garlic	ثَمِين valuable, precious, costly
ثَيِّب matron, widow, divorcee	ثَنَاء praise, eulogy, thankfulness
	ثَنَائي eulogic, laudatory
	ثُنَائي double, twofold, dual
جُؤَار bellow, bellowing, lowing	ثُنَائي الزَّوَايا biangular
جَأَر lowing, mooing, roaring	ثَنْي bending, folding, dissuation

main street, main road جَادّة	emotion, agitation of جَأْش mind
centre of a road جَادّة الطريق	devastating, disastrous, جَائِح destroying,
winning, attractive, جَاذب captivating	disaster, pest, (جَوَائِح) جَائِحة calamity, epidemic
gravitation, جَاذبِيّة magnetism	neighbourhood, جَائِر arbitrary
flowing, running, جَارٍ current	permitted, permissible, جَائِز lawful, legal
neighbour (جِيْران) جار	prize, reward (جَوَائِز) جَائِزة
wounding, cutting, جَارِح stinging	scholarship, جَائِزة دِرَاسِيّة stipend
limb (جَوَارِح) جَارِحة	hungry, starved (جِيَاع) جَائِع
torrential, stormy جَارِف	gatherer, collector, جاب tax-collector
hand mill جَارُوشة	
girl, maid, ship (جَوَارٍ) جَارِية	bonesetter جَابِر
gas, jazz جَاز	pool, basin جابِيَة
decisive, definite, final جَازِم	crouching down, جَاث kneeling
spy (جَوَاسِيس) جَاسُوس	perching, (جُثُم) جَاثِم crouching
hard, rigid, rough جَاسِي	
dry, dried جَافّ	disbeliever, denier, جَاحِد ungrateful
harsh, rough, rude جَاف	
jacket, coat جَاكِتة	serious, earnest جَادّ
cause, causative جَالِب factor, incentive	

flank, side	جَانِح	sitting, participant	جَالِس
rib, bosom	جَانِحَة (جَوَانِح)	gallon	جَالُون
dignity, glory, honour	جَاه	colony of foreigners	جَالِيَة (جَوَالٍ/جَالِيَات)
prepared, ready, readymade	جَاهِز	bowl, cup	جَام
illiterate, foolish, ignorant	جَاهِل (جُهَلَاء /جُهَّال)	unruly, refractory, defiant	جَامِح
well, pit, dungeon	جُبّ (جِبَاب)	solid, hard, stiff, inflexible	جَامِد
omnipotent, tyrant, oppressor	جَبَّار	compiler, gatherer, comprehensive	جَامِع
bonesetting	جبارة	mosque, masjid	جَامِع (جَوَامِع)
coward, cowardly, faint-hearted	جَبَان (جُبَنَاء)	league, university, community, association, federation	جَامِعَة (جَامِعات)
tax, tax-collecting	جِبَاية (جَوَابٍ)	league of nations	جَامِعة الأُمَم
jubbah, an outer open robe	جُبّة	academic, of university	جَامِعي
beehive	جَبْح (جِبَاح)	buffalo	جَامُوس (جَوَامِيس)
artillery depot	جَبْخَانة	jinn, demon	جَانّ
coercion, bonesetting, compulsion	جَبْر	reaper, gatherer	جَانٍ
forcibly, coercively	جَبْراً	criminal, culprit, perpetrator	جَانٍ (جُنَاة)
might, power, potency	جَبَرُوت	side, part, wing, portion	جَانِب (جَوَانِب)

rejection, disbelief, جَحْد denial, refusal	compulsory, جَبْرِي obligatory
hole, burrow, جُحْر (جُحُور) lair	Gabriel جِبْرِيل/جِبْرَئِيل
young donkey جَحْش (جِحاش)	mountain, big جَبَل (جِبال) hill
great army, legion جَحْفَل	iceberg جَبَل جَلِيد
ingratitude, denial, جُحُود disbelief	volcano جَبَل نار
fire, hellfire جَحِيم	temperament, جِبْلَة/جِبِلّة natural disposition, nature
earnestness, diligence, جِدّ eagerness	mountainous, جَبَلِي mountaineer
forefather, جَدّ (أَجْداد) grandfather	cowardice, جُبْن/جَبَانَة faint-heartedness
good fortune, جَدّ (جُدُود) good luck	cheese جُبْن/جُبْنَة
ancestor جَدّ أَعْلَى	forehead, جَبْهَة (جَبَهات/جِباه) brow
very, much, in the extreme جِدًّا	popular front جَبْهَة شَعْبِيّة
wall جِدَار (جُدُر/جُدْران)	front, جَبِين (جُبُن/أَجْبِنة) forehead
worthiness, fitness, جَدَارة competence, efficiency	nightmare, incubus جُثَام
dispute, discussion, جِدَال quarrel, argument	body, corpse, جُثّة (جُثَت) carcass
dearth, barren, جَدْب barrenness	body, corpse, remains جُثْمان
	kneeling, crouching جُثُوّ down

worthy of, deserving جَدِير	novelty, newness, جِدّة
worth mentioning جَدِير بالذِّكْر	modernity
plait, tress (جَدَائل) جَدِيلة	grandmother (جَدَّات) جَدَّة
attractive, charming, جَذَّاب	grave, tomb (أَجْدَاث) جَدَث
captivating	cricket جُدْجُدْ
scraps, slip (جُذَاذَات) جُذَاذة	smallpox جُدَرِي/جَدَرِي
of paper	dispute, controversy, جَدَل
leprosy جُذَام	argument
gravitation, attraction, جَذْب	controversial, جَدَلي
captivation	argumentative
sex appeal جَذْب جنْسي	schedule, (جَدَاول) جَدْوَل
root, stem (جُذُور) جِذْر/جَذْر	chart, list, streamlet
radical جِذْري	working plan, جَدْوَل الأَعْمال
stem, (أَجْذَاع/جُذُوع) جِذْع	agenda
stump	stock list جَدْوَل البُورصة
happy, cheerful, جَذِل	curriculum جَدْوَل دِرَاسي
exhuberant, gay	benefit, advantage, جَدْوَى
exuberance, gaiety, جَذَل	avail
cheerfulness, happiness	serious, earnest جِدِّي
cheerful, happy, جَذْلان	kid, young goat جَدْي
hilarious	seriously, earnestly جِدِّيًّا
stump جُذْمُور	barren, sterile, جَدِيب
pulling, dragging, جَرّ	unfertile
drawing	new, novel, (جُدُد) جَدِيد
	recent, modern

جُرْأَة intrepidity, boldness, forwardness	جُرْح (جُرُوح/ جِراح) wound, cut, injury
جَرّاء runner, racer	جُرْح ذَرِب incurable wound
جُراب sock, stocking	جُرْح مُمِيت fatal wound
جِراب (أَجْرِبة) case, covering, sack, sheath	جَرِد plantless, bleak, desolate
جَرّاح surgeon	جَرْدَل bucket, pail
جَرّاح الأَسْنان dental surgeon	جُرَذ (جُرْذَان/جِرْذان) rat
جِراحة surgery	جَرَس (أَجْراس) bell
جِراحي surgical	جَرَس التَّحْذير alarm-bell
جَرَاد locust	جَرَس المَوْت death-bell, knell
جَرّار huge, tremendous, legion	جَرَس كَهْرَبائي electric bill
جَرّار (جَرّارَات) tractor	جَرْس/جِرْس sound, ring, tone
جَرّارة tractor, scorpion	جِرْسيّة jersey
جَرام gram	جَرْعة/جُرْعَة (جُرَع) draught, gulp, swallow
جَرانيت granite	جُرْف/جُرُف (جُرُوف/أَجْرَاف) clif, bank, precipice
جِرايَة (جِرَايات) rations, food	
جَرَب itch, scabies	جِرْم (أَجْرام) body, bulk
جَرِب itchy, mangy, scabby	جُرْم (أَجْرام) crime, offence, sin
جَرّة earthen vessel, jar	جِرْم فَلَكِي celestial body
جُرّة trace, trail	جُرْن (أَجْران) basin, barn
جُرْثُوم/جُرْثُومة (جَرَاثيم) germ, seed, root	جَرْو/جِرْو cub, pup, whelp

recompense, return, requital	جَزَاء
penal	جَزَائِي
butcher	جَزَّار
shearer, woolshearer	جَزَّاز
randomly, aimlessly, haphazardly	جُزَافاً
abundance, plenty, profusion	جَزَالة
fleece, clip	جُزَّة
purse	جُزْدان/جِزْدان
slaughtering, butchering	جَزْر
ebb-tide	جَزْر البَحْر
carrot	جَزَر/جَزَرة
onyx	جَزْع
anxiety, restlessness, apprehension, despondency	جَزَع
worried, concerned, anxious, uneasy	جَزِع
abundant, lucid, plentiful, eloquent	جَزْل/ جَزِيل
decision, resolution, determination	جَزْم

course, running, flowing	جَرْي
courageous, bold, audacious	جَرِيْء (أَجْرِياء)
flow, flowing, flux	جَرَيَان
wounded, injured	جَرِيح (جَرْحَى)
newspaper, roster, register	جَرِيدة (جَرَائد)
newsreel	جَرِيدَة نَاطِقَة
daily newspaper	جَرِيدَة يَوْمِيَّة
sin, offence	جَرِيرَة (جَرَائر)
crushed, bruised	جَرِيش
huge, bulky, voluminous	جَرِيم
offence, crime, sin	جَرِيمَة (جَرَائِم)
capital crime	جَرِيمَة عُظْمَى
part, section, portion, books division	جُزْء (أَجْزاء)
partial, divisional, trivial, petty	جُزْئِي
partly, in part	جُزْئِيًّا
particulars, details, divisions	جُزْئِيَّات

جِسْمي bodily, corporal, substantial	جَزُوع impatient, restless, anxious
جَسُور bold, daring, plucky, audacious	جِزْيَة (جِزًى) tribute, tax
جَسِيْم (جِسَام) big, huge, bulky, corpulent	جَزِيْرة (جَزَائِر) island, isle
جُشْأَة eructation, belching	جَزِيْرة العَرَب the Arabian Peninsula
جُشاء belching, eructation	جَزِيل الاِحْترام highly respected
جُشَّة huskiness, hoarseness	جَسّ touch, feeling
جَشَع greed, avidity, covetousness	جَسَارة insolence, audacity, forwardness, boldness
جَشِع greedy, covetous, avid	جَسَامة bulkiness, volume, largeness, size
جِصّ gypsum, plaster of paris	جَسَد (أَجْساد) body, corpus
جُعَالة/جِعَالة pay, wages, allowance	جَسَدي bodily, carnal, corporal
جَعْبَة (جِعاب) quiver, gun barrel	جِسْر (جُسُور) bridge, dam
جِعَة beer, ale	جِسْر عَائِم floating bridge
جَعْجاع boisterous, very noisy	جِسْر مُتَحَرِّك drawbridge, movable bridge
جَعْجَعَة rumbling, rumpus, confused sound	جِسْر مُعَلَّق suspension bridge
جَعْدة lock, curl, ringlet of hair	جِسْم (أَجْسام) substance, body, form
جَعْدي curly, frizzed	جُسْمَان body, corpse
	جُسْمَاني bodily, corporal, material

جَلَال glory, sublimity, loftiness, majesty	جَعْفَر rivulet, brook
جَلَالة المَلك His Majesty, the king	جُعْل (أَجْعال) wages, reward, commission
جَلْب bringing, producing, causing, importation	جُغْرَافي geographical, geographer
جَلَب imported, introduced, brought	جُغْرافيَا/جُغْرَافيَة geography
جَلَب/جَلَبَة uproar, tumult	جَفَاء alienation, aversion, estrangement
جِلْباب (جَلَابِيب) gown, dress, outer garment	جَفَاف dryness, desiccation
جُلْجُل (جَلَاجِل) rattle, jinglet, sleigh-bell	جَفْل (جُفُول) shying, startling, fright
جَلْجَلة rattle, resonance, shrill sound	جَفْن (جُفُون/أَجْفان) eyelid, lid
جَلْد flogging, whipping	جَفْو/جَفْوة harshness, roughness, alienation
جَلَد patience, endurance, toleration	جُلّ rose
جِلْد (جُلُود) skin, epidermis, hide	جُلّ/جُلّة most of, the majority of
جِلْد البَقَر cowhide	جَلَاء clarity, plainness, elucidation
جِلْد لَمّاع patent leather	جَلَّاب importer, attractive, charming
جَلْدة lash, whip, scourge, stroke	جُلَاب/جُلَّاب rose water
جَلْسَة gathering, meeting, assembly, session	جَلَاتين jelly
	جَلَّاد executioner, leather merchant

جِلْسَة manner of sitting	momentous, very جَلِيْل الخَطَر important
جَلْسَة عَامَّة plenary session	many, plenty of, crowd جَمّ
جُلْطَة clot, lump	efficacious, جَمّ الأَثَر effective
جُلْطَة دَمَوِيَّة blood clot	lively, full of جَمّ النَّشَاط energy
رِلْف (أَجْلاف) rude, boorish, rough, uncivil	large number or جَمّ غَفِيْر croud
جَلَل great, momentous, important	defiance, restiveness جماح
جَلَم (أَجْلام) shears	inorganic substance, جَمَاد inanimate body
جُلْمُود rock, bolder	Jumada II جُمَادَى الأُخْرَى (name of Islamic month)
جُلُود خام raw leather	Jumada I (name جُمَادَى الأُوْلَى of Islamic month)
جِلَّوْز hazel, hazelnut	total, aggregate جُمَّاع
جُلُوس sitting, sitting down	sexual intercourse, جِمَاع coition
جَلُون gallon	group, جَمَاعة (جَماعات) party, community, company
جَلِي clear, plain, obvious, evident, lucid	collective جَمَاعِي
جَلِيْب imported, foreign	beauty, elegance, grace جَمَال
جَلِيْد ice	relaxation, recreation, جَمَام refreshment
جَلِيْد (جُلَدَاء) sturdy, staunch, steadfast	
جَلِيْدي icy, glacial	
جَلِيْس (جُلَسَاء) companion, associate	
جَلِيل (أَجِلاَّء/ أَجِلَّة) great, exalted, important, glorious, honourable	

جَمْجَمَة	stammering, mumbling
جُمْجُمَة	cranium, skill
جَمْد	freezing, solidification
جَمَد	ice, snow
جَمْر/جَمْرَة	embers, live coal
جُمْرُك (جَمَارِك)	customhouse, customs
جَمْع	gathering, collecting
جَمْع (جُمُوع)	gathering, crowd, throng
جَمْع الشَّمْل	reunion, unity, integration
جَمْع القَوَانِين	codification
جُمْعَة (جُمَع)	Friday, week
جُمْعَة الآلام	Passion Week
جُمْعَة حَزِينَة	Good Friday
جَمْعِيّة (جَمْعِيّات)	association, assembly, society
جَمْعِيّة الأُمَم	league of nations
جَمْعِيّة تَشْرِيعِيّة	legislative assembly
جَمْعِيّة تَعَاوُنِيّة	cooperative society
جَمْعِيّة خَيْرِيّة	welfare society, charitable organization

جَمْعِيّة عَامّة	general assembly
جَمْعِيّة عُمُومِيّة	general assembly
جَمَل (جِمال)	camel
جُمْلَةً	altogether, wholly, on the whole
جُمْلَة (جُمَل)	whole, group, sentence, sum
جُمْلَة آتِيَة	following sentence
جُمْلَة اسْمِيّة	nominal sentence
جُمْلَة شَرْطِيّة	conditional clause
جُمْلَة فِعْلِيّة	verbal sentence
جَمْهَرة	crowd, throng, mass
جُمْهُور (جَمَاهِير)	the public, multitude
جُمْهُوري	republican
جَمُوح	restive, refractory, unruly, defiant
جُمُود	solidity, hardness, rigidity, inaction
جَمِيع	all, total, whole
جَمِيل	beautiful, handsome, pretty, favour, good turn
جِنّ	jinn, demon

side, flank	جِنْح	gardener	جَنائي
darkness, gloom	جُنْح	criminal	جِنائي
misdemeanor	جُنْحَة (جُنَح)	major impurity	جَنابَة
troops, soldiers	جُنْد (جُنُود)	offence, guilt, sin	جُناح
grasshopper	جُنْدُب (جَنادب)	wing, flank	جَناح (أَجنِحَة)
cataract, waterfall	جَنْدَل (جَنادِل)	bier, hearse, funeral procession,	جِنازة/جَنازة (جَنائِز)
militaryman, soldier	جُنْدي (جُنُود)	heart, soul	جَنان
general	جِنْرال	committal of a crime, crime, felony	جِناية (جِنايات)
chain	جِنْزير	capital crime	جِناية كُبْرَى
sex, gender, genus, sort, nature, race	جِنْس (أَجْناس)	impurity, uncleanliness	جُنُب
mankind, human race	جِنْس بَشَري	side, beside	جَنْب (جُنُوب)
strong sex	جِنْس خَشِن	gymnastics	جُنْباز/جُمْباز
fair sex	جِنْس لَطيف	gymnastic	جُنْبازي/جُمْبازي
racial, generic	جِنْسي	region, area	جَنْبَة (جَنَبات)
nationality, citizenship	جِنْسِيّة	madness, mania, obsession	جَنّة
south	جَنُوب	garden, paradise, heaven	جَنّة (جَنّات/جِنان)
southeast	جَنُوب شَرْقي	shield, shelter, screen	جُنّة (جُنَن)
southwest	جَنُوب غَرْبي	land of the Leal	جَنّة الخُلْد
southward, to the south	جَنُوباً	eden, paradise	جَنّة عَدْن

refrigerator	جِهَاز التَّبْرِيد
control apparatus	جِهَاز الضَّبْط
bride's outfit	جِهَاز العَرُوس
carding machine	جِهَاز النَّدْف
digestive system	جِهَاز الهَضْم
television set	جِهَاز تِلْفِزْيُوني
respiratory system	جِهَاز تَنَفُّسي
circulatory system	جِهَاز دَوْري
radio	جِهَاز رَادِيو
sanitary installation	جِهَاز صِحِّي
nervous system	جِهَاز عَصَبي
wireless set, radio	جِهَاز لاَسِلْكي
foolishness, dullness, ignorance	جَهَالة
sullenness, scowl, gloominess	جَهَامة
direction, side, area, part	جِهَة (جِهَات)
exertion, strain, strength	جُهْد
exertion, strain, endeavour, effort	جَهْد (جُهود)

southern	جَنُوبي
frenzy, fury, mania, dementia, madness	جُنُون
kleptomania	جُنُون السَّرِقَة
midsummer madness	جُنُون مُطْبِق
frenzied, crazy	جُنُوني
jinni, demonic	جِنِّي
reaping, gathering	جَنْي
jinniyyah, female demon	جِنِّيَّة
embryo, foetus	جَنِين (أَجِنَّة)
little garden	جُنَيْنَة (جَنَائِن)
Pound	جُنَيْه (جُنَيْهَات)
English Pound	جُنَيْه انْجِلِيزِي
Egyptian Pound	جُنَيْه مِصْرِي
strife, struggle, jihad, holy war	جِهَاد
tough struggle	جِهَاد عَنِيف
military, fighting	جِهَادِي
publicness, openness	جِهَار
publicly, openly	جِهَاراً
appliance, system, equipment, implement, apparatus	جِهَاز (أَجْهِزَة)

steed, race-horse (جِياد) جَوَاد	openness, publicity	جَهْر/جَهْرة
thoroughbred horse	جَوَاد كَرِيم	publicly, openly	جَهْرًا/جَهْرَةً
neighbourhood, vicinity, succour	جِوار	public, open, notorious	جَهْرِي
permit, permissibility, lawfulness	جَوَاز	miscarried foetus, abortive	جِهْض
passport	جَوَاز السَّفَر	ignorance, stupidity, dullness	جَهْل
guava	جُوافة	gross ignorance	جَهْل مُرَكَّب
rover, wanderer, wandering, cruising	جَوَّال	frowning, grim, gloomy	جَهْم
wanderer, cruiser	جَوَّالة	hell, tartarus	جَهَنَّم
travelling, exploration, penetration	جَوْب	infernal, hellish	جَهَنَّمي
pit, hole, opening	جَوْبة (جُوَب)	loud, sonorous	جَهْوَري
broadcloth, cloth	جُوْخ (أَجْواخ)	ignorant, stupid, blockhead	جَهُول
generosity, liberality, munificence	جُود	sullenness, gloominess	جُهُومة
heavy rains	جَوْد	by air	جَوًّا
efficiency, goodness, excellence	جُوْدَة	traveller, explorer	جَوَّاب
		answer, reply (أَجْوِبة) جَوَاب	
injustice, wrong, tyranny, oppression	جَوْر	explicit reply	جَوَاب صَرِيح
		silencing answer	جَوَاب مُفْحِم
		generous, bountiful, liberal	جَوَاد (جُود)

substantial, elemental, essential, jeweller	جَوْهَري	sock, stocking	جَوْرَب (جَوَارِب)
passion, ardent love	جَوَّى	walnut	جَوْز (جَوْزَة)
atmospheric, airy, ethereal, meteoric	جَوِّي	coconut	جَوْز هِنْدي
coming, arrival	جِيْئَة/جَيْئَة	heart, centre, middle	جَوْز/أَجْواز
limekiln	جَيَّارة	spying, espionage	جَوْسَسَة
jeep	جيب	castle, manor	جَوْسَق (جَوَاسِق)
pocket, bosom, hollow	جَيْب (جُيُوب)	hunger, starvation	جُوْع
neck	جيْد (أَجْياد/جُيُود)	hungry, starved	جَوْعَان
good, excellent, well	جَيِّد (جِياد)	hungry (fem.of جَوْعَان)	جَوْعَى
very good	جَيِّد جدًّا	cavity, inside, abdomen, interior	جَوْف (أَجْواف)
excellently, rightly, well	جَيِّدًا	band, troop, group	جَوْق (أَجْواق)
lime	جيْر	troop, group, company	جَوْقَة (جَوْقات)
unslaked lime	جيْر حَيّ	roaming, wandering, roving	جَوَلان
slaked lime	جيْر مُطْفَأ	round, tour, trip, patrol	جَوْلَة
neighbourhood, vicinity	جيْرة	golf	جولف
gyroscope	جَيْرُوسكوب	essence, element, substance, atom	جَوْهَر (جَوَاهِر)
gyroscopic	جَيْرُوسكوبي		
limy, calcareous	جيْري	jewel, gem	جَوْهَرَة

sheltering, veiling, حَاجِب concealing	army, troops (جُيُوش) جَيْش
	Salvation Army جَيْش الإنْقاذ
eyebrow, (حَوَاجِب) حَاجِب brow	invincible army جَيْش مَنِيع
wish, need, necessity, حَاجَة requirement, indigence	agitation, excitement, جَيَشان ebullition
needs,necessities (حوائج)حَاجَة	corpse, (جَيَف/أَجْياف) جِيْفة carcass
urgent need حَاجَة مَاسّة	generation, race, (أَجْيال) جِيْل
obstacle, (حَوَاجِز) حَاجِز hidrance, barrier	epoch
	جِيُوغرافيا= جغرافيا
insurmountable حَاجِز مَنِيع obstacle	geologic-al جيولوجي
	geology جيولوجيا
sharp, keen, acute حَادّ	
sharp-sighted حَادّ البَصَر	
sharp-witted حَادّ الذّهْن	bewildered, startled, حائِر confused
sharp-angled حَادُ الزَّاوِية	
hot tempered, حَادّ الطَّبْع irascible	possessor, holder, حائِز owner
occurring, taking حَادث place	menstruant, حَائِض menstruating
incident, (حَوَادث) حادث accident, mishap	wall حائط (حِيْطان)
	weaver حَائِك (حَاكَة)
incident, (حَوَادث) حَادثة accident, mishap	obstacle, حَائِل (حَوَائِل) impediment, hindrance
traffic accident حَادِثة المُرُور	pilgrim, haji حَاجّ (حُجّاج)

weak-sighted	حَاسِر البَصَر	eleventh	حَادي عشر
bare-headed	حَاسِر الرَّأس	skilful, clever, dexterous, sagacious	حَاذِق (حُذّاق)
decisive, conclusive, final	حَاسِم	hot, pungent, ardent	حَارّ
computer	حَاسُوب	quarter, lane, narrow street	حَارَة (حارات)
crowded	حَاشِد	ploughman	حَارِث (حُرّاث)
battery	حَاشِدة	annoyed, ill-humoured, petulant	حَارِد
edge, border, margin, marginal notes	حَاشِيَة (حَوَاشٍ)	guard, watchman, protector, custodian, keeper	حارِس (حَرَسَة/حُرّاس)
hurricane, storm	حَاصِبة		
harvester, reaper	حَاصِد	night watchman	حَارِث اللَّيل
mowing machine, mower	حَاصِدة	goalkeeper	حَارِس المَرْمَى
result, outcome, returns, product	حَاصِل	resolute, discreet, prudent	حَازِم
present, ready, prepared	حَاضِر	reckoner, calculator	حَاسِب
quick-witted	حَاضِر الذِّهن	computer	حَاسِب عَالِي
ready-witted	حَاضِر الفِكر	sense, sensation	حَاسَّة (حَوَاسّ)
quick-witted	حَاضِر التُّكْتَة	the sense of touch	حَاسَّة اللَّمْس
capital, metropolis	حَاضِرَة (حَوَاضِر)	envious, greedy, grudger	حاسِد
nurse-maid	حَاضِنة	barred, denuded	حاسِر (حَوَاسِر)
wood cutter	حَاطِب		

condition, حَال (أَحْوَال) position, situation, case, circumstance	bare footed حَاف (حُفَاة)
immediately, quickly, حَالاً presently	edge, border, حَافَّة (حَافَّات) verge, margin
ureter حَالِب	verge, brim, حَافَة (حَوَاف/حَافَات) edge, border
condition, state, حَالَة (حَالات) position, case, situation	hoof حَافِر (حَوَافِر)
marital status حَالَة اِجْتِمَاعِيّة	spur, drive, حَافِز (حَوَافِز) incentive
state of alarm حَالَة الْخَطَر	guardian, keeper, حافظ caretaker, custodian,
emergencies, حَالَة الطَّوَارِئ state of emergency	protector
atmospheric حَالَة جَوِّيّة condition	memory حَافِظة full, abundant, حَافِل (حَوَافِل) lavish
the status quo حَالَة رَاهِنَة	autobus حَافِلة (حَوَافِل)
civil status حَالَة مَدَنِيّة	malicious, spiteful, حَاقِد malevolent
pitch dark, pitch حَالِك/حَلِك black	story-teller, narrator, حَاكٍ phonograph
dreamer حَالِم	governor, ruler, حَاكِم (حُكَّام) judge
as soon as حَالَمَا	justice of peace حَاكِم الصُّلْح
present, existing,حَالِي current	umpire, refree حَاكِم الْمُبَاراة
at present, presently, حَالِيًّا actually	governor general حَاكِم عام
heated, burning, حَامٍ passionate, pungent	sovereignty, حَاكِمِيّة domination

حُبّ الاسْتِطْلاع	curiosity, inquisitiveness
حُبّ الذَّات	self-love, selfishness
حُبّ السِّلْم	peace-loving, pacifism
حُبّ الوَطَن	patriotism
حَبّ/حَبّة (حُبُوب)	grains, seed, pills, postules
حِباء	gift, present
حَبار/حِبار	trace, mark
حِبَاكة	weaving, knitting
حِبَالة (حَبَائِل)	snare, net
حَبّة العَيْن	eyeball, pupil of the eye
حَبّة القَلْب	beloved, darling, care of mind
حَبْحَب	water melon
حِبْر	ink
حِبْر/حَبْر (أَحْبار)	bishop, rabbi, pontiff
حَبْري	pontifical
حَبْس	custody, detention, confinement, imprisonment
حِبْس (أَحْبَاس)	dam, weir, bedsheet

حَامٍ (حُماة)	protector, guardian, tutelary
حَامِض	sour, acid, acidulous
حَامِض الفَحْم	carbonic acid
حَامِض كِبْريتي	sulphuric acid
حَامِل (حَمَلَة)	bearer, carrier, holder
حَامِل (حَوَامِل)	pregnant
حَامِل البَريد	courier
حَامِلة	carrier, bearer
حَامِلَة طائرات	aircraft, carrier
حَامِية	patroness, protectress, guardian
حَان/حَائة	bar, wine-shop, tavern
حَانِق	angry, furious, enraged
حَانُوت (حَوَانيت)	store, shop
حَاوٍ	containing, including
حاوٍ (حُوَاة)	snake charmer, juggler
حُبّ	love, affection
حِبّ (أَحْباب)	darling, sweetheart
حُبّ أفلاطوني	platonic love

joy, gaiety, cheerfulness	حُبُور
failure, futility, miscarriage	حُبُوط
loving, friendly	حُبِّي
dear, beloved, friend	حَبِيب (أحْباب/أحِبّة)
little grain, granule	حُبَيْبَة
sweetheart, beloved, darling	حَبِيبَة (حَبَائِب)
confined, imprisoned, locked up	حَبِيس
scraps, scrumbs	حُتَات
bit, scrap, small piece	حِتّة (حِتَت)
death	حَتْف (حُتُوف)
imposing, deciding	حَتْم
resolution, decision, final decision	حَتْم (حُتُوم)
definitely, decidedly	حَتْمًا
definite, final, decisive	حَتْمِي
till, until, even, so that	حَتَّى
until now, by now	حَتَّى الآن
how long, till when	حَتَّى مَتَى

lockup, prison, jail	حَبْس (حُبُوس)
detention, custody	حَبْس احْتِياطِي
solitary confinement	حَبْس انْفِرادِي
penal servitude	حَبْس شَدِيد
orbits	حُبُك
orbits of celestial bodies	حُبُك النُّجُوم
texture, fabric	حَبْكَة
plot of the novel	حَبْكَة الرِّواية
conception, pregnancy	حَبَل
false pregnancy	حَبَل كاذب
cord, rope, thread, line	حَبْل (حِبال/حُبُول)
jogular vein	حَبْل الوَرِيد
navel string, umbilical cord	حَبْل سُرِّي
spinal cord	حَبْل شَوْكِي
spermatic cord	حَبْل مَنَوِي
pregnant, expectant	حُبْلَى (حُبَالَى)
crawling, creeping	حَبْو
gift, present	حِبْوة/حَبْوة

stony, petrified	حَجِر	incitement, instigation, impelling	حَثّ
stone	حَجَر (أَحْجار)	small piece, scrap, bit	حُثْرة
foundation stone, cornerstone	حَجَر أساسي	hajj, pilgrimage to Makka	حَجّ/حِجّة
the Black Stone	حَجَر أَسْوَد	veil, cover, curtain, screen	حِجَاب (حُجُب)
flagstone, paving stone	حَجَر البَلاط	argument, dispute, discussion	حِجَاج
blood stone	حَجَر الدَّم	stone mason, stone cutter	حَجّار
mill stone	حَجَر الرَّحَى		
corner stone	حَجَر الزَّاوِية	limestone	حِجَارَة كِلْسِيّة
mill stone	حَجَر الطَّاحُون	cupper	حَجّام
cornerstone, quoin	حَجَر النَّاصِيَة	cupping, art of cupping	حِجَامة
quarantine	حَجْر صِحِّي	covering, keeping away	حَجْب
precious stone, gem	حَجَر كَرِيم	argument, document, evidence	حُجّة (حُجَج)
limestone	حَجَر كَلْسِي	irrefutable argument	حُجّة دَامِغة
room, chamber	حُجْرة (حُجَرات)		
common room	حُجْرَة الاسْتِراحة	detention, obstruction, restriction, debarment, interdiction	حَجَر
waiting room	حُجْرَة الانْتِظار		
bedroom	حُجْرَة النَّوم	interdicted, forbidden, taboo, lap	حِجْر
stony, hard	حَجَري		

deep mourning حِداد كامِل	prevention, detention, حَجْز
	restraint
ironsmith's business, حِدَادة	
art of smithing	seizure, distraint حَجْز الأَمْوال
love, care, affection حَدَب	anklet (حُجُول) حَجْل/حِجْل
vaulted, curved, bent, حَدِب	partridge حَجَل/حَجَلَة
friendly	size, (حُجُوم/أَحْجام) حَجْم
elavation (أَحْداب) حَدَب	bulk, magnitude
vehemence, sharpness, حِدّة	suitable, appropriate حَجِيّ
anger, fury	intelligence, (أَحْجاء) حِجًى
solitariness, solitude, حِدَة	intellect, discernment
aloneness	kite حِدَأَة
petulance, حِدّة الطَّبْع	limit, end, (حُدُود) حَدّ
irascibility	border, verge, boundary,
occurrence, (أَحْداث) حَدَث	termination
event, novelty, innovation	the minimum حَدّ أَدْنَى
youth, (أَحْداث/حُدْثان) حَدَث	the maximum حَدّ أَعْلَى
juvenile	utmost limit حَدّ النِّهايَة
burden, load حِدْج	newness, novelty, حَدَاثة
rapid recitation of the حَدْر	youth
Quran	youthfulness, حَدَاثة السِّنّ
guess, conjecture, حَدْس	juvenility
supposition	camel saddle (حَدَائِج) حِدَاجة
pupil of the eye حَدَقَة	mourning حِدَاد
occurrence, حُدُوث	ironsmith, blacksmith حَدَّاد
happening, taking place	

حَدِيقَة الْحَيَوَانات	zoo, zoological garden	خُدُور	slope, declivity
حَدِيْقَة السَّطْح	roof-garden	حَدِيث (أَحَادِيث)	speech, talk, report, tradition of the Prophet
حَذَّاء	cobbler, shoemaker	حَدِيث (حِدَاث/حُدَثاء)	new, novel, modern
حِذَاء (أَحْذِيَة)	shoes, boots	حَدِيث السِّنّ	young, juvenile
حِذَاء/حَذْوَ	opposite to, parallel with	حَدِيْث العَهْد	recent, new, young
حَذَاقَة	cleverness, intelligence, acumen	حَدِيث العَهْد بالزَّوَاج	newly-wed
حَذِر	cautious, careful	حَدِيث العَهْد بالوِلَادَة	new-born
حِذْر/حَذَر	caution, care, alertness,	حَدِيْث النَّمَط	new fashioned
حَذْف	deletion, omission, striking off	حَدِيْث الوِلَادَة	newborn
حِذْق	skill, cleverness, dexterity, acumen	حَدِيثاً	recently, newly
حَذْلَقَة	pedantry, dexterity	حَدِيد	iron
حَرّ	heat, warmth	حَدِيد (حَدَائِد)	iron ware, hardware
حُرّ (أَحْرار)	free, liberal, independent, pure, genuine	حَدِيْد (حِداد/أَحِدّة)	sharp, keen, acute
حُرّ العَقِيْدة	free-thinker	حَدِيد خام	iron ore
حُرّ الفِكَر	liberal, frank	حَدِيْد غَشِيْم	raw iron
حَرَّات	ploughman	حَدِيد مَسْبُوك	pig iron
حِرَاثَة	farming, cultivation	حَدِيْقة (حَدَائِق)	garden

heat, ardour, enthusiasm, passion	حَرَارة
watch, care, protection	حِرَاسَة
pungency, acridity	حَرَافة
tinder, touchwood	حُرَاق
burning, hot, pungent	حَرّاق
blanket, rug	حِرَام
interdicted, prohibited, taboo, sacred	حَرَام (أَحْرام)
forbidden, illicit, prohibited, inviolable	حَرَام (حُرُم)
very thirsty, parched	حَرّان
war, battle, fight	حَرْب (حُرُوب)
civil war	حَرْب أَهْلِيَّة
class struggle	حَرْب الطَّبَقَات
guerrilla war	حَرْب العِصَابَات
cold war	حَرْب بَارِدة
civil war	حَرْب دَاخِلِيّة
press feud	حَرْب صَحَافِيّة
fierce war	حَرْب ضَرُوس
world war	حَرْب عُظْمَى
chameleon	حِرْبَاء

lance, spearhead	حَرْبَة (حِرَاب)
martial, warlike, military	حَرْبِي
ploughing, tilling	حَرْث
restriction, narrowness, confinement, difficulty	حَرَج
tight, narrow, close, straitened	حَرِج
wood, thicket	حَرَج (أَحْراج)
ill-humoured, disgruntled	حَرِد
lizard	حِرْذَوْن
fortress, custody, retreat	حِرْز (أَحْراز)
invincible fortress	حِرْز حَرِيز
guard, escort	حَرَس
body-guard	حَرَس شَخْصِي
royal guard	حَرَس مَلَكِي
National Guard	حَرَس وَطَنِي
coarse, rough	حَرِش
forest, thicket	حِرْش/حُرْشى
roughness, coarseness	حُرْشَة/حَرَاشَة
greed, covetousness, avarice, desire	حِرْص

feminist movement	حَرَكَة نِسْوِيّة	edge, border, verge	حَرْف (حِرَف)
excommunication	حِرْم	letter, particle	حَرْف (حُرُوف/أَحْرُف)
deprivation, debarment	حِرْمان	preposition	حَرْف جَرّ
sanctity, sacredness, inviolability	حُرْمَة (حُرُمات)	conjunction	حَرْف عَطْف
wife	حُرْمَة الرَّجُل	vowel	حَرْف عِلّة
pungency, acridity, heartburn, stench	حَرْوَة	interjection	حَرْف نِداء
Alphabet	حُرُوف أَبْجَدِيّة	occupation, profession, trade	حِرْفَة (حِرَف)
Alphabet	حُرُوف الهِجَاء	learned profession	حِرْفَة شَرِيفَة
stubborn, inflexible, refractory, restive	حَرُون	trade	حِرْفَة يَدَوِيّة
suitable, adequate, worthy	حَرِيّ (أَحْرِياء)	literal	حَرْفِي
credible, believable	حَرِي بِالتَّصْدِيق	burn, burning, kindling, setting a fire	حَرْق
worth mentioning	حَرِي بِالذِّكْر	burning, vehemence	حَرْقَة/حُرْقة
freedom, liberty, independence	حُرِّيّة	restless, agile, brisk	حَرِك
freedom of choice	حُرِّيّة الاخْتِيار	acrobatics	حَرَكات بَهْلَوَانِيّة
		tactics	حَرَكات حَرْبِيّة
liberty of the press	حُرِّيّة الصِّحَافَة	movement, motion, vowel point	حَرَكَة (حَرَكات)
		shipping traffic	حَرَكَة المَرَاكِب
		traffic	حَرَكَة المُرُور

safety belt	حِزَام الأَمْن	freedom of worship	حُرِّيّة العِبَادَة
saddle-girth	حِزَام السَّرْج	freedom of thought, liberality	حُرِّيّة الفِكْر
party, group, troop	حِزْب (أَحْزَاب)	freedom of speech	حُرِّيّة الكَلَام
labour party	حِزْب العُمّال	freedom of the press	حُرِّيّة المَطَابِع
nick, nick of time	حَزَّة	silk	حَرِير (حَرَائِر)
guess, conjecture, assessment	حَزْر	synthetic silk	حَرِيْر صِنَاعِي
discretion, resolution, determination, packaging	حَزْم	silky, silken	حَرِيْرِي
package, parcel, bundle	حُزْمَة (حُزَم)	invincible, inaccessible	حَرِيز
sad, grieved, sorrowful	حَزِن	greedy, covetous, avaricious	حَرِيص
grief, sorrow, mourning, sadness	حُزْن (أَحْزَان)	pungent, acrid, hot	حِرِّيْف
June	حَزِيْران	fire, conflagration	حَرِيق/حَرِيْقَة (حَرَائِق)
sad, grieved, mournful	حَزِين	harem, sanctum, sacred place, wife	حَرِيم (حُرُم)
sense, sensation, feeling, sound	حِسّ	notch, incision, nick	حَزّ (حُزُوز)
feeling, sensation	حَسّ	ringworm, dandruff	حَزَاز
calculation, computation, reckoning	حِسَاب	hatred, enmity, rancour	حَزَازة
account, invoice	حِسَاب (حِسَابات)	belt, girdle, girth	حِزَام (حُزُم/أَحْزِمَة)
saving account	حِسَاب التَّوْفِيْر		

grief, distress, sadness, regret	حَسْرَة (حَسَرَات)	current account	حِسَاب جَارٍ
thorn, spikes	حَسَك	suspense account	حِسَاب مُعَلَّق
thorny, spiny	حَسَكي	open account	حِسَاب مَفْتُوح
determination, decision, settlement	حَسْم	blocked account	حِسَاب مَوْقُوف
beauty, loveliness, prettiness, grace	حُسْن	sensitive, sensible, sensual	حَسَّاس
good, beautiful, lovely, excellent	حَسَن (حِسَان)	sword	حُسَام
good performance, good renditions	حُسْن الأداء	reckoning, counting, thinking, consideration	حَسْب
eloquence	حُسْن البَيَان	quantity, measure, amount, noble descent	حَسَب (أَحْسَاب)
discretion	حُسْن التَّصَرُّف	at will	حَسْبَ الإِرَادَة
euphemism	حُسْن التَّعْبِير	as required	حَسْبَ اللُّزُوم
good understanding	حُسْن التَّفَاهُم	reckoning, accounting, computing	حُسْبان
good behaviour, good conduct	حُسْن السُّلُوك	sum, arithmetics	حِسْبَة
good luck	حُسْن الطَّالع	according to	حَسْبَما
good opinion	حُسْن الظَّنّ	envy, covetousness	حَسَد
good intention	حُسْن القَصْد	debility, weak-sightedness	حَسَر
good intention, sincerity	حُسْن النِّيَّة	fatigued, weary, tired	حَسِر
		regretful, grieved, sorry	حَسْرَان

حَشْو	filling, stuffing, insertion
حَشْوَة	stuffing, filling, load
حَشًى (أَحْشَاء)	bowels, entrails, intestines
حَشِيّة (حَشِيّات/حَشَايا)	mattress, cushion
حَشِيْش (حَشَائِش)	weeds, grasses
حَشِيْش الدِّيَار	hops
حَشِيْشة	herb
حَشِيم (حُشَمَاء)	bashful, modest, coy, shy
حَصَاة (حَصَيَات)	little stones, pebbles
حَصَاة بَوْلِيّة	urinary calculus
حَصَاة صَفْرَاوِيّة	gall stone
حِصَاد	harvesting, harvest season
حَصَّاد	harvester, reaper
حَصَّادة	mowing machine
حِصَار	siege, blockage
حَصَافة	sound judgment, prudence, discretion
حِصَان (حُصُن)	horse

حَسَّنًا	well, alright
حَسَنَة (حَسَنات)	charity, good action
حَسْو	soup
حَسْوَة/حُسْوَة	a sip
حَسُود	envious, covetous
حُسُور	near-sightedness, myopia
حَسُوم	fatal, gruelling
حِسِّي	sensuous, perceptible
حَسِيب (حُسَبَاء)	noble, high-born, esteemed
حَسِير	weary, tired, fatigued
حَسِير البَصَر	near-sighted
حَشْد (حُشُود)	assembly, gathering, crowd
حَشْر	crowding, cramming, gathering, insertion
حَشَرَة (حَشَرات)	insect, bug
حَشَرِي	insectival, insectile
حَشَفَة	glans
حَشَم	attendants, servants, satellites
حِشْمَة	decency, modesty, bashfulness

fortress, stronghold, citadel	حِصْن (حُصُون)
stronghold	حِصْن حَصِين
impregnable fortress	حِصْن مَنِيع
pebble, gravel	حَصْوَة
obtainment, acquisition, happening, occurrence	حُصُول
pebbly, stony	حَصَوِي
pebbles, broken stones	حَصًى
harvest, crop	حَصِيد/حَصِيْدة (حَصَائِد)
mat, prison	حَصِيْر (حُصُر)
mat	حَصِيْرة (حَصَائِر)
prudent, judicious, discriminating	حَصِيف
collection, receipts, returns	حَصِيْلة (حَصَائِل)
fortified, strong, firm, immune	حَصِين
exhortation, incitement, inducement	حَضّ
civilization, refinement, culture	حَضَارة

thorough bred horse	حِصَان أصِيل
hippopotamus	حِصَان البَحْر
steed	حِصَان الرُّكُوب
race horse, courser	حِصَان السِّباق
thoroughbred horse	حِصَان كَرِيْم
inaccessibility, invulnerability, chastity	حَصَانة
metal, broken stones	حَصَب
pebbles, gravels, broken stones	حَصْباء
share, portion, quota	حِصَّة (حِصَص)
founders share	حِصّة التَّأْسِيْس
period	حِصّة دِراسِيّة
dividend	حِصّة مَالِيّة
quota	حِصّة نِسْبِيّة
reaping, harvesting	حَصْد
encompassing, confinement, limitation, detention, blockading	حَصْر
retention of urine	حُصْر
shrewd, of sound judgment, judicious	حَصِف

shipwreck حُطَام السَّفِينة	nursing, bringing up, حِضَانة
firewood حَطَب (أَحْطاب)	guardianship
degradation, حِطَّة	incubation حِضَانة البَيْض
debasement, insult	civilization, refinement حَضَر
broken pieces, حِطْمَة	presence حَضْرَة
fragments	your highness, your حَضْرَتكم
wrecked, smashed حَطِيم	honour
luck, fortune, lot, share, حَظّ	civilized, refined, حَضَرِي
affluence	settled
longitude حَظّ الطُّوْل	breast, bosom, (أَحْضَان) حِضْن
bad luck حَظّ عاثِر	embrace
interdiction, prohibition حَظْر	presence, attendance حُضُور
curfew حَظْر التَّجْوال	presence of حُضُور الذِّهْن
favour, good حُظْوة/حِظْوَة	mind
will, high esteem, credit	section, حَضِيرة (حَضَائِر)
concubine, حَظِيّة (حَظَايا)	squod
mistress, favourite	lowland, حَضِيض (حُضُض)
fence, railing, حَظِيرة (حَظَائِر)	perigee
enclosure	embraced, hugged حَضِين
coop, pen حَظِيرة البَهائِم	putting, placing, حَطّ
paradise حَظِيرة القُدْس	belittling, derogation,
fortunate, lucky, حَظِيظ	diminution
happy	woodcutter, wood حَطَّاب
digger, driller, حَفَّار	gatherer
engraver	wreckage, broken حُطَام
	pieces, debris

wedding ceremony	حَفْلَة الزَّوَاج	gravedigger	حَفّار القُبُور
tea-party	حَفْلَة الشَّاي	protection, preservation, guarding	حِفَاظ
marriage ceremony	حَفْلَة العُرْس	truss, bandage, dressing	حِفَاظ (حِفَاظات)
farewell party	حَفْلَة الوَدَاع	sanitary napkin, diaper	حِفَاظ الحَيْض
religious ceremony	حَفْلَة دِيْنِيّة	welcome, kindly reception	حَفَاوَة
dance, dancing party	حَفْلَة رَاقِصَة	digging, engraving, inscription	حَفْر
evening party, evening show	حَفْلَة سَاهِرَة	pit, hole, cavity	حُفْرَة (حُفَر)
motion picture show	حَفْلَة سِينمائِيّة	keeping, guarding, preservation, protection, observance	حِفْظ
concert of vocal music	حَفْلَة غِنَائِيّة		
concert	حَفْلَة مَوْسِيقِيّة	preservation of ancient monuments	حِفْظ الآثار
welcoming, hospitable	حَفِي	hygiene, sanitation, preservation of health	حِفْظ الصِّحَّة
grandson, grandchild	حَفِيد (حَفَدَة)		
grand daughter	حَفِيْدة	party, concert, ceremony, gathering	حَفْلَة (حَفْلات)
dug out, excavated	حَفِير	reception	حَفْلَة الاسْتِقْبَال
protector, preserver	حَفِيظ	commemorative celebration, commemoration	حَفْلَة التَّأْبِين
rustle, restling	حَفِيْف		
right, correct, true, truth, reality	حَقّ	funeral, burial ceremony	حَفْلَة الدَّفْن

experimental fields	حُقُول الاخْتِبَار	pot, small jar, cavity	حُقّ
experimental fields	حُقُول التَّجَارِب	right, claim, law	حَقّ (حُقُوق)
bag, travelling bag	حَقِيْبة (حَقَائب)	veto	حَقّ الاعْتِرَاض
diplomatic pouch	حَقِيْبة دِبْلُومَاسِيّة	patent, permit	حَقّ الامْتِيَاز
hand bag, purse	حَقِيْبة يَد	veto power	حَقّ الفِيْتُو
spite, rancour, malice, ill-will	حَقِيْدة (حَقَائد)	right of veto	حَقّ النَّقْض
abject, low, mean, poor, miserable	حَقِير (حُقَراء)	absolute certainty	حَقّ اليَقِين
worthy, fit, competent	حَقِيق (أَحِقّاء)	really, actually, in fact	حَقًّا
in fact, really, actually	حَقِيْقَةً	lowness, baseness, wretchedness, vileness	حَقارة
reality, fact, authenticity, truth	حَقِيْقة (حَقَائق)	just, upright, proper	حَقّاني
actual, real, true, genuine	حَقِيْقِي	epoch, period, duration	حِقْبَة (حِقَب)
scratching, rubbing, friction	حَكّ	malice, hatred, sprite, ill-will	حِقْد (أَحْقَاد/حُقُود)
lapidary	حَكّاك	field, column	حَقْل (حُقُول)
tale, story, narrative	حِكَاية	oil field	حَقْل البِتْرُول
itch, prurigo	حَكّة	oil field	حَقْل الزَّيْت
		حَقْل النَّفْط= حَقْل الزَّيْت	
		injecting, withholding	حَقْن
		injection, syringe	حُقْنَة (حُقَن)
		spiteful, malicious, resentful	حَقُود
judge, umpire, refree	حَكَم	national rights	حُقُوق وَطَنِيّة

monarchy	حُكُومة مَلكيّة	order, decision, judgment, ordinance, rule	حُكْم (أَحْكام)
interim government	حُكُومَة مُوَقَّتة	reign of terror	حُكْم الإرْهاب
national government	حُكُومة وَطنيّة	acquittal	حُكْم البَرَاءة
governmental, official, of the state	حُكُومي	capital punishment, death sentence	حُكْم بالإعْدام
wise, philosopher, judicious	حَكيم (حُكَماء)	adjudication	حُكْم بالإفْلاس
unbinding, loosening, untying	حَلّ	sentence	حُكْم جِنائي
solution, release compromise, abolition, dissolution	حَلّ (حُلُول)	autonomy, self-determination	حُكْم ذاتي
		martial law	حُكْم عُرْفي
		martial law	حُكْم عَسْكَري
dissolution of a partnership	حَلّ الشَّرِكَة	final judgement	حُكْم نِهائي
		legally, virtually	حُكْمًا
sweetness, deliciousness	حَلَا/حَلَى	wisdom, sagacity, adage	حِكْمَة (حِكَم)
milker, one who milks	حَلَّاب	legal, judicial	حُكْمي
milk maid, dairymaid	حَلَّابة	government, rule, state	حُكُومة
cotton ginner	حَلَّاج القُطْن	federal government	حُكُومَة اتِّحَاديّة
barber, hairdresser	حَلَّاق	autocracy, monocracy	حُكُومَة الفَرْد
shave, shaving	حِلاقة		
legitimate, lawful, licit	حَلَال	Republic	حُكُومة جُمْهُوريّة
sweetness, pleasantness, gracefulness	حَلَاوة	constitutional government	حُكُومة دُسْتُوريّة

palatal, guttural, pharyngeal	حَلْقِي	milking, milk	حَلْب
circular, ring-shaped	حَلَقِي	race-course, race-track	حَلْبَة (حَلَبات)
intense blackness	حُلْكَة	dance floor	حَلْبَة الرَّقْص
puberty, maturity	حُلْم	race-track	حَلْبَة السِّباق
dream	حُلْم (أَحْلام)	garments, dress, vestments	حُلَّة (حُلَل)
mildness, clemency, patience, long suffering	حِلْم (حُلُوم)	formal dress	حُلَّة السَّهْرَة
nipple, teat, mamilla	حَلَم/حَلَمَة	uniform	حُلَّة رَسْمِيّة
sweet, pleasant, delicious	حُلْو	ginning	حَلْج/حِلاَجة
		snail, spire	حَلَزُون
sweetmeats, confection	حَلْوَاء	spiral, voluted	حَلَزُوني
confectioner, tuckshop	حَلْوَائي/حَلْوَاني	ally, alliance, league	حِلْف (أَحْلاف)
lactiferous, milker	حَلُوب	taking the oath	حِلْف اليَمِين
descending, falling, subrogation	حُلُول	military alliance	حِلْف عَسْكَري
sweets, candy, confection	حَلْوَى (حَلاَوَى)	false swearing	حلف كاذب
confectionery, sweets, candies	حَلْوَيَات	swearing, oath	حَلْف/حِلْف
		shave, shaving	حَلْق
jewellery, jewels	حَلْي/حُلِيّ	throat, pharynx	حَلْق (حُلُوق)
		ring, circle, link, course	حَلْقَة/حَلَقَة (حَلَقات/حَلَق)
milk	حَلِيب	throat, gullet, pharynx	حُلْقُوم (حَلاقِيم)

pigeon, dove حَمَام (حَمَامة)	ornament, حِلْيَة (حِلَى/حُلَى) decoration
sea bath حَمَّام بَحْر	confederate, حَلِيْف (حُلَفَاء) ally
vapour-bath حَمَّام بُخَارِي	
swimming bath حَمَّام سِبَاحة	shaved, clean shaven حَلِيْق
sun bath حَمَّام شَمْس	husband, spouse (أَحِلَّاء) حَلِيل
sulfur bath حَمَّام كِبْرِيتِي	wife, mate حَلِيْلَة (حَلَائِل)
heat حَمَاوة	mild, gentle, حَلِيم (حُلَماء) clement
protection, defence, حِمَايَة guard	father-in-law, in-laws of حَم the wife
protectorate حِمَاية دَوْلِيّة	mud, mire, slime حَمَأ/حَمْأة
thermal spring, geyser حَمَّة	mother-in-law (حَمَوَات) حَمَاة
death حِمَّة	donkey, ass حِمَار (حَمِير)
blackness حُمَّة	wild ass, onager حِمار الوَحْش
sting, prick حُمَة	she ass حِمَارة
praise, commendation, حَمْد thanksgiving	enthusiasm, حَمَاس/حَمَاسَة zeal, ardour
red, ruddy حَمْرَاء (fem of أَحْمَر)	stupidity, folly, حَمَاقة foolishness
redness حُمْرَة	porter, carrier حَمَّال
enthusiastic, zealous, حَمِس spirited	work of a porter حِمَالة
acid حَمْض (أَحْماض)	girder, pier حَمَّالة
uric acid حَمْض بَوْلِي	brassiere حَمَّالة للصَّدْر
stupidity, foolishness, حُمْق silliness	bath, bathroom حَمَّام

protection, guard, defence	حِمَى
fever	حُمَّى (حُمَّيَات)
hectic fever	حُمَّى الدِّق
tertian fever	حُمَّى الغِبّ
typhoid fever	حُمَّى تِيْفُودِيّة/ تِيْفِيّة
yellow fever	حُمَّى صَفْرَاوِيّة
gastric fever	حَمَّى مَعِدِيّة
typhoid or enteric fever	حُمَّى مِعَوِية
malaria fever	حُمَّى مَلَارِيَا
zeal, fervour, passion, enthusiasm, vehemence	حَمِيّة
diet	حِمْيَة
chauvinism	حَمِيّة قَوْمِيّة
praiseworthy, commendable, mild	حَمِيد
reputable, famous, respectable	حَمِيد السُّمْعَة
hot water	حَمِيم
intimate, close friend	حَمِيم (أَحِمّاء)
hinna	حِنّاء

carrying, delivering, conveyance	حَمْل
lamb, yearling	حَمَل
pregnancy, gestation	حَمْل (أَحْمال)
load, cargo, burden, weight	حِمْل (أَحْمال)
attack, charge, raid, campaign	حَمْلَة (حَمَلَات)
shareholders	حَمَلَة الأَسْهُم
election campaign	حَمْلَة انْتِخَابِيّة
punitive expedition	حَمْلَة تَأْدِيْبِيّة
military expedition	حَمْلَة حَرْبِيّة
press campaign	حَمْلَة صِحَافِيّة
heat, intense heat	حَمْو/حُمُوّ
praiseworthy, laudable	حَمُود
red, redness	حُمُور
acidity, sourness	حُمُوضَة
long-suffering, mild-tempered	حَمُول
load, cargo, load capacity, freightage	حُمُولة

true, orthodox (حُنَفَاء) حَنِيْف	affection, love, sympathy, pity, compassion حَنان
yearning, craving, longing حَنِين	compassionate, affectionate, kind, sympathetic حَنّان
dialogue, conversation, argument حِوار	sympathy, compassion, pity حَنّة
the five senses حَوَاسّ خَمْس	
assignment, order حَوَالة	
money order حَوَالة بَرِيْدِيّة	perjury, oath-breaking, sin (أَحْناث) حِنْث
travellers's cheque حَوَالة سَفَر	
cheque, draft حَوَالة مَالِيّة	throat, larynx (حَنَاجِر) حَنْجَرَة
about, nearly, approximately حَوَالَيْ	wheat حِنْطَة
	colocynth (حَنْظَلَة) حَنْظَل
bowels, intestines حَوَايا	tap, cock, faucet حَنَفِيّة
sin, offense حَوْبَة	anger, fury, ire, resentment حَنَق
whale, fish (حِيْتان) حُوت	
need, want, necessity, destitution حَوْج	furious, angry, resentful, enraged حَنِق
turning, turn حَوْدَة	bending, twisting, curving حَنْو
cabman, coachman حُوْذِي	twist, bend, curve حِنْو
houri, nymph حُوْرِيّة	compassionate, pitiful, merciful, kind حَنُون
water nymph حُوْرِيّة المَاء	
attainment, acquisition, possession, tenancy حَوْز	twist, twisting, curving حَنْي
possession, tenure حَوْزَة	curvature, camber, crook حَنِيّة

enclosure, fold	حَوْش
rabble, mob	حَوَش
courtyard	حَوْش الدّار
vesica, bladder, pelican	حَوْصَل/حَوْصَلَة
pool, basin, tank, reservoir, dock	حَوْض (حِيَاض/حِيضان)
wash basin	حَوْض التَّشْطيف
dry dock	حَوْض جَافّ
bath tub	حَوْض حَمّام
flower bed	حَوْض زَرْع
floating dock	حَوْض عَوّام
border, edge, verge	حَوْف
change of place	حِوَل
about, around	حَوْل
squint, squinting	حَوَل
might, ability, year	حَوْل (أَحْوال)
yearling, one year old	حَوْلي
yearbook, annals	حَوْلِيَّات
main part, brunt	حَوْمَة
field of battle	حَوْمَة الوَغَى
coil, curl	حَوِيّة

vesicle, belister	حُوَيْصَل/حُوَيْصَلَة
crafty, clever, shrewd	حَوِيط
alive, living, energetic, active, quarter	حَيّ (أَحْياء)
conscientious, scrupulous	حَيّ الضَّمير
shyness, bashfulness, coyness, modesty	حَيَاء
life, existence, vitality	حَيَاة (حَيَوات)
worldly life	حَيَاة الدُّنْيا
country life	حَيَاة الرِّيف
sedentary life	حَيَاة القُعُود
family life	حَيَاة عَائلِيّة
public life	حَيَاة عامّة
practical life	حَيَاة عَمَلِيّة
neutrality	حِياد
neutral	حِيَادي
possession, occupancy, tenure	حِيَازة
protection, care, circumspection	حِيَاطَة
weaving, knitting	حِيَاكة
before, in front of, in view of	حِيَالَ

stratagem	حِيْلة حَرْبِيّة	snake, serpent	حَيّة
judicial separation	حَيْلُولة	where, wherever	حَيْث
time, period, opportunity	حِين (أَحْيان)	wherever, wheresoever	حَيْثُما
then, at that time	حِيْنَئِذ	respect, regard, prestige, dignity	حَيْثِيّة
once, for sometime	حِيْنًا	deviation, turning aside	حَيْد/حَيْدَة
while, when	حِيْنَما	baffled, bewildered,, confused	حَيْران
animals, beast	حَيَوان (حَيْوانات)	embarrassment, confusion, perplexity, uncertainty	حَيْرَة
mammal	حَيَوان لَبُون	field, domain, range, scope	حَيْز/حَيِّز (أَحْياز)
beast of prey	حَيَوان مُفْتَرِس		
rational animal	حَيَوان نَاطِق	evasion, escape, flight	حَيْص/حَيْصَة
domestic animals	حَيَوانات دَاجِنة	menses, menstruation	حَيْض
animality, bestiality	حَيَوانِيّة	caution, provident care	حَيْطَة/حَوْطَة
lively, vital, vigorous	حَيَوي	injustice, inequity, wrong, harm	حَيْف
vitality, vigour	حَيَوِيّة	consequence, result, effect	حَيْق
shy, modest, bashful	حَيِيّ		

faithless, dishonest, perfidious, traitor	خَؤُون	power, strength, might	حَيْل
unsuccessful, frustrated, disappointed	خَائِب	trick, stratagem, shift, policy, artifice	حِيْلَة (حِيَل)

external, foreign, outer خَارِجي	tailor خَائِط
piercing, penetrating خَارِق	fearful, timid, afraid of, scared خائِف (خُوَّف)
unusual, uncommon خَارِق (خَوَارِق)	faithless, disloyal, treacherous خائِن (خُوَّان)
supernatural خَارِق الطَّبِيْعَة	peg, pin, plug خَابُور (خَوَابِير)
exceptional, abnormal خَارِق العَادَة	vat, cask, large vessel خَابِيَة/خَابِئَة (خَوَاب)
preternatural phenomena خَارِق لِلْعَادَة	treacherous, deceiver, perfidious خَاتِر
treasurer خَازِن (خَزَنَة)	wedding ring خَاتَم الزَّوَاج
stake, pole خَازُوق	ring, seal, stamp خَاتِم/خَاتَم (خَوَاتِم)
loser, lost, affected by loss خَاسِر	close, end, conclusion خَاتِمَة (خَوَاتِم)
afraid, fearful, anxious, timid خَاشٍ	lady خَاتُون (خَواتين)
submissive, humble خَاشِع (خَشَعَة)	thickened, clotted, coagulated خَاثِر
special, particular, private, personal خَاصّ	servant, attendant, employee خَادِم (خُدّام/خَدَمة)
characteristic, property, peculiarity خَاصّة (خَوَاصّ)	maid, maidservant خَادِمة
haunch, hip, flank, side خَاصِرَة (خَوَاصِر)	ruiner, destroyer, annihilator خَارِب
property, special quality or trait, particularity, characteristic خَاصِّيَّة (خَصَائص)	outside, external خَارِج
	outside, out of, outward خَارِجَ

attractive, winning, captivating	خَالِب	submissive, humble, yielding	خَاضِع (خُضَّع)
maternal aunt	خَالَة	wrong, sinner, offender	خَاطِئ
scruple, misgiving, sentiment	خَالِجَة (خَوَالِج)	suitor, wooer, fiancé matchmaker	خَاطِب
immortal, eternal, undying, deathless	خَالِد	woman matchmaker	خَاطِبَة
pure, clear, free, unmixed	خَالِص	notion, wish, conception, pleasure	خَاطِر (خَوَاطِر)
post-free	خَالِص الأُجْرَة	rapacious, sudden, quick	خَاطِف (خَوَاطِف)
prepaid	خَالِص الرَّدّ	soft, low, faint, inaudible	خَافِت
tax-exempt	خَالِص الضَّرِيبَة		
creator, maker	خَالِق	throbbing, palpitant	خَافِق
carefree, free from anxiety	خَالِي البَال	secret, mystery	خَافِيَة (خَوَافٍ)
raw, unworked	خَام	empty, vacant, free, disengaged	خَالٍ
putrid, rotten, mouldy	خَامّ		
still, silent, quiet, dying	خَامِد	maternal uncle	خَال (أَخْوَال)
fifth	خَامِس	mole, beauty spot	خَال (خِيْلان)
fifteenth	خَامِس عشر	untenanted, uninhibited	خَالٍ مِن السُّكَّان
unknown, obscure, languid	خَامِل	unemployed, out of work	خَالٍ مِن العَمَل
obscure, unknown	خَامِل الذِّكْر	disinterested	خَالٍ مِن الغَرَض
inn, tavern, hostel	خَان	useless	خَالٍ مِن الفَائِدة

confusion, frenzy, خَبْل/خَبَل perplexity	column, square خَانة
a hidden thing خَبِيئَة (خَبَايا)	strangling, suffocating, خَانِق throttling
wicked, evil, خَبِيث (خُبُث) vicious, malignant	empty, void, vacant, خَاوٍ devastated
stinking, bad خَبِيث الرَّائِحَة smelling	a hidden thing خَبْء/خِبْء
expert, خَبِير (خُبَرَاء) experienced, acquainted	tent, husk خِبَاء (أَخْبِئَة)
medley, mess خَبِيص/خَبِيصة	wickedness, خَبَاثة viciousness, malignancy
treacherous, traitor, خَتَّار perfidious	baker خَبَّاز
end, conclusion, خِتَام termination	bakery, baker's trade خَبَازة
final, concluding, خِتَامي terminal	dissolute, dissipated, خَبَّاص light-minded
circumcision خِتَان/خِتَانة	mental disorder خُبَاط
betrayal, treachery, خَتْر deception	amble, trot خَبَب
trickery, treachery, خَتْل deception	mischievousness, خُبْث wickedness, viciousness
sealing, stamping خَتْم	refuse, scum, dross خَبَث
seal, stamp, خَتْم (أَخْتام/خُتُوم) mark	experience, knowledge خُبْر
postmark خَتْم البَرِيد	news, report, خَبَر (أَخْبار) information
circumcision خَتْن	experience, خِبْرَة acquaintance
son-in-law خَتَن (أَخْتان)	bread خُبْز (أَخْبَاز)
	blow, stroke, knock خَبْطَة
	crazy, insane, mad خَبِل

service, work, employment, job	خِدْمَة (خِدَم)	sediment, dregs	خُثارة
compulsory service	خِدْمَة إِخْبارِيّة	shame, shyness, timidity	خَجَل
social service, social work	خِدمة اِجْتِماعِيّة	shy, timid, bashful	خَجِل
secret service	خِدْمَة سِرِّيّة	ashamed, bashful, shamefaced	خَجْلان
military service	خِدْمَة عَسْكَرِيّة	bashful, ashamed, diffident	خَجُول
confidant, intimate friend	خِدْن/خِدين	cheek	خَدّ (خُدُود)
premature child	خَديج	furrow, groove	خَدّ/خُدّة
deceit, delusion, imposture, treachery	خَديعَة (خَدائِع)	abortion, miscarriage	خِداج
		swindle, imposture, deception, treachery	خِداع
disappointment, abandonment	خِذْلان	servant, attendant	خَدّام
		service, attendance	خَدَامة
excrement, ordure, feces	خُرْء/خَرَاء	numb, benumbed, asleep	خَدِر
ruination, destruction, demolition	خَرَاب	numbness, torpor, insensibility	خَدَر
wreckage, ruins	خَرَابة (خَرائِب)	boudoir, a lady's private room	خِدْر (خُدُور)
land tax, tax	خَرَاج	scratch, abrasion	خَدْش (خُدُوش)
tumour, abscess	خُرَاج		
liar, calumniator	خَرّاص	trick, shift, ruse, deception	خُدْعَة (خُدَع)
turner, boaster, braggart	خَرّاط	servant, attendants	خَدَم

haberdasher, dealer in small wares	خُرْدَجِي	chopping knife	خَرَّاطَة
mustard	خَرْدَل	earthworms	خَرَاطِين
pearls, beads	خَرَز (خَرَزَة)	superstition, legend, fable	خُرَافة (خُرَافات)
dumbness, muteness	خَرَس	superstitious, legendary, fabulous	خُرَافِي
dumb, mute	خَرْسَان	perforator, drill	خَرّامة
erring	خِرِّيص/خُرّص (خِرْصان)	ruination, destruction, devastation	خَرْب
turning, turnery	خَرْط/خِرَاطة	destroyed, ruined, broken, wrecked	خَرِب
cartridge, waste book	خَرْطُوش (خَرَاطِيش)	ruined, destroyed, wrecked	خِرْبان/خَرْبان
trunk, hose	خُرْطُوم (خَرَاطِيم)	ruins, wreckage	خِرْبَة (خِرَب)
shaky, insecure, languid	خَرِع/خَرِيع	confusion, disarrangement	خَرْبَطَة
dotage, imbecility, childishness	خَرَف	drill hole, hole	خَرْت/خُرْت
doting, childish, feeble-minded	خَرِف (خَرْفَان)	rhinoceros	خَرْتِيت/خَرْطِيط
tearing, piercing, perforation	خَرْق	tax, tribute, expenses, outlay	خَرْج
hole, opening	خَرْق (خُرُوق)	saddlebag, wallet	خُرْج
going against common usage	خَرْق العَادَات	projection, protrusion, departure	خَرْجَة (خَرَجات)
folly, stupidity, awkwardness	خُرْق/خُرْقَة	scrap metal	خُرْدَة
rag, tutter, piece of cloth	خِرْقَة (خِرَق)	smallwares, haberdashery	خُرْدَة (خُرْدَوات)

rent, tear, hole خَرْق	shuffling, mixing up خَرْقَشَة
storing, warehousing, خَزْن storage	perforation, boring خَرْم
treasure house, خَزْنَة cupboard	hole, opening خُرْم
	departure, going out خُرُوج
wardrobe, locker خَزْنَة الثِّيَاب	lamb, sheep (خِرَاف) خَرُوف
bookcase خَزْنَة الكُتُب	graduate of a college خِرِّيج or university
shame, disgrace, خِزْي dishonour	murmur, gurgling, خَرِير purling
shameful, disgraceful, خَزْيَان ashamed	map, chart, (خَرَائِط) خَرِيطَة bag
treasury, safe, (خَزَائِن) خَزِينَة treasure house,	autumn, fall خَرِيف
public treasury خَزِينَة الدَّوْلَة	autumnal خَرِيفِي
loss, damage (خَسَائِر) خَسَارة	silkfabric, tissues (خُزُوز) خَزّ of silk
heavy loss خَسَارَة فَادِحَة	potter, dealer in خَزَّاف porcelain
meanness, baseness, خَسَاسَة vileness	pottery, potter's trade خِزَافَة
meanness, lowliness, خِسَّة baseness	nose-ring, nose خِزَام/خِزَامة ornament
loss, damage, perdition خُسْر	water tank, reservoir خَزَّان
perdition, loss, خُسْران depravity	treasury, (خَزَائِن) خِزَانة treasure house
loser, depraved خَسْران	porcelain, pottery خَزَف
humiliation, خَسْف ignominy, disgrace	porcelain, خَزَفِي porcellaneous

خَصَاص interstice, crevice	خُسُوف lunar eclipse
خَصَاصَة destitution, poverty	خَسِيس (أخِسَّاء) mean, base, vile, low
خِصَام dispute, quarrel, contention, litigation	خَشَّاب wood or timber merchant
خِصْب fertility, fruitfulness, abundance	خَشَب (أخْشاب) wood, timber
خَصِب/خَصِيب fertile, fruitful, productive	خَشَبَة (خَشَبات) piece of wood or timber
خَصْر (خُصُور) haunch, hip	خَشَبي wooden, made of wood
خَصْلَة (خِصَال) trait, quality, habit	خَشَبِيّة xylophone
خُصْلَة (خُصَل) tuft, knot, cluster, bunch	خَشْخاش poppy
خَصْم reduction, deduction, discount	خَشْخَشَة rattle, chink, rustle
خَصْم (خُصُوم) opponent, rival, antagonist	خَشْم outlet, vent
خَصْم الكَمْبِيَالات bill discount	خَشِن harsh, coarse, rough
خُصُوبَة fertility, productivity	خَشِن الخُلُق rude, rough, uncouth
خُصُوص respect, regard, specialty	خُشُوع submissiveness, humility, solemnity
خُصُوصاً especially, particularly	خُشُونَة coarseness, rudeness, roughness
خُصُوصي special, particular, private, personal	خَشْيان apprehensive, fearful, timid
خُصُومة dispute, quarrel, controversy	خَشْيَة apprehension, fear
	خُصّ (خُصُوص/خِصَاص) shack, hut, hovel, booth

dyed, coloured	خَضِيب	castrate, castrated	خَصِيّ
green, verdant	خَضِير	testicles	خُصْيَة
quarter, section	خُطّ	characteristic, quality, peculiarity	خَصِيصَة (خَصَائِص)
line, stripe, streak, hand writing	خَطّ (خُطُوط)		
tubeline	خَطّ الأَنَابِيب	opponent, adversary, opposing	خَصِيم (خُصَماء)
equator	خَطّ الاسْتِواء		
longitude	خَطّ الطُّول	dye, paint	خِضَاب
latitude	خَطّ العَرْض	green, greenness	خَضَار
telephone line	خَطّ تلفُوني	green grocer	خَضّار
cursive hand	خَطّ رُقْعَة	greens, herbs	خُضَارة
railroad track	خَطّ سكّة الحَدِيد	jolting, violent shaking	خَضْخَضَة
straight line	خَطّ مُسْتَقِيم		
by mistake, wrongly	خَطَأً	green, verdant	خَضِر
mistake, error, fault	خَطَأ /خَطَاء	vegetables, greens	خَضْراوات
typographical error	خَطَأ مَطْبَعِي	greenness, verdure	خُضْرَة
		greens, vegetables	خُضْرَة (خُضَر)
speech, public address, letter	خِطَاب (أَخْطِبَة)	greengrocer	خُضَرِي
letter of credit	خِطَاب اعْتِماد	wet, moist	خَضِل
rhetorical speech	خِطَاب بَلِيغ	greenness, green colouration	خُضُوب
welcoming address	خِطَاب تَرْحِيب	humility, submission, obedience	خُضُوع
letter of recommendation	خِطَاب تَوْصِيَة	submissive, humble, obedient	خَضُوع

danger, peril, risk	خَطَر (أَخْطَار)	registered letter	خِطَاب مُسَجَّل
impending danger	خَطَر مُحْدِق	oratory, speech, address	خَطَابَة
swinging, oscillation	خَطَرَان	calligrapher	خَطَّاط
notion, strut, gait	خَطْرَة (خَطَرات)	robber, snatcher	خَطَّاف
kidnapping, abduction, snatching	خَطْف	hook, fishhook	خُطَّاف
a grab, a snatching	خَطْفَة (خَطَفات)	noseband	خِطَام (خُطُم)
prattle, silly talk	خَطَل	matter, mishap, condition, calamity	خَطْب (خُطُوب)
prattler, foolish, given to silly talk	خَطِل	engagement, betrothal, proposal	خِطْبَة
muzzle, snout	خَطْم	sermon, lecture, speech, discourse	خُطْبَة (خُطَب)
engagement, betrothal	خُطُوبة	opening address	خُطْبَة الافْتِتَاح
	خَطْوَة (خَطَوَات)=خُطْوَة	farewell discourse	خُطْبَة الوَدَاع
pace, step, footstep, stride	خُطْوَة (خُطُوات/خُطًى)	function, affair, condition	خُطَّة
decisive step	خُطْوَة حَاسِمَة	plan, policy, project, course	خُطَّة (خُطَط)
step by step	خُطْوَةً فَخُطْوَة		خَطَّة (خِطَط) = خُطَّة
gravity, weight, seriousness, importance	خُطُورة	work plan	خُطَّة العَمَل
airlines	خُطُوط الطَّيَران	gravity, importance, momentousness	خَطَر
airlines	خُطُوط جَوِّية	dangerous, risky, serious, grave	خَطِر

dexterity, sleight of خِفَّة الْيَد hand	خَطِّي handwritten, linear
bashfulness, shyness, خَفَر prudence	خَطِيْئَة (خَطَايا) sin, offence, fault, wrong
shy, bashful, modest, خَفِر timid	خَطِيْئَة عَرَضِيّة venial sin
coast guard خَفَر السَّوَاحِل	خَطِيْئَة مُمِيْتَة mortal sin, deadly sin
guard, guarding, خَفْر/خَفَر watching	خَطِيْب (خُطَباء) orator, lecturer, speaker
day blindness خَفَش	fiancée, betrothed خَطِيْبة
lowering, reducing, خَفْض lessening	خَطِيّة =خَطِيْئة
lowering of the خَفْض الصَّوْت voice	momentous, grave, خَطِير important
easy life خَفْض العَيْش	of great خَطِير الشَّأْن importance
devaluation خَفْض القِيْمَة	slipper, خُفّ (خِفَاف/أَخْفاف) half boots
throbbing, beating, خَفْق pulpitation	secrecy, hiddenness خَفَاء
beating, throbbing, خَفَقَان palpitation	guard, watch خفَارة
palpitation of خَفَقان القَلْب the heart	bat خُفّاش (خَفَافيش)
beat, throb, خَفْقَة (خَفَقات) rap	lightness, levity, خِفَّة frivolity
fading, faintness خُفُوت	agility, خِفَّة الحَرَكَة nimbleness
hidden, secret, خَفِيّ concealed, latent	vivacity, خِفَّة الرُّوح liveliness
	thoughtlessness خِفَّة العَقْل

mixer, mixing machine خَلَاط/خَلَاطة	secretly, stealthily خُفْيَة/خِفْيَة
wantonness, profligacy, dissipation خَلَاعة	watchman, guard خَفِير (خُفَرَاء)
dissimilarity, disagreement, difference, contradiction خِلَاف	low, subdued, faint خَفِيض
caliphate, succession, deputyship خِلَافَة	light, slight, thin, nimble خَفِيف (خِفَاف/أَخِفَّاء)
controversial, disputed, contested خِلَافِي	nimble, agile, active, light خَفِيف الحَرَكة
during, through interval خِلَالَ	nimble-footed خَفِيف الرِّجل
toothpic, skewer خِلَال	lively, vivacious, light-spirited, cheerful خَفِيف الرُّوح
claw, finger nail خِلْب (أَخْلاب)	feeble-minded, light-headed خَفِيف العَقْل
characteristic, attribute, property, habit خَلَّة (خِلَال)	nimble,-fingered, dexterous خَفِيف اليَد
friendship, intimacy خُلَّة (خُلَل)	vinegar خَلّ
anklet, ankle ring خَلْخَل/خَلْخَال	intimate friend, friend خُلّ/خِلّ (أَخْلال)
eternity, perpetuity, immortality خُلْد	empty space, vacuum, open country خَلَاء
mole خُلْد	captivating, alluring, attractive, deceptive خَلَّاب
soul, heart, spirit خَلَد (أَخْلاد)	misgiving, doubt خَلَاج
occasion, opportunity خُلْسَة	deliverance, rescue, redemption خَلَاص
stealthily, secretly, furtively خُلْسَةً	substance, summary, extract خُلَاصة

tatter, rag	خَلَقة	mixing up, blending, mingling	خَلْط
creation, nature, disposition, countenance, constitution	خِلْقَة (خلق)	mixture, combination	خِلْط (أَخْلاط)
natural, inborn, innate, constitutional	خِلْقِي	pell-mell, motley, confused	خَلْط مَلْط
disorder, confusion, disturbance, flaw, interstice	خَلَل	blend, mixture	خَلْطَة
devoid, empty, vacant	خِلْو	taking of, undressing, deposition	خَلْع
emptiness, vacuity	خُلُوّ	robe of honour	خِلْعَة (خِلَع)
privacy, seclusion, retreat, solitude	خَلْوَة	back, rear or hinder part	خَلْف
eternity, perpetuity, immortality	خُلُود	behind, after, at the back	خَلْفَ
purity, sincerity, clearance	خُلُوص	successor, substitute, descendant	خُلَف (أَخْلاف)
rustic, rural, solitary, isolated	خَلَوِي	difference, dissimilarity	خِلْفَة
free, empty, void	خَلِي (أَخْلِياء)	back, hinder, hind	خَلْفِي
carefree, free from anxiety	خَلِيّ البال	background	خَلْفِيّة الصُّورة
cell	خَلِيّة (خَلايا)	creation, creature, nature	خَلْق
beehive, hive	خَلِيّة النَّخْل	worn out, ragged, shabby	خَلَق
gulf, bay	خَلِيج (خُلُج)	desposition, temper, nature	خُلْق/خُلُق (أَخْلاق)
sincere, loyal, pure	خَلِيص (خُلَصاء)	by nature	خِلْقَةً

fifty خَمْسُون	combination, blend, خَلِيْط blended, mixed
scratch, scar (خُمُوش) خَمْش	
sluggish, languid خَمِل	companion, (خُلَطاء) خَلِيْط associate, friend
nap, fibers خَمْل/خَمْلَة	profligate, (خُلَعاء) خَلِيْع wanton, rake, deposed
extinction, stillness, خُمُود silence	
indolence, languor, خُمُول luggishness, drowsiness	caliph, (خُلَفاء) خَلِيْفة successor
obscurity, خُمُول الذِّكر humility	suitable, fit, (خُلَقاء) خَلِيْق competent
leaven, leavened bread خَمِيْر	creature, nature خَلِيْقَة
leaven, yeast, (خَمَائِر) خَمِيْرة ferment	intimate friend, (أَخِلّاء) خَلِيْل bosom friend
brewer's yeast خَمِيْرَة البِيْرا	sweetheart, concubine, خَلِيْلَة girl friend
baker's yeast خَمِيْرَة العَجِين	
Thursday خَمِيْس	after effect of wine خُمَار
empty-bellied, خَمِيْص البَطْن hungry	wine shop keeper خَمَّار
	veil, cover (خُمُر) خِمار
devil, whisperer خَنَّاس	wine shop خَمَّارة
diphtheria, suffocation خُنَاق	scratch, scar خُمَاشَة
strangling, strangling خِنَاق cord, fight	wine, (خُمُور) خَمْر/خَمْرة liquor
nasal twang خُنَّة	smooth wine خَمْرَة سائِغَة
hermaphrodite خُنْثَى	one fifth (أَخْماس) خُمْس
dagger, (خَنَاجِر) خَنْجَر poniard	five خَمْس/ خَمْسَة
	fifteen خَمْسة عشر/خمس عشرة

weakness, faintness, lassitude	خَوَر	trench, ditch	خَنْدَق (خَنَادِق)
inlet, bight, bay	خَوْر (أَخْوار)	pig, swine	خِنْزِير (خَنَازِير)
choir, chorus	خُورس	sow	خِنْزِيرَة
palm leaves	خُوص (خُوصة)	little finger	خِنْصَر (خَنَاصِر)
plunge, diving, rushing, penetration	خَوْض	nasality, nasal twang	خَنَف
fear, fright, dread	خَوْف	suffocation, strangulation	خَنْق
property in cattles and slaves	خَوَل	effeminacy	خُنُوثَة
little brother	خُوَيّ	piglet	خِنَّوْص (خَنَانِيص)
cucumber	خِيار	servility, humbleness, submissiveness	خُنُوع
choice, option, refusal	خِيَار	servile, humble, submissive	خَنُوع
optional, voluntary	خِيَارِي	hunger, inanition, vacuity	خَوَاء/خَوًى
tailor	خَيّاط		
tailoring, needle work	خِيَاطَة	mooing, bellowing, lowing	خُوَار
dress maker, seamstress	خَيّاطَة	fearful, timid, coward	خَوّاف
imagination, fancy, shadow, vision	خَيَال (أَخْيلَة)	unfaithful, disloyal, traitor	خَوّان
spectre, ghost	خِيَالَة	table	خُوَان/خِوَان
imaginary, conceptual, ideal	خَيَالِي	dressing table	خِوَان الزِّينَة
tent maker	خَيّام	brotherliness, fraternity, brotherhood	خُوّة
dishonesty, disloyalty, faithlessness, treason	خِيَانة	peach, plum	خَوْخ/خَوْخَة
		helmet	خُوذَة

horse	خَيْل (خُيُول)
race-horses	خَيْل الرِّهَان
conceit, vanity, haughtiness	خُيَلاَء
haughtiness, pride, snobbery	خَيْلُولة
tent, bower, pavilion	خَيْمَة (خِيَم)
raw fibres	خُيُوط خام

د

perseverance, assiduity, habit	دَأْب
perseverance, assiduity, persistence	دَأْب
persistence, assiduity	دُؤُوب
preserving, untiring, assiduous	دَؤُوب
disease, malady	دَاء (أَدْواء)
incurable disease	دَاء عَيَاء
giddy, dizzy	دَائِخ
circular, circulating, turning	دَائِر
circle, ring, zone, sphere, range	دَائِرَة (دَوَائِر)
appellate court	دَائِرَة اسْتِئْنَافِيّة

breach of faith or trust	خِيَانَة الأَمَانَة
breach of promise	خِيَانَة العهود/الوعود
failure, frustration, miscarriage	خَيْبَة
disappointment	خَيْبَة الأَمَل
mirage	خَيْدَع
munificent, liberal, generous, charitable	خَيِّر
good, better	خَيْر (خِيار)
wealth, riches, affluence, good	خَيْر (خُيُور)
choice, best part, pick	خِيرة
good deed	خَيْرة (خَيْرَات)
benevolent, charitable	خَيْري
bamboo, reed	خَيْزُران
canvas, sack cloth	خَيْش
nose, gills	خَيْشوم
thread, cord, line	خَيْط (خُيُوط)
first glim of dawn	خَيْط أَبَيض
thread of hope	خَيْط أَمَل
twine, string	خَيْط القنَّب
threadlike, fibrous	خَيْطي
fear, fright, apprehension	خِيفة

inside, interior	دَاخِل الشَّيْء	domain, scope of competence	دَائِرة الاخْتِصَاص
inwards, inside	دَاخِلاً	information bureau	دَائِرة الاسْتِخْبَارَات
inside, interior, inner part	دَاخِلَة (دَوَاخِل)	tropic	دَائِرة الائْقلاب
inner, internal, private	دَاخِلي	encyclopedia	دَائِرة المَعَارِف
inside, inwards, internally	دَاخِليًّا	constituency	دَائِرة انْتِخَابِيّة
interior	دَاخِليّة	short circuit	دَائِرة قَصِيرة
interior, inland	دَاخِليّة البلاد	electric circuit	دَائِرة كَهْرَبَائِيّة
chimney, smokestack	دَاخِنَة (دَوَاخِن)	circular, round	دَائِري
knowing, acquainted with, aware	دَارٍ	permanent, continual, perpetual	دَائِم
home, abode, residence, country	دار (دُوْر/دِيَار)	evergreen	دَائِم الاخْضِرار
the everlasting adobe	دار آخِرة	always	دَائِمًا
museum	دَارُ الآثار	everlasting, eternal, perpetual	دَائِمي
orphanage	دَارُ الأَيْتَام	creditor	دَائِن
the hereafter, heaven, the eternal abode	دَارُ البَقَاء	animals, live-stock	دَابّة (دَوَابّ)
hell	دَار البَوَار	past, elapsed, root, extremity	دَابِر
commercial house	دارُ التِّجَارة	dark, obscure, gloomy	دَاجٍ
playhouse, opera-house, theatre	دَارُ التَّمْثِيل	tamed, tame, domesticated	دَاجِن
maternity home	دَارُ التَّوْلِيْد	belonging, pertaining, coming in	دَاخِل

obliterated, effaced دَارِس (دَوَارِس)	war zone, enemy territory دَارُ الْحَرْب
armour-clad دَارِع	day nursery دَار الْحَضَانة
screw-propeller دَاسِر	paradise دَار الْخُلْد
cause, motive, inviter دَاعٍ (دُعَاة)	presidential palace دَارُ الرِّئَاسَة
playful, jolly, gay دَاعِب	mint دَارُ السِّكَّة
licentious, vicious, lewd, bawdy دَاعِر	police station دَارُ الشُّرْطَة
propagandist, one who invites دَاعِيَة	mint دَارُ الضَّرْب
motive, cause دَاعِيَة (دَوَاعٍ)	the perishable abode دَارُ الْفَنَاء
brand دَاغ (دَاغَات)	the hereafter دَار القَرَار
repelling, repulsive, resisting, pushing, payer دَافِع	court of justice, tribunal دَار القَضَاء
motive, impulse دَافِع (دَوَافِع)	library دَارُ الكُتُب
tax-payer دَافِع الضَّرَائِب	public library دَارُ الكُتُب العُمُوْمِيّة
electromotive دَافِع كَهْرَبَائِي	custom house دَارُ المُكُوس
breaking out, gushing دَافِق (دَوَافِق)	clubhouse دَارُ النَّادِي
dark, dark-coloured دَاكِن	publishing house دَار النَّشْر
pointing to, indicative of, directing دَالّ	solar halo, corona دَارَة الشَّمْس
liberty, familiarity دَالَّة	halo, lunar halo دَارَة القَمَر
bleeding دَامِ	current, in circulation, popular, common دَارِج

safety pin, pin (دَبَابِيس) دَبُّوس	dusky, pitch dark دَامِس
drawing pin دَبُّوس رَسْم	close, near, low دَان
hairpin دَبُّوس شعْر	crafty, cunning, دَاهٍ (دُهَاة)
breastpin, brooch دَبُّوس صَدْر	shrewd, subtle
creeping, crawling دَبِيب	resourceful person, دَاهِيَة
blanket, cover (دُثُر) دِثَار	cunning
obliteration, extinction دُثُور	misfortune, دَاهِيَة (دَوَاه)
thrush, throstle دُجّ	calamity, catastrophe
chickens, fowls, دَجَاج	midwife, wet nurse دَايَة
poultry	bear, bruin (أَدْباب) دُبّ
hen, fowl دَجَاجة	creeping, crowling, دَبّاب
imposter, swindler, دَجَّال	reptant
humbug, quack	tank, armoured car دَبَّابَة
obscurity, intense دُجّة	tanner دَبَّاغ
darkness	tanning دِبَاغَة
deceit, trickery, treason دَجْل	sand hill, mound دَبّة
obscurity, darkness, دُجْنَة	patter, sound of دَبْدَبَة
gloom	footsteps
darkness, obscurity, دُجًى	rump, backside, (أَدْبار) دُبْر/دُبُر
gloom	posteriors, buttocks, tail
refutation, دَحْض	lime, birdlime دِبْق
confutation, disproof	sticky, viscous, limy دَبِق
ins and outs of دَخَائِل الأُمُور	diploma دِبْلُوم/دِبْلُومة
the things	diplomatic, دِبْلُوماسِي
smoke, tobacco (أَدْخِنَة) دُخَان	diplomat
dolphin دُخَس	diplomacy دِبْلُوماسِيّة

armoured, cruiser	دَرَّاعَة (دَرَّاعَات)	return, revenues, misgiving, interference, insanity	دَخْل
knowledge, cognizance, acquaintance	دِرَايَة	disorder, disturbance, dementia	دَخَل
track, path, road	دَرْب (دُرُوب)	decent income	دَخْل كَرِيْم
door bolt, bolt	دِرْبَاس (دَرَابِيْس)	deceit, trickery	دَخْمَسَة
practice, experience, habit	دُرْبَة	smoke, vapour, fume	دَخَن
balustrade, handrail	دَرْبَزِين/دَرَابِزِين	entry, entering, getting in, penetration	دُخُول
pearl	دُرَّة (دُرَر)	inner, internal	دَخِيْل
recording, entering	دَرْج	foreign, stranger, alien	دَخِيْل (دُخَلَاء)
roll, scroll	دَرْج	inmost being, heart, mind, inner self	دَخِيْلَة (دَخَائِل)
drawer	دُرْج (أَدْرَاج)	secret	دَخِيْلَة الأَمْر
stairs, staircase	دَرَج (أَدْرَاج)	jewel, gem, pearl	دُرّ/دُرّة
spiral staircase	دَرَج لَوْلَبِي	bicycle	دَرَّاجَة (دَرَّاجَات)
class, stage, grade, degree, stairs, mark	دَرَجَة (دَرَجَات)	motorcycle	دَرَّاجَة نَارِيّة
first class, first rate	دَرَجَة أُوْلَى	classical studies	دِرَاسَات قَدِيْمَة
freezing point	دَرَجَة الجَمْد	study	دِرَاسَة (دِرَاسات)
degree of temperature	دَرَجَة الحَرَارَة	secondary education	دِرَاسَة ثَانَوِيّة
level of intelligence	دَرَجَة العَقْل	higher studies	دِرَاسَة عَالِية
		scholastic, educational	دِرَاسِي

intriguer, conspirator, دَسَّاس plotter	academic degree دَرَجَة عِلْميّة
stopper, plug دِسَام	special class, دَرَجَة مُمْتَازَة distinction
greasiness, fatness دَسَامَة	prattling, roaring دَرْدَرَة
constitution, (دَسَاتِير) دُسْتُور statute	vortex, whirlpool دُرْدُور
constitutional دُسْتُوري	pipe-seam (دُرُوز) دَرْز
fat, grease, greasiness دَسَم	obliteration, دَرْس effacement
greasy, fat, rich دَسِم	lesson, class, (دُرُوس) دَرْس study
December دِسمْبِر	
richness, fatness, دُسُومة greasiness	armour, armour (دُرُوع) دِرْع plate
intrigue, plot, (دَسَائس) دَسِيسَة conspiracy	flank, side دَرْف
shower, douche, bath دُشّ	dolphin دَرْفِيل
invocation, (أَدْعِيَة) دُعَاء prayer, request	thyroid دَرَقِي
	bottom, lowest (أَدْرَاك) دَرَك level
playful, funny, jolly دَعَّاب	filth, dirt, (أَدْرَان) دَرْن tuberculosis
fun, joke, (دُعَابات) دُعَابة banter	
	tubercule, tubercle دَرَنَة
licentiousness, دَعَارة/دِعَارة debauchery, indecency	tubercular, tuberculous دَرَني
support, prop, (دَعَائم) دِعَامة pillar	dirhem (دَرَاهِم) دِرْهَم
	protecting wall درْوَة
publicity دَعَاوَة	lustrous, glittering دُرِّي
sportive, playful, دَعِب frolicsome	target, object دَرِيئَة
	dozen دَزِينَة

warmth, heat	دفْء
warm	دَفْآن
warmth, heat	دَفَاءة
propelling, impelling	دَفّاع
defence, vindication	دفَاع
defensive, protective	دفَاعي
rushing out, bursting forth	دَفّاق
leaf of a door	دَفّة البَاب
cover of a book	دَفّةُ الكِتَاب
rudder	دَفّة المَرْكَب
notebook, register	دَفْتَر (دَفَاتِر)
charge sheet	دَفْتَر الأَحْوَال
letter book, folder	دَفْتَر الخِطَابات
report card	دَفْتَر الدَّرَجَات
cashbook	دَفْتَر الصُّنْدُوق
waste-book	دَفْتَر المُسَوَّدة
diary, daybook, journal	دَفْتَر اليَوْميّة
stench, fetidness	دَفَر
repulsion, repellence, rebuttal, payment	دَفْع
push, drive, instalment, payment	دَفْعَة (دَفْعات)

meekness, gentleness	دَعَة
debauchery, immorality, license	دَعَر
lewd, licentious, immoral	دَعِر
support, stay, prop	دِعْمَة (دِعَم)
call, claim, invitation, case, suit	دَعْوَة
supplication, prayer	دَعْوَة (دَعْوَات)
claim, case, allegation, lawsuit	دَعْوَى (دَعَاوٍ)
civil action	دَعْوَى مَدَنِيّة
pretender, swindler, braggard, show-off	دَعِيّ (أَدْعِياء)
assault, attack	دَغْر
dusk, darkness	دَغَش
corruption, decay	دَغَل
bushy, corrupt, decayed	دَغِل
thicket, bush	دَغَل (أَدْغال)
tambour, tambourine	دُفّ (دُفُوف)
side	دَفّ/دَفّة

flour, meal	دَقيق	spurt, gush	دُفْعَة (دُفَعات)
thin, fine, subtle, minute, delicate, accurate	دَقيق (دقَاق)	effusion, influx, pouring	دَفْق
sensitive	دَقيق الشُّعُور	gush, spurt	دُفْقَة
penetrating, sensitive	دَقيق النَّظَر	burial, interment	دَفْن
particle, minute, intricacy	دَقيقَة (دَقَائق)	buried, hidden, concealed	دَفِين (دُفَناء)
demolition, subversion	دَكّ	hidden treasure	دَفِينَة (دَفَائن)
level ground	دَكّ (دُكُوك)	warm	دَفِيء
beating flat, levelling	دَكّ الأَرْض	beating, knocking, grinding	دَقّ
shop, store	دُكّان (دَكَاكِين)	thin, fine, delicate	دق
ballast	دَكّة (دَكّات)	ringing of the bell	دَقّ الجَرَس
bench	دكّة (دكَك)	intricacies of the things	دَقَائق الأُمُور
dictator	دكْتَاتُوْري	pounder, grinder	دَقَّاق
dictatorship	دكْتَاتُوْرِيّة	knocker, clapper, pestle	دَقَّاقة البَاب
doctor	دُكْتُور (دَكَاترَة)		
doctor of laws	دُكْتُور في الحُقُوق	knock, rap, beat	دَقّة
doctor of medicine	دُكْتُور في الطِّب	fineness, thinness, minuteness, accuracy, precision	دقّة
doctorship, doctorate	دُكْتُوراه	powder	دُقّة
honourary doctorate	دكتوراه فَخْرِيّة	sensitiveness, sensibility	دقّة الشُّعُور
		heartbeat	دَقّة القَلْب

blood	دَم (دِماء)	دَلّ	flirtation, coquetry, coquettishness
noble blood	دَم كَرِيم	دَلَال	coddling, coquetry
mildness, tenderness	دَمَاثَة	دَلَّال	broker, agent, public crier
gentleness, mildness	دَمَاثة الأَخْلاق	دَلَالَة	guidance, direction, meaning, indication
ruin, destruction, devastation	دَمَار	دِلَالَة	brokery, brokerage, commission
darkness, duskiness	دَمَاسَة	دُلْفِين (دَلافِين)	dolphin
brain, essence	دِمَاغ (أَدْمِغة)	دَلْك	rubbing, scrubbing, touching
liniment, ointment, paint	دِمَام	دَلْو (دِلاَء)	bucket, pail
ugliness, unsightliness	دَمَامة	دُلُوف	toddling, walking slowly
manure, dung, fertilizer	دَمَان	دُلُوك	setting, going down (sun)
gentle, mild, good-natured	دَمِث الأَخْلاق	دُلُوك	ointment, liniment
rumble, growl	دَمْدَمة	دَلِيل (دَلائِل/أَدِلّة)	guide, index, directory, evidence, token
hot ashes, cinders	دِمْس	دَلِيل ظَرْفِي	circumstantial evidence
tears	دَمْع (دُمُوع)	دَلِيل قَاطِع	conclusive evidence
abundant tears	دَمْع مِدْرار	دَلِيل نَاصِع	evident proof
tear, teardrop	دَمْعَة	دَمّ	paint, pigment, ointment
stamp, mark, brand	دَمْغَة		
hall-mark	دَمْغَة الذَهَب		
democrat, democratic	دُمُقَراطي		

nearness, closeness, proximity دُنُوّ	democracy دمُقْرَاطِيّة
close, near, mean, lowly دَنِيّ (أَدْنِياء)	boil, tumour, abscess, pimple, postule دُمَّل (دَمَامِل)
mean, low, base, abject, vile دَنِيء (أَدْنِياء)	bracelet, armlet دُمْلُج (دَمَالِج)
world, universe, earth, wordly دُنْيا	manure, dung دمْن/دمْنَة (دمَن)
worldly, earthly, temporal دُنْيَوِي	ruins or vestiges of a dwelling دمْنَة (دمَن)
shrewdness, astuteness, subtlety دَهَاء	tearful, watery دَمُوع
painter, house-painter دَهَّان	crocodile tears دُمُوع الرِّياء
ointment, unguent, paint دهَان (دهَانات/أَدْهِنَة)	bloody, sanguinary دَمَوِي
age, epoch, era, time دَهْر (دُهُور)	doll, effigy, painting دُمْيَة (دُمًى)
atheist, sceptic دَهْرِي	ugly, unsightly, pigmy دَمِيْم
surprise, wonder, perplexity دَهَش	buzzing, humming دَنّ/دَنِين
surprised, stunned, astonished دَهِش	meanness, lowliness, baseness دَنَاءَة
astonishment, surprise, bafflement دَهْشَة	nearness, closeness, meanness, baseness دَنَاوة
corridor, hall way دهْلِيْز (دَهَالِيْز)	meanness, vileness, baseness دَنَايَة
mob, masses, common people دَهْمَاء	filth, dirt, impurity, uncleanliness دَنَس (أَدْنَاس)
	unclean, impure, defiled دَنِس (أَدْنَاس)
	serious and long illness دَنَف

top, spinning top	دُوَّامَة	blackness, pitchiness	دُهْمَة
whirlpool, vortex	دُوَّامَة المَاء	oiling, greasing	دَهْن
tall and lofty trees	دَوْحَة	fat, grease (أَدْهان/دِهَان)	دُهْن
giddiness, dizziness, nausea	دَوْخَة	desert	دَهْنَاء
sea-sickness	دَوْخَة البَحْر	oily, greasy, fatty	دُهْنِي
air-sickness	دَوْخَة الهَوَاء	oils, fats	دُهْنِيات
worm, larva, maggot	دُود/دُوْدة (دِيْدَان)	medicine, medicament, cure	دَوَاء (أَدْوِيَة)
cheese-maggot	دُوْدَة الجُبْن	government circles	دَوَائِر الحُكُومة
silk-worm	دُوْدَة الحَرِير	political circles	دَوَائِر سِيَسِيَّة
tapeworm	دُوْدَة الشَّرِيط	medicinal, curative	دَوَائِي
cochineal insect	دُوْدَة القِرْمِز	inkwell	دَوَاة (دَوَيات)
cotton worm	دُوْدَة القُطْن	dizziness, vertigo	دُوَار
vermiform, wormlike	دُوْدِي	revolving, rotating, circulating	دَوَّار
round, turn, floor, period, age, role, stage	دَوْر (أَدْوار)	sea-sickness	دُوَار البَحْر
ground floor	دَوْر أَرْضِي	sunflower	دَوَّار الشَّمْس
leading role	دَوْر أَوّل	air-sickness	دُوَار الهَوَاء
motion picture theatres	دُوْر السِّينما	whirlpool, vortex	دَوَّارَة
brothels	دُوْر الفِسْق	weather vane	دَوَّارة الهَوَاء
night clubs, amusement centers	دُوْر اللَّهْو	pedal	دَوَّاسَة
leading role, leading part	دَوْر رَئِيسِي	permanence, durability, continuance	دَوَام
		permanently, perpetually	دَوَامًا

the great powers دُوَل عُظْمَى	دَوْر نِهَائِي final round
دُوْلاب (دَوَالِيب) cupboard, closet, wheel	دَوَرَان rotation, circulation, revolution
دُوْلاب سَائِب free wheel	دَوْرَة (دَوْرَات) turn, round, revolution, circulation, patrol, trip, rotation, period
دُوْلاب كُتُب book case	
دُوْلاب لِلْمَلابَس wardrobe	دَوْرَة المِياه lavatory
دُوْلاب هُدُوم wardrobe	دَوْرَة تَشْرِيعِيَّة legislative period
دُوْلاب هَوَائِي wind wheel	
دُولار (دُولارات) dollar	دَوْرَة جَوِّيَّة air circulation
دَوْلَة tumult, clamour, confusion	دَوْرَة دَمَوِيَّة blood circulation
دَوْلَة (دُوَل) state, dynasty, government, kingdom, rotation	دَوْرَة زِرَاعِيَّة crop rotation
	دَوْرَة مَالِيَّة fiscal year
دَوْلَة الاِنْتِدَاب mandatory power	دَوْرِي periodic, circulatory, patrolling
دَوْلَة فيْدَراليَّة federal states	دَوْرِيَّة patrol, round
دَوْلَة مُنْتَدَبَة mandatory power	دَوْزَنَة tuning
دُوَلِي international	دُوْزِينة dozen
دَوْم permanence, continuance, constancy	دَوْس tread, step
دَوْمًا always, continually	دُوْش shower, douche
دُوْمان helm, rudder	دُوْشَة uproar, noise, din
دُونَ below, under, without	دُوْق duke
دَوِيّ clang, ring, echo, sound	دُوْقَة duchess
	دُوَل أَعْضَاء the member states

priviledged debt	دَيْن مُمْتاز	disease, sickness	دَوًى (أَدْوَاء)
bad debt	دَيْنَ مَيْت/هَالك	obscurities, shadows, dark	دَيَاجِي
dinar	دِيْنار (دَنَانِيْر)	monk, monastic	دَيّار
dynamo	دِيْنَامو	pious, devout, godly	دَيَّان
dynamite	دِيْنَامِيْت	religion, denomination	دِيَانة
religious, devotional	دِيْنِي	silk brocade	دِيْبَاج (دَبابِيْج)
council, cabinet, administrative office, sofa, court of justice	دِيْوان (دَوَاوِيْن)	prelude, preface, introduction, visage	دِيْبَاج/دِيْبَاجَة
collection of poems, anthology	دِيْوان شعْر	blood money, blood fine	دِبَة (دِيَات)
pimp, pander, procurer	دَيُّوث	sentinel, sentry	دَيْدُبان
war debts	دُيُون الحَرْب	monastery, convent, abbey	دَيْر (أَدْيرة/أَدْيار)

ن

		monastic, friar	دَيْرَانِي
		region, area, locality	دِيْرَة
		monasterial, monastic	دَيْرِي
tuft, lock of hair	ذُؤَابة (ذُوَائب)	December	دِيْسمْبر
wolf	ذِئْب (ذِئَاب)	cock, rooster	دِيْك (دُيُوك)
this	ذا	دِيْكْتَاثُوري=دكْتَاثُوري	
melted, dissolved, dissoluble	ذَائب	stage decoration	دِيْكُور (دِيْكُورات)
protector, defender	ذَائد	ديموقراطي= دمُقراطي	
widespread, circulating	ذَائع	devout, religious, pious	دَيِّن
		religion, faith	دِيْن (أَدْيان)

fading, discoloured	ذَاهِب اللَّوْن	famous, renowned, noted, celebrated	ذَائِع الصِّيْت
distracted, confused, absent-minded	ذَاهِل	taste, sense of taste	ذَائِقَة
withered, faded	ذَاوٍ	withered, withering, fading	ذَابِل
horsefly, gadfly	ذُبَاب قَارِص	self, same, personality (fem. of ذو)	ذَات (ذَوَات)
fly	ذُبَاب/ذُبَابة (ذِبَّان/أَذِبَّة)	disagreement, dissension	ذَات البَيْن
slaughterer, butcher	ذَبَّاح	pleurisy	ذَات الجَنْب
fly, sight	ذُبَانة	pneumonia	ذَات الرِّئَة
slaughter, sacrifice	ذَبْح	to the left	ذَات الشِّمَال/ اليَسَار
sacrificial victim	ذِبْح	the same thing	ذَات الشَّيْء
pendulation, oscillation	ذَبْذَبَة	secret thoughts	ذَات الصَّدْر
withering, wilting	ذُبُول	to the right	ذَات اليَمِين
slaughtered, slaughtered animal	ذَبِيح	once, one time	ذَات مَرّة
sacrifice, offering, slaughtered animal	ذَبِيحَة (ذَبَائِح)	one day, once	ذَاتَ يَوْم
rancour, retaliation, resentment	ذَحْل (ذُحُول)	personal, spontaneous, automatic	ذَاتِي
treassure, store	ذُخْر (أَذْخَار)	personally, spontaneously	ذَاتِيًّا
treasure, store, fund	ذَخِيْرَة (ذَخَائِر)	personality, identity	ذَاتِيّة
prinkling, scattering	ذَرّ	that	ذَاكَ
arm, limb, cubit	ذِرَاع (أَذْرُع)	memory	ذَاكِرة

male, penis	ذَكَر (ذُكُور)	diarrhea	ذَرَب
reminiscence, recollection, memory	ذِكْرَى (ذِكْرَيَات)	sharp, cutting, malignant	ذَرِب
intelligent, acute, sharp-witted	ذَكِيّ (أَذْكِيَاء)	atom, particle, whit	ذَرَّة
sweet-smelling, fragrant	ذَكِيّ الرَّائِحَة	maize	ذُرَة
disgrace, humility, ignominy, shame	ذُلّ	capability, ability	ذَرْع
loquacity, glibness	ذَلاَقَة	excrement of birds	ذَرْق
baseness, vileness, meanness, humiliation	ذِلَّة	summit, peak, top, zenith, acme	ذُرْوَة/ذِرْوَة
tip, tip of the tongue	ذَلْق	powder	ذَرُور
loquacious, glib, eloquent	ذَلْق/ذَلِق	powdery, pulverous	ذَرُورِي
tractable, docile	ذَلُول	protection, shelter	ذَرًى
low, abject, servile, despised, humble	ذَلِيل (أَذلاَّء)	atomic	ذَرِّي
blame, censure, criticism, disparagement	ذَمّ	progeny, offspring, descendants	ذُرِّيَّة (ذَرَارِي)
honour, reputation	ذِمَار	quick, rapid, lively	ذَرِيع
security, protection, responsibility, guarantee	ذِمَّة	means, medium	ذَرِيعَة (ذَرَائِع)
zimmi, a non-Muslim subject who lives in a Muslim country and enjoys freedom and safety	ذِمِّي	deadly, sudden	ذُعَاف
		panic, fright, terror	ذُعْر/ذَعَر
		chin, beard	ذِقَن/ذَقَن (ذُقُون/أَذْقَان)
		intelligence, acuteness, sagacity, wit	ذَكَاء
		remembrance, mention, fame, invocation	ذِكْر

powerful, influential	ذُو الْيَد	censored, blamed, dispraised	ذَمِيْم
mighty, strong, valorous	ذُو بَأْس	tail, end	ذَنَب (أَذْناب)
notable, considerable	ذُوْ بال	crime, guilt, sin, offence	ذَنْب (ذُنُوب)
effective, effectual, efficacious	ذُو تَأْثِير	going, passing, departure	ذَهَاب
dangerous, perilous	ذُو خَطَر	up and down	ذَهَاباً وإِيَابًا
important, significant	ذُوْ شَأْن	gold	ذَهَب
healthy	ذُوْ صِحّة	platinum	ذَهَب أَبْيَض
intelligent	ذُو عَقَل	glittering gold	ذَهَب وَهَّاج
valuable, worthy	ذُوْ قِيْمة	golden, of gold	ذَهَبِي
wealthy, rich	ذُو مَال	mind, brain, intellect	ذِهْن (أَذْهان)
destitute, poor, indigent	ذُو مَتْرَبة	mental, intellectual	ذِهْنِي
influential	ذُو نُفُوذ	mentality	ذِهْنِيَّة
taste, inclination, epicure	ذَوَاق	distraction, dismay, confusion of mind	ذُهُوْل
dissolution, melting	ذَوْب/ذَوَبان	possessor, owner	ذُو (ذَوُو/أُولو)
snow break	ذَوَبَان الثَّلْج	qualified for, fit, suitable	ذو أَهْلِيَّة
defence, protection	ذَوْد/ذِياد	Zul-Hijjah, the last month of Islamic calender	ذُو الْحِجّة
well-to-do, wealthy	ذُوْسَعَة	relative, relation, kins	ذُو القُرْبَى
taste, flavour, liking, tact	ذَوْق (أَذْواق)		
good taste	ذَوْق سَلِيْم		

رَأْس مالي/رَأْسمالي	capitalistic, capitalist	ذَوْقِي	gustatory, gustative
رَأْس مالية/رَأْسمالية	capitalism	ذَوُو الأَرْحَام	relatives of maternal side
رَأْسًا	directly, at first hand	ذَيْل (ذُيُول)	tail, extremity, end, appendix
رَآفَة	mercy, pity, compassion	ذَيْلِي	caudal
رَأْفَة	mercy, compassion, clemency	ذُيُوع	spreading, circulating, dispersion, promulgation
رِئْم (أَرْآم)	white antelope		

رُؤُوسُ أَمْوَال	capital, fund		
رَؤُوف	merciful, clement, compassionate	رِئَاء	hypocrisy, insincerity, dissimulation
رَؤُوم	loving, kind, tender	رِئَاسَة	presidency, leadership, direction
رِئَوِي	pulmonic, pulmonary	رِئَاسَة الوُزَرَاء	premiership
رَأْي (آرَاء)	opinion, idea, view, suggestion	رِئَة (رِئَات)	lung
رَأْي صَرِيح	candid opinion	رَئْد (أَرْآد)	contemporary
رَأْي عَامّ	public opinion	رَأْس (رُؤُوس)	head, mind, chief, summit, top
رُؤْيَا (رُؤَى)	dream, vision	رَأْس الآفات	the root of all evils
رُؤْيَة	vision, visibility, view, sight	رَأْس السَّنَة	new year
رَئِيس (رُؤَسَاء)	president, head, chief, leader	رَأْسُ الشَّهْر	new moon
		رَأْس القَوْم	chief, leader
رَئِيس الإِدَارة	administrator, manager, boss	رَأْس الكِتَاب	letter-head
رَئِيس الأَساقفة	archbishop	رَأْس مَال/رَأْسُمَال	capital

imposing thing (رَوائِع) رائِعة	mayor	رَئيس البَلْدية
clear, pure	رائِق	editor-in-chief	رَئيس التَّحْرير
step father	رابّ	speaker of the lower house	رَئيس النّوّاب
step mother	رابّة	Prime Minister, premier	رَئيس الوُزَراء
gainer, gainful, profitable, advantageous	رابِح	president, chairman	رَئيس جَلْسَة
binding, tying, connecting	رابِط	abbot	رَئيس دَيْر
cool, calm, composed, collected	رابط الجَأْش	headmaster, principal	رَئيس مَدْرَسَة
connection, tie, (رَوابِط) رابِطَة bond, union, league	directress, manageress	رَئيسة
Muslim league	رابِطة إسْلاميّة	chief, main, principal, leading	رَئيسي
fourth	رابِع	viewer, onlooker, observer, seer	رَاءٍ
fourthly	رابِعًا	curdled milk	رائِب
comfortable, pleasant	رابِغ	in circulation, current, widespread, in demand	رائِج
hill	(رَواب) رابِية	smell, odour	(رَوائِح) رائِحَة
salary, pay, wages	(رَواتِب) راتِب	stench, stink	رائِحَة خَبيثَة
hopeful, expectant	راجٍ	scent, perfume	رائِحَة ذَكِيّة
preferable, preponderant	راجِح	scout, pioneer, explorer, leader	(رُوّاد) رائِد
returning, reverting, belonging	راجِع	wonderful, charming, delightful, awe-inspiring	رائِع
walking, going on foot	راجِل		

content, pleasant, satisfied رَاضٍ	rest, leisure, repose رَاحَة
damp, wet, moist رَاطِب	palm of the hand رَاحَة اليَد
shephered, herdsman, patron, guardian رَاعٍ (رُعَاة)	leaving, departing رَاحِل (رُحَّل)
dreadful, terrible, horrible رَاعِب	female riding camel رَاحِلَة (رَوَاحِل)
desirous, full of desire رَاغِب (رَغْبَة)	radar رَادَار
unwilling, hesitant, reluctant رَاغِم	restraint, curb, obstacle رَادِع (رَوَادِع)
support, prop رَافِد (رَوَافِد)	radical رَادِيكَالي
bearer رَافِع	radio رَادِيو
crane, hoist رَافِعَة (رَوَافِع)	radiology رَادِيولوجي
floating crane رَافِعَة عَائمَة	radium رَادِيوم
rising, high, advanced رَاقٍ	anchored, firm, immovable رَاسٍ (رَوَاسٍ)
layer, stratum رَاق (رَاقَات)	رَاس (رَوَاس/رَاسِيَات) immovable or unshakable mountains
sorcerer, charmer, magician رَاقٍ (رُقَاة)	sediment, dregs, residue رَاسِب (رَوَاسِب)
sleeping, recumbent, resting رَاقِد (رُقَّد)	firm, stable, fixed, firmly rooted رَاسِخ
dancer, dancing رَاقِص	briber رَاشٍ
female dancer رَاقِصَة	major, mature, reasonable, guided رَاشِد
passenger رَاكِب (رُكَّاب)	spy, watcher رَاصِد
horseman, rider رَاكِب (رُكْبَان)	

quadric, quadruple رُبَاعي	stagnant, dull, sluggish رَاكد
quadriliteral رُبَاعي الأَحْرُف	bowing to the رَاكع (رُكَّع) ground
quadruped, رُبَاعي الأَرْجُل fourfooted	marksman, good رَامٍ (رُمَاة) shot, thrower
quadrilateral رُبَاعي الأَضْلاَع	monk رَاهب (رُهْبان)
plumpness, fleshiness رَبَالة	nun رَاهبَة
captain, skipper رُبَّان	pledger, present, رَاهن current, fixed
captain of the رُبَّان السَّفيْنَة ship	narrator, reporter, رَاوٍ (رُوَاة) story-teller
divine, godly رَبَّاني	banner, flag رَايَة (رَايَات)
mistress, lady رَبَّة	lord, master رَبّ (أَرْباب)
landlady رَبَّة البَيْت	rob, jam رُبّ (رِبَاب/رُبُوب)
lady of the house رَبَّة المَنـــزْل	creditor رَبُّ الدَّيْن
advantage, profit, رِبْح (أَرْبَاح) gain	head of the family رَبّ العَائلَة
simple interest رِبْح بَسيط	usury, interest رِبًا
compound رِبْح مُرَكَّب interest	surplus, excess رَبَاء
fold, pen رَبَض (أَرْبَاض)	lordship, mastership رِبَابة
outskirts, رَبَضُ المَديْنَة environments, suburb	tie, ribbon, رِبَاط (رِبَاطات/رُبُط) bandage, bond
binding, joining, tying رَبْط	shoe-lace رِبَاط الحذَاء
financial allocation رَبْط مَالي	tie, necktie رِبَاط الرَّقَبَة
bundle, parcel, رَبْطَة (رِبَاط) bandage	calmness, رِبَاطَة الجَأْش coolness, composure

Rabi II (name of رَبِيع الثَّاني third month of Islamic calendar)	necktie رَبْطَة الرَّقَبَة
	garter رَبْطَة السَّاق
	money purse رَبْطَة النُّقُود
vernal رَبِيعي	quarter, fourth رُبْع (أَرْباع) part
gate, gateway رِتَاج (رُتُج)	
grade, rank, رُتْبَة (رُتَب) category, class, degree	region, area, رَبْع (رُبُوع) mansion
mending, patching up رَتْق	quarterly رُبْعي
queue, file رَتَل	noose رَبْقَة/رِبْقَة
ragged, worn out, رَثّ (رِثَاث) old, shabby	entanglement, رَبَك confusion, embarrassment
lamentation, bewailing رِثَاء	entangled, confused رَبِك
shabbiness, raggedness رَثَاثَة	plump, fleshy, رَبِل/رَبِيل corpulent
shabbiness, raggedness رُثُوثَة	sometimes, possibly رُبَّمَا
bewailing, lamenting, رَثْي bemoaning	lordship, رُبُوبة/رُبُوبِيّة mastership, deity
shabby, ragged, worn رَثِيث out, threadbare	hill, hillock رَبْوَة/رِبْوَة (رُبَّى)
	usurious رِبَوي
shaking, agitating, رَجّ convulsion	foster son, foster رَبِيب father
side, رَجًا/رَجَاء (أَرْجاء) direction, quarter	foster daughter, foster رَبِيبة mother
hope, expectation, رَجَاء solicitation	spring, spring tide رَبِيع
expectation, hope, رَجَاة anticipation	Rabi I (name of رَبِيع الأَوّل third month of Islamic calendar)

رِجْس (أَرْجَاس)	dirt, filth, atrocity	رَجَّاج	tremulous, quivering, trembling
رَجَس (أَرْجَاس)	filth, impurity, dirt	رَجَاحَة	leniency, equanimity
رَجْع	coming back, returning	رَجَّاف	quaking, quivering, trembling
رَجْعُ الصَّدَى	echo	رِجَال الأَدَب	men of letters, literati
رَجْعَة	return, revocation	رِجَال الإِسْعَاف	first-aid men
رَجْعِي	retroactive, obscurant	رِجَال الإِطْفَاء	firemen
رَجْفَة	quiver, shiver, tremour, convulsion	رِجَال الأَمْن	police men
رَجِل	pedestrian, on foot	رِجَال الحِفْظ	police
رِجْل (أَرْجُل)	foot, leg	رِجَال الدَّوْلَة	statesmen
رَجُل (رِجَال)	man	رِجَال الكَهَنُوت	the clergy, the ministry
رَجُل أَعْمَال	businessman		
رَجُل الصِّنَاعَة	industrialist	رِجَال المَطَافِئ	the firemen
رَجْم	stoning	رَجَب	Rajab, the seventh month of Islamic calendar
رَجْم بالْغَيْب	guess work, conjecture, divination		
		رَجّة	convulsion, rocking, concussion
رُجْمَة (رُجَم)	tombstone, gravestone		
		رُجْحَان	preponderance, outweighing, preference
رُجُوع	return, coming back		
رُجُولَة/رُجُولِيّة	manhood, manliness, virility	رَجْرَاج	tremulous, quivering
رَجِيْع	excrement	رِجْز/رُجْز	filth, impurity, dirt, punishment
رَجِيْم	accursed, cursed, damned		
		رَجِس	dirty, foul, impure

merciful, compassionate رَحمن	vastness, roominess, spaciousness رَحَابَة
rotatory, rotating رَحَوِي	roaming, roving, traveller رَحَّال
handmill, quern رَحًى (رُحِيّ)	traveller, explorer رَحَّالة
nectar, sweet drink رَحِيْق	spacious, wide, roomy رَحْب
departure, going, setting out رَحِيْل	wideness, roominess, spaciousness رُحْب/رَحَب
merciful, compassionate رَحِيْم (رُحَمَاء)	generous, open-handed رَحْب البَاع
light shower رَخّ	spacious, unconfined رَحْبُ الجَوَانِب
prosperity, opulence, abundance, comfort رَخَاء	open-handed, generous رَحْب الذِّرَاع
gentle breeze رُخَاء	liberal, broad-minded, generous رَحْب الصَّدْر
comfortable, easy رَخَاخ	square, open space رَحْبَة/رَحَبَة
marble رُخَام	luggage, camel saddle رَحْل (رِحَال)
marble slab رُخَامَة	journey, tour, excursion, trip رِحْلَة
flaccidity, laxity, slackness رَخَاوَة	destination, place of destination رُحْلَة
soft, tender رَخْص	womb, uterus, relation رَحِم/رِحْم (أَرْحَام)
permission, leave, permit, license رُخْصَة (رُخَص)	mercy, pity, compassion, grace رَحْمَة
driving license رُخْصَة قِيَادَة السَّيَّارَات	
soft, lax, flaccid رَخْو/رِخْو	
languid, cozy رَخِيّ	
cheap,inexpensive,low رَخِيْص	

رَخِيم melodious, soft, mellow	رَدْهَة الْمُحَاضَرات lecture room
رَدّ return, reply, denial, refutation, repulsion	رَدَى ruin, destruction, devastation
رَدّ الْحِيَازَة reintegration, re-entry	رَدِيْء (أَرْدِياء) bad, evil, wicked, malicious
رَدّ الفِعْل reaction	رَدِيْء التَّرْبِيَة ill-bred
رِدْء (أَرْدَاء) support, help, prop	رَدِيء السُّمْعَة of ill repute
رَدًّا على in response to	رَدِيْء الطَّبْع ill-natured, ill-tempered
رِدَاء (أَرْدِيَة) mantle, cloak, robe	رَدِيْف rear man, tandem
رَدَاءَة badness, wickedness, evil	رَذَاذ drizzle, fine misty rain
رِدَاف croup, rump	رَذَالَة meanness, vileness
رَدَّة bran, reverberation	رَذْل rejection, discarding
رِدَّة عَنِ الإِسْلَام apostasy from Islam	رَذْل (رُذُول) despicable, low, mean
رَدْغَة mire, mud	رَذِيل (رُذَلَاء) mean, base, vile
رِدْف (أَرْدَاف) posterior, hinder, rump, rearman	رَذِيلَة vice, evil, depravity
رَدْم debris, rubbish	رُزّ rice
رُدْن (أَرْدَان) sleeve	رُزْء (أَرْزَاء) misfortune, heavy loss
رَدْهَة (رَدَهَات) hall, entrance hall, lobby	رَزَّاق the Provider, the Maintainer
	رَزَانَة sedateness, gravity, seriousness, calmness
رَدْهَة الاسْتِقْبَال drawing room	رَزَّة (رَزَّات) staple, ringed screw

رَسْم الجُمْرُك	customs duty	رِزْق (أَرْزاق)	livelihood, sustenance, nourishment, rations
رَسْم الدُّخُول	admission fee		
رَسْم بَيَاني	illustrative figure	رِزْق مَوْرُوث	patrimony
رَسْم تَخْطِيطِي	rough draft	رِزْمَة (رِزَم)	packet, parcel, bundle
رَسْم شَمْسي	photograph		
رَسْم هَزْلِي	caricature, cartoon	رَزِيئَة/رَزِيّة (رَزَايا)	disaster, damage, loss
رَسْمي	formal, official		
رَسْميًّا	officially, formally	رَزِين	sedate, staid, calm, serious
رُسُوب	failure, sediment		
رُسُوخ	stability, firmness	رِسَالَة (رَسَائِل)	message, letter, epistle, treatise
رَسُول (رُسُل)	messenger, envoy, courier		
		رِسَالَة بَرْقِيّة	telegram
رُسُوم دِرَاسِيّة	tuition fees	رِسَالَة طَاعِنَة	lampoon
رَسِيْل (رُسَلَاء)	messenger, runner	رِسَالَة غَرَامِيّة	love letter
		رِسَالَة مُسَجَّلَة	registered letter
رَشّ	spraying, sprinkling	رَسَّام	illustrator, artist, painter
رَشَاد	maturity, good sense, reason		
		رُسْغ (أَرْسُغ)	wrist
رَشَّاشَة	rose, watering can	رَسْل	fluent, flowing, loose, gentle
رَشَاقَة	agility, nimbleness, elegance, slimness		
		رَسْم (رُسُوم)	sketch, drawing, trace, description, formality, tax
رَشْح	leakage, filtration, perspiration		
		رَسْم الإِنْتَاج	excise tax
رُشْد	maturity, sense, consciousness	رَسْم التَّقْيِيد	registration fee

on hand	رَشَد consciousness, forthrightness
رَصِيص compact, compressed	رَشْفَة sip of a drink
رَصِيف sound, solid, firm	رَشْو bribery, dishonesty
رَصِيف (أَرْصِفَة) pavement, platform	رَشْوَة/رُشْوَة/رِشْوَة (رِشَّى/رُشَّى) bribery, bribe
رَصِيف (رُصَفَاء) colleague, fellow	رَشِيد rational, mature, reasonable, guided
رَصِين sedate, composed, staid	رَشِيق nimble, swift, elegant, lissome
رَضّ bruise, contusing	رَشِيق الحَرَكَة nimble, swift, agile
رِضا/اِرْضًى consent, content, acceptance, assent	رَصَاص lead, bullets
رِضَاء consent, approval, agreement, contentment	رَصَاصَة bullet, ball
رُضَاب saliva, spittle	رَصَاصِي leaden, leady
رَضَّاعَة feeding bottle, feeder	رَصَافَة solidity, firmness, soundness
رَضَاعَة sucking, sucking period	رَصَانَة sedateness, staidness, composure
رَضْخ/رَضْخَة scanty allowance	رَصَد (أَرْصاد) ambush, look out, watcher
رَضْرَاض pebbles, gravels, metal	رَصْد/رَصَد (أَرْصاد) close observation, watch
رِضْوَان consent, favour, sanction, approval	رَصْف paving, macadamizing
رُضُوخ surrender, yielding, submission	رَصِيد (أَرْصِدَة) balance, stock

pastoral, bucolic رَعَوي	pleasant, satisfied, رَضِيّ content
repentance, رَعْوَى/رُعْوَى amendment	bruised, broken رَضِيْض
nationality, رَعَوِيّة citizenship	suckling, رَضِيْع (رُضَعَاء) nursing infant
taking care, watching, رَعْي guarding, protection	damp, wet, moist, رَطْب mellow
flock, herd, رَعِيّة (رَيَاعا) subjects	ripe dates رُطَب (رِطَاب)
	rotl رَطْل
comfort, ease, رَغَادَة opulence	dampness, wetness, رُطُوبَة moisture
dust, earth, mould رَغَام	moist, humid, wet, رَطِيْب damp
froth, foam رُغَاوَة	nosebleed رُعَاف
desire, wish, رَغْبَة (رَغَبَات) eagerness, longing	care, regard, attention, رِعَايَة patronage
ease, comfort, affluence رَغَد	fright, dismay, alarm رُعْب
easy, comfortable, رَغْد affluent, pleasant	thunder رَعْد (رُعُود)
in spite of, despite رَغْمَ	tremour, shaking, رَعْدَة/رِعْدَة shudder
foam, froth رَغْوَة/رُغْوَة	flourishing, in رَعْرَع/رُعْرُع full bloom
suckling رَغُوث	tremour, shiver رَعْش/رَعْشَة
desire, object رَغِيْبَة (رَغَائب) of desire	orgasm رَعْشَة الجماع
comfortable, pleasant رَغِيْد	frivolity, رُعُونَة thoughtlessness
loaf of a bread رَغِيْف (أَرْغِفَة)	

رَفّ (رُفُوف)	shelf, ledge, rack
رِفَاء	harmony, concord, love
رُفَات	mortal remains, corpse
رِفَادة	bandage, dressing
رَفَّاس/رَقّاص	steamboat, steam launch
رَفَاه	luxury, comfort of life
رَفَاهَة/رَفَاهِيّة	comfort, ease, luxury, coziness
رَفْت	discharge, dismissal
رَفْتِيّة	certificate of discharge
رَفْتِيَّة الجُمْرُك	clearance certificate
رَفَث	obscenity
رِفْد (رُفُود)	support, prop, gift
رَفْرَف (رَفَارِف)	cushion, eyeshade
رَفْسَة	kick
رَفْش	spade, shovel
رَفْض	rejection, refusal
رَفْع	raising, lifting, erection, removal
رِفْعَة	high rank, dignity, elevation

رِفْق	kindness, gentleness, clemency
رِفْقَة/رُفْقَة (رِفَق)	company, group, society
رِفْل	train, trail
رِفْه	luxury, ease and comfort
رَفِيْض	rejected, refused, dismissed
رَفِيْع	high, elevated, lofty, sublime
رَفِيْع الشَّأْن	exalted, eminent, high-ranking
رَفِيْع القَدْر	eminent, prominent
رَفِيْق (رُفَقَاء)	companion, friend, associate, comrade, mild
رَفِيْق المَدْرَسَة	school mate
رَفِيْقَة	mistress, girl friend, companion
رِقّ	slavery, bondage
رَقّ (رُقُوق)	turtle
رَقّاء	charmer, magician
رَقَابَة	supervision, control
رُقَاد	sleep, recumbence
رَقّاص	dancer

sleep, reclining, رُقُود recumbency	رَقَّاصَة woman dancer, dancing girl
development, progress, رُقِي advancement	رَقَاعَة silliness, foolishness, shamelessness
observer, (رُقَبَاء) رَقِيْب vigilant, watchful, guardian	رُقَاق loaf of a bread
	رِقْبَة vigilance, observation, heed
incantation, (رُقَّى) رُقْيَة charm, spell	رَقَبَة (رِقَاب) neck, slave
impudent, shameless رَقِيْع	رِقَّة fineness, thinness, delicacy, gentleness
thin, fine, slim, (رِقَاق) رَقِيْق delicate, tender, slave	رقَّة الشُّعُور sensitiveness
amiable, gentle رَقِيْق الجَانب	رَقَّة الطَّبْع gentleness, kindness
amiable, friendly رَقِيْق الحَاشِيَة	رقَّة القَلْب tender-heartedness
sensitive رَقِيْق الشُّعُور	رَقْرَاق misty, glittering, gleaming, resplendent
gentle, mild, kind رَقِيْق الطَّبْع	رَقْص dance, dancing
soft-hearted, رَقِيْق القَلْب tender-hearted	رَقْص البَطْن belly dance
gentle-hearted رَقِيْق المِزَاج	رَقْص مُتَنَكِّر masked ball
letter, message رَقِيْم	رَقْصَة (رَقَصَات) dance
riding animal, (رُكُب) رِكَاب stirrup	رُقْعَة (رُقَع) patch, piece of cloth, lot
buried treasures like رِكَاز gold, silver or ore etc	رَقْم (أَرْقام) number, numeral
racer, runner رَكَّاض	رَقْم مُتَسَلْسِل consecutive number
feeble, weak, insecure رُكَاك	رُقُوب anticipation, expectation

kneeling	رُكُوع	colourlessness, feebleness, unsoundness	رَكَاكَة
confidence, trust	رُكُون	heap, pile, lump	رُكَام
post, poll, support, treasure	رَكِيزَة (رَكَائِز)	convoy, caravan, horsemen	رَكْب
colourless, pallid, feeble, rickety	رَكِيك	retinue, escort	رُكْبَان
steady, firm, fixed, sedate	رَكِين	knee	رُكْبَة (رُكَب)
repair, reparation	رَمّ	weakness, feebleness, unsoundness	رِكَّة
lancer, spearman	رَمَّاح	sound, tone	رِكْز
ashes, cinders	رَمَاد (أَرْمِدَة)	pause, stop, break	رَكْزَة
ashy, ash-coloured	رَمَادِي	rakah, part of prayer	رَكْعَة
pomegranate	رُمَّان/رُمَّانَة	kick	رَكْلَة
hand grenade	رُمَّانَة يَدَوِيَّة	lump, pile, heap	رَكَم
raft, float	رَمَث (أَرْمَاث)	support, basis, nook, staff	رُكْن (أَرْكَان)
spear, lance	رُمْح (رِمَاح)	riding animal, mount	رَكُوب
inflammation or soreness of the eye	رَمَد	riding, mounting, boarding	رُكُوب
sore-eyed	رَمِد	navigation	رُكُوب البَحْر
indication, sign, symbol, hint	رَمْز (رُمُوز)	aviation	رُكُوب الهَوَاء
symbolic	رَمْزِي	coffee pot	رَكْوَة (رَكَوَات)
tomb, grave, pit	رَمْس (رُمُوس)	stagnation, standstill, stillness	رُكُود
eyelashes	رِمْش (رُمُوش)		
wink, blink	رَمْشَة	running, race	رُكُوض

رَهْط/رَهَط (أَرْهاط) troop, group, flock	رَمَض parchedness, scorchedness
رَهف/رَهيْف thin, slim	رَمْضَاء intense heat, sun-baked ground
رَهِل soft, tender, flaccid	
رَهْن (رِهان) pledge, hostage, mortgage	رَمَضان Ramadan, the ninth month of Islamic calendar
رَهْو calm, quiet, tranquil	رَمَق (أَرْماق) spark of life, breath of life
رَهِيْب fearful, dreadful, aweful	
	رَمَق أَخِيْر the last breath
رَهِين mortgaged, pledged	رَمْل (رِمَال) sand
رَهِيْنَة (رَهَائن) pledge, hostage, security	رَمْلي sandy, sabulous
رَوَاء fresh water	رَمْي throwing, tossing, flinging
رُوَاء sightlines, comliness, beauty	رَمْيَة throw, fling
رِوَائي playwright, novelist	رَمِيْم decayed, cankered, rotten
رَوَابط الصَّدَاقة bonds of friendship	رَنَّان ringing, echoing, resounding
رَوَاج circulation, currency	رَنَّة echo, resonance, reverberation
رَوَاح departure, going out	
رَوَاغ dodge, cunning trick, artifice	رَنِيْن echo, reverberation, ring
رِوَاق/رُوَاق (أَرْوقَة) portico, porch, dormitories	رِهَان betting, wagering
رَواقي stoic, stoical	رَهْبَة owe, fear, dread, terror
	رَهْبَنَة/رَهْبَانيّة monasticism
رِوَاية (رِوايات) story, tale, narration, report	رَهْبَى/رُهْبَى fear, fright, alarm

رَوْضَة (رَوْض/رِيَاض) meadow, garden	detective story	رِوَاية بُوْلِيْسِيّة
رَوْضَة الأَطْفَال kindergarten, nursery school	play, drama	رِوَاية تَمْثِيْلِيّة
رَوَع beauty, charm	romance, fiction	رِوَاية خَيَالِيّة
رَوْع/رَوْعَة fear, fright, awe, surprise	motion picture, movie, film	رِوَاية سِيْنمائِيّة
رَوْم wish, desire, purpose, intention	novel	رِوَاية قصَصِيّة
رَوْنَق splendour, brilliancy, beauty	serial story	رِوَاية مُتَسَلْسَلَة
رَوِيّة deliberation, consideration, meditation	tragedy	رِوَاية مُحْزِنَة
رُوَيْدًا slowly, gently	play, stage play	رِوَاية مَسْرَحِيّة
	comedy	رِوَاية مُضْحكة
رِيّ/رَيّ watering, irrigation	sound film	رِوَاية ناطقة
رِيَاء hypocrisy, dissimulation, insincerity	comedy, comical story	رِوَاية هَزْلِيّة
رِيَاسَة presidency, leadership, direction	curds	رَوْب
رِيَاسِي presidential	rupee	رُوْبِيّة (رُوْبِيّات)
رِيَاضَة (رِيَاضَات) practice, exercise, physical training	dung, droppings	رَوْث
رِيَاضِي mathematic, mathematician, sportsman	refreshment, relief	رَوْح
رِيَاضِيّات mathematics	spirit, soul	رُوْح (أَرْوَاح)
رِيَال Riyal	the Holy Spirit or ghost	رُوْح القُدْس
	spiritual, divine, holy	رُوْحَاني
	spirituality	رُوْحَانِيّة
	spiritual, divine	رُوْحي
	exploration, survey	رَوْد

watered, lush, succulent	رَيَّان
doubt, suspicion	رَيْب/رِيبَة

mercury, quicksilver	زِئْبَق
wind, odour, smell	رِيح (رِيَاح)
roaring, bellowing	زَئِير
exceeding, excessive, superabundant, extra, surplus	زَائِد
mansoon	رِيح دَوْرِيَّة
violent wind	رِيح صَرْصَر
appendix, appendage	زَائِدَة (زَوَائِد)
storm, violent wind	رِيح عَاصِفَة
vermiform appendix	زَائِدَة دُوْدِيَّة
monsoon, trade wind	رِيح مَوْسمِيّة
visitor, guest	زَائِر (زُوّار)
sweet basil	رَيْحَان
divergent, deviating, distorted	زَائِغ
feathers, quill, plumage	رِيش/رِيشَة
counterfeit, false, forged, artificial	زَائِف
feathered, plumed	رِيْشِي
vanishing, passing, evarescent	زَائِل
product, income, best part	رَيْع (رُيُوع)
mercury, quicksilver	زَاؤُوق
the prime of youth	رَيْع الشَّبَاب
restraint, check, impediment, scruple	زَاجِر
prime, best portion	رَيْعَان
restriction, check, prevention	زَاجِرَة (زَوَاجِر)
the prime of youth	رَيْعَان الشَّبَاب
creaping, crawling	زَاحِف
country, countryside, field	رِيف (أَرْيَاف)
reptiles	زَاحِف (زَوَاحِف)
rural, rustic	رِيْفِي
brimful, replete	زَاخِر
saliva, spittle	رِيْق (أَرْيَاق)
	foam, froth, addax
	رِيْم

زَبَّال	sweeper, garbage man
زُبَالة	rubbish, garbage
زَبَد (أَزْباد)	foam, froth, scum
زُبْدَة	butter, cream
زُبْر	penis
زَبَرْجَد	chrysolite
زَبَط	mud, slime, mire
زِبْل/زِبْلَة	dung, droppings, manure
زَبُون (زَبَائِن)	client, customer
زَبُون دَائِم	regular customer
زَبِيب	raisins, dried grapes
زُبْيَة (زُبًى)	climax
زُجَاج	glass
زَجَّاج	glazier
زُجَاجَة	bottle, piece of glass
زُجَاجِي	vitreous, glassy, glazier
زَجْر	rebuke, reprimand, check, restraint
زَجْرِي	penitentiary, reformatory
زُحَار	groaning, moaning
زَحَّاف	creeping, crawling
زَحّافَة	reptile, leveller

زَاد (أَزْوِدة)	provisions, supplies
زَارِع (زُرَّاع)	farmer, peasant
زَارُوب (زَوَارِيْب)	narrow lane, alley
زَاغ (زِيغان)	crow
زَانٍ (زُناة)	adulterer, seducer, fornicator
زَانِيَة (زَوَانٍ)	adulteress, prostitute, whore
زَاهٍ	splendid, shining, radiant
زَاهِر	shining, bright, luminous
زَاوُوق	mercury, quicksilver
زَاوِيَة (زَوَايا)	angle, nook, corner
زَاوِيَة الانْعِكَاس	angle of reflection
زَاوِيَة حَادّة	acute angle
زَاوِيَة خَارِجيّة	exterior angle
زَاوِيَة دَاخِليّة	interior angle
زَاوِيَة قَائِمَة	right angle
زَاوِيَة مُتَتَامَّة	complementary angle
زَاوِيَة مُتَكاملة	supplementary angle

horticulture زِرَاعَة البَسَاتِين	throng, crowd زِحَام
agricultural, agrarian زِرَاعِي	march, proceeding زَحْف
in groups and زَرَافَات ووُحْدَانًا alone	Saturn زُحَل
in groups, in (زَرَافَات) زَرَافة flocks	slide زَحْلُقة
	skiing, skating زَحْلُوْقة
giraffe زَرَافة/زُرَافة	crowd, throng زَحْمَة
contempt, scorn, زِرَايَة disdain	groaning, moaning زَحِير
	vanities of this زَخَارِفُ الدُّنْيا world
chain link زَرَدَة
starling زُرْزُر	brimful, replete زَخَّار
sowing, growing, زَرْع cultivation	heavy (زَخَّات) زَخَّة downpour
crop, seed (زُرُوع) زَرْع	زُخْرُف (زَخَارف)
blueness, blue زَرَق/زُرْقَة colour	embellishment, ornament, vain show
blue (fem. of أَزْرَق) زَرْقَاء	decoration, (زَخْرَفَات) زَخْرَفَة ornamentation
tapestry, brocade زَرْكَش
despicable, زَرِيّ contemptible, miserable	decorative, زُخْرُفِي ornamental
pen, fold for (زَرَائب) زَرِيبَة cattle	stinking, tainted زَخِم
	stench, bad smell زَخَمَة
leadership, chiefdom زَعَامَة	button, bud (أَزْرار) زِرّ
inconvenience, زَعَج uneasiness	flower bud, bud زِرّ الزَّهْرَة
	farmer, cultivator زَرَّاع
peevish, ill- (زَعَارِير) زُعْرُور natured, irascible	cultivation, agriculture زِرَاعَة

corridor, alley, narrow lane	زُقَاق (أَزِقَّة)	convulsion, concussion	زَعْزَعَة (زَعَازِع)
chirping, cheeping	زَقْزَقَة	saffron	زَعْفَرَان
a thorn tree, balanites	زَقُّوم	screaming, shrieking	زَعْق
purity, chastity, integrity	زَكَاء	shriek, scream, yell	زَعْقَة
alms, charity, sanctity, purity	زَكَاة/زكوة	annoyance, anger, vexation	زَعَل
cold in head, catarrh	زُكَام/زَكْمَة	vexed, angry	زَعِل/زَعْلان
sinless, guiltless, pure	زَكِيّ (أَزْكِيَاء)	supposition, assumption, claim	زَعْم
slipperiness, smoothness	زَلَاقَة	yelling, screaming	زَعِيق
fresh cold water, albumen	زُلَال	leader, chief	زَعِيم (زُعَمَاء)
albuminous	زُلَالي	nap, fuzz, soft hair	زَغَب
lapse, slip	زَلَّة	fuzzy, downy	زَغِب
slip of pen	زَلَّة قَلَم	counterfeit money	زَغَل
slip of tongue	زَلَّة لسَان	infant, baby	زُغْلُول (زَغَالِيل)
slippery, smooth	زَلِج/زَلِيج	nuptial feast	زِفَاف
convulsion, concussion	زِلْزَال	procession	زَفَّة
earthquake	زَلْزَلَة (زَلَازِل)	pitch	زِفْت
pebbles, gravels	زَلَط	nuptial procession	زَفَّة العُرْس
sycophancy, servile flattery	زَلَف	grease, greasy food	زَفَر
		rancid, dirty	زَفِر
		deep sigh, moan	زَفْرَة
		sighing, exhalation	زَفِير

زُلْفَة/زُلْفَى	flattery, sycophancy
زَلِق	slippery, smooth
زَلَّقَة	slip, sideslip
زَمَّار	piper
زَمَّار الرَّمْل	sandpiper
زَمَّارَة	pipe, flute, reed
زَمَالة	companionship, fellowship
زَمَالَة دِرَاسِيّة	scholarship, stipend
زِمَام (أَزِمّة)	rein, halter, bond, limit, boundary
زِمَام الأَمْر	reins of power
زَمَان (أَزْمِنَة)	time, duration, period
زَمَائِنة	chronic illness
زَمَانِي	temporal, wordly, transitory
زُمْرَة (زُمَر)	group, troop, band
زُمْرَة دَمَوِيّة	blood group
زُمُرُّد	emerald
زَمْزَم	Zamzam, well in Makkah
زَمْزَمَة	rumbling of thunder

زُمْلَة	companionship, association
زَمَن (أَزْمان)	time, period, age
زَمَنِي	temporal, wordly, transitory
زَمْهَرِيْر	severe cold
زَمِيْل	companion, colleague, associate
زَمِيْل الْمَدْرَسَة	school-fellow
زَمِيْلة	woman companion, girl friend
زَنّ	buzz, buzzing
زُنّار	belt, girdle, waistband
زِنَاق	neckband, collar
زُنْبُور (زَنَابِيْر)	hornet, wasp
زِنَة	weight, weighing
زَنْجَبِيْل	ginger
زِنْجِيْر	chain
زَنِخ	rank, rancid, fusty
زَنَخ	rancidity, fustiness
زَنْدَقَة	atheism, sanctimony
زِنْدِيْق (زَنَادِقَة)	atheist, unbeliever
زِنْك	zinc
زِنًى/زِنا	adultery, fornication

wedding, marriage	زَوَاج	mean, ignoble, outsider	زَنِيم
doubling, duplication	زَوَاج	splendour, brilliancy	زَهَاء
morganatic marriage	زَوَاج مَرْغَنْطِي	florist	زَهَّار
civil marriage	زَوَاج عُرْفِي	asceticism, abstinence, apathy	زُهْد
provisions, supplies	زَوَاد/زُوَّادَة	daisy	زَهْر اللُّؤْلُؤ
adornment, embellishment	زَوَاق	flower, blossom	زَهْر/زَهْرَة (أَزْهار/زُهُور)
cessation, extinction, passage	زَوَال	brightness, splendour, brilliancy, beauty	زُهْرَة
storm, hurricane	زَوْبَعَة	Venus	زُهْرَة
couple, pair, husband	زَوْج (أَزْواج)	passion flower	زَهْرَة الآلام
brother-in-law	زَوْج الأُخْت	pansy	زَهْرة الثَّالُوث
son-in-law	زَوْج الابْنَة	primrose	زَهْرَة الرَّبِيع
wife, consort	زَوْجَة	honey-suckle	زَهْرَة العَسَل
sister-in-law	زَوْجَة الأَخ	daisy	زَهْرَة اللُّؤْلُؤ
daughter-in-law	زَوْجَة الابْن	flower pot	زَهْرِيّة
double, in pairs, conjugal	زَوْجِي	fedidness, offensive smell	زُهْمَة/زُهُومة
matrimony	زَوْجِيّة (زَوْجِيّات)	ostentation, vain show, vanity, splendour	زَهْو/زُهُوّ
lie, falsehood, false	زُور	perishing, dying	زَهُوق
visit, call	زَوْرَة	splendid, brilliant, sumptuous	زَهِيّ
boat, rowboat	زَوْرَق (زَوَارِق)	trifling, trivial, paltry, insignificant	زَهِيد

زِينَة adornment, decoration, make-up	زَوْرَق الصَّيْد fishing boat
زِينَة الوَجْه make-up	زَوْرَق النَّجَاة lifeboat
	زَوْرَق بُخَارِي steam launch
س	زُوْلُوجِي zoological
	زُوْلُوجِيا zoology
سُؤَال (أَسْئِلَة) question, request, demand	زُوْم sap, juice
سَأَّال/سَؤُول inquisitive, curious	زِيّ (أَزْيَاء) fashion, style, shape, style of dress
سُؤْر/سُؤْرة remnant, rest, leftover	زَيَّات oilman, oilseller
سُؤْل/سُؤْلَة request, demand	زِيَادَة increase, addition, surplus
سَئِم tired, weary	زِيَارَة visit, call
سَآمَة disgust, weariness, ennui, tedium	زَيْت (زُيُوت) oil
سَؤُوم tired, weary, disgusted	زَيْت الغاز kerosene
	زَيْت خام crude oil
سائب free, loose, unconfined, left	زَيْتُون olive, olive tree
سائح flowing, running	زَيْتُونِي olive-coloured, olive like
سائح (سُوَّاح/سيَّاح) tourist, traveller	زَيْتِي oily, oilbearing
سائد prevalent, predominant, ruling	زِيجِي matrimonial, conjugal
سائر rest, remaining	زَيْغ/زَيَغَان deviation, divergence, departure
سائر current, running, moving	زَيْف counterfeit, forged, spurious, artificial
	زَيْن nice, beautiful, graceful, good

composer of rhymed prose	ساجِع	سائِس (سُوَّاس/سَاسَة)	administrator, stableman
drawer	ساحِب	سائِغ	permissible, palatable, smooth
courtyard, open space	سَاحَة (سَاحَات)	سائِق	driving, driving force
playground, athletic field	سَاحَة الأَلْعَاب	سائِق (سَائِقُون/سَاقَة)	driver
battlefield	سَاحَة القِتَال	سائِق السَّيَّارَة	driver, chauffeur
tribunal	سَاحَة القَضَاء	سائِل	fluid, liquid
magician, wizard, sorcerer	ساحِر (سَحَرة)	سائِل (سُؤَّال)	questioner, mendicant, petitioner, beggar
witch, sorceress	سَاحِرَة (سَوَاحِر)	سائِمَة (سَوَائِم)	livestock
crushing, overwhelming	ساحِق	سَابِح	swimmer
coast, seashore	سَاحِل (سَوَاحِل)	سَابِحات	floating (race horses)
littoral, coastal	سَاحِلي	سَابِحَة	glider, cargo glider
angry, indignant, displeased	سَاخِط	سَابِع	the seventh
hot, warm	سَاخِن	سَابِع عشر	seventeenth
obstructive	سَادّ	سَابِغ (سَوَابِغ)	complete, full, ample
plain, simple	سَادَة	سَابِق	previous, former, precedent
ladies and gentlemen	سَادَتي وسَيِّدَاتي	سَابِقَة	precedent, precedence, previous, conviction
the sixth	سَادِس	سَاتِر	screen, folding screen
		سَاجٍ	calm, quiet, tranquil
		سَاجِد/سَجَّاد	prostrator, worshiper

wrist watch	سَاعَة اليَد	sixteenth	سَادِس عشر
striking clock, repeater	سَاعَة دَقَّاقة	sixthly	سَادِسًا
sandglass, hour-glass	سَاعَة رَمْليّة	custodian, keeper	سَادِن (سَدَنَة)
sundial	سَاعَة شَمْسيَّة	guileless, simple, ingenious, homely	سَاذِج
wrist watch	سَاعَة معْصَم	delightful, pleasant, joyful	سَارّ
forearm	سَاعِد (سَوَاعِد)	effective, in force, night reveller	سَارٍ (سُرَاة)
tributary	سَاعِدَة (سَوَاعِد)		
postman, mailman	سَاعِي البَرِيد	free, unrestrained	سَارِح
starving, hungry	سَاغِب	absent-minded, dreamy	سَارِح الفِكْر
unveiled, uncovered	سَافِر	thief, robber	سَارِق (سُرَّاق/سَرَقَة)
lowly, mean, despicable	سَافِل	rocket	سَارُوخ (سَوَارِيْخ)
cupbearer, butler	سَاقٍ (سُقَاة)	mast, column	سَارِيَة (سَوَارِي)
leg, thigh	سَاقٌ (سُوق/سِيْقان)	shining, bright, luminous	سَاطِع (سَوَاطِع)
trunk	سَاق الشَّجَرَة		
stem, stalk	سَاق النَّبَات	chopper, cleaver	سَاطُور (سَوَاطِيْر)
rear, stern	سَاقَة	messenger, calumniator	سَاعٍ (سُعَاة)
rear-guard	سَاقَة الجَيْش		
falling, base, degraded, low	سَاقِط (سُقَّاط)	watchmaker	سَاعَاتِي
barmaid	سَاقِيَة	hour, clock, time, watch	سَاعَة (سَاعَات)
streamlet, rivulet, irrigation canal	سَاقِيَة (سَوَاق)	pocket watch	سَاعَة الجَيْب

forgetful, inattentive, negligent	سَاه	silent, quiet, reticent	ساكت
sleepless, awake	ساهد	dweller, occupant, resident	ساكِن (سُكّان)
awake, watchful, sleepless	ساهِر	still, quiet, motionless, silent	ساكِن (سَكَنة)
vituperator, reviler	سَبّاب	negative, negatory	سَالِب
abuse, insult, vituperation	سِباب	predecessor, previous, bygone	سَالِف (سَلَف)
index, fore flinger	سَبّابة	forementioned, forecited	سَالِف الذِّكر
slumber, coma, lethargy	سُبات	previously, formerly	سَالِفًا
lethargic, carotid	سُباتي	trodden, passable, unimpeded	سَالِك
swimmer	سَبّاح/سَبُوح	safe, secure, sound, integral	سَالِم
swimming	سِباحة	poisonous, venomous	سَامّ
manure, fertiliser	سِباخ (أَسْبِخة)	high, sublime, elevated	سَامٍ (سُمَاة)
dump, bunch, cluster	سُباطة	jovial partner, companion in conversation	سَامِر (سُمّار)
sevenfold, seven-lettered	سُباعي	hearer, listener	سَامِع
race, competition, contest	سِباق	towering, lofty	سَامِق
arms race	سِباق التَّسَلُّح	high-principled	سَامي المَبادئ
horse-race	سِباق الخَيْل	auspicious, favourable	سَانِح (سَوانِح)
boat race	سِباق القَوارب		
boat races	سِباق المَراكب		
founder, smelter	سَبّاك المَعادن	opportunity, occasion	سَانِحة

beast of prey	سَبْع (سُبوع/أَسْبُع)
seven	سَبْع/سَبْعَة
seventeen	سَبْعَة عَشَر/سَبْع عشرة
seventy	سَبْعُون
precedence, priority	سَبْق
race, stake in a race	سَبَق (أَسْباق)
stake in a race	سُبْقَة
founding, forming, casting	سَبْك
metal casting, founding	سَبْك المَعَادن
stable manure, droppings	سَبْلَة
mustache	سَبَلَة (سِبَال)
blackboard, slate	سَبُّورَة
captivity, capture	سَبْي
prisoner of war, captive	سَبِيّ (سَبَايا)
way, road, course, path	سَبِيل (سُبُل)
sixteen	ستّ عشرة
six	ستّ/ستّة
curtain, veil, cover, drape	سَتَار (سُتُر)

spinach	سَبَائخ
cause, reason, motive, origin	سَبَب (أَسْباب)
compelling reason	سَبَب قَهْري
Saturday	سَبْت
September	سِبْتمْبر
swim, swimming	سَبْحَة
beads	سُبْحَة (سُبُحات)
rosary, chaplet	سُبْحَة الصَّلاَة
manure, droppings, fertilizer	سَبَخ
briny, wet and salty	سَبِخ
chemical manure	سَبَخ كِيْماوي
moorland, salt marsh	سَبْخَة/سَبَخَة (سِباخ)
probing, sounding, fathoming	سَبْر
grandson, grandchild, tribe	سِبْط (أَسْباط)
open-handed, generous	سَبْط اليَدَيْن
lank, soft and straight	سَبْط/سَبَط (سِباط)
seventh part	سُبْع (أَسْباع)
سُبْع (سِباع) = سَبْع	

prostration, bowing, سُجُود worship	silver screen سِتَار فِضِّي
temper, nature, (سَجَايا) سَجِيَّة disposition, characteristic	veil, curtain, (سَتَائِر) سِتَارَة cover, drape
imprisoned, (سُجَنَاء) سَجِين prisoner	veils, cover, (سُتُور/أَسْتار) سِتْر curtain, shelter
state prisoner سَجِين سِيَاسِي	jacket (سُتَر) سُتْرَة
meningeal سِحَائِي	buttocks, backside سَتْه/سِتْه
clouds سَحَاب/سَحَابَة	sixty سِتُّون
magician, sorcerer, سَحَّار enchanter	carpet, (سَجَاجِيد) سَجَّادة prayer rug
witch, sorceress سَحَّارة	cigarette (سَجَائِر) سِجَارَة
lesbianism سِحَاق	jailer, gaoler سَجَّان
meninx, cortex سِحَايَة	sajdah, position of سَجْدَة prostration in prayer
withdrawing, سَحْب withdrawal, pulling	rhyming, rhymed سَجْع prose
ill-gotten (أَسْحَات) سُحْت	سَجْف/سِجْف (أَسْجاف/سُجُوف) veil, curtain
witchcraft, سِحْر bewitchment, fascination	register, (سِجِلَّات) سِجِلّ scroll
dawn, early (أَسْحَار) سَحَر morning	imprisonment, سَجْن detention
magic-al سِحْرِي	prison, jai, (سُجُون) سِجْن goal
crushing, pounding, سَحْق bruising	life imprisonment سَجْن مُؤَبَّد
remoteness, vastness سُحْق	solitary سَجْن مُنْفَرِد confinement
tatter, rag (سُحُوق) سَحْق	

blackness, malice	سَحَم/سُخْمَة	blackness, black colour	سَحَم/سُحَام
hot, warm, feverish	سُخْن	black colour, blackness	سُحْمَة
heat, warmth, fever	سُخُونَة	expression, appearance, mien	سَحْنَة/سَحَنَة
generous, liberal, open-handed	سَخِيّ (أَسْخِيَاء)	daybreak meal	سُحُور
flimsy, weak-minded, frivolous, insipid	سَخِيف (سِخَاف)	remote, faraway	سَحِيق
		generosity, liberality	سَخَاء
silly, stupid, fool	سَخِيف (سُخَفاء)	frivolity, feeble-mindedness, insipidity	سَخَافة
malice, ill-will, hatred	سَخِيمَة (سَخَائِم)	boiler, geyser	سَخَّان
closing, stopping, blocking	سَدّ	heat, warmth	سَخَانة
obstruction, hindrance, block, dam	سَدّ (سُدُود)	bath heater, geyser	سَخَّانة
warp	سَدَاة	generosity, open-handedness	سَخَاوَة
appositeness, appropriateness	سَدَاد	laughing stock, butt	سُخْرَة
plug, stopper, obturator	سِدَاد (أَسِدَّة)	laughing stock, ridiculous	سُخْرِي
plug	سَدَّاد التَّوْصِيل	sarcasm, mockery, object of ridicule	سُخْرِيّة
stopper, cork	سِدَادَة	resentment, displeasure, rage, anger	سُخْط/سَخَط
sixfold	سُدَاسي	flimsiness, weak-mindedness, frivolity, idiocy	سُخْف/سَخَف
block, barricade, obstacle	سَدّة	lamb	سَخْلَة

prosperity and adversity	سَرّاء والضَّرّاء	gate, door	سُدَّة
mirage, phantom	سَراب	clogging, block	سَدَد
saddler	سَرّاج	nabk tree, lotus tree	سِدْر/سِدْرَة (سِدَر)
lamp, night light	سِراج (سُرُج)	one sixth	سُدْس (أَسْداس)
glowworm	سِراج اللَّيْل	twilight, dusk	سَدَف (أَسْداف)
dismissal, release	سَراح	dusk, darkness	سُدْفَة
canopy, pavilion	سُرادِق	curtain, veil, hangings	سُدْل/سِدْل (سُدُول)
quickly, hurriedly	سِراعًا	grief, sorrow, sadness	سَدَم
palace	سَرايَة (سَرايَات)	in vain, uselessly, ineffectually	سُدًى
flock, herd, swarm, group, throng	سِرْب (أَسْراب)	apposite, appropriate, relevant	سَدِيد
tunnel, subterranean passage	سَرَب (أَسْراب)	mist, haze	سَدِيم (سُدُم)
dress, garment, shirt, apparel	سِرْبال (سَرابِيل)	nebular, nebulous	سَدِيمي
herd, flock, swarm	سُرْبة (سُرَب)	simplicity, plainness, guilelessness	سَذاجَة
umbilical cord, navel-string	سُرَّة (أَسِرَّة)	secret, secrecy, mystery	سِرّ (أَسْرار)
saddle	سَرج (سُرُوج)	navel, umbilicus	سُرّ (سُرَر)
wolf	سِرْحان	profound secret	سِرّ غامِض
citation, quotation, presentation	سَرْد	in secret, secretly, privately	سِرًّا
tunnel, subterranean passage	سِرْداب (سَرادِيب)	prosperity, good fortune	سَرّاء

umbilical	سُرِّي	crab, cancer	سَرَطَان
magnanimous, high-minded, noble	سَرِيّ (أَسْرِياء)	reins	سُرْع/سِرْع (أَسْرَاع)
effectiveness, penetration, applicability	سَرَيَان	rapidity, speed, quickness	سُرْعَة
concubine, mistress	سُرِّيَّة (سَرَارِي)	sensitiveness, sensibility	سُرْعَة التَّأَثُّر
detachment, squadron	سَرِيّة (سَرَايَا)	credulity	سُرْعَة التَّصْديق
street vendor, peddler, hawker	سَرِيح	presence of mind	سُرْعَة الخَاطِر
bed, bedstead	سَرِير (سُرُر)	rate of speed, velocity	سُرْعَة السَّيْر
throne	سَرِير المَلك	theft, stealing, plundering	سَرِقَة
secret, heart	سَرِيرَة (سَرَائِر)	piracy	سَرِقَة البِحَار
fast, quick, rapid, speedy	سَرِيع	plagiarism	سَرِقَة التَّأْليف
inflammable, combustible	سَرِيع الاحْتِراق	circus	سِرْك
inflammable	سَرِيع الالْتِهاب	rectum, anus	سُرْم (أَسْرَام)
easily affected, sensitive	سَرِيع التَّأَثُّر	eternity, endless time	سَرْمَد
credulous	سَرِيع التَّصْديق	eternal, endless	سَرْمَدِي
very changeable, capricious	سَرِيع التَّقَلُّب	drawers, trousers	سِرْوَال (سَرَاويل)
quick-witted	سَرِيعُ الخَاطِر	baggy trousers	سِرْوَال فَضْفَاض
ephemeral, vanishing, transient	سَرِيع الزَّوَال	delight, joy, happiness, pleasure	سُرُور
		secret, clandestine, private, mysterious	سِرِّي

flat, stretched, prostrate	سَطِيح	rapid-fire	سَرِيع الطَلَق
happiness, good fortune, felicity	سَعَادَة	fragile, easily injured, perishable	سَرِيع العَطَب
true happiness	سَعَادة حَقَّة	quickly, in a short time	سَرِيعًا
cough	سُعَال	plug, stopper, poker	سِطَام
whooping cough	سُعَال دِيكيّ	plane, surface, level, roof	سَطْح (سُطُوح)
calumny, slander	سِعَايَة	sea level	سَطْح البَحْر
spaciousness, capacity, capability, profusion, extent	سَعَة	house-top, terrace	سَطْح البَيْت
luck, good fortune	سَعْد (سُعُود)	inclined plane	سَطْح مَائِل
madness, frenzy, rabies	سُعْر	outward, external, superficial, shallow	سَطْحِي
rate, price	سِعْر (أَسْعار)	superficially	سَطْحِيًّا
rate of interest	سِعْر التَّسْلِيف	superficiality, shallowness	سَطْحِيَّة
wholesale price	سِعْر الجُمْلَة	line, row	سَطْر (سُطُور)
discount rate, bank rate	سِعْر الخَصْم	radiance, brilliance, brightness, diffusion	سَطْع
market price	سِعْر السُّوق	thud, sound of fall	سَطَع
exchange rate	سِعْر الصَّرْف	bucket, pail	سَطْل (أَسْطال)
rate of interest	سِعْر الفَائدَة	assault, attack, burglary	سَطْو
rate of exchange	سِعْر القَطْع	influence, autority, power	سَطْوَة
rate of exchange	سِعْر الكَمْبِيو	radiance, brightness, glow	سُطُوع
palm leaves or branches	سَعَف		

quince	سَفَرْجَل	cough	سُعْلَة
nonsense, silly talk	سَفْسَفَة (سَفَاسِف)	effort, attempt, run	سَعْي
burned spot	سَفْع	happy, blissful, fortunate, auspicious	سَعِيْد (سُعَدَاء)
black spot	سُفْعَة (سُفَع)	blaze, fire, hell	سَعِيْر
shedding, pouring out	سَفْك	starvation, hunger	سَغَب /سَغَابَة
bloodshed	سَفْكُ الدِّمَاء	blood-shedder, murderer	سِفّاح
bottom, lower part, depth	سُفْل	lewdness, debauchery, fornication	سِفَاح
low, lower	سُفْلِي	embassy, mediation	سَفَارَة
stupidity, foolishness, insolence, prodigality	سَفَه	blood shedder	سَفَّاك
skewer, pin	سَفُّود (سَفَافِيْد)	baseness, meanness, lowliness	سَفَالَة
unveiling, uncovering	سُفُور	ship builder	سَفَّان
powder	سَفُوف	ship building	سِفَائَة
ambassador, intercessor	سَفِيْر (سُفَرَاء)	stupidity, silliness, impudence	سَفَاهَة
ship, boat	سَفِيْنَة (سَفُن)	foot of a mountain	سَفْح الجَبَل
spaceship	سَفِيْنَة الفَضَاء	leaving, departure	سَفْر
steamer, steamship	سَفِينة بُخَارِيّة	journey, travel	سَفَر (أَسْفَار)
cargo boat	سَفِيْنَة تِجَارِيّة	religious book, scripture	سِفْر (أَسْفَار)
battle ship	سَفِيْنَة حَرْبِيّة	trip, tour, journey	سَفَر (سَفَرَات)
sailing boat	سَفِيْنَة شِرَاعِيّة		
gun boat	سَفِيْنَة مِدْفَعِيّة	provision, dining table	سُفْرَة

loss of hair	سُقُوط الشَّعْر	foolish, stupid, insolent	سَفِيْه (سُفَهَاء)
irrigation, watering	سَقْي	scaffold	سَقَالَة
hail	سَقِيْط	illness, sickness, leanness	سَقَام
roofed gallery, shed	سَقِيْفَة (سَقَائِف)	irrigation, watering, watering place	سِقَايَة
ill, sick, lean	سَقِيْم (سِقَام/سُقَمَاء)	hell	سَقَر
lovesick	سَقِيْم الغرام	cheeping, chirping	سَقْسَقَة
reticence, silence	سُكَات	dew, hail	سَقْط
cigarette	سِكَارَة (سَكَائِر)	miscarriage, abortive	سِقْط
shoemaker, cobbler	سَكَّاف	offal, refuse, unsound	سَقَط (أَسْقَاط)
shoemaking	سِكَافَة	rubbish, trash, waste, refuse	سَقَط المَتَاع
cutler	سَكَّان	errata, misprints	سَقَطَات الطِّبَاعَة
pouring out, spilling	سَكْب	fall, slip, lapse	سَقْطَة (سَقَطَات)
silence, reticence	سَكْت	roof, ceiling	سَقْف (سُقُوف)
coin, road, street	سِكَّة (سِكَك)	palate	سَقْف الحَلْق
railroad	سِكَّة الحَدِيد	sickness, illness	سَقَم/سُقْم (أَسْقَام)
coulter, plough iron	سِكَّة المِحْرَاث		
stroke, apoplexy, seizure	سَكْتَة	fall, downfall, collapse, decline	سُقُوط
drunkenness	سُكْر		
sugar	سُكَّر		
raw sugar	سُكَّر خام		
powdered sugar	سُكَّر نَاعِم	rainfall	سُقُوط الأَمْطار

consumption	سُل/سِل	intoxicated,	سَكْران (سُكارَى)
tuberculosis	سِلّ تَدَرُّني	inebriated, drunk	
pulmonary consumption	سِلّ رِئَوي	inebriety, intoxication	سَكْرَة (سَكَرات)
basket	سَل/سَلّة (سِلال)	death pang, agony of death	سَكْرَة المَوْت
mourning clothes, black clothes	سِلاب (سُلُب)	secretary	سكْرتير
weapon, arm	سِلاح (أَسْلِحة)	secretary general	سكْرتير عامّ
armour, defensive arm	سِلاح الدِّفاع	secretariat	سكْرتيريّة
air force	سِلاحُ الطَّيَران	sugary, saccharine	سُكَّري
cavalry	سِلاح الفُرْسان	dwelling, dwelling place, abode	سَكَن
firearm	سِلاح ناري	legal residence	سَكَن شَرْعي
armourer	سِلاحي	dwelling, inhabiting	سُكْنَى
salad	سَلاطة	silence, reticence	سُكُوت
impudence, glibness, sauciness	سَلاطة	reticent, taciturn, silent	سَكُوت
scurrility, foul-mouthedness	سَلاقة	reticent, taciturn, silent	سُكُوتي
fluency, pliability, tractability	سَلالة	stillness, silence, quiescence	سُكُون
offspring, progeny, family, lineage	سُلالة (سُلالات)	taciturn, habitually silent	سِكِّيت
fluency, smoothness	سَلالة الكَلام	drunkard, hard drinker	سِكِّير
genealogical, family	سُلالي	knife	سِكِّين (سَكاكين)
		quietude, peace tranquillity, calmness	سَكِينة (سَكائن)

cascade, fresh water سَلْسَل	peace, peacefulness, سَلَام intactness
chain, train, (سَلَاسِل) سِلْسِلَة series	greeting, (سَلَامَات) سَلَام salutation
chain of سِلْسِلَة الجِبَال mountains	military salute سَلَام عَسْكَرِي
backbone سِلْسِلَة الظَّهْر	intactness, safety, سَلَامَة security, faultlessness
pedigree, سَلْسَلَة النَّسَب ancestral lineage, family tree	good taste سَلَامَة الذَّوْق
spine, vertebral سِلْسِلَة فَقَارِية column	sincerity, سَلَامَة النِّيَّة simplicity, artlessness
vertebral column سِلْسِلَة فَقْرِيّة	plundering, robbing, سَلْب negation
authority, power, سُلْطَان dominion	loot, booty, (أَسْلَاب) سَلَب offal
ruler, (سَلَاطِين) سُلْطَان sovereign	negative, negatory سَلْبِي
imperial, royal سُلْطَانِي	basket (سِلَال) سَلَّة
jacket سُلْطَة	wastebasket سَلَّة المُهْمَلَات
salad سَلَطَة	turnip سَلْجَم
authority, (سُلْطَات/سُلَط) سُلْطَة power, influence	excrements, dung سَلْح
legislative سُلْطَة تَشْرِيعِيَّة power	tortoise, (سَلَاحِف) سُلَحْفَاة turtle
executive power سُلْطَة تَنْفِيذِيَّة	skinning, flaying, سَلْخ detaching
military سُلْطَة عَسْكَرِية authority	smooth, fluent, سَلِس compliant
judicial power سُلْطَة قَضَائِيَّة	tractable, docile سَلِس القِيَاد
	a spring in Paradise سَلْسَبِيل

peace, tranquillity, quietude, safety	سِلْم/سَلَم	local authorities	سُلْطَة مَحَلِّيَّة
step, stair	سُلَّمَة	absolute power	سُلْطَة مُطْلَقَة
peaceful, pacifistic	سِلْمي	sultanate	سَلْطَنَة
cylinder	سِلِنْدَر	crack, fissure, chap	سَلْع (سُلُوع)
consolation, comfort, oblivion	سُلْوَان	commodity, articles	سِلْعَة (سِلَع)
distraction, diversion, pastime	سُلْوَة	brother-in-law	سِلْف (أَسْلَاف)
behaviour, conduct, attitude	سُلُوك	in advance, forehand	سَلَفًا
solace, consolation, ease	سَلْوَى	sulphate	سُلْفات
quail	سَلْوَى (سَلَاوَى)	loan	سُلْفَة (سُلَف)
stolen, looted	سَلِيْب	inner sole	سُلْفَة الحِذَاء
skinned, flayed, vapid	سَلِيْخ	thread, string, wire	سِلْك (أَسْلَاك)
impudent, saucy, glib	سَلِيْط	ground wire	سِلْك أَرْضِي
instinct, intuition	سَلِيْقَة (سَلَائِق)	filament	سِلْك حَرَارِي
descendant, scion, unsheathed, drawn	سَلِيْل	diplomatic corps	سِلْك سِيَاسِي
		wire rope, cable	سِلْك مَبْرُوم
sound, safe, healthy, faultless	سَلِيْم	antenna, aerial	سِلْك هَوَائِي
sane, sound in mind	سَلِيْم العَقْل	thread, string, wire	سِلْكَة (سِلَك)
		wire (adj)	سِلْكي
sincere, artless, undesigning	سَلِيْم النِّيَّة	ladder, staircase	سُلَّم (سَلَالَم)
		escalator	سُلَّم مُتَحَرِّك
		escalator	سُلَّم مِيْكَانِيْكي

rough, awkward, ugly	سَمْج/سَمِج	poison, venom	سَمّ (سُمُوم)
kindness, tolerance, liberality	سَمْح	deadly poison	سُمّ زُعَاف
generous, liberal, kind	سَمْح (سِمَاح)	deadly poison	سَمّ قَاضٍ
pleasing chat, evening chat	سَمَر (أَسْمَار)	sky, heaven, firmament	سَمَاء (سَمَاوَات)
brown, dark (fem. of أَسْمَر)	سَمْرَاء	heavenly, celestial	سَمَائي/سَمَاوِي
brownness	سُمْرَة	ugliness, rudeness, roughness	سَمَاجَة
broker, agent	سِمْسَار (سَمَاسِرَة)	generosity, kindness, liberality, permission	سَمَاح
stockbroker	سِمْسَار الأَسْهُم	magnificence, tolerance, kindness	سَمَاحَة
brokerage	سَمْسَرة	fertilizer, manure	سَمَاد (أَسْمِدَة)
hearing, audition	سَمْع	table, table clothe	سِمَاط
reputation, fame	سُمْعَة	hearing, listening	سَمَاع
good repute	سُمْعَة حَمِيدَة	receiver, earphone	سَمَّاعَة
evil reputation, infamy	سُمْعَة سَيِّئَة	audible, acoustic	سَمَاعِي
acoustic, auditory	سَمْعِي	fisherman	سَمَّاك
roof, ceiling	سَمْك	thickness	سَمَاكَة
thickness	سُمْك	butter merchant	سَمَّان
fish	سَمَك (سَمَكَة)	mark, stamp, impression	سِمَة (سِمَات)
tinsmithing	سَمْكَرَة	way, path, manner, mode	سَمْت (سُمُوت)
tinsmith, tinker	سَمْكَري		

سِنّ التَّقَاعُد	superannuation age, age of retirement	سَمَل (أَسْمال)	tatters, rags
سِنّ الرُّشْد	majority, full age	سَمْن (سُمُون)	cooking butter
سَنّ الشَّرَائِع	enactment of laws	سَمَن/سِمْنَة	fatness, fleshiness
سِنّ الفِيل	tusk, ivory	سمنتو	cement
سِنُّ القَلَم	tip, point	سُمُوّ	height, highness, loftiness, eminence
سِنّ اللَّبَن	milk tooth	سُمُوّ الأَخْلاَق	nobility of character
سِنّ اليَأْس	climacteric, menopause	سَمُوق	lofty, towering
سَنَاء	sublimity, splendour	سَمُوم (سَمَائِم)	hot wind, simoom
سِنَّارَة (سَنَانِير)	fishhook	سَمِيّ	elevated, exalted, lofty
سَنَام (أَسْنِمَة)	hump	سَمِيج (سِمَاج)	ugly, clumsy, disgusting
سِنَان (أَسِنَّة)	spearhead	سَمِيح (سُمَحَاء)	liberal, generous, tolerant
سُنْبُل (سَنَابِل)	ear of a corn, spike	سَمِير	entertainer, jovial partner
سِنْت	cent	سَمِيرَة	woman entertainer or companion
سِنَة	slumber, doze, sleep	سَمِيع (سُمَعَاء)	hearer, listener
سُنَّة (سُنَن)	law, tradition, practice	سَمِيك	thick
سَنَة (سِنُون/سَنَوات)	year	سَمِين (سِمَان)	fat, fleshy, corpulent
سَنَة دِرَاسِيَّة	academic year	سِنّ (أَسْنَان)	tooth, age
سَنَة شَمْسِيَّة	solar year	سِنّ الإِدْرَاك	maturity, age of discretion
سَنَة ضَوْئِيَّة	light-year		
سَنَة قَمَرِيَّة	lunar year		

insomnia, sleeplessness سُهَار	leap year	سَنَة كَبِيسَة
insatiable thirst سُهَاف	fiscal year	سَنَة مَالِيَّة
wakefulness, vigilance سَهَر	Christian ear	سَنَة مِيلَادِيَّة
watchful, awake سَهْرَان	centimetre	سِنْتِمِتْر
evening party سَهْرَة	squirrel	سِنْجَاب
easy, simple, plain, level سَهْل	ash-coloured	سِنْجَابِي اللَّوْن
level ground, plain سَهْل (سُهُول)	weight	سَنْجَة (سِنَج)
easy to handle سَهْل الاِسْتِعْمَال	rancid, fusty	سَنِخ
tractable, docile سَهْل المَرَاس	rancidity, fustiness	سَنَخ/سَنَاخة
attainable, within reach, easy to get سَهْل المَنَال	support, stay, prop	سَنَد (أَسْنَاد)
easily digested, digestible سَهْل الهَضْم	documents, papers	سَنَد (سَنَدات)
arrow, share, portion سَهْم (أَسْهُم)	sarsenet, silk brocade سُنْدُس	
rocket سَهْم نَارِي	tinsmith, tinker	سَنْكَرِي (سَنَاكِرَة)
forgetfulness, negligence, inadvertence سَهْو	cat	سِنَّور (سَنَانِير)
inattententively, negligently سَهْوًا	annual, yearly	سَنَوِي
	yearly, annually	سَنَوِيًّا
forgetful, absent minded, inadvertent سَهْوَان	splendid, sublime, brilliant	سَنِيّ
facility, convenience, easiness سُهُولة	splendour, brilliance	سَنًى/سَنًا
	sleeplessness, insomnia	سُهَاد/سُهْد

disgrace, shame, shameful deed, private parts	سَوْءَة/سَوْأَة
equity, equality, fairness	سَوَاء
straight path	سَوَاء السَّبِيل
equally, indiscriminately	سَوَاء بِسَوَاء
tourist, traveller	سَوّاح
blackness, majority	سَوَاد
the great majority, the mass	سَوَاد أَعْظَم
eyeball	سَوَاد العَيْن
suburbs, outskirts	سَوَاد المَدِيْنَة
the masses, the common people	سَوَاد النَّاس
bracelet, armlet	سِوَار/سُوَار (أَسْوِرَة)
driver	سَوّاق (سَوّاقُون)
toothbrush, toothstick	سِوَاك
black (fem. of أَسْوَد)	سَوْدَاء
melancholic, depressed	سَوْدَاوِي
fence, wall, railing	سُوْر (أَسْوَار)
violence, vehemence, intensity	سَوْرَة

evil, ill, mischief, misfortune, iniquity	سُوْء (أَسْوَاء)
mismanagement, maladministration	سُوْء الإِدَارَة
misuse, abuse	سُوْء الاِسْتِعْمَال
bad luck, misfortune	سُوْء البَخْت
misbehaviour	سُوْء التَّصَرُّف
malnutrition	سُوْء التَّغْذِيَة
misunderstanding	سُوْء التَّفَاهُم
bad luck, misfortune	سُوْء الحَظّ
ill-nature, bad temper	سُوْء الخَلْق
ill-temper, ill nature	سُوْء الخُلُق
misbehaviour, misconduct	سُوْء السُّلُوك
suspicion, mistrust, bad opinion	سُوْء الظَّنّ
misunderstanding, misapprehension	سُوْء الفَهْم
evil intention	سُوْء القَصْد
mistreatment	سُوْء المُعَامَلَة
evil intent	سُوْء النِّيَّة
indigestion	سُوْء الهَضْم

small market	سُوَيْقة	سُورَة (سُوَر)	Surah, chapter of the Holy Quran
similar, equal	سِيّ (أَسْوَاء)	سَوْرَة البَرْد	intensity of cold
evil, ill, bad	سَيِّئ	سُوسَة (سِيسَان)	mouthworm, woodworm
ill-bred	سَيِّئُ التَّرْبِية	سَوْسَن	lily
unlucky, unfortunate	سَيِّئ الحَظّ	سَوْط (أَسْوَاط/سِيَاط)	whip, scourge, lash
ill-natured, ill-tempered	سَيِّئ الخُلُق	سُوفِسْطَائِي	sophistic
ill-natured, ill-tempered	سَيِّئ الخُلُق	سُوفِيَات	Soviet
infamous, ill-reputed	سَيِّئ السُّمْعَة	سُوفِيَاتِي	Soviet
unlucky, unfortunate	سَيِّئ الطَّالِع	سَوْق	driving, conscription
ill-tempered, ill-natured, ill-disposed	سَيِّء الطَّبْع	سُوق (أَسْواق)	market, bazaar
sin, misdeed, offence	سَيِّئة (سَيِّئَات)	سُوق أَسْوَد	black market
fence, hedge, enclosure	سِيَاج (أَسْيَاج)	سُوق حُرَّة	free market
tourist, traveller	سَيَّاح	سُوق خَيْرِية	charity bazaar
tour, travel, tourism	سِيَاحَة	سُوق دَوْرِية	periodical market
sovereignty, rule, dominion	سِيَادَة	سُوقِي	common, vulgar
circulating, moving	سَيَّار	سِوَى	except, save
car, motorcar	سَيَّارة (سَيَّارَات)	سَوِيّ (أَسْوِيَاء)	right, straight, intact, even
		سُوًى/سِوًى	equality, sameness
		سَوِيًّا/سَوِيَّة	jointly, together
		سَوِيق	fine flour

سَيِّدَة (سَيِّدَات) mistress, lady	سَيَّارَة الأُجْرَة taxi cab
سَيِّدَتي madam	سَيَّارَة الإِسْعَاف ambulance
سَيِّدي sir	سَيَّارَة الشَحْن truck, lorry
سَيْر walk, march, travel, trip	سَيَّارَة النَّقْل truck, lorry
سِيْرَة (سِيَر) conduct, behaviour, biography	سَيَّارَة دَوْرِيَة patrol car
سِيْرك circus	سَيَّارَة مُدَرَّعَة armoured car
سَيْطَرَة domination, power, supremacy, rule	سَيَّارَة مُصَفَّحَة armoured car
سِيْف seaside	سِيَاسَة administration, policy
سَيْف (سُيُوف/أَسْيَاف) sword, sabre	سِيَاسَة التَّوَسُّع policy of expansion
سيفون siphon	سِيَاسَة التَّوْسِيْع policy of expansion
سِيْكارة (سَكَائِر) cigarette	سِيَاسَة عَمَلِيّة practical policy
سِيْكُورتاه insurance, assurance	سِيَاسِي political, diplomatic
سيكورتاه الحَرِيْق fire insurance	سِيَاسِي (سَاسَة) politician, statesman, diplomat
سيكورتاه الحياة life insurance	سَيَّاف swordsman, executioner
سيكولوجي psychologic-al	
سَيْكُولوجِيَا psychology	سَيَّالَة rivulet, water course
سَيْل (سُيُول) flood, torrent, rushing stream	سِيْجار cigar
سَيَلَان flowing, running	سِيْجَارَة (سَجَائِر) cigarette
سَيْلَة water course, runlet, stream	سِيْخ skewer, spit, bar
سِيْما/سِيْمَاء mark, sign	سَيِّد (سَادَة) chief, head, lord, master

thorny, spiny, spiky شَائك	cinema, motion سِيْنما picture
disgraceful, شَائن dishonourable	sound film سِيْنما صَائتَة/نَاطقة
disformed, disfigured, شَائه ugly	silent film سِيْنما صَامَتَة
youthful, young (شُبّان) شَابّ	cinematic, actor سِيْنمائي
young woman, (شَوَابّ) شَابة maiden	cinematograph سِيْنماتوغراف
	liquidity, fluidity سُيُولَة
sheep, ewe (شِيَاه) شَاة/شاء	
pale, (شَوَاحِب) شَاحِب pallied, wan	
far, remote, distant شَاحط	root شَأْفَة
loaded, freighted شَاحن	evil omen, bad luck شُؤْم
truck, lorry شَاحنَة	affair, concern, (شُؤُون) شَأْن condition, relation
glazed, fixed شَاخص	social affairs شُؤُون اجْتماعيّة
educated, trained شَاد	grey-haired, white- شَائب haired
warehouse, tent شَادِر	
singer, songster شَادِيَة	suspicion, (شَوَائب) شَائبَة blemish, effect, fault
abnormal, rare, (شَوَاذّ) شَاذّ unusual, curious, peculiar	wide-spread, شَائع circulated, common
eccentric, شَاذّ الأَطْوَار peculiar	widespread, شَائع الذُّيُوع widely-known
eccentric, crazy شَاذّ الطَّبْع	rumour, (شَوَائع) شَائعَة hearsay
mustache (شَوَارِب) شَارِب	
mark, token, (شَارَات) شَارَة sign	stimulating, desire, شَائق desirable

poet شَاعِر (شُعَراء)	sign of the cross شَارَة الصَّليب
poet- laureate شَاعِر الدَّوْلَة	commentator, شَارِح explainer, expounder
vacant, unoccupied, شَاغِر empty	fugitive, شَارِد (شَوَارِد) runaway, astray
preoccupation, (شَوَاغِل) شَاغِل distraction, concern	distracted, شَارِد الفِكْر absent-minded
curative, tending to شَافٍ cure, satisfactory	anomaly, شَارِدَة (شَوَارِد) peculiarity
pre-emptor, mediator, شَفِيع intercessor	legislator, law-maker شَارِع
tedious, hard, tiresome, شَاقّ troublesome	street شَارِع (شَوَارِع)
doubtful, skeptical, شَاكّ complainant, plaintiff	commercial شَارِع تِجَارِي street
thankful, grateful شَاكِر	main street, شَارِع رَئِيْسِي thoroughfare
manner, mode, flank شَاكِلَة	public street, شَارِع عَامّ thoroughfare
hammer شاكوش (شَوَاكِيش)	distant, remote, far شَاسِع away
shawl شَال (شِيْلان)	muslin, white cloth شَاشَة
shooting, lodge, شَاليه cabana	screen شَاشَة بَيْضَاء
sense of smell, شَامَّة olfaction	beach, shore, (شَوَاطِئ) شَاطِئ coast
mole, beauty شَامَة (شَامَات) spot, birth mark	seashore, coast شَاطِئُ الْبَحْر
malicious, شَامِت (شَوَامِت) malevolent	cunning, crafty, شَاطِر shrewd

شَبَح الحَرْب	war-cloud
شَبَح الخَوْف	spectre of fear
شِبْر (أَشْبَار)	span, span of hand
شِبْراً فَشِبْراً	inch by inch
شَبْرَقَة	pocket money
شِبْشِب (شَبَاشب)	slipper, mule
شَبَع	satisfaction, satiety, saturation
شِبْع	thing that fills or satisfies
شَبْعان	satisfied, full
شَبَق	lust, lewdness, licentiousness
شَبِق	lewd, lustful, lecherous
شَبَكَة	snare, net, network
شَبَكَة لاَسلْكِيّة	radio network
شَبَكي	reticular, retinal
شِبْه/شَبَه (أَشْبَاه)	resemblance, similarity, likeness, portrait
شِبْه الكُرَة	globoid, spheroid
شِبْهُ جَزِيرة	peninsula
شِبْه قَارّة	subcontinent
شُبْهَة (شُبْهات/شُبُهات)	doubt, suspicion, obscurity

شَامِخ (شَوَامخ)	lofty, high, towering
شَامِخ الأَنْف	haughty, arrogant, proud
شَامس	sunny, exposed to sun
شَامل	comprehensive, comprising, general
شَاهد (شُهُود)	witness, present
شَاهد (شَوَاهد)	evidence, testimony, attention
شَاهد السَّمْع	ear witness
شَاهد العَيْن/العِيَان	eyewitness
شَاهد عِيَاني	eyewitness
شَاهدَة (شَوَاهد)	grave stone, tomb stone, duplicate
شَاهق (شَوَاهق)	high, lofty, elevated, height
شَاي	tea
شَبَاب	youth, youthfulness
شُبَاط	February
شُبّاك (شَبَابيك)	window, counter, net work
شُبّاك العَرْض	show window
شَبَث (شِبْثان)	spider
شَبْح/شَبَح (أَشْبَاح)	ghost, spectre, shadow

skull fracture	شَجَّة	like, similar, resembling	شَبِيه (شِبَاه)
tree, shrubs	شَجَر (أَشْجار)	dispersed, scattered	شَتّ (أَشْتات)
tree, shrub	شَجَرَة (شَجَرَات)	winter, rainy season	شِتَاء
cotton plant	شَجَرَة القُطْن	scattered, dispersed	شَتَات
genealogical tree	شَجَرَة النَّسَب	insolent, abusive	شَتّام
sorrow, grief, anxiety	شَجَن (شُجُون)	transplant, nursery plant	شَتْلَة
distress, anxiety, grief	شَجْو	abuse, insult, vilification	شَتْم
distressed, grieved, worried	شَجَوِي	hibernal, wintry	شَتْوِي/شِتَوِي
anxious, distressed, worried, pathetic	شَجِيّ	scattered, dispersed, separated	شَتِيت (شَتَّى)
shrub, bush	شُجَيْرَة	insulted, abused, reviled	شَتِيم
courageous, brave, valorous	شَجِيع (شُجَعَاء/شُجْعَان)	abuse, vituperation	شَتِيمَة (شَتَائِم)
avarice, stinginess, covetousness	شُحّ	door-bolt, quarrel, dispute	شِجَار
importunate beggar	شَحّاذ	brave, courageous, valorous	شِجَاع/شُجَاع (شُجْعان)
pappy, pulpy	شَحِم	courage, valour, bravery	شَجَاعَة
fat, grease, lubricant	شَحْم (شُحُوم)	destruction, affliction	شَجْب
pieace of suet or fat	شَحْمَة	affliction, grief, distress	شَجَب
earlobe	شَحْمَة الأُذُن		
eyeball	شَحْمَة العَين		

singing, chanting شَدْو	freight, cargo, شَحْن shipment
strong, شَديد (أَشدّاء) powerful, intense, fierce	cargo, freight, (شَحَنَات) شَحْنَة shipment, charge
highly شَديد الإحْساس sensitive	paleness, wanness شُحُوب
courageous, شَديد البَأْس valorous, brave, bold	stingy, شَحيح (أَشحّاء) niggardly, covetous, avaricious
relentless, شَديد الشَّكيمَة obstinate, stubborn, unyielding	fatty, fat, greasy شَحيم
cruel, fell, fierce شَديد الوَطْأَة	urine, piss, water شَخّ/شَخَاخ
hardship, شَديدَة (شَدائد) misery, adversity, misfortune	person, شَخْص (أَشْخَاص) individual
fragrance, scent شَذَر	personal, private شَخْصي
helter-skelter, شَذَر مَذَر dispersed and scattered	personally, in person شَخْصيًّا
fragment, شَذْرَة (شَذَرَات) small piece	personality, شَخْصيَّة individuality, identity
fragrance of musk شَذْو	magnetic شَخْصيّة جَذّابَة personality
curiosity, anomaly, شُذُوذ irregularity, eccentricity	tightness, strain, شِدَّة intensification
fragrant, aromatic شَذي	strength, intensity, شِدَّة violence, severity
evil, bad, wicked (أَشْرَار) شَرّ	adversity, شِدَّة (شَدائد) hardship, distress, calamity
evil, ill, mischief, (شُرُور) شَرّ wickedness	energy, vigour شِدَّة الأَسْر
buying, purchasing شِرَاء	inside of the cheek, شِدْق jawbone

شَرْخ (شُرُوخ)	crack, fissure, split	شَرَاب (أَشْرِبَة)	drink, syrup, beverage
شِرْذَمَة (شَرَاذِم)	group, gang, company	شَرَاب اللَّيْمُون	lemonade
شَرَر/شَرَرَة	sparks	شَرَّار	sparkling, emitting sparks
شَرِس	malicious, ferocious, mischievous	شَرَار/شَرَارَة	sparks
شَرْشَف (شَرَاشِف)	bed sheet	شَرَاسَة	malice, viciousness, ill-naturedness
شَرَط (أَشْرَاط)	sign, portent	شِرَاع (أَشْرِعَة)	sail, tent
شَرْط (شُرُوط)	condition, term, provision	شِرَاعِي	sailing, sail
شَرْطَة	dash, hyphen, stroke	شِرَاك (شُرُك)	shoelace
شُرْطَة	police, policemen	شَرَاهة	ravenousness, avidity, gluttony, greediness
شُرْطَة المُرُور	traffic police	شُرْب	drinking, absorption
شَرْطِي	conditional	شُرْبَة	drink, draught, dose
شُرْطِي	policeman	شَرَج (أَشْرَاج)	anus, loop
شَرْطِيّة	agreement, contract	شَرَجِي	anal
شَرْع	law, statute	شَرْح	explanation, commentation, description
شِرْعَة	law, revealed law	شَرْح (شُرُوح)	commentary
شَرْعِي	legal, lawful, legitimate	شَرْحَة	slice, slat, rasher
شَرْعِيًّا	lawfully, rightfully, legally	شَرْحِي	explanatory, explicatory
شَرْعِيَّة	legitimacy, legality	شَرْخ	prime of life
شَرَف	dignity, nobility, honour		

partnership, association	شِرْكَة/شَرِكَة	balcony, terrace (شُرَف)	شُرْفَة
rift, split, cleft	شَرْم (شروم)	eastward	شَرْقًا
covetousness, gluttony, greediness	شَرَه	the Middle East	شَرْق أَوْسَط
greedy, avaricious, glutton	شَرِه	east, sunrise	شَرْق
honey	شَرْو	eastern, oriental	شَرْقِي
trousers, drawers	شِرْوال (شَرَاوِيل)	polytheism, idolatry	شِرْك
deviation, straying, wandering	شُرُود	snare, trap	شَرَك/شِرَاك
fleeing, running away, astray	شُرُود (شُرُد)	company, corporation	شَرِكَة (شَرِكات)
distractedness, wandering of the thoughts	شُرُود الفِكْر	broadcasting corporation	شَرِكَة الإِذَاعَة
commencement, beginning	شُرُوع	insurance company	شَرِكَةُ التَّأْمِين
rise, shining	شُرُوق	cooperative society	شَرِكَة التَّعَاوُن
sunrise	شُرُوق الشَّمْس	insurance company	شَرِكَة الضَّمَان
purchase, buy	شِرًى (أَشْرِيَة)	limited company	شَرِكَة المُسَاهَمَة
artery	شِرْيان (شَرَايِين)	trading company, corporation, firm	شَرِكَة تِجَارِيّة
arterial	شِرْيَانِي	limited company	شَرِكَة مَحْدُودة
slice, slat, rasher	شَرِيْحَة	joint-stock company	شَرِكَة مُسَاهَمَة
fugitive, wanderer, vagrant	شَرِيد		

dividing, bisecting, halving	شَطْر
portion, half, division, direction	شَطْر (شُطُور)
chess	شَطْرَنْج
excess, encroachment	شَطَط
chip, splinter, piece	شُطْفَة
steak, sandwich	شَطِيْرَة
hard, difficult, austere	شَظِف
hardship, difficulty	شَظَف (شِظَاف)
splinter, chip, sliver	شَظِيَّة (شَظَايا)
beams, rays	شُعّ
motto, emblem, mark, characteristic	شِعَار (شُعُر)
trade mark	شِعَار تِجَاري
beams, rays, spokes	شُعَاع (أَشِعَّة)
mountain pass or trail	شِعْب (شِعَاب)
people, nation, folk	شَعْب (شُعُوب)
Shaban, name of eighth month of Islamic calendar	شَعْبَان

very bad, malicious, vicious	شِرِّير
bad, evil, wicked	شَرِير (أَشِرَّاء)
tape, ribbon, stripe, cord, lace	شَرِيط (أَشْرِطَة)
mourning band	شَرِيط الحِدَاد
tape measure	شَرِيط القِيَاس
sound film	شَرِيط نَاطِق
condition, provision	شَرِيطَة
law of Islam	شَرِيعَة
law, drinking place	شَرِيعَة (شَرَائِع)
natural law	شَرِيعَة الضَّمِير
noble, honourable, high born	شَرِيف (شُرَفاء/أَشْراف)
partner, associate, participant	شَرِيك (شُرَكاء)
askance	شَزْرًا
shore, coast	شَطّ (شُطُوط)
seashore, seacoast	شَطّ البَحْر
cunningness, shrewdness, cleverness	شَطَارَة
slash, slit, scratch, eraser	شَطْب
strapping, tall	شَطْب (شُطُوب)

شُعُور مُشْتَرَك community spirit	شُعْبَة (شِعَاب) branch, ramification, division, section, department, twig
شُعُوري conscious, emotional	شَعْبِي national, popular
شَعِير barley	شُعَبِي bronchial
شَعِيرَة (شَعَائِر) rite, religious ceremony	شَعْبِيَّة popularity
شَغَّاب troublesome, riotous	شَعِث matted, unkempt
شَغْب/شَغَب turmoil, broil, affray, disturbance	شِعْر (أَشْعَار) poem, poetry, verse
شَغَف passion, ardent love, amorousness	شَعْر/شَعَر (أَشْعَار) hair
شَغِف infatuated, enamoured	شَعْر خَشِن bristles
شُغْل distraction, detention, occupancy	شَعْر فِلْفِلِي crisp hair
	شَعْر نَاعِم glossy hair
شُغْل (أَشْغَال) work, job, occupation, business	شَعْرَة (شَعْرات) hair
شُغْل الإِبْرَة needle work, embroidery	شَعْرِي hairy, hirsute
شُغْل اليَد handwork, manual work	شِعْرِي poetic, poetical
	شَعْفَة (شِعَاف) peak, summit
شُغْل شَاقّ hard work	شُعْلَة (شُعَل) blaze, flame, fire
شُغْل يَدَوِي manual work, hand work	شَعْوَاء outspreading, devastating
شَغُوب troublous, riotous	شَعْوَذَة conjury, jugglery, magic
شُغُور vacancy, emptiness	شُعُور feeling, perception, consciousness, sensibility
شَغُوف infatuated, enamoured	شُعُور بالذَّات self-consciousness

شَفَق قُطْبِي	polar light
شَفَقَة	compassion, kindness, pity, sympathy
شَفَهِي/شِفَاهِي	labial, oral, verbal
شَفَهِيًّا/شِفَاهِيًّا	orally, verbally
شُفُوف	transparency, translucence
شَفُوق	compassionate, affectionate, sympathetic
شَفَوِي	labial, oral
شَفَوِيًّا	orally, verbally
شَفِير	edge, palpebral margin
شَفِيع (شُفَعاء)	pre-emptor, intercessor, mediator
شَفِيف	transparent, flimsy, translucent
شَفِيق	kind, compassionate, affectionate
شِقّ	side, portion, part, difficulty
شَقّ (شُقُوق)	split, fissure, rift, crack
شَقًا/شَقَاء	wretchedness, misery, misfortune, unhappiness
شِقَاق	dissension, discord, separation

شَغِيل	worker, labourer
شَفًا (أَشْفَاء)	brink, verge, edge
شِفَاء	remedy, recovery, restoration to health
شِفَاء (أَشْفِيَة)	medication, remedy
شِفَائِي	medicative, curative
شَفَّاطَة	siphon
شَفَّاطَة الغُبَار	vacuum cleaner
شَفَاعَة	intercession, mediation
شَفَّاف	transparent, flimsy, translucent
شَفَّافِيَّة	transparency, translucence
شَفَة (شفاه)	lip, edge
شَفْر	edge, edge of the eyelid
شُفْر (أَشْفَار)	edge, fringe, rim
شَفْرَة	verge, brink, blade
شِفْرَة/شِفْر	cipher, code
شَفْع	even, double
شُفْعَة	right of pre-emption
شَفَف	transparency, translucence
شَفَق	evening twilight

many thanks شُكْرًا جَزِيلًا	misery, distress, شَقَاوَة/شَقْوَة
thanks, thank you شُكْرًا لك	misfortune, nastiness
thanks, gratitude, شُكْرَان	rift, fissure, cleft, crack شَقّة
gratefulness	difficulty, toil, (شُقَق) شُقّة
surly, peevish, (شُكْس) شَكِس	hardship
petulant, malicious	flat, apartment (شقَق)شُقّة/شَقّة
figure, shape, (أَشْكَال) شَكْل	fairness, redness شَقَر/شُقْرَة
fashion, mode, form	chirping, twittering شَقْشَقَة
in form, formally شَكْلًا	peep of day, شَقْشَقَة النَّهَار
formal شَكْلِي	daybreak
complaint, grievance شَكْوَة	sherds شَقَف/شِقْفَة
very thankful, very شَكُور	somersault (شَقْلَبَات) شَقْلَبَة
grateful	miserable, (أَشْقِيَاء) شَقِيّ
chocolate شَكُولاته	wretched, distressed,
complaint, (شَكَاوَى) شَكْوَى	unhappy
grievance	full brother (أَشِقّاء) شَقِيق
complaint, grievance شَكِيّة	full sister (شَقَائِق) شَقِيقَة
obstinacy, (شَكَائِم) شَكِيمَة	doubt, suspicion, (شُكُوك) شَكّ
disdain, unyieldingness	misgiving
waterfall, cataract شَلَّال	petulance, surliness, شَكَاسَة
paralysis, palsy شَلَل	peevishness, malice
decayed limb, (أَشْلَاء) شِلْو	complaint, grievance, شِكَايَة
decayed corpse	suffering
strawberries شَلِيك	thanks, praise, (شُكُور) شُكْر
smelling, olfaction, شَمّ	gratitude
sense of smell	profuse thanks شُكْر جَزِيل

beet-root	شَمَنْدَر
olfactory	شَمِّي
making an attack	شَنَّ غَارَة
hate, strong dislike	شَنَآن/شَنَآن
ignominy, disgrace	شَنَار
ugliness, disgrace, hideousness	شَنَاعة
mustache	شَنَب (أَشْنَاب)
suitcase, bag, satchel	شَنْطَة (شُنَط)
handbag	شَنْطَة اليَد
ugly, unsightly, hideous, horried	شَنِع
ugliness, horridness, hideousness	شُنْعَة
erring	شَنَف (شُنُوف)
hanging, execution by hanging	شَنْق
rope, cord	شَنَقَ
ignominious, disgraceful, shocking, ugly	شَنِيع
meteor, falling star, blaze	شِهَاب (شُهُب)
witness, testimony, evidence, certificate, martyrdom	شَهَادة (شَهَادات)

good qualities	شَمَائِل
malicious joy, malice, malevolence	شَمَات/شَمَاتَة
wax-chandler	شَمَّاع
left, left hand	شِمَال
north, north wind	شِمَال/شَمَال
northward, to the north	شِمَالاً
northern, northerly	شِمَالِي
sweet melon	شَمَّام
fennel	شَمْرَة/شُمْرَة
sun	شَمْس (شُمُوس)
sunny, solar	شَمْسِي
sunshade, umbrella	شَمْسِيَّة
parachute	شَمْسِيَّة الطَّيَّار
sealing wax	شَمْع الخَتْم
wax, candles	شَمْع/شَمَع (شُمُوع)
wax, wax candle	شَمْعَة/شَمَعَة
candlestick	شَمْعَدَان
waxy, waxen	شَمْعِي/شَمَعِي
unity, union	شَمْل
superciliousness, haughtiness, disdain	شَمَم

monthly, per month	شَهْرِيًّا	primary certificate	شَهَادة اِبْتِدائية
monthly salary	شَهْرِية	marriage lines	شَهَادة الزَّوَاج
whoop, moaning, groaning	شَهْقَة	false testimony	شَهَادة الزُّور
quick, nimble, expeditious	شَهِل	birth certificate	شَهَادة الوِلَادَة
audacious, gallant, astute, shrewd	شَهْم (شِهَام)	certificate of good conduct	شَهَادَة حُسْن السُّلُوك
lecherous, lewd, lustful, covetous	شَهْوَان	irrefutable testimony	شَهَادة دَامِغة
lustful, covetous, lascivious	شَهْوَاني	diploma	شَهَادة عَالِية
passion, lust, longing, appetite, carnal appetite	شَهْوَة	sagacity, audacity, gallantry, boldness	شَهَامَة
bestial passion	شَهْوَة بَهِيمِيَّة	grayness, gray colour	شَهَب/شُهْبَة
tasty, agreeable, desirable, appetizing	شَهِيّ	honey, honey-comb	شُهْد/شَهْد (شِهَاد)
appetite	شَهِيَّة	month, publication	شَهْر (شُهُور/أَشْهُر)
witness, martyr	شَهِيد (شُهَدَاء)	next month	شَهْر آتٍ
famous, renowned, celebrated	شَهِير	honeymoon	شَهْر العَسَل
bray, sigh, sob, inhalation	شَهِيق	lunar month	شَهْر قَمَرِي
grilled meat	شِوَاء/شُوَاء	lunar month	شَهْر هِلَالِي
anomalies of a language	شَوَارِد اللُّغَة	reputation, fame, renown, popularity	شُهْرَة
		world-wide fame	شُهْرَة عَالَمِيّة
		monthly, every month	شَهْرِي

grilled, roasted ‏ شَوِي	disorder, confusion, ‏ شَوَاش
a little, a bit ‏ شُوَيَّة	muddle
thing, something (أَشْيَاء) شَيْء	blaze, flame, passion ‏ شُوَاظ
gradually, little by شَيْئًا فَشَيْئًا	Shawwal, name of the ‏ شَوَّال
little	tenth month of Islamic
community ‏ شِيَاع	calendar
porter, carrier ‏ شَيَّال	grill, gridiron ‏ شَوَّايَة
hoariness, greyness of ‏ شَيْب	mixture, blemish, hot ‏ شَوْب
the hair, old age	wind, sirocco
mottle, spot, (شِيَات) شِيَة	soup ‏ شُورْبة/شُورْبا
mark, blemish	counsel, advice, ‏ شُورَى
shaikh, chief, old man ‏ شَيْخ	consultation, suggestion
chief of a tribe ‏ شَيْخ القَبِيلَة	advisory, consultative شُورِي
old age, senility ‏ شَيْخُوخَة	lock, tuft ‏ شُوْشَة
satan, devil (شَيَاطِين) شَيْطان	object, aim, (أَشْواط) شُوْط
satanic, demonic, ‏ شَيْطانِي	round, distance
devilish	longing, strong (أَشْواق) شَوْق
the Shiites ‏ شِيعَة	desire, craving
sect, faction, (شِيَع) شِيعَة	thorns, spines, (أَشْواك) شَوْك
denomination	prickles
disciples, ‏ شِيعَة الرَّجُل	thorn, prick, spike, ‏ شَوْكَة
followers	prong
sectarian, Shiitic ‏ شِيعِي	thorny, spiky, spiny ‏ شَوْكِي
chiffon ‏ شِيفُون	garner, granary (شُوَن) شُوْنَة
desirous, yearning, ‏ شَيِّق	beet root, chard ‏ شَوَنْدَر
covetous	disfigurement, ugliness, ‏ شَوَه
	deformity, distortion

patient, enduring	صَابِر	cheque	شِيْك (شِيْكات)
dyer, Baptist	صَابِغ	traveller's cheque	شِيْك السِّيَاحَة
soap	صَابُون	chocolate	شيكولاته
shaving soap	صَابُون الحِلَاقَة	load, burden	شَيْلَة (شَيْلات)
soap-ball, a cake of soap	صَابُونَة	disposition, nature, habit	شِيمَة (شِيَم)
soapy, saponaceous	صَابُونِي	whirlpool, vortex	شِيْمِيَّة (شِيَامِي)
cloudless, bright, serene	صَاحٍ	disgrace, dishonour, bad	شَيْن
wakeful, vigilant, conscious	صَاحٍ (صُحَاة)	publicity, circulation	شُيُوع
companion, friend, associate	صَاحِب (أَصْحَاب/صُحُب)	communist, communistic	شُيُوعِي
employer	صَاحِب الأَعْمَال	communism	شُيُوعِيَّة
ruler, master, boss	صَاحِب الأَمْر		
His Majesty	صَاحِب الجَلَالَة	appropriate, right, correct, apposite	صَائِب
creditor	صَاحِب الدَّيْن	sound, of sound	صَائِت
His Excellency	صَاحِب السَّعَادَة	goldsmith, jeweller	صَائِغ (صَاغَة)
His Eminence	صَاحِب السَّمَاحَة	fasting, one who fasts	صَائِم (صُوَّم)
artisan, craftsman	صَاحِب الصَّنَائِع	keeper, preserver, protective	صَائِن
craftsman, artisan	صَاحِب الصَّنْعَة	juvenile, youthful	صَابٍ

صَاعَة	salon, parlour
صَاعِد	ascending, rising
صَاعِقَة (صَوَاعِق)	thunderbolt, lightning
صَاغ	proper, right, standard
صَاغٍ	disposed, attentive, hearkener
صَاغِر	low, servile, humiliated
صَافٍ	clear, pure, limpid, sheer
صَافِي النِّيَّة	sincere, honest, candid
صَالَة (صَالَات)	hall, large room
صَالَة رَقْص	dancing hall
صَالِح	good, pious, valid, efficient, usable
صَالِح (صَوَالِح)	good, benefit, advantage, welfare
صَالِح عَامّ	public welfare
صَالِح لِلزَّوَاج	marriageable
صَالِحات	good deeds
صَالُون	saloon, parlour
صَالُون الحِلَاقَة	barbershop
صَامِت	silent, quiet

صَاحِب العَظَمَة	His Highness
صَاحِب العَمَل	employer
صَاحِب الفَضْل	meritorious
صَاحِب الفِكْر	originator of an idea
صَاحِب المَعَالِي	His Excellency
صَاحِب المَنْزِل	landlord
صَاحِبَة (صَوَاحِب)	woman companion, girl friend
صَاحِبَة الجَلَالَة	Her Majesty
صَاخِب	clamorous, noisy, vociferous
صَادِر	issued, come out, exported
صَادِرات	exports, exported goods
صَادِق	truthful, faithful, sincere, genuine
صَارِم	hard, harsh, severe, violent
صَارُوخ (صَوَارِيخ)	rocket
صَارِي العَلَم	flag pole
صَارِي/صَارِيَة (صَوَارٍ)	mast, pole
صَاع	measure of capacity
صَاعًا بِصَاع	tit for tat

pretty, graceful صَبْحَان	maker, worker (صُنَّاع) صَانِع manufacturer, craftsman
breakfast, morning meal صُبْحَة	shoemaker صَانِع الأَحْذِيَة
beautiful صَبْحَى (fem. of صبحان)	pouring out, effusion, صَبّ gush, casting
patience, endurance, صَبْر perseverance	east wind (أَصْبَاء) صَبًا
heap, pile صُبْرَة	boyhood, صِبًا/صَبَاء childhood, youth
dye, colour, (أَصْبَاغ) صِبْغ paint, stain	ardent love, strong صَبَابَة longing
dye, colour, tincture, صِبْغَة paint, baptism	morning صَبَاح
tincture of صِبْغَة الأَفِيون opium	beautiful, pretty, صُبَاح handsome
tincture of iodine صِبْغَة اليُود	good morning صَبَاح الخَيْر
chromosomes (صِبْغِيَّات) صِبْغِي	this morning صَبَاح اليَوْم
yearning, longing, صُبُوّ youthful passion	in the morning صَبَاحاً
longing, yearning, صَبْوَة passion, sensual desire	grace, beauty, صَبَاحَة comliness
boyhood, childhood, صُبُوَّة youth	perseverant, very صَبَّار patient
enduring, steadfast, صَبُور long suffering	severe cold صَبَارَة
	dyer, tinter صَبَّاغ
boy, youth (صِبْيَان/صِبْيَة) صَبِيّ	dye, dyestuff, (أَصْبِغَة) صِبَاغ colour
boyish, childish صِبْيَانِي	dying, tinting صِبَاغَة
poured out, shed, blood صَبِيب	morning, (أَصْبَاح) صُبْح daybreak

صَحْن الدَّار	courtyard, patio	صَبِيَّة (صَبَايَا)	young girl, maid, lass
صَحْن السَّجَائِر	ashtray	صَبِيح (صِبَاح)	beautiful, handsome, comely
صَحْو	cloudless, clarity, cloudlessness	صَبِيحَة	morning, forenoon
صَحْوَة	consciousness, wakefulness	صَحَابَة	companions of the Prophet
صِحِّي	sanitary, hygienic, healthful	صَحَابِي	companion of the Prophet
صَحِيح (صِحَاح)	right, correct, genuine, sound, authentic	صِحَافَة	journalism, press
صُحَيْفَة	saucer	صِحَافِي	newsman, journalist
صَحِيفَة (صُحُف)	newspaper, journal, surface	صِحَافِي مُحْتَرِف	professional journalist
صَخَّاب	boisterous, clamorous, roaring	صُحْبَة	company, friendship, companionship, association
صَخَب	clamour, crying, shouting, yelling	صِحَّة	health, soundness, rightness, reality, authenticity
صَخِب	clamorous, noisy, boisterous, yelling	صَحْرَاء (صَحْرَاوَات)	desert, steppe
صَخِر	stony, rocky	صَحْرَاوِي	desolate, desert
صَخْر (صُخُور)	rocks, boulders	صَحْفَة (صِحَاف)	bowl, dish, trencher
صَخْرَة	rock, boulder	صُحُفِي	journalist, journalistic
صَخْرِي	rocky, stony	صَحْن (صُحُون)	plate, dish, surface
صَدّ	resistance, repulsion, checking, hindering		
صَدَأ	rust, smut		

accidentally, by chance	صُدْفَةً	rusty, shabby	صَدِئ
chance, accident, coincidence	صُدْفَة (صُدَف)	echo, resounding	صَدًا/صَدًى (أَصْدَاء)
truth, truthfulness, faithfulness, sincerity	صِدْق	rust, rustiness	صَدَاءَة
verily, truly, really	صِدْقًا	waistcoat, bodice	صِدَار/صُدْرَة
alms, charity	صَدَقَة (صَدَقَات)	presidency, chairmanship	صَدَارَة
blow, shock, jolt, concussion	صَدْمَة (صَدَمَات)	headache	صُدَاع
appearance, issuance	صُدُور	marriage contract	صِدَاق/صَدَاق (أَصْدِقَة)
true, truthful, sincere	صَدُوق	bridal dower	صِدَاق/صَدَاق (صُدُق)
matter, suppuration	صَدِيد	friendship, intimacy	صَدَاقَة
purulent, suppurative	صَدِيدِي	banner	صَدَح
righteous, just, upright	صِدِّيق	respect, regard, object, end	صَدَد
friend, true friend	صَدِيق (أَصْدِقاء)	chest, breast, bosom, part, beginning	صَدْر (صُدُور)
clarity, plainness, unambiguousness, frankness	صَرَاحَة	daybreak	صَدْر النَّهَار
clearly, openly, frankly, unambiguously	صَرَاحَةً	break, cleft, fissure, split	صَدْع (صُدُوع)
shouting, crying, screams	صُرَاخ	temple, earlock	صُدْغ (أَصْدَاغ)
cricket	صَرّار	temporal	صُدْغِي
		shells, sea shells	صَدَف (أَصْدَاف)

shout, screams, shriek صَرِيخ	path, way, road صِرَاط
squeaking, chirping صَرِير	wrestling, fighting صِرَاع
epileptic, felled صَرِيع	money changer, banker, cashier صَرَّاف
difficult, hard, ardulous صَعْب	vigour, sharpness, severity صَرَامَة
hard to please, fastidious صَعْب الإِرْضَاء	bundle, packet, wrapper (صُرَر) صُرَّة
insupportable, unbearable صَعْب الاحْتِمال	cash remittance صُرَّة النُّقُود
intractable, refractory صَعْب المَرَاس	palace, castle, edifice (صُرُوح) صَرْح
unattainable, hard to get صَعْب المَنَال	shout, shouting, outcry, yell صَرْخَة
height, altitude صُعْد	cricket صَرْصَار
thunder صَعَق	turning away, changing, spending, expenditure صَرْف
thunderstruck, dumfounded صَعِق	mere, pure, unadulterated صِرْف
pauper, beggar, vagabond (صَعَالِيك) صُعْلُوك	money changing صَرْفُ النُّقُود
difficulty, hardship صُعُوبَة	severance, cutting away صَرْم
ascent, ascending, rising صُعُود	vicissitudes of time, adversities صُرُوف الدَّهْر
upland, high land (صُعُد) صَعِيد	clear, obvious, frank, pure صَرِيح
trivialities, trifles صَغَائِر	self-evident صَرِيح بِذَاتِه
smallness, paltriness, lowliness صَغَارَة	

warning siren صَفَّارَة الإنْذَار	smallness, paltriness, صِغَر insignificance
quality, attribute, (صِفَات) صِفَة description, adjective	youthfulness, صِغَر السِّنّ juvenility
distinguishing صِفَة مُمَيِّزَة quality	smaller, younger صُغْرَى (fem. of أَصْغَر)
forgiveness, pardon, صَفْح surface	inclination, disposition صَغْو
page, sheet, (صَفَحَات) صَفْحَة surface	small, young, (صِغَار) صَغِير insignificant, paltry
title page صَفْحَة العُنْوَان	young, juvenile صَغِير السِّنّ
fetters, shackles (أَصْفَاد) صَفَد	mean-spirited, صَغِير النَّفْس low-minded
brass, bronze صُفْر	venial sin صَغِيرَة (صَغَائِر)
Safar, name of the صَفَر second month of Islamic calendar	arranging, putting in صَفّ order
empty-handed صِفْر اليَدَيْن	line, row, queue (صفوف) صَفّ
empty, void, صُفْر/صَفْر/صِفْر vacant, nothing, zero	blood group صَفّ الدَّم
gall, bile صَفْرَاء	rocks, صَفَا/صَفَاة (صَفَوات) stones
choleric, bilious صَفْرَاوِي	clarity, clearness, صَفَاء purity, sincerity
yellowness, paleness صُفْرَة	door panel صَفَائِح المِصْرَاع
desolate, waste, صَفْصَف barren	fetters, bond صِفَاد
slap, spank, blow صَفْعَة	hand cuff صِفَاد اليَد
clap of hands, (صَفَقَات) صَفْقَة bargain, deal	whistle, صَفَّارَة (صَفَّارَات) siren

burnishing, polishing صَقْل	bad bargain صَفْقَة خَاسِرَة
polishing of صَقْل الأَذْهان minds	good bargain صَفْقَة رَابِحَة
frost, ice صَقِيع	clearness, sincerity, صَفْو cloudlessness, serenity
burnished, shining, صَقِيل polished	choice, select, صَفْوَة/صُفْوَة cream
document, (صُكُوك) صَكّ deed, title-deed	forgiving, ready to صَفُوح pardon
insurance policy صَكُّ التَّأْمِين	pure, clear, cloudless, صَفِي limpid
hardness, rigidity, صَلَابَة solidity, firmness	bosom friend, (أَصْفِيَاء) صَفِي best friend
salat, (صَلَوَات) صَلَاة/صلوة Islamic prayer	lion's share (صَفَايَا) صَفِيَّة
morning prayer صَلَاةُ الصُّبْح	broadside, tinplate صَفِيح
goodness, rightness, صَلَاح fitness, piety	leaf, plate, (صَفَائِح) صَفِيْحَة sheet
suitability, صَلَاحِيّة applicability, usefulness, efficiency	whistle, whistling صَفِير
	sapphire صَفِير
hard, stiff, rigid صُلْب	thick, heavy صَفِيق
backbone, (أَصْلَاب) صُلْب loins	brazen-faced, صَفِيق الوَجْه impudent
stubborn, صُلْب الرَّأْي obstinate	scaffold, gangplank صَقَالَة
connection, (صِلَات) صِلَة relation, tie	falcon, hawk (صُقُور) صَقْر
peace, reconciliation, صُلْح friendliness	region, (أَصْقَاع) صُقْع locality, area
	frost, bitter cold صَقْعَة

hardness, stiffness, rigidity	صَمْل	preventive settlement	صُلْح تَحَفُّظي
deafness	صَمَم	arbitrative, arbitrational	صُلْحي
silent, quiet	صَمُوت	hard, rigid, solid	صَلْد (أَصْلَاد)
real, true, genuine, heart	صَمِيم	dry clay	صَلْصَال
cordial, hearty	صَمِيمي	sauce	صَلْصَة
fishhook, hook, angle	صِنَّارَة (صَنَانير)	rattle, clank	صَلْصَلَة
trade, industry, art, craft, profession	صِنَاعَة (صِنَاعات/صَنَائِع)	baldness	صَلَع
		swaggering, boasting, bragging	صَلَف
printing	صِنَاعَة الطَّبْع	solidity, rigidity, hardness	صُلُودَة
architecture	صِنَاعَة العِمَارَة	cross	صَلِيب (صُلُب)
handicraft	صِنَاعَة يَدَوِيّة	Red Cross	صَلِيب أَحْمَر
artificial, synthetic, industrial	صِنَاعي	rattle, clatter, clink	صَلِيل
water faucet, cock	صُنْبُور (صَنَابير)	plug, cork, valve	صِمَام (صِمَامَات)
sandals	صَنْدَل	safety valve	صِمَام الأَمَان
box, chest, suitcase, pay office	صُنْدُوق (صَنَاديق)	plug, stopper	صِمَّة
post office box	صُنْدُوق البَرِيد	silence, quiet	صَمْت/صُمُوت
savings bank	صُنْدُوق التَّوْفِير	eternal, everlasting	صَمَد
dustbin, garbage can	صُنْدُوق الزُّبالَة	everlasting, eternal	صَمَداني
		gum, resin	صَمْغ (صُمُوغ)
		gummy, mucilaginous	صَمْغي

brother-in-law, صِهْر (أَصْهَار) son-in-law	garbage can صُنْدُوق القُمَامَة
water tank, cistern صِهْرِيج	mail box صُنْدُوق المَكَاتِيب
horse's back صَهْوَة	صُنْدُوق النَّقْد الدُّوَلِي International Monetary Fund
scorching heat صَهِيد/ صُهُود	
neigh, whinny صَهِيل	cash box صُنْدُوق النُّقُود
Zion صَهْيُون/صِهْيُون	public treasure صُنْدُوق عُمُومِي
Zionism صَهْيُونِيَّة/صِهْيُونِيَّة	
right, correct, just, صَوَاب rightness, properness	brave, valiant (صَنَادِيد) صِنْدِيد
rightly, properly, صَوَابًا justly	handmade, صُنْع اليَد handwork
wool merchant صَوَّاف	making, صُنْع/صَنْع manufacturing
personal interest صَوَالِح شَخْصِيَّة	craft, work, trade, صَنْعَة occupation, workmanship
cupboard, chest, case صِوَان	صِنْف/صَنْف (أَصْنَاف/صُنُوف) sort, kind, category
wardrobe صِوَان الثِّيَاب	idol, image (أَصْنَام) صَنَم
book-case صِوَان الكُتُب	twin, twin brother (صِنْوَان) صِنْو
correct, right, direction صَوْب	act, action, deed صَنِيع
sound, voice, (أَصْوَات) صَوْت vote, noise	favour, good (صَنَائِع) صَنِيعَة turn, good deed
vocal, sonic, sonant, صَوْتِي phonetic	heat, blaze صَهْد
phonetics صَوْتِيَّات	relationship by صِهْر marriage
soda صُودا	

fast, fasting, abstinence	صَوْم	caustic soda	صُودا كَاوِيَة
hermitage (صَوَامِع)	صَوْمَعَة	sodium	صُودِيوم
preservation, safeguard, maintenance	صَوْن	horn, bugle	صُور
cry, clamour	صِياح	picture, form, figure, image, copy	صُورَة
shooter, hunter, fisher	صَيَّاد	formally	صُورَةً
fisher man, kingfisher	صَيَّاد السَّمَك	overall picture	صُورَة جَامِعَة
forming, shaping, wording	صِياغَة	snapshot	صُورَة خَاطِفَة
fast, fasting	صِيام	photo, photograph	صُورَة شَمْسِيَّة
protection, safeguarding, preservation	صِيانة	true copy, exact replica	صُورَة طِبْق الأَصْل
fame, renown, reputation	صِيت	motion picture, film	صُورَة مُتَحَرِّكَة
crying, shouting	صِيح	enlargement, blowup	صُورَة مُكَبَّرَة
shout, cry	صَيْحَة	reflected image	صُورَة مُنْعَكِسَة
war cry	صَيْحَة الحَرْب	fictitious, formal, fallacious, imaginary	صُوَرِي
hunt, hunting	صَيْد	fashioning, molding, shaping	صَوْغ
fishing	صَيْد السَّمَك	wool (أَصْواف)	صُوف
druggist, pharmacist	صَيْدَلاَني	woolen	صُوفي
pharmacy, pharmacology	صَيْدَلَة	authority, influence, force, assault	صَوْلَة (صَوْلات)
pharmacist, chemist, druggist	صَيْدَلي	scepter, mace	صَوْلَجان (صَوَالِجَة)

regulator, controlling device ضَابِط	licensed pharmacist صَيْدَلِي قَانُونِي
officer ضَابِط (ضُبّاط)	pharmacy, drug-store صَيْدَلِيَّة
canon, rule ضَابِط (ضَوَابِط)	fissure, crack صِيْر
senior officer ضَابِط آمِر	cashier, money changer صَيْرَف (صَيَارِف)
liaison officer ضَابِط ارْتِبَاط	becoming, upshot, termination, end صَيْرُورَة
vicinity, outskirts ضَاحِيَة (ضَوَاحٍ)	form, shape صِيْغَة (صِيَغ)
harmful, hurtful, injurious ضَارّ	summer صَيْف (أَصْيَاف)
ferocious, savage, voracious ضَارٍ	smoother, polisher صَيْقَل (صَيَاقِلَة)
compressor ضَاغِط	a large metal plate, turnplate صِينِيَّة (صَوَانِي)
abundant, ample, overflowing ضَافٍ	
straying, wrong, pervert, erroneous ضَالّ	
object of strong wish ضَالّة	tininess, smallness, scantiness ضَآلَة
skinny, slim ضَامِر	sheep ضَأْن
warrantor, guarantor, bailor ضَامِن	thin, small, tiny, slight ضَئِيْل (ضِئَال)
mastigure, lizard ضَبّ (ضِبَاب)	lost, missing ضَائِع
fog, thick mist ضَبَاب	straits, predicament, poverty ضَائِقَة (ضَوَائِق)
file ضَبَارَة/ضُبَارَة	financial straits ضَائِقَة مَالِيَّة
control, detention, accuracy, precision ضَبْط	

forenoon	ضُحًى/ضَحِيَّة	record, entry, protocol	ضَبْط (ضُبُوط)
slaughter animal, victim	ضَحِيَّة (ضَحَايا)	confiscation	ضَبْط الأَمْوَال
largeness, bigness, hugeness, bulkiness, vuluminosity	ضَخَامة	self-restraint	ضَبْط الشَّهْوَة
		self-control	ضَبْط النَّفْس
big, voluminous, bulky, huge	ضَخْم (ضِخَام)	police, police station	ضَبْطِيّة
		noise, cry, clamour, uproar	ضَجَّة
opposite, adversary, contrary	ضِدّ (أَضْدَاد)	fretfulness, vexation, restlessness, discontent	ضَجَر
damage, harm, injury	ضَرّ/ضُرّ	vexed, restless, fretful, weary	ضَجِر
polygamy	ضُرّ/ضِرّ	lying down, recumbency	ضَجْعَة
adversity, distress	ضَرَّاء	roaring, crying, clamorous	ضَجُوج
blaze, burning, ignition	ضِرَام	uproar, outcry, noise, cry	ضَجِيج
ferocity, voracity	ضَرَاوَة	bedfellow, companion	ضَجِيع
beating, hitting, striking	ضَرْب	frequently laughing	ضَحَّاك
kind, sort, specimen,	ضَرْب (ضُرُوب)	laughter, laugh	ضَحْك/ضِحْك
imposition of tax	ضَرْب الضَّرَائِب	laugh, laughter	ضَحْكَة
coining, minting	ضَرْب النُّقُود	forced laugh	ضَحْكَة مُتَكَلَّفَة
stroke, blow, punch, jolt	ضَرْبَة	shallow, shoal	ضَحْل
sunstroke	ضَرْبَة الشَّمْس	laughing, laugher	ضَحُوك

property tax	ضَرِيبَة العَقار	fatal blow	ضَرْبَة قَاضِية
entertainment tax	ضَرِيبَة المَلاهِي	udder	ضَرَّة
grave, tomb	ضَرِيح (ضَرائِح)	loss, damage, harm	ضَرَر (أَضْرار)
blind	ضَرِير	molar tooth	ضِرْس (أَضْراس)
humiliation, lowliness, inferiority	ضَعَة/ضِعَة	alike, similar	ضَرْع
demolition, dilapidation	ضَعْضَعَة	udder, bag, teat	ضَرْع (ضُرُوع)
double, twice as much	ضِعْف (أَضْعاف)	hound, hunting dog	ضِرْو
weakness, frailty, feebleness	ضَعْف/ضُعْف	necessarily, perforce	ضَرُورَةً
weakness of will	ضَعْف الإرَادَة	necessities, needs, indigence	ضَرُورَة (ضَرُورات)
neurasthenia	ضَعْف عَصَبِي	necessary, essential, imperative	ضَرُورِي
weak, feeble, frail, faint	ضَعِيف (ضُعَفاء)	necessities, necessaries	ضَرُورِيّات
weak-willed	ضَعِيف الإرَادة		ضَرُورِيّات الأَحْوال
delicate constitution	ضَعِيف البُنْية	requirements of situation	
weak-minded	ضَعِيف العَقْل	necessities of life	ضَرُورِيّات الحَياة
weak-hearted, faint-hearted	ضَعِيف القَلْب	ruinous, pernicious, destructive	ضَرُوس
bouquet, bunch	ضِغْث (أَضْغاث)	struck, beaten, hit	ضَرِيب
pressure, stress, compulsion, squeezing	ضَغْط	tax, levy, duty	ضَرِيبَة (ضَرائِب)
		war tax	ضَرِيبَة الحَرْب
		income tax	ضَرِيبَة الدَّخْل

robust, sturdy, strong, skilled	ضَلِيع	blood pressure	ضَغْط الدَّم
joining, amalgamation, addition, collecting	ضَمّ	air pressure	ضَغْط الهَوَاء
bandage, bandaging, dressing	ضِمَاد	atmospheric pressure	ضَغْط جَوِّي
bandage, dressing	ضِمَادَة	high voltage, high tension	ضَغْط عَالٍ
guarantee, surety, warrant, liability	ضَمَان	rancorous, malicious, malevolent	ضَغِن
collective security	ضَمَان جَمَاعِي	spite, malice, ill will	ضِغْن (أَضْغَان)
collective security	ضَمان مُشْتَرَك	spite, malice, grudge	ضَغِينَة (ضَغَائِن)
surety, guarantee	ضَمَائة	crowd, throng	ضَفَّة
leanness, slimness, emaciation	ضُمْر/ضُمُور	bank, shore	ضَفَّة/ضِفَّة (ضِفاف)
within, inside	ضِمْن	frog	ضَفْدَع/ضِفْدَع (ضَفَادِع)
implied, hidden, implicit	ضِمْنِي	girth	ضَفْر (ضُفُور)
conscience, heart, mind	ضَمِير (ضَمَائِر)	easy or comfortable life	ضَفْوَة العَيْش
supplement, addition	ضَمِيمَة (ضَمَائِم)	braid, plait	ضَفِيرة (ضَفَائِر)
liable, responsible, warrantor	ضَمِين (ضُمَنَاء)	sturdiness, robustness	ضَلَاعة
		straying, deviation from right path	ضَلَال
		error, delusion	ضَلَالَة
		attachment, affection	ضَلَع
straits, hardship, poverty	ضَنْك	rib, side	ضِلْع/ضَلَع (ضُلُوع/أَضْلاَع)

guest, visitor (ضُيُوف) ضَيْف	weakness, emaciation, ضَنَى consumption
narrowness, restriction, ضِيْق tightness, paucity, distress	stingy, avaricious, ضَنِين scanty
narrow, tight, confined ضَيِّق	similar, alike ضَهِيّ
impatient, restless ضَيِّق الخُلُق	light, glow (أَضْواء) ضَوْء
impatient, restless ضَيِّق الخُلُق	sunlight, ضَوْء الشَّمْس sunshine
disgruntled, ضَيِّق الصَّدْر depressed, annoyed	moonlight ضَوْء القَمَر
narrow-minded ضَيِّق العَقْل	daylight ضَوْء النَّهار
narrow scope, ضَيِّق النِّطاق confined, restricted	luminary ضَوْئِي
laboured ضِيق النَّفَس breathing, asthma	suburbs, ضَواحي المَدينة outskirts
paucity, poverty, ضِيق اليَد destitution	uproar, hubhub, ضَوْضَاء noise, din
injustice, wrong, (ضُيُوم) ضَيْم injury, grievance	uproar, din, noise, ضَوْضَى hubhub
	light, glow ضِيَاء
ط	loss, ruin ضَيَاع
	loss of time ضَيَاع الوَقْت
aviator, pilot طَائِر	hospitality, ضِيَافة entertainment of a guest
bird, omen (طَائِرات) طَائِر	harm, injury, damage, ضَيْر prejudice
song bird طَائِر مُغَرِّد	
aeroplane, (طَائِرات) طَائِرَة aircraft	loss ضَيْع
dive bomber طَائِرَة الاِنْقِضَاض	farm, estate, (ضِيَاع) ضَيْعَة hamlet

stamp, impress, impression, seal	طَابَع (طَوَابِع)
fingerprint	طَابَع الأَصَابِع
postage stamp, stamp	طَابَع البَرِيد
postage stamp	طَابَع البَرِيد
commemorative stamp	طَابَع تَذْكَارِي
ground floor	طَابِق أَرْضِي
story, floor	طَابَق/طَابِق (طَوَابِق)
queue, line, column	طَابُور (طَوَابِير)
fort, fortress	طَابِيَة (طَوَاب)
grinder, molar	طَاحِن/طَاحِنة
grinder, mill	طَاحُون/طَاحُونة
windmill	طَاحُونة الهَوَاء
foreign, extraneous, accidental, contingent	طَارِئ
incident, mishap, emergency	طَارِئَة (طَوَارِئ)
knocking, beating, night visitor	طَارِق (طُرَّاق)
calamity, disaster	طَارِقَة (طَوَارِق)
fresh	طَازِج
drinking cup, bowl	طَاس/طَاسَة

combat plane	طَائِرَة المُقَاتَلَة
transport plane	طَائِرَة النَّقْل
seaplane	طَائِرَة بَحْرِيّة
glider, sailplane	طَائِرَة شِرَاعِيّة
helicopter	طَائِرَة عَمُودية
seaplane	طَائِرَة مَائِيّة
pursuit plane, interceptor	طَائِرَة مُطَارِدَة
bomber	طَائِرَة مُقَنْبِلَة
rash, heedless, thoughtless, inconstant	طَائِش
obedient, submissive, compliant	طَائِع
wandering, roving, itinerant	طَائِف
party, group, faction, sect	طَائِفَة (طَوَائِف)
sectarian, sectional	طَائِفِي
sectarianism, confessionalism	طَائِفِيّة
big, huge, immense	طَائِل
powerful, mighty	طَائِل الصَّدْلَة
use, avail, power, ability	طَائِل/طَائِلَة
printer	طَابِع

longing, aspiring, covetous	طَامِح	obedience, submission, compliance	طَاعَة
cook	طَاه (طُهَاة)	plague, pestilence	طَاعُون
clean, pure, chaste	طَاهِر	oppressor, tyrant	طَاغٍ (طُغَاة)
upright, innocent, blameless, undefiled	طَاهِر الذَّيْل	false god, tempter	طَاغُوت
windmill	طَاهُون الرِّيح	despot, tyrant	طَاغِيَة
table	طَاوِلَة	superficial, floating	طَافٍ
peacock	طَاوُوس (طَوَاويس)	flowing over, replete	طَافِح
medicine, medical treatment	طِبّ	floating iceberg	طَافِيَة
dentistry	طِبّ الأَسْنَان	layer, arch	طَاق (طَاقَات)
veterinary science	طِبّ بَيْطَري	power, energy, capacity, capability	طَاقَة (طَاقَات)
forensic medicine	طِبّ شَرْعي	output capacity	طَاقَة انْتَاجِيّة
paediatrics	طِبّ طِفْلي	atomic energy	طَاقَة ذَرِّيَّة
psychiatry	طِبّ نَفْسَاني	accumulated energy	طَاقَة مُدَّخَرَة
medical treatment	طَبَابَة	crew, set, series	طَاقِم
cook	طَبَّاخ	seeker, applicant, candidate, student	طَالِب
cookery	طَبَاخَة	suitor	طَالِب زَوَاج
chalk	طَبَاشير	student, pupil	طَالِب عِلْم
chalky, creataceous	طَبَاشيري	bad, wicked, vicious	طَالِح
printer	طَبَّاع	rising, going up, ascending	طَالِع (طَوَالِع)
printing	طِبَاعَة	often, frequently	طَالَما
lithography	طِبَاعَة الحَجَر		

eardrum	طَبْلَة الأُذَن	typographic	طِبَاعي
pistol	طَبَنْجَة	in accordance with	طِبَاق
medical	طِبِّي	tobacco	طَبَاق/طُبَاق
medical doctor, physician	طَبِيْب (أَطِبَّاء)	drummer	طَبَّال
dentist	طَبِيب الأَسْنَان	cooking, cookery	طَبْخ
neurologist	طَبِيب الأَمْرَاض العَصَبِيَّة	chalk	طَبْشُوْرَة
gynaecologist	طَبِيب الأَمْرَاض النِّسَائِيَّة	stamp, nature, impression, disposition	طَبْع (طِبَاع)
eye specialist	طَبِيب العُيُون	typography	طَبْع الحُرُوف
veterinarian	طَبِيب بَيْطَري	printing	طَبْع الكُتُب
surgeon	طَبِيب جَرَّاح	naturally, certainly, of course	طَبْعًا
private physician	طَبِيب خَاصّ	edition, issue, print	طَبْعَة
psychiatrist	طَبِيب نَفْسَاني	plate, dish, layer	طَبَق (أَطْبَاق)
lady doctor, doctress	طَبِيْبَة	air layers	طَبَقات الجَوّ
nature, temper, natural disposition	طَبِيعَة (طَبَائِع)	air layers	طَبَقات جَوِّية
natural, normal, ordinary	طَبِيعِي	the middle classes	طَبَقَات وُسْطَى
physics, natural science	طَبِيعِيات	layer, stratum, category	طَبَقَة (طَبَقَات)
spleen, milt	طحَال (طُحُل)	upper class	طَبَقَة رَاقِية
miller	طَحّان	middle class	طَبَقَة مُتَوَسِّطَة
green moss, water moss	طُحْلُب	drum, drum beat	طَبْل
flour, meal	طِحْن/طَحِين	drum	طَبْلَة

parcel, package (طُرُود) طَرْد	fresh, new طَرِئ
expulsion, repulsion, a chase طَرْدَة	all without exception طُرًّا
kind, make, model, fashion, method (طُرُوز) طَرْز	chase, pursuit, hunt طِرَاد
paper, sheet of paper (أَطْراس) طِرْس	cruiser طَرّاد/طَرّادة
white washing طَرْش	model, style, sort, fashion (أَطْرِزَة) طِرَاز
deafness طَرَش	first rate, first class طِرَاز أَوَّل
pickles طُرْشِي	hand-operated model طِرَاز يَدَوِي
eye, look طَرْف	novelty, oddness, peculiarity طَرَافَة
side, edge, fringe (أَطْرَاف) طَرَف	freshness, moistness, tenderness طَرَاوَة
witty saying, curiosity, a present (طُرَف) طُرْفَة	gentleness of character طَرَاوَة الخُلْق
twinkling of the eye طَرْفَة عَيْن	joy, delight, pleasure (أَطْرَاب) طَرَب
knock, rap طَرْقَة	delighted, enraptured, joyous (طِرَاب) طَرِب
merry, lively, delighted طَرُوب	cap, tarboosh (طَرَابِيش) طَرْبُوش
fresh, moist, succulent طَرِيّ	throwing away, expulsion, repudiation, rejection طَرْح
delicate to the touch طَرِيّ الجَسّ	miscarried foetus, abortion طِرْح
thrown, cast down, rejected, expelled طَرِيح	miscarriage طَرْح الجَنِين
bedridden طَرِيح الفراش	expulsion, dismissal, rejection طَرْد

taste, flavour, relish طَعْم (طُعُوم)	outcast, expelled, ousted, fugitive طَرِيد
stabbing, piercing, defamation طَعْن	chased game طَرِيدَة (طَرَائِد)
thrust, stab, vilification طَعْنَة	rare, curious, exquisite طَرِيف
flood, inundation طُغْوَان	exquisite thing, curiousity طَرِيفَة (طَرَائِف)
oppression, tyranny, deluge, flood طُغْيان	way, path, road, track, passage طَرِيْق (طُرُق)
babyhood, childhood, infancy طَفَالَة	sea route طَرِيْق البَحْر
floating, floatage طَفَاوَة	air route طَرِيْق الجَوّ
overflowing, repletion, superabundance طَفْح	main road طَرِيْق رَئِيسِي
skin eruption, rash طَفْح جِلْدِي	thoroughfare, public road طَرِيْق عَامّ
replete, overfull, brimful طَفْحَان	public road, thoroughfare طَرِيْق عُمُومِيّة
skipping, leaping طَفْر	manner, system, way, mode طَرِيْقَة (طُرُق/طَرَائِق)
bounce, leap, upturn طَفْرَة	dozen طَزِيْنَة
in one leap طَفْرَةً	basin, washbowl طَسْت/طِسْت
clay, argil طَفْل	washbasin, washbowl طَشْت/طِشْت
baby, child طِفْل (أَطْفَال)	
female child طِفْلَة	food, diet, meal طَعَام (أَطْعِمَة)
childish, childlike طِفْلِي	graft, bait طُعْم
repletion, superabundance طُفُوح	vaccine طُعْم (طُعُوم)

طَلَب (طَلَبات)	requirement, demand, order, claim, petition	طُفُولة/طُفُولِيّة	childhood, babyhood
طَلَب العِلْم	craving for knowledge	طُفُولي	childlike, childish
طَلَبَة	request, desire, application	طَفِيف	trivial, slight, trifling, insignificant
طِلَّسْم	talisman, charm	طُفَيْلي	sponger, intruder, meddler
طَلْعَة	appearance, look, aspect	طَقْس	weather, climate, manner
طَلْق	open, free, unrestrained	طَقْس (طُقُوس)	rites, rituals, customs
طَلَق (أَطْلَاق)	race, shot	طَقْم (طُقُوم)	set, series, suit of clothes
طَلْق اللِّسَان	eloquent, fluent	طَلّ (طِلَال)	thick mist, drizzle, fine rain
طَلْق اللِّسَان	eloquent, loquacious	طِلَاء	coat, paint, covering layer
طَلْق المُحَيّا	bright-faced, frank		
طَلْق الوَجْه	with a bright or cheerful face	طَلَاق	divorce
طَلْق اليَدَيْن	open-handed, free-handed	طَلَاقَة	relaxedness, openness
طَلْق نَاري	gunshot	طَلَاقَة اللِّسَان	eloquence, fluency, loquacity
طَلْقَة (طَلَقَات)	divorce	طَلَاقَة الوَجْه	cheerfulness, gaiety
طَلْقَة/طَلَقَة نَارية	shot		
طَلَل (أَطْلَال)	remains, traces	طَلَاوَة	beauty, elegance, grace
طُلُمْبَة	pump	طَلَب	seeking, looking for, search
طُلُمْبَة الهَوَاء	air pump		

ambitious, covetous, desirous طَمُوح	rise, rising, ascent, appearance طُلُوع
ton طُنّ (أطْنان)	daybreak طُلُوع النَّهَار
resounding, echoing, humming, tinkling طَنَّان	beautiful, becoming, graceful طَلِي
tent rope, tendon طُنُب (أطْناب)	front row, foremost طَلِيْعَة (طَلاَئِع)
tinkling, jingling, buzzing طَنْطَنَة	vanguard, advance guard طَلِيْعَة الجَيْش
summit, top, peak طُنْف/طُنُف (طُنُوف)	free, released طَلِيق (طُلَقَاء)
tinkling, buzzing طَنِين	divorcee, divorced woman طَلِيْقَة
cleanliness, purity, sanctity, holiness طَهَارَة	repose, tranquillity, serenity, peace طُمَأْنِيْنَة
innocence, blamelessness, probity طَهَارَة الذَّيْل	covetous, desirous, high aspiring طَمَّاح
cooking, cook's trade طِهَايَة	tomato طَمَاطِم
purity, cleanness, holiness طُهْر	covetous, avaricious, greedy طَمَّاع
clean, cleansing, pure, circumcision طَهُور	tranquillity, calmness, composure, serenity طَمَان
adversities of fate طَوَائِح	menses, menstruation طَمْث
brickmaker, tilemaker طَوّاب	obliteration, effacement طَمْس
eunuch طَوَاشِى (طَوَاشِية)	greed, avidity, covetousness, avarice طَمَع (أطْمَاع)
round trip, circumambulation طَوَاف	aspiration, ambition, craving, coveting طُمُوح

life buoy	طُوْق للنَّجَاة	going rounds, ambulant, roving	طَوّاف
collar-like, ring-shaped	طَوْقِي	patrol boat	طَوّافَة
power, might	طَوْل	throughout, during	طِوَال/طَوَال
length, height	طُوْل (أَطْوَال)	fry-pan	طَوّايَة
tallness	طُوْل القَامَة	bricks	طُوْب
farsightedness	طُوْل النَّظَر	artilleryman, gunner	طُوبْجي
all day long	طُوْل النَّهَار	artillery, ordnance	طُوبْجِيّة
scroll, roll	طُوْمَار (طَوَامِيْر)	beautitude, blessedness	طُوبَى
fold, pleat, intention, design	طَوِيَّة (طَوَايَا)	high mountain	طَوْد (أَطْوَاد)
long, tall, high, lengthy	طَوِيْل (طِوَال)	phase, time, stage, state	طَوْر (أَطْوَار)
long term	طَوِيْل الأَجَل	mountain	طُوْر (أَطْوَار)
patient, tolerant, long-suffering	طَوِيْل الأناة	obedience, spontaneity	طَوْع
powerful, mighty, capable	طَوِيْل البَاع	tractable, docile	طَوْع العنان
long-sighted, presbyopic	طَوِيْل البَصَر	willingly, voluntarily	طَوْعًا
long, lengthy	طَوِيْل الذَّيْل	raft, wall, round, patrol	طَوْف
patient, long-suffering	طَوِيْل الرُّوْح	flood, deluge, inundation	طُوْفَان
insolent, foul-tongued	طَوِيْل اللِّسَان	ability, capability, faculty	طَوْق
far-sighted	طَوِيْل النَّظَر	neckband, collar, necklace	طَوْق (أَطْوَاق)

bird, fowl	طَيْر (طُيُور)	long-breathed	طَوِيْل النَّفَس
flight, flying, aviation	طَيَرَان	fold, folding, hiding	طَيّ
gliding	طَيَرَان شِرَاعِي	flying, floating, volatile	طَيَّار
commotion, agitation	طَيْرَة	flyer, aviator, aircraftsman	طَيَّار (طَيَّارُون)
evil omen, portent	طِيَرَة	aircraft, airplane	طَيَّارَة
recklessness, rashness, thoughtlessness	طَيْش	glider	طَيَّارَة شِرَاعِيَّة
thoughtlessness, rashness, inconstancy	طَيَشَان	bomber	طَيَّارَة قَذَّافَة
		seaplane	طَيَّارَة مَائِيَّة
obedient, submissive	طَيِّع	good, well, alright, pleasant, hale	طَيِّب
phantom, phantasm, spectre	طَيْف	perfume, scent	طِيب (طُيُوب)
spectral	طَيْفِي	good-natured	طَيِّب الخُلُق
porcelain clay	طِين خَزَفِي	nice-smelling, fragrant	طَيِّب الرَّائِحَة
clay, mud	طِين/طِيْنة	simple-hearted	طَيِّب السَّرِيْرَة
barnyard fowls	طُيُور دَاجِنَة	noble descent	طِيْب العِرْق
		high born, of noble descent	طَيِّب العِرْق

		good-humoured, cheerful	طَيِّب النَّفْس
victorious, successful	ظَافِر		
unjust, unfair, transgressor, oppressor	ظَالِم	goodness, good temper	طِيْب/طِيْبَة
thirsty, parched	ظَامِئ	good things	طَيِّبات
obvious, manifest, evident, exterior	ظَاهِر	pleat, fold, design	طَيَّة
phenomenon, external symptom	ظَاهِرَة (ظَوَاهِر)	design, intention	طِيَّة

victorious, triumphant ظَفِر	meteor ظَاهِرة جَوِّية
fingernail, nail (أَظْفار) ظُفُر	external, outer, ظَاهِري
shade, shadow, (ظِلَال) ظِلّ	exterior
shelter	gazelle (ظِبَاء) ظَبْي
darkness, duskiness ظَلَام	female gazelle, doe ظَبْيَة
intense darkness ظَلَام دَامِس	wittiness, elegance, ظَرَافة
wrong, (ظُلَامات) ظُلَامَة	gracefulness
injustice, iniquity	elegance, cleverness, ظَرْف
awning, tent, (ظُلَل) ظُلّة	cheerfulness
canopy	envelope, (ظُرُوف) ظَرْف
wrong, tyranny, ظُلْم	cover, receptacle, vessel
oppression, inequity,	conditions, ظُرُوف
injustice	circumstances
darkness, (ظُلُمَات) ظُلْمَة	existing ظُرُوف رَاهِنَة
obscurity, gloom	condition, status quo
shady, umbrageous ظَلِيل	compulsory ظُرُوف قَهْرِيَّة
thirst, parchedness ظَمَأ/ظَمَاء	circumstances
thirsty, parched ظَمْآن	extenuating ظُرُوف مُخَفَّفَة
supposition, (ظُنُون) ظَنّ	circumstances
suspicion, opinion	aggravating ظُرُوف مُشَدَّدَة
suspicious, mistrustful ظَنُون	circumstances
supposed, presumptive ظَنِّي	elegant, (ظُرَفَاء) ظَرِيف
suspected, ظَنِين	graceful, lovely, witty
untrustworthy	journey, trek ظَعْن
outside, rightside ظِهَارة	woman sitting in (ظُعُن) ظَعِينَة
	a sedan chair
noon, midday (أَظْهَار) ظُهْر	victory, triumph ظَفَر

عَابِث frivolous, jocular, futile	ظَهْر (ظُهُور) back, rear part
عَابِد (عُبَّاد) worshipper, adorer	ظَهْر المَرْكَب deck
عَابِر passing, traversing, transitory	ظُهُور appearance, ostentation, show
عَابِر (عَابِرون) passer by	ظَهِير assistant, supporter, helper
عَابِر الطَّرِيق wayfarer	ظَهِيرَة midday, noon
عَابِس frowning, austere, gloomy	

عَابِق redolent, fragrant	
عَات arrogant, oppressive, violent, impudent	عَائِد returning, recurrent
عَاتِق (عَوَاتِق) shoulder	عَائِد (عُوَّاد) visitor, caller
عَاج ivory	عَائِدَة benefit, advantage, profit
عَاجِز incapable, disable, impotent	عَائِز indigent, needy, poor
عَاجِل wordly, temporal	عَائِق obstacle, impediment, hindrance
عَاجِلاً soon, immediately	عَائِق مَنِيع insurmountable obstacle
عَاجِلاً أو آجِلاً sooner or later	
عَاجِي ivory	عَائِقَة (عَوَائِق) obstacle, hindrance, impediment
عَاد aggressive, assailing, assaulting	عَائِل bread winner, supporter, sustainer
عَادَةً usually, ordinarily	
عَادَة (عَادَات) habit, practice, usage, custom	عَائِلَة (عَوَائِل) family, household
عَادَة (عَوَائد) taxes, duties, fees	عَائِم swimming, floating, natant

player, musician	عَازِف	masturbation	عَادَة سِرِّيَّة
pianist	عَازِف على البيانُو	established usage	عَادَة مَرْعِيَّة
resolved, resolute, determined	عَازِم	just, upright, straightforward	عَادِل
lover, fan	عَاشِق (عُشَّاق)	usual, ordinary, normal	عَادِي
rebel, insurgent, rebellious, disobedient, sinful	عَاص (عُصَاة)	adversity, offense, wrong	عَادِيَة (عَوَادٍ)
stormy, windy	عَاصِف	disgrace, shame, ignominy	عَار (أَعْيَار)
storm, violent wind, tempest	عَاصِفَة (عَوَاصِف)	naked, nude, stripped, bare	عَارٍ (عُرَاة)
thunder storm	عَاصِفَة رَعْدِيَّة	exhibitor, demonstrator	عَارِض (عَارِضُون)
guardian, protector, preserver	عَاصِم	obstruction, obstacle, impediment, casualty	عَارِض (عَوَارِض)
capital, capital city	عَاصِمَة (عَوَاصِم)	girder, side of the face	عَارِضَة (عَوَارِض)
fragrant, aromatic	عَاطِر	accidental, occasional	عَارِضِي
thirsty, craving, covetous	عَاطِش	knowing, acquainted, familiar	عَارِف
compassionate, affectionate, kind	عَاطِف	huge, tremendous, violent	عَارِم
feeling, sympathy, sentiment	عَاطِفَة (عَوَاطِف)	barefooted	عَارِي الأَقْدَام
sentimental, affectionate, emotional	عَاطِفِي	lack, need, want	عَازَة
devoid of, jobless, inactive	عَاطِل		

عَالَمِي worldly, universal, international	عَاف obliterated, wiped out
عَالِي الهِمّة high-minded, high-aspiring	عَافِيَة good health, force, vigour
عَامّ public, general, common	عَاقّ disobedient, refractory
عَامّ (أَعْوَام) year	عَاقِبَة (عَوَاقِب) consequence, end, result, outcome
عَامّة (عَوَامّ) the people, the masses	عَاقِر sterile, barren
عَامّة النَّاس the common people, the masses	عَاقِل (عُقَلاَء) wise, intelligent, rational, sane
عَامِر populated, inhabited, cultivated	عَاكِس/عَاكِسَة reflector
عَامِل (عُمّال) doer, worker, employee, maker	عَاكِف (عُكُوف) bent on, engaged, busy
عَامِل (عَوَامِل) motive, factor, regimen	عَالٍ high, elevated, exalted
عَامِل لاَسِلْكِي wireless operator	عَالَم world, universe
عَامِّي common, current, popular, vulgar	عَالِم knowing, acquainted, aware of
عَانٍ servile, submissive, miserable	عَالِم (عُلَماء) learned, man of learning, scientist
عَائة pubes, pubic region	عَالِم أَثَرِي archeologist
عَاهِر (عُهّار) adulterer, fornicator, debauchee	عَالَم الغَيْب invisible world
	عَالِم الغَيْب the all-knowing
	عَالَم الوُجُود this world
عَاهِر/عَاهِرة (عَوَاهِر) adulteress, prostitute, whore	عَالِم طَبِيعِي natural scientist, physicist
	عَالِم نَفْسَانِي psychologist
	عَالِمَة woman scholar, learned woman

عَبْقَري (عَبَاقِرَة) ingenious, gifted person	عَاهِل (عَوَاهِل) prince, ruler, emperor
عَبْقَرِيّة ingenuity, genius	عِبْء (أَعْبَاء) burden, charge, load
عُبُوّة container, fill, package	عِبْء الضَّرِيبَة burden of taxation
عُبُودِيّة slavery, servitude, worship	عَبَاء/عَبَاءَة aba, oriental cloak
عُبُور passage, crossing, traversing	عُبَاب waves, torrents
عُبُوس frown, stern look	عَبّاد الشَّمْس sunflower
عَبُوس frowning, stern, sullen, gloomy	عِبَادَة worship, devotion, adoration
عَبِير perfume, scent, fragrance	عَبَّادة الشَّمْس sunflower
عِتَاب rebuke, reprimand, reproach	عِبَارَة (عِبَارَات) expression, phrase, explanation
عَتَاقَة vintage, age	عَبَث play, sport, pastime, futile, useless
عَتّال carrier, porter	عَبَثًا uselessly, in vain
عَتَالة porterage, carriage	عَبْد (عِبَاد) servant, man
عَتَامَة darkness, opaqueness	عَبْد (عَبِيد) slave, bondsman
عَتَاهَة idiocy, imbecility	عَبْر crossing, passing, traversing
عَتْب reproof, censure, reprimand	عِبْرَة (عِبَر) lesson, advice, admonition, warning
عَتَبَة (أَعْتَاب) threshold, step, stair	عَبْرَة (عَبَرَات) tear drop, tear
عِتْق emancipation, liberty, vintage	عَبِق redolent, fragrant
	عَبْقَر fairyland, home of jinns

wonder, astonishment عَجَب	darkness, gloom, عَتَمَة obscurity
omelet عُجَّة	
arrogance, pride, عَجْرَفَة haughtiness	first third of the night عَتَمَة
	idiocy, imbecility عَتَه/عُتْه
disability, incapacity, عَجْز impotence	arrogance, haughtiness, عُتُوّ tyranny
haste, hurry, speed عَجَل	arrogance, impertinence, عُتِيّ haughtiness
calf عِجْل (عُجُول)	
sea calf عِجْل البَحْر	impertinent, عَتِيّ (أَعْتاء) insolent, unruly
haste, precipitancy عَجَلَة	prepared, ready, عَتِيد approaching
wheel, عَجَلَة (عَجَلات) bicycle	ancient, old, outmoded, عَتِيق free, liberated
steering wheel عَجَلَة التَّوْجِيه	
steering wheel عَجَلَة القِيَادَة	old-fashioned عَتِيق الطِّرَاز
motorcycle عَجَلَة نَارِية	old-fashioned, عَتِيق النَّمَط outmoded
non-Arabs عَجَم	moth, moth عُثّ/عُثّة (عُثَت) worm
non-Arab, burbarian عَجَمِي	
oldman or woman عَجُوز	fall, slip, stumble عَثْرَة
quick, rash, fast, swift عَجُول	discovery, detection عُثُور
odd, miraculous, عَجِيْب wonderful, amazing	crying, yelling, shouting عَجّ
miracle, عَجِيْبَة (عَجَائِب) marvel, wonder	wonderful, عُجَاب astonishing, marvellous
clamour, crying, cry عَجِيْج	clamouring, roaring, عَجّاج yelling
posteriors, buttocks عَجِيْزَة	conceit, vanity عُجْب

lentils	عَدَس	paste, dough	عَجِين
lens, glass	عَدَسَة (عَدَسات)	pasty, doughy	عَجِينِي
lenticular	عَدَسِي	reckoning, counting, enumeration, calculation	عَدّ
equity, justice, fairness, impartiality	عَدْل	enmity, hostility	عَدَاء
upright, just, equitable	عَدْل (عُدُول)	inimical, hostile	عَدَائِي
judicial, legal	عَدْلِي	justice, equity, fairness	عَدَالَة
administration of justice	عَدْلِيَّة	enmity, animosity	عَدَاوَة
nothingness, nonentity, non-existence, absence	عَدَم	severl, numerous	عِدّة
impossibility, improbability	عَدَم الإمْكان	promise	عِدَة
nonaggression	عَدَم الاعْتِدَاء	appliance, equipment, instrument	عُدّة (عُدَد)
inattention, inadvertence	عَدَم الالْتِفَات	several times	عِدّة مَرَّات
indifference, inattention	عَدَم الاهْتِمام	number, figure	عَدَد (أَعْدَاد)
non-intervention	عَدَم التَّدَخُّل	regular number,	عَدَد أَصْلِي
disproportion, disharmony	عَدَم التَّناسُب	prime number	عَدَد أَوَّلِي
distrust, mistrust	عَدَم الثِّقَة	ordinal number	عَدَد تَرْتِيبِي
non-existence, non-being	عَدَم الوُجُود	special number	عَدَد خَاصّ
ruthlessness, mercilessness	عَدَم رَحْمَة	even number	عَدَد شَفْعِي
		whole number	عَدَد صَحِيح
		abstract number	عَدَد مُبْهَم
		composite number	عَدَد مُرَكَّب
		special issue	عَدَد مُمْتَاز
		numerical, numeral	عَدَدِي

insensitive, apathetic	عَديم الشُّعُور	nihilist	عَدَمِي
unkind, ruthless, cruel, merciless	عَديم الشَّفَقَة	Eden, the paradise	عَدْن
dull, inactive, gloomy	عَديم النَّشَاط	run, race	عَدْو
unique, matchless	عَديم النِّظْر	enemy, foe	عَدُوّ (أَعْدَاء)
matchless, peerless, unique	عَديم النَّظِير	mortal or bitter enemy	عَدُوّ أَلَدّ
weightless, insignificant	عَديم الوَزْن	aggression, hostility, injustice	عُدْوَان
torture, chastisement, agony, anguish	عَذَاب	aggressive, hostile	عُدْوَاني
sweet, fresh	عَذْب	side, bank	عُدْوَة
excuse, apology	عُذْر (أَعْذَار)	refraining, abstention	عُدُول
virgin, chaste	عَذْرَاء (عَذَارَى)	contagion, infection	عَدْوَى
virginity, virginhood	عُذْرَة	many, numerous	عَديد
bunch, cluster	عذْق (أَعْذَاق)	equal, like	عَديل
sweetness, freshness	عُذُوبَة	deprived of, devoid of	عَديم
open air, open space, bareness, nakedness	عَرَاء	ill-mannered, ill-bred	عَديم الأَدَب
godfather, sponsor	عَرَّاب	unimportant, of no importance	عَديم الأَهَمِّيَّة
godmother, sponsor	عَرَّابَة	ineffective, inefficacious	عَديم التَّأْثِير
fortuneteller, diviner	عَرَّاف	lifeless, inanimate	عَديم الحَيَاة
woman fortuneteller, diviner	عَرَّافَة	smelless, odourless	عَديم الرَّائِحَة
		ruthless, merciless	عَديم الرَّحْمَة

spouse, عِرْس (أَعْرَاس) husband or wife	divination, fortune عَرَافَة telling
throne, thatch, عَرْش (عُرُوش) canopy	fight, combat, struggle عِرَاك
throne of grace عَرْش الرَّحْمَة	Arabs عَرَب
showing, exposing, عَرْض staging, presentation, exhibition	cart, carriage, عَرَبَة (عَرَبَات) vehicle
accident, عَرَض (أَعْرَاض) chance, contingent	hackney عَرَبَة الأُجْرَة
	dining car عَرَبَة الأَكْل
honour, عِرْض (أَعْرَاض) dignity	spinkler, water عَرَبَة الرَّشّ cart
width, breadth عَرْض (عُرُوض)	dust car عَرَبَة الزُّبَالة
fashion show عَرْض الأَزْيَاء	freight car عَرَبَة الشَّحْن
target, object, purpose عُرْضَة	sleeping car, عَرَبَة النَّوْم sleeper
transverse, latitudinal عَرْضِي	handcart عَرَبَة اليَد
accidental, casual, عَرَضِي contingent	riot, uproar, عَرْبَدَة contentiousness
custom, tradition, عُرْف beneficence	pledge, token عُرْبُون (عَرَابِين) money, handsel
perfume, sweet scent عَرْف	Arabic, Arab عَرَبِي
crest, comb عُرْف الدِّيْك	Arabic language عَرَبِيَّة
cognition, awareness, عِرْفَان acquaintance	contentious, riotous, عِرْبِيْد quarrelsome
	lameness عَرَج
thankfulness, عِرْفَان الجَمِيْل gratitude	wedding, عُرْس (أَعْرَاس) marriage

application, petition	عَرِيْضَة (عَرَائِض)	customary, conventional	عُرْفِي
notice of appeal	عَرِيْضَة الِاسْتِئْناف	sweet, sweating, perspiration	عَرَق
acquainted with, aware, monitor	عَرِيْف (عُرَفاء)	race, descent, root	عِرْق (عُرُوق)
firmly-rooted, inveterate	عَرِيْق	hindrance, handicap, obstacle	عَرْقَلَة (عَرَاقِيْل)
of noble birth, high born	عَرِيْق النَّسَب	combat, fight, battle	عَرْكَة
disposition, temper	عَرِيْكَة	violent, terrific, huge	عَرِم
lion's den, thicket	عَرِيْن (عُرُن)	heap, pile, huge amount	عُرْمَة (عُرَم)
dignity, glory, power	عِزّ	loop, buttonhole, handle	عُرْوَة (عُرًى)
comfort, consolation, condolence	عَزَاء	firm grip	عُرْوَة وُثْقَى
household effects	عَزَال	bridegroom	عَرُوس (عُرُس)
single, unmarried, bachelor	عَزَب (عُزّاب)	bride, doll	عَرُوسَة (عَرَائِس)
bachelorhood, celibacy	عُزْبَة/عُزُوبَة	prosody	عَرُوض
dignity, glory, honour, might, power	عِزّة	nudity, nakedness	عُرْي/عُرْيَة
self-respect, self-esteem	عِزّة النَّفْس	nude, naked, bare	عُرْيَان (عَرَايا)
reprimand, reproof	عَزْر	star naked, completely naked	عُرْيَان مَلْط
removal, dismissal, separation, segregation	عَزْل	nudism	عُرْيَانِيّة
		bridegroom	عَرِيْس
		vast, wide, broad	عَرِيْض

troops, army (عَسَاكِر) عَسْكَر	عُزْلَة privacy, seclusion, solitude, retirement
military, army, soldier عَسْكَرِي	resolution, decision, عَزْم determination, strong will
honey (عُسُول) عَسَل	determined, resolute عَزُوم
twig, sprig (عَسَالِج) عُسْلُج	entertainment, عُزُومَة invitation, banquet
twig, sprig, (عَسَالِيج) عُسْلُوج small shoot	mighty, powerful, عَزِيز honourable, noble, dear
despot, tyrant, oppressor عَسُوف	mighty, powerful عَزِيز الجَانِب
hard, distressing, عَسِير difficult	resolution, (عَزَائِم) عَزِيمَة determination, strong will
nest (أَعْشَاش) عُشّ	oppressor, tyrant عَسَّاف
night-blindness, عَشَاً/عَشَاوَة nyctalopia	beehive عَسَّالَة
evening, nightfull عِشَاء	gold عَسْجَد
dinner, supper عَشَاء	difficulty, distress, عُسْر/عُسُر straits, poverty
grassy, herby عَشِب	distressing, hard, عَسِر difficult
grass, herb, (أَعْشَاب) عُشْب herbage	dismenorrhoea عُسْر الطَّمْث
herb, plant عُشْبَة	dyspepsia عُسْر الهَضْم
herbal, herbaceous عُشْبِي	indigestible, عَسِر الهَضْم heavy to digest
hovel, bower, (عُشَش) عُشَّة arbour	financial straits عُسْر مَالِي
one tenth (أَعْشَار) عُشْر	hardship, difficulty عُسْرَة
ten عَشْر/عَشَرَة	oppression, tyranny, عَسْف despotism
tens, decades عَشَرَات	

عُصْبَة/عَصَبَة (عَصَبَات/عُصَب) band, gang, group, league, union	association, intercourse, society عِشْرَة
عَصَبِي nervous, sinewy	twenty عِشْرُون
عَصَبِي المِزَاج nervous, nervy	decimal عُشْرِي
عَصَبِيَّة nervosity, nervousness	passion, passionate love عِشْق
عَصَبِيّة (عَصَبِيّات) racialism, partisanship, relationship	darkness, gloom عَشْوَة/عَشْوَاء
عَصْر squeezing, pressing	evening عَشِي
عَصْر (عُصُور) age, period, time	late evening عَشِيّة
عَصْر تَلْجِي ice age, glacial period	عَشِير (عُشَرَاء) associate, companion, friend
عَصْر جَلِيْدِي the Ice Age, glacial epoch	عَشِيرَة (عَشَائِر) clan, tribe
عَصْر حَاضِر present time	lover, sweetheart عَشِيْق
عَصْر حَجَرِي Stone Age	beloved, sweetheart عَشِيْقَة
عَصْرِي contemporary, modern, new	rod, staff, stick عَصًا/عَصَاة
عَصْف blast, blowing of wind	عِصَابَة (عَصَائِب) bandage, dressing
عَصْفَة a blast or gust of wind	عِصَابَة (عِصَابات) league, association, band, group
عُصْفُر safflower	juice, sap عُصَار/عُصَارَة
عُصْفُور (عَصَافِيْر) sparrow	chaff, straw عُصَافَة
عُصْفُور دُوْرِي house sparrow	عِصَام (عُصُم/أَعْصِمَة) strap, thong, braces
	عَصَب (أَعْصَاب) nerve, sinew, tendon
	عُصْبَة الأُمَم the League of Nations

عُضْو فخْري	honorary member
عَضُوض	biting, mordacious
عُضْوي	organic
عُضْويّة	organism, membership
عَطًا/عَطَاء	gift, present, offer
عَطَّار	perfumer, druggist
عطَارَة	perfumery, drugs
عُطَارد	Mercury
عُطَاس	sneeze, sneezing
عَطَالَة	unemployment
عَطَب	destruction, damage, wreck
عَطِر	aromatic, fragrant, sweet-smelling
عِطْر (عُطُور)	perfume, scent, essence
عِطْري	sweet-smelling, fragrant
عَطَش	thirst, thristiness
عَطِش	thirsty, longing, dry
عَطْشَان	thirsty, craving, covetous
عَطْف	inclination, curvature, propensity, sympathy

عُصْمَة	necklace
عِصْمَة	prevention, modesty, protection, preservation
عُصُور وُسْطَى	the Middle Ages
عَصِي (أَعْصِيَاء)	refractory, rebel, insurgent
عِصْيَان	refractoriness, rebellion, disobedience
عَصِيب	intensely hot, critical
عُصَيَّة	little rod
عَصِيدة	porridge, gruel
عَصِير البُرْتُقال	orange juice
عَصِير اللَّيْمُون	lime juice
عَصِير/عَصِيرَة	juice, extract
عَضَّاض	biting, mordacious
عُضَال	irremediable, chronic
عَضّة	a bite
عَضُد	aid, assistance, backing, support
عَضُد (أَعْضاد)	arm, strength
عَضَلَة (عَضَلات)	muscle
عَضَلي	muscular, strong
عُضْو (أَعْضَاء)	member, organ, limb
عُضو أَصْلي	regular member

greater, bigger (fem. of أَعْظَم)	عُظْمَى
bony, osseous	عَظْمِي
great, grand, glorious, magnificent	عَظِيم
of paramount importance	عَظِيم الأَهَمِّيَّة
calamity, great misfortune	عَظِيمَة (عَظَائِم)
decent, pure, chaste, honest	عَفّ
obliteration, effacement	عَفَاء
dust-earth	عُفَار/عَفَر
chastity, modesty, purity, decency	عِفَّة
devil, mischievous, cunning	عِفْرِيْت (عَفَاريت)
luggage, rubbish, refuse	عَفْش
acrid, astringent	عَفِص
putrid, rotten, mouldy	عَفِن
putridity, rottenness, mould	عَفَن/عُفُوْنَة
pardon, forgiveness, favour, obliteration	عَفْو
amnesty	عَفْو عَامّ

turn, twist	عَطْفَة
loss, damage, defectiveness, devoid of	عُطْل
unemployment	عَطَل
vacation, holidays, unemployment	عُطْلَة
weekend	عُطْلَة الأُسْبُوع
official holiday	عُطْلَة رَسْمِيّة
weekend	عُطْلَة نِهَايَة الأُسْبُوع
rotten, stinking	عَطِن/عَطِين
kind, compassionate, affectionate	عَطُوف
attachment, affection	عُطُوفَة
gift, present	عَطِيّة (عَطَايا)
sermon, lesson, admonition	عِظَة
bone	عَظْم (عِظَام)
shinbone	عَظْم السَّاق
marrow-bone, medulla	عَظْم مُخّ
greatness, grandeur, importance	عُظْم/عِظَم
majesty, sublimity, magnificence, pride	عَظَمَة
greatness, grandeur, magnitude	عَظَمُوت

heel, offspring, child (أَعْقاب) عَقِب/عَقْب	عَفْواً pardon me, not at all, spontaneously
steep track, mountain road (عِقاب) عَقَبَة	عُفُوْصَة acridity, pungency
obstacle, hindrance, difficulty (عَقَبَات) عَقَبَة	عَفْوِي spontaneous
consequence, end, outcome عُقْبَى	عَفِيْف modest, chaste, upright decent
tyning, knotting, holding, contraction عَقْد	عَفِيْف النَّفْس selfless, unselfish
agreement, contract, document, circle (عُقُود) عَقْد	عَقّ undutiful, disobedient
necklace, chaplet (عُقُود) عِقْد	عُقَاب eagle
contract of rent, lease عَقْد إِيْجار	عِقَاب punishment, penalty, pursuit
contraction of marriage عَقْد الزَّوَاج/القِرَان	عِقَابِي punitive, penal
private contract عَقْد عُرْفِي	عُقَار residue
knot, problem, difficulty, puzzle (عُقَد) عُقْدَة	عَقَار (عَقَارات) real estate, real property
barren, childless عُقْر	عَقَّار (عَقَاقِيْر) drug, medicament
sterility, barrenness عَقْر/عُقْر	عَقَارِي landed, consisting in real estate
scorpion (عَقَارِب) عَقْرَب	عِقَال (عُقُل) shackles, tethers
hand, pointer عَقْرَب السَّاعَة	عَقِب subsequent, coming after
magpie عَقْعَق	عَقِبَ subsequent to
sense, mind, understanding, memory (عُقُول) عَقْل	عُقْب (أَعْقَاب) consequence, result, outcome

muddy, turbid, feculent عَكِر	knot, joint, knob (عُقَل) عُقْلَة
muddiness, turbidity, sediment عَكَر	sterility, barrenness عُقْم/عَقْم
reflection, reversion, contrast عَكْس	sterility, barrenness عُقْمَة
averse, contrary, contrasting عَكْسِي	punishment, penalty (عُقُوبات) عُقُوبَة
highness, exaltedness عَلاَء/عَلْيَاء	corporal punishment عُقُوبة بَدَنِيّة
cure, treatment عِلاَج	punitive, penal عُقُوبِي
effective remedy عِلاَج نَاجِح	disobedience, refractoriness عُقُوق
extreme remedy عِلاَج نِهَائِي	intelligent, sensible, understanding عَقُول
seller of forage عَلاَّف	subsequent, following عَقِيب
coat hanger عَلاَّق	eaglet, small eagle عُقَيِّب
public relations عَلاَقات عَامّة	contractor, contracting party (عُقَدَاء) عَقِيد
friendly relations عَلاَقَات وُدِّيّة	creed, faith, belief (عَقَائِد) عَقِيدَة
suspension rope(عَلائِق) عَلاَقَة	braid, plait (عَقَائِص) عَقِيصَة
relation, connection, attachment (عَلاَقَات) عَلاَقَة	barren, sterile, ineffective, fruitless (عُقُم) عَقِيم
illicit amour, liaison عَلاَقة غَرامِيّة	sultry, sweltering عَكّ/عَكِيك
well-informed, thoroughly knowing عَلاَّم	dregs, lees, sediment عَكَارَة/عِكَارَة
quotation marks عَلاَمَات التّنصِيص	staff, crutch عُكّاز/عُكّازَة
	cobweb, spider-web عُكَاشَة/عُكّاشَة

flag, sign, mark, signpost	عَلَم (أَعْلام)	erudite, very learned, well-informed	عَلَّامَة
science	عِلْم (عُلُوم)	mark, sign, symptom, emblem	عَلَامَة (عَلَامَات)
archeology	عِلْم الآثار القَديمة	question mark	عَلَامَة الاستِفْهَام
biology	عِلْم الأَحْياء	quotation mark	عَلَامَة الاقْتِبَاس
ethics, morals	عِلْم الأَخْلاق	exclamation point	عَلَامَة التَّعَجُّب
phonetics	عِلْم الأَصْوَات	quotation mark	عَلَامَة التَّنْصِيص
theology	عِلْم الإلهيات		
pathology	عِلْم الأَمْرَاض		
sociology	عِلْم الاجْتِمَاع	parantheses	عَلَامَة الحَصْر
etymology	عِلْم الاشْتِقَاق	trade mark	عَلَامَة تِجَارِيّة
economics	عِلْم الاقْتِصَاد	openness, publicity	عَلَانِيّة
political economy	عِلْم الاقْتِصَاد السِّيَاسي	publicly, overtly	عَلَانِيَّةً
rhetoric	عِلْمُ البَدِيع	extra, addition	عِلاوَة
rhetoric or elocution	عِلْم البَلاغة	in addition to	عِلاوَةً عَلَى
elocution, rhetoric	عِلْم البَيَان	box, case, milk can	عُلْبَة (عُلَب)
history	عِلْم التاريخ	weakness, defect, illness, cause	عِلّة (عِلَل)
orthography	عِلْم التَّجْوِيد	fodder, forage	عَلَف (أَعْلاف)
pedagogy	عِلْمُ التَّرْبِية	precious object	عِلْق/عَلْق (أَعْلاَق)
anatomy	عِلْم التَّشْرِيح	mastic, chewing gum	عِلْك
theology	عِلْم التَّوْحِيد	knowledge, perception, acquaintance, information	عِلْم
algebra	عِلْم الجَبْر		

عِلْم الوِلادَة	obstetrics, midwifery	عِلْم الحِسَاب	arithmetics
عِلْم اليَقِين	certain knowledge	عِلْم الحَشَرَات	entomology
عِلْم دِيْني	science of religion	عِلْم الحَيَاة	biology
عِلْم طَبَقَات الأَرْض	geology	عِلْم الحَيَوَان	zoology
عِلْم قِرَاءَة الكَفّ	palmistry	عِلْم الشَّرِيْعَة	the law, Islamic Jurisprudence
عَلْمَانِي	laic, secular	عِلْم الطِّبّ	medical science
عِلْمِي	scientific, erudite	عِلْم الطَّبِيْعَة	physics, natural science
عَلَن	open, public, patent		
عَلَنًا	openly, in public	عِلْم الغَيْب	divination
عَلَنِي	open, public	عِلْم الفَرَائِض	law of descent and distribution
عُلُوّ	height, highness, attitude, elevation	عِلْم الفَلَك	astronomy, astrology
عُلُوّ الصَّوْت	sound intensity	عِلْم الكَلَام	scholastic theology
عُلُوّ الكَعْب	high rank, dignity	عِلْم الكِيْمِياء	chemistry
عُلُوم تَطْبِيقِيّة	applied sciences	عِلْم اللَّاهُوت	theology
عُلْوِي/عَلَوِي	heavenly, upper	عِلْم اللُّغَة	linguistics, philology, lexicography
عُلًى	height, highness, sublimity, attitude	عِلْم المَعَادِن	mineralogy
عَلَى	on, above, upon, at	عِلْم المَعَانِي	rhetoric
عَلِي	high, exalted, sublime	عِلْم النَّبَات/النَّبَاتَات	botany
عَلَى أَثَرِه	immediately after	عِلْم النَّفْس	psychology
عَلَى الأَقَلّ	at least	عِلْم الهَنْدَسَة	geometry
عَلَى التَّقْرِيْب	almost, approximately		

عَمَايَة	ignorance, folly
عَمَّة	aunt, paternal aunt
عَمْد	intention, deliberation, purpose
عَمْدًا	intentionally, deliberately
عُمْدَة	prop, support, pillar
عَمْدي	intentional, deliberate, premeditated
عُمْر (أَعْمَار)	age, life, life span
عُمْر مَدِيد	great age
عُمْرَان	populousness, civilization, structure
عُمْرَاني	civilizational, cultural
عُمْرَة	umrah, minor hajj
عَمْرَة	headdress, tire, overhauling
عُمْق/عَمْق (أَعْمَاق)	depth, profundity, bottom
عَمَل (أَعْمَال)	act, action, work, deed, job
عَمَل الخَيْر	benevolence, charity
عَمَل كِتَابِي	clerical work

عَلَى التَّوَالِي	successively, continuously
على السَّوَاء	equally, likewise
عَلَى المَلَأ	publicly, openly
عَلَى حِدَة	isolated, detached, alone, apart from others
عَلَى حَيْدة	apart, aside
عَلَى مَهْل	slowly, gently, leisurely
عُلِّيّة/علِّيّة	upstairs room, attic
عُلَّيْق	blackberry, raspberry
عَلِيق (عَلَائِق)	fodder, provender
عَلِيم (عُلَمَاء)	knowing, all knowing, omniscient
عِلِّيُّون	uppermost heaven
عَمّ (أَعْمَام)	uncle, paternal uncle
عِمَاد (عَمَد)	column, pillar, prop
عِمَارَة (عَمَائِر/عِمَارَات)	building, structure, edifice, lot
عَمَالَة (عَمَالات)	wages, commission
عِمَامَة (عَمَائِم)	turban

head, principal, dean	عَمِيد (عُمَدَاء)
profound, deep	عَمِيق
client, customer, agent	عَمِيل (عُمَلَاء)
general, common, universal	عَمِيم
toil, drudge, trouble, pains	عَنَاء
obstinacy, resistance, pertinacity	عِنَاد
embracing, hugging	عِنَاق
reins, bridle	عِنَان (أَعِنَّة)
care, attention, concern, heed	عِنَايَة
medical care	عِنَايَة طِبِّيَّة
grapes	عِنَب (أَعْنَاب)
ambergris	عَنْبَر
perfumed with ambergris	عَنْبَري
impotence, impotency	عُنَّة
distress, adversity, affliction	عَنَت
near, on, upon	عِنْدَ
in case of need	عِنْدَ الاقْتِضَاء
on demand	عِنْدَ الطَّلَب

currency, money	عُمْلَة
counterfeit money	عُمْلَة زَائِفَة
soft currency	عُمْلَة سَهْلَة
standard currency	عُمْلَة صَاغ
hard currency	عُمْلَة صَعْبَة
practical, applied	عَمَلي
practically	عَمَلِيًّا
operation, work, procedure	عَمَلِيَّة (عَمَلِيَّات)
surgical operation	عَمَلِيَّة جِرَاحِيَّة
post, pole, column	عَمُود (عُمُد)
vertebral column	عَمُود شَوْكي
vertebral column	عَمُود فِقْري
columnar, vertical	عَمُودي
brokerage, commission	عُمُوْلَة
generality, totality, universality	عُمُوم
generally, in general	عُمُومًا
unclehood	عُمُوْمَة
general, public, common	عُمُومي
blindness, ignorance	عَمًى

impotent	عِنِّيْن	if necessary	عِنْد اللُّزُوم
adultery, fornication, prostitution	عَهَارَة	then, at that time	عِنْدَئِذ
pledge, promise, contract, obligation, era, period	عَهْد (عُهُود)	nightingale	عَنْدَلِيْب (عَنَادل)
		when, whenever	عِنْدَمَا
transition period	عَهْد انْتِقَالي	goat	عَنْز/عَنْزَة
responsibility, charge, custody	عُهْدَة	element, origin, ingredient, race	عُنْصُر (عَنَاصِر)
adultery, prostitution, debauchery	عِهْر	racial, elemental	عُنْصُري
ally, allied person, confederate	عَهِيْد	race, racial theory	عُنْصُرِيّة
		violence, vehemence, severity, roughness	عُنْف
yelling, howling, howl	عُوَاء	prime, bloom	عُنْفُوَان
custom duties	عَوَائِد الجُمْرُك	neck	عُنْق/عُنُق (أَعْنَاق)
house taxes	عَوَائِد مَبَان	fabulous bird, griffin	عَنْقَاء
fault, flaw, defect	عَوَار/عِوَار	hawker, peddler	عِنْقَاش
swimmer	عَوَّام	bunch, cluster	عُنْقُود (عَنَاقِيْد)
buoy, raft	عَوَّامَة	spider	عَنْكَبُوت (عَنَاكِب)
life-buoy	عَوَّامَة للنَّجَاة	address, heading, title	عُنْوَان (عَنَاوِين)
crook, bend, crookedness	عِوَج/عَوَج	force, violence, coercion	عَنْوَة
return, repetition, recurrence	عَوْد	forcibly, by force	عَنْوَةً
wood, stick, lute	عُوْد (أَعْوَاد)	obstinate, stubborn, opinionated	عَنِيْد
peony	عُوْد الصَّلِيْب	violent, severe, harsh, rough	عَنِيْف

powerless, faint, incapable, weak عَيّ (أَعْيَاء)	matchstick, match عُوْد الكِبْرِيْت
disability, weakness, faintness, lassitude عَيَاء	return, reversion عَوْدَة
	taking shelter or refuge عَوْذ
clinic, consultation room عِيَادَة (عِيَادَات)	refuge, shelter, asylum عَوَذ
policlinic, outdoor patient عِيَادة خَارِجيّة	charm, spell عُوْذَة
	fault, defect, genitals عَوْرَة
indoor patient عِيَادَة دَاخِليَّة	want, need, lack, poverty عَوْز
taking refuge عِيَاذ	
standard, standard measure عِيَار	needy, destitute, poor عَوِز
	substitute, recompense, return عِوَض
straggler, vagabound, scoundrel عَيَّار	
	hindering, detaining, retarding عَوْق
bread-seller عَيَّاش	
yelling, howling, screaming عِيَاط	wailing, lamenting, support, maintenance عَوْل
tired, fatigued, عَيَّان	reliance, dependence عِوَل
viewing, witnessing عِيَان	floating, swimming عَوْم
defect, flaw, fault, blemish, foible عَيْب (عُيُوب)	assistance, aid, help, relief عَوْن
physical defect عَيْب جسْمي	assistant, helper عَوْن (أَعْوَان)
leather bag, suitcase, trunk عَيْبَة	abstruse, difficult, deep, recondite عَوِيص
feast, festival عِيْد (أَعْيَاد)	wailing, lament عَوِيْل
Feast of Immolation عِيْد الأضْحَى	eyeglasses, spectacles عُوَيْنَات

eminent or notable person	عَيْن (أَعْيَان)	Feast of breaking fast	عيْد الفِطْر
eye, hole, spring, source	عَيْن (عُيُون)	Christmas Day	عيْد المِيْلاد
suspicious glance	عَيْن شَزْرَاء	All Saints Day	عيْد جَمِيْع القِدِّيْسين
sample, specimen	عَيِّنة (عَيِّنَات)	New Year's Day	عيْد رَأْس السَّنَة
ocular, optic	عَيْنِي	anniversary	عيْد سَنَوِي تَذْكَارِي
		All Saints Day	عيْد كل القِدِّيْسين
غ		anniversary, centennial	عيْد مئَوِي
absent, hidden, invisible	غَائِب	feast's gift	عيْديّة
hallow, sinking	غَائِر	wild ass	عَيْر (أَعْيَار)
excrements, stool	غَائِط	caravan	عِيْر (عِيرَات)
calamity, disaster	غَائِلة (غَوَائِل)	living, livelihood, way of living	عَيْش
cloudy, clouded	غَائِم	easy life	عَيْش بَارِد
forest, jungle, thicket, wood	غَابَة (غَابَات)	life of comfort and ease	عَيْش رَغْد
past, bygone	غَابِر	hard life	عَيْش ضَنْك
young girl, damsel	غَادَة	comfortable life	عَيْش نَاعِم
treacherous, faithless, deceitful	غَادِر	life, way of life	عِيْشَة
		pleasant life	عِيْشَة رَاضِيَة
cave, cavern	غَار (غِيْرَان)	loathing, disgust	عَيْف
rolling attacks	غَارَات مُتَوَاصِلَة	family members, dependents	عَيِّل (عِيَال)

most likely	غَالِبًا	invasion, raid, incursion	غَارَة (غَارَات)
sorrowful, sad, grievous	غَامّ	air raid or attack	غَارَة جَوِّيَّة
abundant, overflowing, plentiful	غَامِر	drowned, sunk, immersed	غَارِق
obscure, ambiguous, mysterious, recondite	غَامِض	gas, petroleum	غَاز (غَازَات)
mystery, secret, enigma	غَامِضَة (غَوَامِض)	invader, warrior, ghazi	غَازٍ (غُزَاة)
dark colour	غَامِق	poison gases	غَازَات سَامَّة
successful	غَانِم	gaseous, gas like	غَازِي
seducer, alluler, tempter	غَاوٍ	soap, shampoo	غَاسُول
purpose, aim, intention, objective, extremity	غَايَة (غَايَات)	unjust, oppressor, wrongdoer	غَاشِم
consequence, issue, effect, outcome	غِبّ	disaster, calamity, pericardium	غَاشِيَة (غَوَاش)
stupidity, foolishness, ignorance	غَبَاء/غَبَاوَة	usurper, robber	غَاصِب (غُصَّاب)
dust, dust cloud	غُبَار	angry, furious, raged, annoyed	غَاضِب
dust, dust colour	غُبْرَة/غَبَرَة	draf, draught	غَاطِس
darkness, duskiness	غَبَش	negligent, neglectful, inadvertent	غَافِل
opaque, dark, dusky	غَبِش	expensive, dear, high-priced	غَالٍ
exultation, rapture, happiness, felicity	غِبْطَة	majority of, most of	غَالِب
stupidity, foolishness	غَبَن	victor, conqueror, prevalent	غَالِب (غَلَبَة)
criminal fraud	غُبْن فَاحِش		

pond, pool, brook, rivulet	غَدِير (غُدُر)	wrong, injustice, fraud, deceit	غَبْن/غُبْن
food, aliment, nourishment	غِذَاء (أَغْذِيَة)	silly, foolish, stupid, ignorant	غَبِي (أَغْبِيَاء)
alimentary, nutritious	غِذَائِي	lean, thin, emaciated, meager	غَثّ/غَثِيث
feeding, nurture, nourishment	غَذْو	scum	غُثَاء
gullible, green horn, inexperienced	غِرّ (أَغْرَار)	leanness, thinness, meagreness	غَثَاثَة
glue	غَرًا/غِرَاء	nausea, sickness	غَثْي/غَثَيَان
crow, raven	غُرَاب (غِرْبان)	following day	غَد
curiosity, oddness, strangeness	غَرَابَة	tomorrow	غَدًا
edge of a sword	غِرَار	lunch, breakfast	غَدَاء (أَغْدِيَة)
deceptive, delusive	غَرَّار	early morning	غَدَاة (غَدَوَات)
inexperience, thoughtlessness, gullibility	غَرَارَة	treacherous, perfidious, faithless	غَدَّار
cultivation, growing	غِرَاسَة	raven	غُدَاف
gram	غَرَام	gland	غُدَّة (غُدَد)
fondness, passion, ardent love, infatuation	غَرَام	thyroid gland	غُدَّة دَرَقِيّة
fine, penalty, compensation	غَرَامَة	glandular	غُدَدِي
		treachery, betrayal, perfidy	غَدْر
collective fine	غَرَامة إِجْمالِيّة	abundant, copious	غَدِق
a fine	غَرَامَة مَالِيّة	lassitude, languor, limpness	غَدَن/غُدْنَة
passionate, amorous	غَرَامي	early morning	غُدْوَة

room, chamber, unit, ward	غُرْفة (غُرَف)	glue pot	غَرَّايَة
dining room	غُرْفَة الأَكْل	west, occident, remoteness, sharpness	غَرْب
combustion chamber	غُرْفَة الاحْتِراق	toward the west	غَرْبًا
reception, parlour	غُرْفَة الاسْتِقْبال	sieve	غِرْبال (غَرَابيل)
cold-storage room	غُرْفَة التَّبْريد	expatriation, exile, away from home	غُرْبَة
chamber of commerce	غُرْفَة التِّجَارَة	western, occidental	غَرْبِي
dressing room	غُرْفَة الزِّينَة	blaze, whiteness, the best of	غُرَّة
operating theatre	غُرْفَة العَمَلِيّات الجِراحِيّة	inattention, inadvertence	غِرّة
bedroom	غُرْفَة النَّوْم	twittering, worbling, singing	غَرَد
drowned	غَرْقَان	stitch	غُرْزَة (غُرَز)
loss, damage	غُرْم	plant, planting, seedling	غَرْس
crane	غُرْنُوق (غَرَانيْق)	plant, seedling, layer	غَرْس/غِرْس (أَغْراس)
sunset	غُرُوب الشَّمْس	plant, nursery plant	غَرْسَة
conceit, vanity, delusion, deception	غُرُور	piastre	غِرْش/غُرْش (غُرُوش)
delusive, deceptive, fallacious	غَرُور	target, aim, goal, purpose, advantage, desire	غَرَض (أَغْراض)
self-deception, self-delusion	غُرُور بِنَفْسِه	guinea fowl	غُرْغُر
strange, peculiar, curious, extraneous, unusual	غَرِيب (غُرَباء)	gargle, gargling	غَرْغَرَة

dalliance, flirtation, love poetry	غَزَل	eccentric, queer, odd, cranky	غَرِيب الأَطْوَار
spun yarn or thread	غَزْل (غُزُول)	twittering, singing (bird)	غِرِّيد
attack, invasion, assault	غَزْو	deceived, deluded, beguiled	غَرِير
abundant, plentiful, ample	غَزِير	instinct, natural impulse, intuition	غَرِيْزَة (غَرَائِز)
washerman, laundryman	غَسَّال	natural, instinctive	غَرِيْزِي
washerwoman, washing machine	غَسَّالَة	nursery plant, layer	غَرِيْسَة (غَرَائِس)
dusk, twilight, dark of night	غَسَق	tender, fresh	غَرِيض
washing, cleansing	غَسْل	drowned, immersed	غَرِيق (غَرْقَى)
washing of the whole body	غُسْل	creditor, debtor, rival	غَرِيْم
lotion, detergent	غَسُول	invasion, incursion, military expedition	غَزَاة/غَزْوَة (غَزَوَات)
washed, washed clothes	غَسِيْل	abundance, plenty, profusion, copiousness	غَزَارَة
cheating, deceiving	غُشّ	gazelle	غَزَال
deception, fraud, deceit, cheat	غِشّ	spinner	غَزَّال
cover, envelope, membrane	غِشَاء (أَغْشِيَة)	female gazelle, doe	غَزَالَة
maidenhead, hymen, virginal membrane	غِشَاء البَكَارَة	spider	غَزَّالَة
mucous membrane	غِشَاء مُخَاطِي	profusion, abundance, plenty	غَزْر
		spinning	غَزْل

olive branch	غُصْن الزَّيْتُون	serous membrance	غِشَاء مَصْلِي
sprout, small twig	غُصْنَة	nuclear membrane	غِشَاء نَوَوِي
fresh, tender, lush, succulent	غَضّ	cheat, swindler, impostor	غَشَّاش
freshness, luxuriance, affluence, opulence	غَضَارَة	veil, cover, wrap	غِشَاوَة/غَشَاوَة
freshness, juiciness, tenderness, succulence	غَضَاضَة	oppression, wrong, injustice	غَشْم
anger, rage, fury, indignation	غَضَب	covering, veil, envelope	غَشْوَة
angry, annoyed, enraged, furious	غَضِب	oppressor, tyrant, unjust	غَشُوم
irate, infuriated, enraged	غَضْبان	inexperience, gullibility, stupidity	غُشُومَة
abundant, lush, opulent, exuberant	غَضِر	swooning, fainting fit	غَشَيان
cartilage, gristle	غُضْرُوف (غَضَارِيْف)	swoon, fainting fit	غَشْيَة
wrinkles, crease, ridges	غَضْن/غَضَن (غُضُون)	inexperienced, untrained, green horn	غَشِيم
lion	غَضَنْفَر	usurpation, compulsion, coercion	غَصْب
peevish, irritable, irascible	غَضُوب	forcibly, by force	غَصْبًا
freshness, softness, juiciness, succulence	غُضُوضَة	grief, distress, torment, choker	غُصَّة (غُصَص)
fresh, green, lush, luxuriant	غَضِير	agony of death	غُصَّة المَوْت
		branch, bough, twig	غُصْن (غُصُون/أَغْصَان)

inadvertence, غَفَل inattention, indifference, carelessness	fresh, tender, soft, غَضِيْض juicy, succulent
careless, negligent, غَفْلَان inattentive	immersion, plunging, غَطّ dipping
negligence, غَفْلَة inadvertence, heedlessness	cover, wrap, (أَغْطِيَة) غِطَاء envelope
forgiving, ready to غَفُور forgive	headgear غِطَاء الرَّأْس
large, huge غَفِيْر	diver, dipper غَطَّاس
grudge, spite, rancour غِلّ	haughtiness, غَطْرَسَة snobbishness, arrogance
fetters, shackles (أَغْلَال) غُلّ	haughty, (غَطَارِيْس) غِطْرِيْس snobbish, conceited
burning thirst, ardent غُلّ/غُلَّة desire	great or (غَطَارِف) غِطْرِيف noble man
victorious, غَلَّاب conquering, triumphant	dipping, diving, غَطْس plunging
thikness, roughness غِلَاظَة	a dip غَطْسَة
cover, wrapper, (غُلُف) غِلَاف envelope	dim-sightedness, غَطْش obscurity
boy, lad, youth, (غِلْمَان) غُلَام servant	snore, snoring غَطِيْط
boiler, (غَلَّايَات) غَلَّايَة cauldron	forgiving, much غَفَّار forgiving
conquering, beating, غَلَب overcoming	pardon, forgiveness غَفْر
victory, conquest غَلَبَة	forgiveness, pardon غُفْرَان
crops, produce, product غَلَّة	cover, lid غُفْرَة
	anonymous, devoid of, غُفْل undesignated

glycerine	غْلِيسَرِين	vintage	غَلَّة الكَرْم
thick, coarse, rude, rough, harsh	غَلِيظ (غِلاظ)	darkness, dusk before dawn	غَلَس
water pipe, galleon	غَلْيُون	error, mistake	غَلَط (أَغْلاط)
tobacco pipe	غَلْيُون التَّدْخِين	erring, erroneous, wrong	غَلْطان
sorrow, grief, sadness	غَمّ (غُمُوم)	error, mistake	غَلْطَة (غَلَطات)
dimple	غَمَّازَة	clerical error	غَلْطَة كِتابيّة
blink, wink	غِمَاض	typographical error, misprint, printer's error	غَلْطَة مَطْبَعِيَّة
clouds	غَمَام (غَمَائِم)		
sorrow, grief, anxiety	غُمَّة	thickness, coarseness, roughness, harshness	غِلَظ
sheath, scabbard	غِمْد (أَغْماد)		
deluge, flood, inundation, submersion	غَمْر	thickness, crudeness, roughness, harshness	غِلْظَة
pangs of death	غَمَرَات المَوْت	foreskin, prepuce	غُلْفَة
agony, throe, hardship	غَمْرَة (غِمار)	ambiguous, obscure, recondite	غَلِق
submersion, deluge, flood	غَمْرَة (غَمَرات)	lock, padlock	غَلَق (أَغْلاق)
wink, hint, sign	غَمْزَة (غَمْزَات)	lewd, lustful, lascivious	غَلِم
plunging, dipping, immersion	غَمْس	lust, carnal desire	غُلْمَة
sleep, slumber	غُمْض	excess, extravagance, exaggeration	غُلُوّ
wink, blink	غُمْضَة	youth, youthfulness, adolescence	غُلُومَة
mumble, cry	غَمْغَمَة		
distressful, disastrous	غَمُوس	boiling, ebullition	غَلْي/غَلَيَان

غَنِيْمَة باردة easy prey, easy come	غُمُوض/غُمُوضَة obscurity, abstruseness, ambiguity
غَوَّاص diver, pearl diver	غَمْي swoon, fainting fit, unconsciousness
غَوَّاصَة submarine	
غَوَايَة seduction, enticement, error	غَمِيْزَة shortcoming, blemish
غَوْث help, appeal for help, succour	غَنَاء wealth, riches, affluence, sufficiency
غَوْر (أَغْوَار) fathom, depth, bottom	غِنَاء singing, song, chanting
	غِنَائي singing, vocal
غَوْص diving, plunging	غَنَّام shepherd, herder of sheep
غَوْط (غِيْطان) hallow, cavity	غُنَّة nasal pronunciation or sound
غَوْغَاء clamour, din, uproar, rabble	
غُوْل demon, jinni, goblin	غُنْج dalliance, flirtation, coquetry
غَوِيْص deep	غُنْدُر plump, chubby
غَوِيْط deep	غُنْدُور dandy, fop
غَيّ seduction, enticement, offence	غَنْغَرِيْنَا gangrene
غِيَاب absence, concealment	غُنْم booty, spoils, profit
غِيَاب الشَّمْس sunset	غَنَم (أَغْنَام) sheep, goat
غِيَابَة (غَيَابَات) depth, bottom	غِنًى wealth, riches, abundance, satisfaction
غِيَاث help, succour, aid	غَنِي (أَغْنِيَاء) rich, wealthy, prosperous
غَيْب absence, unseen, hidden	غَنِيْمَة (غَنَائِم) booty, spoils, loot, gain
غَيْبَة absence, concealment	

unprecedented	غَيْر مَسْبُوق	calumny, slander	غَيْبَة
inaudible	غَيْر مَسْمُوع	distraction, absent-mindedness, unconsciousness	غَيْبُوبة
illicit, unlawful	غَيْر مَشْرُوع		
unreasonable, absurd	غَيْر مَعْقُول	hidden, unseen, invisible	غَيْبِي
unconfined, unlimited, unrestricted	غَيْر مُقَيَّد	error, sin	غَيَّة
inattentive, heedless, inadvertent	غَيْر مُلْتَفِت	ghetto	غِيتُو
impossible, improbable	غَيْر مُمْكِن	rain	غَيْث (غُيُوث)
irregular, errotic	غَيْر مُنَظَّم	softness, tenderness	غَيْد
invisible, unseen	غَيْر مَنْظُور	except, save, not	غَيْرَ
incessant, continual	غَيْر مُنْقَطِع	vicissitudes of time	غَيَر الدَّهْر
nonexistent	غَيْر مَوْجُود	unofficial	غَيْر رَسْمِي
zealousy, zeal, fervour	غَيْرَة	inorganic	غَيْر عُضْوِي
abortion, premature foetus	غَيْض	illegal, unlawful	غَيْر قَانُونِي
thicket, wood, jungle	غَيْضَة	harmless, innocent, inoffensive	غير مُؤْذٍ
anger, rage, fury	غَيْظ	uncommon, unusual	غير مَأْلُوف
guile, deceit, assassination	غِيْلَة	unsafe, insecure	غير مَأْمُون
clouds	غَيْم (غُيُوم)	indirect	غير مُبَاشِر
		heedless, careless	غير مُبَالٍ
zealous, enthusiastic, jealous	غَيُور	unaffected	غير مُتَأَثِّر
		boundless, unlimited, infinite, endless	غَيْر مُتَنَاهٍ
		unlimited, boundless, infinite	غَيْر مَحْدُود

languid, listless, flagged فاتِر الهِمَّة	
assassin, killer, murderer فَاتِك	heart فُؤَاد (أَفْئِدَة)
seductive, fascinating, charming فَاتِن (فَوَاتِن)	group, party, band, category فِئَة (فِئَات)
invoice, bill فَاتُورَة (فَوَاتِير)	mouse, rat فَأْر (فِئْرَان)
pro-forma invoice, فَاتورةَ أَوَّلِيَّة	mouse فَأَرة/فَارَة
sudden, surprising فَاجِئ	axe, hatchet فَأْس/فَاس (فُؤُوس)
debauchee, wanton, profligate فَاجِر (فُجَّار/فَجَرَة)	good omen, auspices فَأْل (فُؤُول)
adulteress, prostitute, whore فَاجِرَة (فَوَاجِر)	passing away, transient, transitory فَائِت
disaster, catastrophe, misfortune فَاجِعَة (فَوَاجِع)	benefit, advantage, use, profit فَائِدَة (فَوَائِد)
obscene, abominable, enormous, exorbitant فَاحِش	successful, victorious فَائِز
prostitute, whore, adulteress فَاحِشَة	flowing, abundant, profuse فَائِض
monstrosity, adultery, abomination فَاحِشَة (فَوَاحِش)	interest, benefit فَائِض (فَوَائِض)
examiner فَاحِص	superior, outstanding, excellent فَائِق
auditor فَاحِص الحِسَابَات	factory, plant فَابْرِيْكَة (فبارك)
jet-black, black فَاحِم	victor, conqueror فَاتِح
jet-black, coal black فَاحِم السَّوَاد	opening, beginning, commencement فَاتِحَة (فَوَاتِح)
	lukewarm, tepid, slack فَاتِر

fascist, fascistic	فاشِسْتي/فاشِيْسْتي	magnificent, excellent, outstanding, boastful	فاخِر
fascism	فاشِسْتيّة	redeemer	فاد
worthless, futile	فاشِل	oppressive, serious, grievous, exorbitant	فادِح
fascist	فاشِي	disaster, calamity	فادِحَة (فَوَادِح)
separating, conclusive, decisive	فاصِل	plummet, plumbline	فادِن (فَوَادِن)
interspace, interval, dash	فاصِلَة (فَوَاصِل)	fugitive, fleeing	فارّ
bean	فاصُوليا	mouse, rat	فار (فِيْران)
vacant, empty, free	فاضٍ	knight, horseman, cavalier	فارِس (فُرْسَان)
infamous, notorious ignominious, disgraceful	فاضِح	void, vacant, unoccupied	فارِغ
surplus, left over, remnant	فاضِل	distinctive, discriminative, distinguishing	فارِق
learned, excellent, outstanding	فاضِل (فُضَلَاء)	agile, nimble, swift, pretty	فارِه
creator	فاطِر	turquoise	فارُوز
actor, doer	فاعِل	discriminator, sagacious	فارُوق
worker, labourer	فاعِل (فَعَلَة)	vaseline	فازْلِيْن
efficacy, effectiveness	فاعِليّة	spoiled, corrupt, decayed, foul	فاسِد
indigence, want, poverty	فاقَة	dissolute, debauchee, impious, sinful, adulterer	فاسِق (فُسّاق/فَسَقة)
deprived of, devoid of, loser	فاقِد		
senseless, unconscious, insensible	فاقِد الشُّعُور		

murderous, lethal فَتَّاك	فَاقِد الضَّمير conscienceless, unconscionable, unscrupulous
cordmaker, twister فَتَّال	
fascinating, captivating, فَتَّان seducer	bright yellow فَاقِع
opening, beginning فَتْح	cheerful, gleeful, فَاكِه joyful, funny
victory, (فُتُوح/فُتُوحات) فَتْح conquest, triumph	fruit seller فَاكِهَاني
opening of a فَتْح الاعْتِمَاد credit	fruits (فَوَاكِه) فَاكِهَة
	escaped, free, loose فَالِت
opening, hole, (فُتَح) فُتْحَة breach	paralysis, hemiplegia فَالِج
lassitude, languor, فَتْرَة slackness	successful, progressive, فَالِح lucky
intermission, (فَتَرَات) فَتْرَة interval, period	perishable, evanescent, فَانٍ ephemeral
transition period فَتْرَة الانْتِقَال	flannel فَانِلَة
recess, rest, break فَتْرَة الرَّاحَة	lantern (فَوَانِيس) فَانُوس
crack, cleft, (فُتُوق) فَتْق fissure, rip	magic lantern فَانُوس سِحْري
	factory, plant فَاوَرِيقَة
assassination, murder فَتْك	February فَبْرَايِر
twisting, twining فَتْل	youth, adolescence فَتَاء
a twist, thread فَتْلَة	crumbs, fragments فُتَات
trial, sedition, (فِتَن) فِتْنَة affliction, captivation	young girl, girl (فَتَيَات) فَتَاة
	opener, beginner فَتَّاح
youth, youthfulness, فُتُوَّة adolescence	investigator, examiner, فَتَّاش inspector
	hernia, rupture فِتَاق

air pocket	فَجْوَة هَوَائِيَّة	lassitude, slackness, languor	فُتُور
debauchery, immorality, dissipation	فُجُور	lassitude, languor, flagging	فُتُور الهِمَّة
grievous, painful, distressing	فَجُوع	fatwa, legal decision	فَتْوَى (فَتَاوٍ/فَتَاوَى)
disaster, calamity	فَجِيعَة (فَجَائِع)	youth, young, juvenile	فَتَى (فِتْيَة/فِتْيَان)
shameless, obscene, lewd, indecent	فَحَّاش	crumbs, smithers	فَتِيت
enormity, obscenity, abomination	فُحْش	youthfulness, juvenility	فَتِيَّة
adultery, lewdness, enormity	فَحْشَاء	ripped, rent, ruptured	فَتِيق
test, check up, investigation, examination	فَحْص (فُحُوص)	twisted, entwined, coiled	فَتِيل
audit	فَحْص الحِسَابَات	wick, filament	فَتِيلَة (فَتَائِل/فَتِيلَات)
bull, male of the animal	فَحْل (فُحُول)	unripe, green	فِجّ
coal, charcoal	فَحْم	suddenly, unexpectedly	فَجْأَةً/فُجَاءَةً
lump of coal	فَحْمَة	sudden, unexpected	فُجَائِي
meaning, import, sense	فَحْوَى	daybreak, dawn	فَجْر
jet-black	فَحِيم	glutton, voracious	فَجْعَان
glory, pride, vanity	فَخَار	gluttony	فَجْعَة/فَجَاعَة
earthenware, crockery	فَخَّار	braggart, windbag, imposter	فَجْفَاج
magnificence, splendour, greatness, eminence	فَخَامَة	radish	فُجْل
		opening, interstice, crevice	فَجْوَة (فَجَوَات)

seed separator	فَرَّازَة آلية	thigh, leg	فَخْذ
horsemanship, chivalry	فَرَاسَة	glory, honour, vanity	فَخْر
discernment, perspicacity	فِرَاسَة	honorary	فَخْري
office boy, peon, attendant	فَرّاش	magnificent, grand, stately, luxurious	فَخْم
mattress, bed, cushion	فِرَاش (أَفْرِشَة/فُرُش)	proud, boastful	فَخُور
sickbed	فِرَاش المَرَض	release, redemption, ransom	فِدَاء
deathbed	فِرَاش المَوْت	fedayeen, commando	فِدَائي
butterfly, moth	فَرَاش/فَرَاشَة	exorbitance, burdensomeness	فَدَاحَة
vacuum, void	فَرَاغ	yoke of oxen	فَدّان
leisure	فَرَاغ البَال	redemption, release, ransom	فِدَّى/فَدَّى
departure, separation, difference	فِرَاق	redemption, release, ransom	فِدْيَة (فدَيات)
baker	فَرّان	single, unique, unusual	فَذّ (فُذُوذ)
nimbleness, agility	فَرَاهَة	furrier	فَرّاء
strawberry	فَرَاوَلَة	sweet, fresh	فُرَات
interstice, opening, aperture, vulva	فَرْج (فُرُوج)	singly, one by one	فُرَادًا/فُرَادَى
relief, ease, comfort, pleasure	فَرَج/فُرْجَة	flight, escape	فِرَار
interstice, opening, aperture, hole	فُرْجَة (فُرَج)	fugitive, runaway, quick silver	فَرّار
joy, happiness, gladness, mirth	فَرَح	sorter, separator	فَرّاز

فَرْش (فُرُوش) furniture, house furniture, bedding	فَرِح cheerful, joyful, happy
فُرْشَاة brush, paintbrush	فَرْحَان delighted, happy, joyful, cheerful
فُرْشَة bed, mattress	فَرْحَة joy, happiness
فُرْشَة (فُرَش) brush, paintbrush	فَرْخ (أَفْرَاخ/فِرَاخ) the young of birds
فُرْشَة الأَسْنَان tooth brush	فَرْخَة (فِرَاخ) poultry, fowls, hen
فُرْشَة الحَلاَقَة shaving brush	
فُرْشَة الشَّعْر hair brush	فَرْد (أَفْرَاد/فُرَادَى) individual, alone, single, unique
فُرْشَة رِيش feather duster	فَرْدًا فَرْدًا singly, one by one
فِرْصَاد mulberry, mulberry tree	فِرْدوس paradise, garden
فُرْصَة (فُرَص) chance, recess, opportunity, occasion	فَرْدِي individual, solitary, single
فُرْصَة عَظِيْمَة golden opportunity	فَرْدِيَّة individualism, individuality
فَرْض (فُرُوض) obligation, duty, ordinance, assumption	فَرْز sorting, selecting, isolation, detachment
فَرْض عَيْن individual duty	فِرْزَان (فَرَازِين) queen (in chess)
فَرْض كِفَايَة collective duty	فَرَس (فِرَاس) horse, mare, knight
فَرْض مَدْرَسِي task, home work	
فُرْضَة gap, crevice, interstice	فَرَس البَحْر sea-horse, hippopotamus
فُرْضَة بَحْرِيَّة seaport, harbour	فَرَس الرِّهَان race horse
فَرْضِي conjectural, suppositional, speculative	فَرْسَخ (فَرَاسِخ) parasang, league

detachment, division فِرْقَة عَسْكَرِيّة	exaggeration, excess, فَرْط intensity
music band, orchestra فِرْقَة مُوسِيقِيّة	فَرْط الإِحْسَاس hypersensitiveness
explosion, blast, crack فَرْقَعَة	brunch, division, (فُرُوع) فَرْع twig, bough
rubbing, scrubbing فَرْك	
decree, firman (فَرَامِين) فَرْمَان	Pharaoh (فَرَاعِنَة) فِرْعُون
brake (فَرَامِل) فَرْمَلَة	minor, secondary, فَرْعِي subsidiary
oven, bakery (أَفْرَان) فُرْن	
agile, lively, swift فَرِه	empty, vacant, void فَرِغ
fur, skin فَرْو/فَرْوَة	convenience, comfort فَرْفَشَة
horsemanship, فُرُوسة/فُرُوسِيّة knighthood	parting, separating فَرْق
	division, section, unit فِرْق
voidness, vacuity فُرُوغ	fright, dismay, terror فَرَق
fearful, timorous, فُرُوق terrified	fearful, terrified فَرِق
unprecedented, unheard فَرِي	difference, (فُرُوق) فَرْق dissimilarity, remainder
fabricated lie, (فِرًى) فِرْيَة slander	proof, convincing فُرْقَان evidence
unique, incomparable, فَرِيد alone	separation, disunion فُرْقَة
precious gem (فَرَائِد) فَرِيْدَة	group, party, (فِرَق) فِرْقَة band, troop, sect
victim, prey (فَرَائِس) فَرِيسَة	firing squad فِرْقَة الإِعْدَام
obligation, (فَرَائِض) فَرِيضَة religious duty, precept	fire brigade فِرْقَة المَطَافِئ
party, company, (فُرُوق) فَرِيق unit, team	company of فِرْقَة تَمْثِيلِيّة actors

physiology	فَسْلَجَة	caution, scare crow	فَزَّاعَة
physiological	فَسْلَجِي	bolt, start, spring	فَزَّة
wide, spacious, ample	فَسِيح	fearful, scared, frightened, terrified	فَزِع
physiologist	فسيولُوجِي		
physiology	فسيولُوجيا	fright, fear, panic, terror	فَزْع (أَفْزَاع)
braggart, vain boaster	فَشَار		
bragging, boasting	فُشَار/فَشْر	frightful, fearful, terrified	فَزْعان
failure, flop, disappointment	فَشَل	puzzle, riddle	فَزُّورة
faint-hearted, cowardly	فَشِل	corruption, invalidity, deterioration, decomposition	فَسَاد
eloquence, fluency	فَصَاحَة		
blood-letting, venesection	فَصْد/فِصَاد	lady's gown or dress	فُسْتَان (فَسَاتِين)
phosphate	فُصْفَات	wide space, open space	فُسْحَة (فُسَح)
phosphorus	فُصْفُور		
parting, separating, division	فَصْل	abrogation, annulment, abolition, cancellation	فَسْخ
class, section, chapter, part	فَصْل (فُصُول)	abrogative, nullifying	فَسْخِي
final decision	فَصْل الخِطاب	tent, pavilion, marquee	فُسْطَاط (فَسَاطِيط)
comma	فَصْلَة	فُسْطان (فَسَاطِين) = فُسْتَان	
semicolon	فَصْلَة مَنْقُوطَة	phosphate	فُسْفَات
bean	فَصُوليا	phosphorus	فُسْفُور
eloquent, fluent, pure	فصِيح (فُصَحَاء)	debauchery, sin, adultery, dissoluteness	فِسْق

officiousness, meddling, curiousity	فُضُول
officious, meddlesome, inquisitive	فُضُولِي
silvery, like silver	فِضِّي
disgraceful, ignominious, exposed	فَضِيْح
shame, disgrace, ignominy	فَضِيْحَة (فَضَائِح)
excellent, eminent, distinguished	فَضِيْل (فُضَلاء)
excellence, exquisitiveness, merit	فَضِيْلَة (فَضَائِل)
weaning	فِطَام
intelligence, cleverness, smartness	فَطَانَة
mushrooms, fungi	فُطْر
rift, crack, fissure, split	فَطْر (فُطُور)
nature, disposition, instinct, creation	فِطْرَة
natural, instinctive	فِطْرِي
intelligent, astute, clever	فَطِن
astuteness, cleverness, intelligence	فِطْنَة (فِطَن)
breakfast	فُطُور

young camel	فَصِيْل (فِصَال)
group, squad, platoon, detachment	فَصِيْلَة (فَصَائِل)
execution squad	فَصِيْلَة الإِعْدَام
blood group	فَصِيْلَة دَم
opening, disclosing, breaking up	فَضّ
defloration	فَضّ البَكَارَة
vast and empty space, sky	فَضَاء
refuse, residue, remnant	فُضَالَة
silver	فِضَّة
disgracing, humiliation	فَضْح
loose and waving, flowing (robe)	فَضْفَاض
favour, grace, kindness, superiority	فَضْل
merit, credit, honour, gift	فَضْل (أَفْضَال)
surplus, superfluity, remnant	فَضْل (فُضُول)
residue, remnant, excrement, remainder	فَضْلَة (فَضَلات)

actually, indeed	فِعْلاً	immature, unbaked	فَطير
deed, act	فَعْلَة (فَعَلات)	pastry, bread	فَطيرَة (فَطَائر)
practical, actual, factual	فِعْلي	strangled, suffocated	فَطيس
mouth of a valley	فُغْرَة (فُغَر)	weaned	فَطيم
spine, vertebra	فَقَار	clever, intelligent, bright	فَطين
vertebral, spinal	فَقَاري	rough, rude, harsh, uncivil	فَظّ
bubble, air-cell	فُقَّاعَة		
loss, act of losing, breavement	فَقْد	rudeness, harshness, crudeness	فَظَاظَة
unconsciousness	فَقْد الإدْراك	enormity, horror, hideousness	فَظَاعَة (فَظَائع)
loss, breavement	فُقْدان/فِقْدَان		
loss of memory, amnesia	فُقْدَان الذَّاكرَة	horrible, hideous, terrible	فَظع
unconsciousness, senselessness	فُقْدان الشُّعُور	shocking, horrid, horrible, terrible	فَظيع
poverty, need, indigence	فَقْر	active, effective, powerful	فَعَّال
abject poverty, penury	فَقْر مُدْقع	efficacy, effectiveness, efficiency	فَعَّاليّة
sentence, paragraph, vertebra	فِقْرَة (فِقَر/فِقْرَات)	doing, activity, performance	فِعْل
vertebral, spinal	فِقْري	feasts, great deeds	فِعْل (أَفَاعيل)
only	فَقَط		
phoenix	فُقْنُس	deed, effect, verb	فِعْل (أَفْعَال)
comprehension, understanding, knowledge	فقْه	benevolence, charity	فِعْل الخَيْر

Arabian jasmine	فَلّ/فُلّ	Islamic Jurisprudence	فِقْه إِسْلَامِي
debauchee, licentious, rake	فَلَاتِي	juristical, doctrinal	فِقْهِي
success, progress, welfare	فَلَاح	missing, lost, deceased	فَقِيْد
farmer, peasant	فَلَّاح	poor, needy, pauper	فَقِير (فُقَرَاء)
farming, tillage, cultivation	فِلَاحَة	jurisprudent, expert in Islamic Jurisprudence	فَقِيه
highway robber	فَلَّاق	unbinding, untying	فَكّ
so-and-so	فُلَان	jaw, jawbone	فَكّ (فُكُوك)
escape, release	فَلَت	redemption	فَكّ الرّهْن
slip, lapse	فَلْتَة (فَلَتَات)	redemption, emancipation	فَكَاك
slip of pen	فَلْتَة قَلَم	jesting, joking, funmaking	فُكَاهَة
slip of tongue	فَلْتَة لِسَان		
cleft, fissure, crevice	فَلْج (فُلُوج)	humorous, humorist	فُكَاهِي
piece, slice	فِلْذَة (أَفْلاذ/فِلَذ)	idea, thought, contemplation	فِكْر (أَفْكَار)
metal, mineral	فِلِزّ	thought, idea, opinion, concept	فِكْرَة (فِكَر)
mite, fils (coin)	فَلَس (فُلُوس)		
philosophy	فَلْسَفَة	intellectual, speculative	فِكْرِي
ethics, moral science	فَلْسَفَة أَخْلاَقِية	cheerful, merry, gay, jovial	فَكِه
ethics, moral sciences	فَلْسَفة أَدَبِيّة	thoughtful, meditative	فِكّير
philosophical	فَلْسَفِي	notch, dent	فَلّ (فُلُول)

strategy, art of war فَنّ حَرْبِي	فَلْع/فِلْع (فُلوع) crack, fissure, cleft
evanescence, cessation, فَنَاء perdition, mortality	فِلْفِل أَحْمَر red pepper
فِنَاء (أَفْنِيَة) courtyard, open space	فِلْفِل أَسْوَد black pepper
lighthouse فَنَار	فِلْفِل/فُلْفُل pepper
artist فَتَان	فَلْفَلَة peppercorn
cup, tea cup فِنْجَان (فَنَاجِين)	فَلَق dawn, daybreak
hotel, inn فُنْدُق (فَنَادِق)	فَلْق (فُلوق) crack, cleft, fissure
cistern, water فِنْطَاس (فَنَاطِيس) tank	فُلْك ship, Noah's Ark
phonograph فُنُغْرَاف	فَلَك (أَفْلاك) orbit, sphere
branch, twig فَنَن (أَفْنَان)	فَلَكِي astronomical, astronomer
fine arts فُنُون جَمِيلَة/لَطِيفَة	فِلْم/فِيْلم (أَفْلام) film, motion picture
the fine arts فُنُون رَفِيعَة	فلم مُصَغَّر micro film
artistical, technical, فَنِّي artist, technician	فِلْم مُلَوَّن colour film
lynx فَهْد (فُهُود)	فِلْم نَاطِق sound film
فِهْرِس/فِهْرِسْت (فَهَارِس) contents, catalogue, index	فِلْو (أَفْلاء) colt, foal
فِهْرِس المَوْضُوعَات table of contents	فَلُور fluorine
understanding, فَهْم comprehension, intelligence	فَلْيُون godchild
	فَم (أَفْوَاه) mouth, orifice
discerning, of acute فَهِم discernment	فَنّ (فُنون) art, field of work, specimen, profession
	فَنّ الخِطَاب rhetoric, oratory

phosphate	فوسفات
phosphorous	فُوصفور
chaotic, anarchic, anarchist	فَوْضَوِي
anarchism, anarchy	فَوْضَوِيَّة
chaos, disorder, confusion, anarchy	فَوْضَى
serviette, napkin, towel	فُوطَة (فُوَط)
bath towel	فُوطَة الحَمَّام
fragrance, aroma	فَوْعَة
prime of life	فَوْعَة الشَّبَاب
up, above, upon	فَوْق
past all bearing	فَوْق الاحْتِمال
supernatural	فَوْق الطَّبِيعَة
extraordinary, unusual, uncommon	فَوْق العَادَة
higher, upper	فَوْقَانِي
beans	فُول
peanuts	فُول سُودَانِي
steel	فُولَاذ
made of steel, steel-hard	فُولَاذِي
volt	فُولت
garlics	فُوم

intelligent, sagacious, judicious	فَهِيم
boiling up, bubbling, effervescent	فَوّار
fountain, spring	فَوّارَة
hiccough, death rattle	فَوَاق
losing, missing, passing	فَوْت/فَوَات
photographic, photographer	فُوتُوغَرَافِي
photography	فُوتُوغَرَافِيا
detachment, group, crowd	فَوْج (أَفْوَاج)
breath of fragrance, emanation	فَوْحَة
boiling over, ebullition, effervescence	فَوْر
at once, immediately	فَوْرًا
boiling up, ebullition	فَوَرَان
outburst, flare-up	فَوْرَة
shaving brush	فُرْشَة الحِلاَقَة
immediate, instant, prompt	فَوْرِي
triumph, victory, success	فَوْز
ultimate triumph	فَوْز نِهَائِي

abundance, exuberance, flood, inundation	فَيْض	phonograph	فُوُنُوغَراف
stream	فَيْض (فُيُوض)	opening, orifice, mouth	فُوْهَة (أَفْواه/فُوْهات)
flood, deluge, over flowing	فَيَضَان	crater, mouth of a volcano	فُوْهَة البُرْكان
elephant	فِيْل (أَفْيال/فِيلة)	in, at, on, during	فِي
villa, cottage, country house	فِيْلا (فِيْلات)	during, at the time of	فِي إِبَّان
philosopher	فَيْلَسُوف (فَلاَسِفَة)	after, on his track	فِي أَثَرِه
army corps	فَيْلَق (فَيَالِق)	last of all, after all	فِي الآخِر
philology	فِيْلُولُوجِيا	per cent	فِي المِئَة
while, as	فِيمَا	in hand, available	فِي اليَد
afterwards, later	فِيما بَعْد	shade, shadow	فَيْء (أَفْياء)
time, moment	فَيْنَة	bountiful, exuberant, effusive	فَيَّاض
Venus	فِينُوس	vitamin	فِيتَامِين
		veto	فِيتُو
ق		federalistic	فِيْدَرَالِي
		turquoise	فِيْرُوز
docile, tractable	قَؤُوْد	virus	فَيْروس
leader, chief, head	قَائِد (قَادَة/قُوّاد)	physics	فِيْزياء
commander-in-chief	قَائِد أَعْلَى	physical	فِيْزِيائِي
admiral of a fleet	قَائِد الأُسْطُول	physiology	فِيْسِيولُوجِيا
		arbiter, umpire, decisive	فَيْصَل

dissoluble, meltable	قَابِل للذَّوَبَان	commander of an army	قَائِد الجَيْش
curable, remediable	قَابِل للشِّفَاء	wing commander	قَائِد جَنَاح
mortal	قَابِل للْمَوْت	supreme commander	قَائِد عَامّ
midwife, receptacle	قَابِلَة (قَوَابِل)	telling, teller, sayer	قَائِل
ability, capability, fitness, aptitude	قَابِليّة	standing, erect, existing, upright	قَائِم
nightmare	قَابُوس	right-angled	قَائِم الزَّاوِية
stingy, parsimonious	قَاتِر	catalogue, list, index	قَائِمَة (قَائِمَات)
killing, murderous, fatal	قَاتِل	post, pillar, leg, stanchion	قَائِمَة (قَوَائِم)
killer, murderer, assassin	قَاتِل (قَتَلَة/قُتَّال)	price list	قَائِمَة الأَسْعَار
		bill, account	قَائِمَة الحِسَاب
black, dark, obscure	قَاتِم	menu	قَائِمَة الطَّعَام
dry, arid, droughty	قَاحِل	quantity, measure	قَاب
powerful, mighty, able, capable	قَادِر	holding, grasping, embarrassing, recipient	قَابِض
coming, arriving	قَادِم	capable, liable, next, coming	قَابِل
scoop, bucket	قَادُوس (قَوَادِيس)	inflaming, combustible	قَابِل الالْتِهَاب
bomber	قَاذِفَة القَنَابِل	combustible	قَابِل للْالْتِهَاب
flame thrower	قَاذِفَة اللَهَب	divisible	قَابِل للتَّجْزِئَة
		conductive	قَابِل للتَّوْصِيْل
rubbish, garbage, squalor	قَاذُوْرَة	soluble, solvable	قَابِل للْحَلّ

legally minor	قَاصِر (قُصَّر)	standing, settled, sedentary, fixed	قَارّ
helpless, powerless, without power	قَاصِر اليَد	villager, countryman	قَارّ
sharp, cutting, keen	قَاصِل	pitch, tar	قَارٌ
breaking, crushing	قَاصِم (قَوَاصِم)	reciter, reader	قَارِئ (قُرَّاء)
decisive, conclusive, finishing	قَاضٍ	boat, skiff	قَارِب (قَوَارِب)
judge, justice	قَاضٍ (قُضَاة)	lifeboat	قَارِب النَّجَاة
committing judge	قَاضِي الإحَالَة	gunboat	قَارِب مُسَلَّح
judge of summary justice	قَاضِي الأُمُور المُسْتَعْجَلَة	motorboat	قَارِب نَارِي
justice of peace	قَاضِي الصُّلْح	hill, hillock	قَارَة
chief justice	قَاضِي القُضَاة	continent	قَارّة (قَارّات)
locomotive, engine	قَاطِرَة	chilly, freezing, biting	قَارِس
sharp, cutting, convincing, decisive	قَاطِع	pinching, biting, painful	قَارِص
ticket seller, conductor	قَاطِع التَّذَاكِر	calamity, adversity	قَارِعَة
highway robber, brigand	قَاطِع الطَّرِيق	vial, flask, bottle	قَارُورَة (قَوَارِير)
circuit breaker	قَاطِعَة	hard, harsh, cruel, relentless	قَاسٍ (قُسَاة)
inhabitant, dweller	قَاطِن (قُطَّان)	distributor, divider	قَاسِم
desolate area	قَاع صَفْصَف	hard-hearted, cruel, pitiless	قَاسِي القَلْب
		remote, far, distant	قَاصٍ
		straight, short, easy	قَاصِد
		unable, incapable, confined	قَاصِر

stature, build, frame قَامَة	hall, entrance قَاعَة (قَاعَات) hall, big room
dictionary, (قَوَامِيس) قَامُوس lexicon, ocean	banquet hall قَاعَة الأَفْرَاح
hunter, huntsman قَانِص	ballroom قَاعَة الرَّقْص
gizzard قَانِصَة (قَوَانِص)	lecture hall قَاعَة المُحَاضَرَات
desperate, disheartened قَانِط	reading room, قَاعَة المُطَالَعَة study hall
contented, satisfied قَانِع	seated, sitting قَاعِد (قُعُود)
rule, regulation, (قَوَانِين) قَانُون statute	rule, principle, (قَوَاعِد) قَاعِدَة pattern, mode, base
statute, basic قَانُون أَسَاسِي rule or law	naval base قَاعِدَة بَحْرِيّة
penal code قَانُون الجَرَائِم	airbase قَاعِدَة جَوِّيَّة
penal code قَانُون العُقُوبات	base of operation قَاعِدَة حَرْبِيّة
code of قَانُون المُرَافَعَات procedure	general rule قَاعِدَة عَامَّة
commercial or قَانُون تِجَارِي mercantile law	general rule قَاعِدَة مُطَّرِدَة
	caravan, convoy (قَوَافِل) قَافِلَة
penal law, قَانُون جِنَائِي criminal law	naval convoy قَافِلَة السُّفُن
constitutional قَانُون دُسْتُورِي law	naval convoy قَافِلَة بَحْرِيّة
	rhyme, pun قَافِيَة (قَوَاف)
international law قَانُون دُوَلِي	mold, form, (قَوَالِب) قَالَب/قَالِب matrix
retroactive law قَانُون رَجْعِي	sugar loaf قَالِب سُكَّر
common law قَانُون عُرْفِي	a cake of soap قَالِب صَابُون
civil law قَانُون مَدَنِي	galoche, galosh, over- قَالُوش shoe

handle, hilt	قَبْضَة (قِبَاض)	positive law	قَانُون وَضْعِي
plough-tail	قَبْضَة المِحْرَاث	lawful, legal, statutory	قَانُونِي
captain	قُبْطَان		
hat, cap	قُبَّعَة (قُبَّعَات)	vanquisher, conquerer	قَاهِر
patten, wooden clogs	قَبْقَاب (قَبَاقِيْب)	braised mutton or beef	قَاوِرْمَة
before, earlier, previous to	قَبْل	hub, nave	قَبّ (أَقُبّ)
power, ability, capability	قِبَل	distance, space	قَبَاء
previously, before time	قَبْل الآن	an outer garment	قَبَاء (أَقْبِيَة)
before Christ (BC)	قَبْل المِيْلاَد	ignominy, insolence, ugliness	قَبَاحَة
front, fore part	قُبْل/قُبُل	responsibility, liability, guarantee, contract	قَبَالَة
kibla, prayer direction	قِبْلَة	midwifery, obstetrics	قِبَالَة
kiss	قُبْلَة (قُبُلات/قُبَل)	collar	قَبّة
tribal	قَبَلِي	dome, cupola	قُبَّة (قُبَب)
vault, arched ceiling	قَبْو (أَقْبِيَة)	belfry, bell tower	قُبَّة الجَرَس
vault, small vault	قَبْوَة	ugliness, infamy, disgust	قَبْح/قُبْح
acceptance, admittance, approval, reception	قَبُول/قُبُول	grave, tomb	قَبْر (قُبُور)
		firebrand, brand, live coal	قَبَس
ugly, disgusting, disgraceful, obscene	قَبِيْح (قَبْحَى)	brand, firebrand	قَبْسَة
		a pinch of snuff	قُبْصَة/قَبْصَة
abomination, shameful deed, vice	قَبِيْحَة (قَبَائِح)	grasping, holding, seizure	قَبْض

torrential, sweeping قَحَاف	shortly before, prior to قَبْيْل
torrent	guarantor, bailor, sort, قَبِيل
prostitute, قَحْبَة (قِحَاب)	specimen
whore	tribe قَبِيلَة (قَبَائِل)
impudence, insolence, قِحَة	slanderer, calumniator قَتَات
shamelessness	murderous, fatal قَتَال
famine, dearth, قَحْط	fight, battle, war قِتَال
drought, aridity	darkness, gloom قَتَام
brainpan, skull(قُحُوف) قِحْف	parsimony, stinginess, قَتَر
dryness, aridity, قُحُولَة	stint
drought	killing, assassination, قَتْل
physique, stature, قَدّ (قُدُود)	homicide
size	foe, enemy قِتْل (أَقْتَال)
fire iron, flint قَدَّاح	fraticide قَتْل الأخ
holiness, sanctity, قَدَاسَة	infanticide قَتْل الأَطْفَال
saintliness	accidental قَتْل الخَطَأ
front part, fore part قُدَّام	homicide
ruler, rail قِدَّة (قِدَد)	suicide, self قَتْل الذّات
dispraise, slander, قَدْح	murder
censure, defamation	murder, قَتْل العَمَد
tumbler, goblet (أَقْدَاح) قَدَح	premeditated murder
worth, value, قَدْر (أَقْدَار)	darkness, gloom قُتْمَة/قَتَمَة
amount, quantity, grade	killed, casualty قَتِيل (قَتْلَى)
destiny, fate قَدَر (أَقْدَار)	cucumber قِثَّاء/قُثَّاء
pot, cooking pot قِدْر (قُدُور)	pure, red, genuine قُحّ
ability, power, قُدْرَة	
potency, strength	

sanctity, holiness	قُدْس/قُدُس	defamatory, slanderous	قذِفي
holy, sacred	قُدْسِي	dainty, fastidious	قَذُور
oldness, antiquity, olden times	قِدَم	speck, mote	قَذَى
foot, step	قَدَم (أَقْدَام)	fine dust	قَذًى (أَقْذَاء)
example, model	قُدْوَة/قِدْوَة	eye sore, a speck in the eye	قَذًى في العَيْن
most holy	قُدُّوس/قَدُّوس	bomb, shell	قَذِيفَة (قَذَائِف)
arrival, coming	قُدُوم	hand grenade	قَذِيفَة يَدَوِيَّة
daring, audacious, brave	قَدُوم	cold, chilly	قَرَّ
tasty, platable	قَدِي	coldness, chilliness	قُرَّ
cured meat, jerked meat	قَدِيد	menses, menstruation	قُرْء (قُرُوء)
powerful, omnipotent	قَدِير	reading, recitation	قِرَاءَة (قِرَاءَات)
saint, saintly	قِدِّيس	palmistry	قِرَاءَة الكَفّ
old, ancient, antique	قَدِيم (قُدَمَاء)	sheath, case, receptacle	قِرَاب (أَقْرِبَة)
old-fashioned	قَدِيم الطِّرَاز	relation, relationship	قَرَابَة
dirtiness, filthiness, impurity	قَذَارَة	uterine relation	قَرَابَةُ رَحْم
bomber	قَذَّاف	stability, steadiness, sedentation, abode	قَرَار
dirtiness, uncleanliness	قَذَر	modifying regulations	قَرَارَات التَّعْدِيل
dirt, filth	قَذَر (أَقْذَار)	bottom, depth	قَرَارَة
filthy, dirty, unclean	قَذِر/قَذْر	pincers, nippers	قَرَّاصَة
defamation, accusation, calumniation	قَذْف		

discoid, disk-shaped	قرْصِي	scraps,	قُرَاضَة (قُرَاضَات)
loan	قَرْض (قُرُوض)	chips, clippings	
domestic loan	قَرْض أَهْلِي	cemetery, burial ground	قَرَافَة
interest-free loan	قَرْض حَسَن	carpet, curtain	قِرَام
monetary loan	قَرْض مَالِي	marriage, wedding, close union	قَرَان
erring, eardrop	قُرْط (أَقْرَاط/قُرُوط)	nearness, proximity	قُرْب
paper, sheet of paper	قِرْطَاس (قَرَاطِيس)	sacrifice, immolation, offering	قُرْبَان
stationery	قِرْطَاسِيَّة	saddlebow	قَرَبُوس
paper, sheet of paper	قَرْطَس	relationship, kinship	قُرْبَى
knocking, beating, whipping	قَرْع	delight of the eye	قُرَّة العَيْن
baldness, bareness	قَرَع	ulcerated, ulcerous	قَرِح
gourd, pumpkin	قَرْع/قَرْعَة	wound, ulcer	قَرْح (قُرُوح)
knock, blow, rap	قَرْعَة	ulcer, sore	قَرْحَة
lot, ballot ball	قُرْعَة (قُرَع)	bedsore	قَرْحَة الفِرَاش
disgust, detestation	قَرَف	mokey, ape	قِرْد (قُرُود)
crust, bark	قِرْفَة	piaster	قِرْش (قُرُوش)
squirrel	قَرْقَذَان	disc, sheave, tablet	قُرْص (أَقْرَاص)
uproar, clattering, rumbling	قَرْقَعَة	honeycomb	قُرْص عَسَل
cartilage	قَرْقُوش	pirate, buccaneer, corsair	قُرْصَان
kermes	قِرْمِز	pinch, nip	قَرْصَة
crimson, scarlet	قِرْمِزِي		

content, delighted قَرِيرُ العَيْن	red bricks, قِرْمِيد (قَرَامِيد) tiles, plaster
eulogy, praise قَرِيظ	match, equal, قِرْن (أَقْرَان) like, peer
companion, قَرِين (قُرَنَاء) consort, combined	century, horn, قَرْن (قُرُون) peak
wife, consort قَرِينَة	cauliflower قَرْنَبِيط
context, قَرِينَة (قَرَائِن) indication, relation	carnation قَرَنْفُل
silk, raw silk قَزّ (قُزُوز)	the Middle Ages قُرُون وُسْطَى
silk merchant قَزَّاز	rural, rustic قَرَوِي
dwarf, pygmy قُزْعَة	countryman, قَرَوِي (قَرَوِيُّون) villager
dwarf, pygmy, قَزَم (أَقْزَام) midget	hospitality, قِرًى entertainment
priest, قِسّ/قَسّ (قُسُوس) clergyman	near, close to قَرِيب
cruelty, mercilessness, قَسَاوَة severity, harshness	relative, قَرِيب (أَقْرِبَاء) relation
pitilessness, قَسَاوَة القَلْب weak-heartedness	new, recent, قَرِيب العَهْد young
compulsion, constraint, قَسْر coercion	soon, recently, shortly قَرِيبًا
forcibly, compulsorily قَسْرًا	yard قَرْيَة (قَرَايا)
justice, equity, قِسْط equitability	village, small قَرْيَة (قُرًى) town
portion, share, قِسْط (أَقْسَاط) amount, installment	clear, pure قَرِيح
balance, scales قِسْطَاس	intuition, قَرِيحَة (قَرَائِح) genius, intellect

قِشْر (قُشُور) cover, shell, peel, husk	قِسْم (أَقْسَام) section, part, division, department, kind
قِشْر الرَّأْس scurf, dandruff	قَسَم (أَقْسَام) oath
قِشْر السَّمَك scales	قِسْم التَّرْفِيْه recreation department
قِشْرَة paring, peel, shelt, crust, skin	قِسْم التَّنْفِيْذ executive division
قِشْري scaly, scurfy	قِسْم المُحَاسَبَة accounting department
قِشْطَة cream	قَسَمًا I swear
قِشْفَة (قِشَف) crust	قِسْمَة share, protion, allotment
قُشْلاَق barracks	قِسْمَة ضِيْزَى unfair decision
قَشِيْش garbage, refuse	قَسْو hardness, harshness, austerity
قَصّ cutting, clipping	قَسْوَة cruelty, inclemency, harshness
قَصًا/قَصَاء remoteness, distance	قُسُوسَة priesthood, ministry
قَصَّاب butcher, slaughterer	قَسِيّ hard, solid, grim
قِصَابَة butchery	قِسِّيْس priest, clergyman
قَصَّاج pincers, nippers	قَسِيْم (أَقْسِمَاء) allotment, share, portion
قَصَّاص story teller, shearer, tracer of footsteps	
قِصَاص requital, penalty, punishment	قَسِيْم (قُسَمَاء) partner, sharer
قُصَاصَة cuttings, clippings, scrap	قَسِيْمَة coupon, receipt
قَصّال sharp, keen, cutting	قَشّ chaff, straw, hay
قَصَب reed, cane, brocade	قِشْدَة cream

narrative, epic قَصَصي/قَصَصي	gold brocade قَصَب الذَّهَب
large wooden قَصْعَة (قَصَعَات) bowl, tencher	sugar cane قَصَب السُّكَّر
roaring, snapping, قَصْف revelry	reed, cane, flute قَصَبَة
peal of thunder, قَصْف الرَّعْد thunderclap	forelock, lock قُصَّة (قُصَص) of hair
fragile, frail, قَصِف/قَصيْف brittle	story, tale, قِصَّة (قِصَص) narrative
brittle, breakable, قَصِم/قَصيْم fragile	fable قِصَّة خُرَافِيّة
deficiency, قُصُور insufficiency, short coming, laxity	novel, fiction قِصَّة خَيَالِيّة
	purpose, intent, aim قَصْد
	intentionally, قَصْدًا deliberately
revelry, orgy قُصُوف	intentional, deliberate قَصْدي
remote, distant قَصِي (أَقْصَاء)	shortness, slothfulness, قَصْر negligence, reduction, confinement
intended, desired قَصيْد	
poem قَصيْدة (قَصَائد)	shortness, brevity, قِصَر inadequacy
short, small قَصيْر (قَصَار)	negligence, laziness, قَصَر slackness
short-lived, قَصير الأَجَل short-term	
short-term, short-lived قَصير الأَمَد	palace, castle قَصْر (قُصُور)
	short-sightedness قِصَر النَّظَر
powerless, قَصير البَاع incapable, incompetent	flower pot, chamber قَصْرية pot
short-sighted, قَصير البَصَر myopic	cuttings, clippings قَصَص
	bamboo قَصَص هِنْدي

express train	قِطَار سَرِيع	short-sighted	قَصِير النَّظَر
local train	قِطَار عَادِي	short-breathed	قَصِير النَّفَس
section, sector	قِطَاع	pebbles, gravel	قَضّ/قَضِيض
cross section	قِطَاع عَرْضِي	completion, execution,	قَضَاء
cotton merchant	قَطَّان	settlement, judgement, judiciary, destiny	
pole, pivot, axis	قُطْب (أَقْطَاب)	inevitable destiny	قَضَاء مُبْرَم
south pole	قُطْب جَنُوبِي	fate and divine decree	قَضَاء وقَدْر
north pole	قُطْب شَمَالِي	by fate and divine decree	قَضَاءً وقَدْرًا
polar	قُطْبِي	judicial, judiciary	قَضَائِي
female cat	قِطَّة	clippings, prunings	قُضَابَة
dripping, falling in drops	قَطْر	pruning, edible herbs	قَضْب
region, zone, country	قُطْر (أَقْطَار)	judgement, decision	قَضَى
drops, driblets, rain	قَطْر (قِطَار)	rod, stick, twig, branch, penis	قَضِيب (قُضْبَان)
railway trains	قَطْر (قُطُورَات)	issue, affair, matter, case	قَضِيّة (قَضَايا)
tar	قَطْرَان	never	قَطّ
drop	قَطْرَة (قَطَرَات)	cat, tom cat	قِطّ (قِطَط)
regional, diametrical	قُطْرِي	trail, railroad	قِطَار (قُطُر)
cutting, amputation, disconnection	قَطْع	freight train	قِطَار البِضَاعَة
		passenger train	قِطَار الرُّكَّاب
size, format	قَطْع (أَقْطَاع)	railroad train	قِطَار حَدِيْدِي
section, division	قِطْع (قُطُوع)	special train	قِطَار خَاصّ

pellicle, film	قطمير	settlement of amount	قَطْع الحِسَابَات
cotton	قُطْن	despair	قَطْع الرّجاء
unginned cotton	قُطْن خَام	highway robbery, waylaying	قَطْع الطّريق
absorbent cotton	قُطْن طِبّي	severance of relations	قَطْع العَلَائِق
cotton, made of cotton	قُطْني	definitely, decidedly, unmistakably	قَطْعًا
frowning, scowling	قَطُوب		
driblet, droplet	قُطَيْرَة	piece, segment, section	قِطْعَة (قِطَع)
kitten	قُطَيْطَة		
flock, herd	قَطِيع (قِطَاع)	a piece, a cut, lot, patch of land	قُطْعَة (قُطَع)
breach, strangement, separation	قَطِيعَة		
velvet, plush	قَطِيفَة	segment of a circle	قِطْعَة الدَّائِرَة
sitting, postures, buttocks	قَعْدة	vocal piece	قِطْعَة غِنَائِيّة
bottom, depth	قَعْر (قُعُور)	work of art	قِطْعَة فَنّيّة
cavity, pit, hole	قَعْرَة	stage play	قِطْعَة مَسْرَحِيّة/تَمْثِيْلِيّة
magpie	قَعْقَع/قُعْقُع	piece of music	قِطْعَة مَوْسِيْقِيّة
clank, rattling	قَعْقَعَة	definite, decided	قَطْعي
young camel	قَعُود	categorically, decidedly	قَطْعيًّا
sitting, abstention	قُعُود		
companion, guardian, keeper	قَعِيْد	plucking, twitching, picking	قَطْف
woman companion, wife	قَعِيْدَة (قَعَائِد)	plucked fruit	قِطْف
deep, profound	قَعِيْر	scratch	قَطْف (قُطُوف)

reversal, alteration, قَلْب transformation, changing	back, back of the قَفَا (أَقْفِيَة) head
changeable, inconstant قُلَّب	back, nape قَفَاء
heart, centre, قَلْب (قُلُوب) essence	glove قُفَّار
with heart and soul قَلْبًا وقَالِبًا	locksmith قَفَّال
cardial, cardiac, hearty, قَلْبِي warm	large basket قُفَّة (قُفَف)
apex, top, summit قُلَّة	desert, wasteland قَفْر (قِفَار)
pitcher, jug قُلَّة (قُلَل)	leaping, jumping قَفْز
insensitivity, قِلَّة الإِحْسَاس obtuseness	long jump قَفْز طَوِيْل
shamelessness, قِلَّة الحَيَاء insolence	high jump قَفْز عَال
impatience قِلَّة الصَّبْر	a leap, a jump قَفْزَة
rarity, scarcity قِلَّة الوُجُود	chatter, prattling قَفْش
extracting, pulling out قَلْع	cage, pen قَفَص (أَقْفَاص)
sail قِلْع (قِلَاع)	caftan, an قُفْطَان (قَفَاطِيْن) outer garment
fort, fortress, قَلْعَة (قِلَاع) citadel	lock, pad- قُفْل (قُفُول/أَقْفال) lock
prepuce, foreskin قُلْفَة	beehive قَفِيْر (قُفْرَان)
unrest, anxiety, worry, قَلَق restlessness	cafiz (a drymeasure) قَفِيز
anxious, worried, قَلِق restless, concerned	littleness, scarceness, قِلّ/قُلّ insignificance
convulsion, قَلْقَلَة (قَلَاقِل) commotion, disturbance	necklace قِلَادَة (قَلَائِد)
	caulking قِلَافَة
	cuttings, clippings قُلَامَة
	frying vessel or pan قَلَّايَة

unfortunate, unlucky	قَلِيل البَخْت	pen, writing, style, bureau	قَلَم (أَقْلَام)
impertinent, uncivil	قَلِيْل التَّرْبِيَة	head office	قَلَم الإدَارة
shameless, impudent	قَلِيْل الحَيَاء	information bureau	قَلَم الاسْتِعْلاَمَات
discourteous, incivil	قَلِيْل الذَّوْق	reed pen	قَلَم البَسْط
impatient	قَلِيْل الصَّبْر	editors' office	قَلَم التَّحْرِير
few, small in number	قَلِيْل العَدَد	fountain pen	قَلَمُ الحِبْر
rare, scarce	قَلِيْل الوُجُود	traffic bureau	قَلَم الحَرَكَة
insignificant, lowly, inferior	قَمِئ	accounting department	قَلَم الحِسَابات
lowliness, inferiority, insignificance	قَمَاءَة	travel agency	قَلَم السِّيَاحَة
gambling, bet	قِمَار	drawing pen	قَلَم رَسْم
trash, garbage, refuse	قُمَاش	pencil, lead pencil	قَلَمُ رَصَاص
cloth merchant, drapper	قَمَّاش	reed pen	قَلَم قَصَب
fabric, textile, cloth	قُمَاش (أَقْمِشَة)	rarely, scarcely	قَلَّما
furniture, household effects	قُمَاش البَيْت	cap, headgear	قَلَنْسُوَة (قَلاَنَس)
diaper, swaddle	قِمَاط (قُمُط)	adaptable, changeable, agile	قَلُوب
garbage, sweepings, rubbish	قُمَامَة	little, small, thin, scanty, insufficient	قَلِيْل
		insensitive, dull	قَلِيل الإحْسَاس
		impolite, ill-bred, rude , discourteous	قَلِيل الأدَب

chicken coop	قَنّ (قِنَان)	top, peak, summit	قِمَّة (قِمَم)
canal, waterway, tube, spear	قَنَاة (قَنَوات)	crown of the head	قِمَّة الرَّأْس
huntsman, shooter	قَنَّاص	wheat	قَمْح
arms, weapons, armour	قِنَاع (قُنُع)	wheat kernel	قَمْحَة
		moon, satellite	قَمَر (أَقْمَار)
content, satisfaction, contentment	قَنَاعَة	customs	قُمْرُق
lark	قُنْبُر	moon-shaped, moonlike	قَمَري
bomb, grenade, bomb shell	قُنْبُلَة (قَنَابِل)	turtledove	قُمْري
hand grenade	قُنْبُلَة اليَد	bookcase, satchel	قِمَطْر (قَمَاطِر)
hydrogen bomb	قُنْبُلَة ايدروجينية	repression, suppression, subdual	قَمْع
hydrogen bomb	قُنْبُلَة حَيْدُرُوجِينِّية	funnel	قَمْع/قِمْع (أَقْمَاع)
tear gas bomb	قُنْبُلَة دَمْعِيّة	scent bottle	قُمْقُم/قُمْقُمَة
atomic bomb	قُنْبُلَة ذَرِّيَّة	lousy, infested with lice	قَمِل
time bomb	قُنْبُلَة زَمَنِيّة	louse	قَمْل (قَمْلَة)
rocket bomb	قُنْبُلَة صَارُوخِيّة	worthy, deserving, fitting	قَمِن/قَمِين
gas bomb	قُنْبُلَة غَازِية	shirt, dress, cover	قَمِيص (قُمْصان/أَقْمِصَة)
explosive bomb	قُنْبُلَة مُنْفَجِرة	night gown, night dress	قَمِيص النَّوْم
hand grenade	قُنْبُلَة يَدَوِيّة		
hunch, hump	قُنْبُور	kiln, furnace	قَمِين/قَمِينَة
cauliflower	قُنَّبِيط	serf, serfdom	قِنّ (أَقْنان)

desperate, despondent, hopeless قَنُوط	beaver, castor قُنْدُس
satisfied, content, temperate قَنُوع	lamp, chandelier قِنْدِيْل (قَنَادِيْل)
slavery, serfdom قُنُونَة	tuft of hair قَنْزَعَة
bottle, flask قِنِّيْنَة (قَنَانٍ)	hunting, shooting قَنْص
conquering, the Almighty, vanquishing قَهَّار	consul قُنْصُل (قَنَاصِل)
sudual, subjugation, overcoming, coercion قَهْر	consul general قُنْصُل عَامّ
by force, forcibly قَهْرًا	consular قُنْصُلي
coercion, force, compulsion قُهْرَة	consulate قُنْصُلِيَّة
	consulate general قُنْصُلِيَّة عَامّة
butler, steward, housekeeper قَهْرَمان	kantar, central قِنْطَار (قَنَاطِيْر)
coercive, forcible, compelling قَهْري	arched bridge, archway, arch قَنْطَرَة (قَنَاطِر)
retrogression, recession, retreat قَهْقَرَى/قَهْقَرَة	shield, armour, weapon قِنْع
	content, satisfaction, temperance قَنَع
laud guffaw, large burst of laughter قَهْقَهَة	satisfied, content قَنِع
	hedgehog قُنْفُذ
coffee, café قَهْوَة	kangaroo قَنْقَر
unsweetened coffee, coffee without sugar قَهْوَة سَادَة	bunch of dates قِنْو/قُنْو (قُنْوَان/أَقْنَاء)
	piety, devoutness قُنُوت
coffee house keeper قَهْوَجِى	acquisition, possession, property قُنْوَة/قُنْيَة
wasteland, desert قَوَاء/قُوَاء	despair, hopelessness, despondency قُنُوط

steam power	قُوّة بُخَارِيّة	reserves	قُوّات احْتِيَاطِيّة
ground forces	قُوّة بَرِّيّة	naval forces	قُوّات بَحْرِيّة
air forces	قُوّة جَوِّيّة	air forces	قُوّات جَوِّيّة
memory, recollection	قوة حَافِظَة	armed forces	قُوّات مُسَلَّحَة
horse power	قُوّة حصان	pander, procurer	قَوّاد
propulsive force, impulse, impetus	قُوّة دَافِعَة	bowman, archer, shooter	قَوّاس
reason, intuitional faculty	قُوّة عَاقِلَة	garrulous, itinerant, singer	قَوّال
brute force	قُوّة غَاشِمَة	straightness, directness, consistence, stamina, support	قَوَام
superior force	قُوّة قَاهِرَة		
coercive power	قُوّة قَهْرِيّة	caretaker, custodian, manager	قَوّام
potential ability	قُوّة كَامِنَة		
central force	قُوّة مَرْكَزِيّة	guardianship, support	قِوَامَة
morale, moral courage	قُوّة مَعْنَوِيّة	food, sustenance, nutriment	قُوت (أَقْوَات)
pandering, pimping	قَوْد	power, force, strength, capability	قُوّة (قُوّات/قُوًى)
preserved or cooked meat	قَوُرْمَة	will power	قُوّة الإِرَادَة
bow, arch, vault	قَوْس (أَقْوَاس)	inertia	قُوّة الاسْتِمْرَار
bow, violin bow	قَوْس الكَمَنْجَة	purchasing power	قُوّة الشِّرَاء
teasing bow	قَوْس النَّدْف	volume, intensity	قُوّة الصَّوْت
rainbow	قَوْس قُزَح	legal force	قُوّة القَانُون
		growth faculty	قُوّة النَّبْت

vomit, vomiting فَيْء/قَيَاء	parenthesis قَوْسَان
leadership, guidance, direction قِيَادَة	saying, utterance, speech, word قَوْل (أَقْوَال)
measure, measurement, scale, analogy قِيَاس	proverb, saying قَوْل مَأْثُور
world record قِيَاس عَالَمِي	by word and deed قَوْلاً وَعَمَلاً
fallacy, sophism قِيَاس فَاسِد	colic قَوْلَنْج
logical, comparative, regular قِيَاسِي	colon قُولُون
regularly قِيَاسِيًّا	nation, tribe, people قَوْم (أَقْوَام)
tracking, following the tracks قِيَافَة	uprising, revolt قَوْمَة
rise, rising, standing, awakening قِيَام	national, racial قَوْمِي
rising, resurrection, upheaval, custody قِيَامَة	nationality, nationalism قَوْمِيَّة
suppuration, pus قَيْح	common citizenship قَوْمِيَّة مُشْتَرَكَة
fetters, shackles, bond, restriction قَيْد (قُيُود)	icon, image قُوْنَة
kerat (a dry measure) قِيرَاط	strong, powerful, vigorous قَوِي (أَقْوِيَاء)
carvan قَيْرَوَان	sturdy, strong قَوِي البُنْيَة
Caesar, emperor قَيْصَر (قَيَاصِر)	energetic, vigorous قَوِي الشَّكِيمَة
emperial, Caesarean قَيْصَرِي	stout-hearted, courageous قَوِي القَلْب
exchange, bartering قَيْض/قِيَاض	hunger, starvation قَوًى/قَوَاء
	right, upright, straight, erect قَوِيم (قِيَام)

nightmare, phantom كَابُوس (كَوَابِيس)	scorching heat of summer قَيْظ
writer, clerk, secretary كَاتِب (كُتَّاب)	daytime heat قَيْظ النَّهَار
stenographer كَاتِب اخْتِزَال	gossips, idle talk قِيْل وقال
secretary of state كَاتِب الدَّوْلَة	midday nap, siesta قَيْلُولَة
secretary, private secretary كَاتِب السِّرّ	straight, right, custodian, valuable قَيِّم
bookkeeper, accountant كَاتِب حِسَابَات	worth, value, price قِيْمَة (قِيَم)
novelist, writer كَاتِب قِصَصِي	face value, nominal value قِيْمَة اسْمِيَّة
cathedral كَاتِدْرَائِيّة	the Eternal, the Everlasting قَيُّوم
private secretary كَاتِم السِّرّ	
catholic كَاثُولِيْكِي	
ankle bone كَاحِل (كَوَاحِل)	grief, distress, depression, sorrow, gloom كَأْب/كَأْبَة/كَآبَة
cadre, skeleton, organization كَادِر	sad, sorrowful, gloomy, depressed كَئِب/كَئِيْب
false, untrue, deceptive, liar كَاذِب	distress, sadness, gloominess كَأْدَاء
profession, work, job, business كَار (كَارَات)	glass, tumbler كَأْس (كُؤُوْس)
carton كَارْتُون (كَارْتُونات)	as if, as though كَأَنَّ
grievous, sorrowful, painful كَارِث	existing, located, situated كَائِن
disaster, calamity, catastrophe كَارِثَة (كَوَارِث)	creature, created things كَائِن (كَائِنَات)

camphor	كَافُوْر	cardinal	كَارْدِيْنَال
as follows	كَالآتِي	preacher	كَارِز
austere, stern, gloomy	كَالِح	foot, trotter	كَارِع
gallon	كَالُون	unwilling, reluctant	كَارِه
rate of exchange	كَامْبِيْو	misogamist	كَارِه النِّسَاء
pickles, sauce	كَامَخ/كَامِخ (كَوَامِخ)	caricature, cartoon	كَارِيْكَاثُورِيّة
gloomy, worried, sad, swarthy	كَامِد	casino	كَازِيْنُو
complete, completed, perfect, whole, full	كَامِل	drinking cup	كَأْس/كَأْس
concealed, hidden	كَامِن	earner, winner	كَاسِب
hidden factors, latent depths	كَامِن (كَوَامِن)	listless, stagnant, dull	كَاسِد
camera	كَامِيْرا	rapacious, savage	كَاسِر (كَوَاسِر)
post exchange, canteen	كَانْتِيْن	stone break	كَاسِر الحَجَر
stove, hearth	كَانُون (كَوَانِيْن)	depressed, dejected, gloomy	كَاسِف
December	كَانُون الأَوَّل	uncoverer, discoverer, investigator, revealing	كَاشِف
January	كَانُون الثَّانِي		
upper part of the back, withers	كَاهِل (كَوَاهِل)	sufficient, enough, capable	كَافٍ
fortune-teller, soothsayer, priest	كَاهِن (كُهَّان/كَهَنَة)	entirety, totality	كَافّة
		all without exception	كَافَّةً
caustic	كَاوٍ	unbeliever, infidel, atheist	كَافِر (كُفَّار/كَفَرَة)
overturn, capcizing	كَبّ	supporter, protector, breadwinner	كَافِل (كُفَّل)

intercalation كَبْس السَّنَة	grilled or broiled meat كِباب
raid, sudden attack كَبْسَة	liver ailment كُباد
capsule, كَبْسُول/كَبْسُولَة detonator	senior officers كِبَار الضُّبَّاط
ram, كَبْش (كِباش/أَكْباس) sheep	senior officials كِبَار المُوَظَّفِين
	very big, huge كُبَار/كِبَار
grasp, handful, scoop كَبْشَة	cabaret كَبارِيه
handcuffs, كَبْل/كِبْل (كُبُول) manacles	ball, ball of thread كُبّة
hood, hooded cloak, كَبُّوت overcoat	suppression, كَبْت repression, curbing
trip, stumble, misstep كَبْوَة	restraint, curbing, كَبْح control
big, great, كَبِير (كِبار) important, enormous, old	liver, كَبْد/كَبِد (أَكْباد/كُبُود) centre, interior
bulky, of great كَبِير الحَجْم size	haughtiness, arrogance, كِبْر insolence, greatness
old, aged كَبِير السِّنّ	greatness, eminence, كُبْر bulk, principal part
chief justice كَبِير القُضاة	old age, bigness, كِبَر greatness
high-minded, كَبِير النَّفْس high spirited	arrogance, pride, كِبْرِياء glory, majesty
atrocity, grave كَبِيرة (كَبائِر) sin	matches, sulfur كِبْرِيت
pickled, preserved, كَبِيس conserved, intercalated	sulfate كِبْرِيتات
simmering, gentle كَتّ/كَتِيت hissing	sulfureous كِبْرِيتي
	pressure, preservation كَبْس

concealing, concealment, secrecy	كِتْمان	book, record, document, letter	كِتَاب (كُتُب)
smut, soot	كَتَن	credentials	كِتَاب الاعْتِمَاد
discreet, reticent	كَتُوم	marriage contract	كِتَاب الزَّوَاج
booklet, pamphlet	كُتَيِّب	class book	كِتَاب مَدْرَسِي
battalion, regiment	كَتِيبَة (كَتَائِب)	writing, inscription, paper, record	كِتَابَة
thick, dense	كَثّ/كَثِيْث	writings, essays	كِتَابَة (كِتَابَات)
thickness, heaviness, density	كَثَافَة	historiography	كِتَابَة التَّارِيخ
thickness of population	كَثَافَة السُّكَّان	clerical, scriptural, literary	كِتَابِي
thickness, density	كَثَث	handcuffs, shackles	كِتَاف (كُتُف)
much, abundance, multiplicity, majority	كَثْرَة	catalogue	كَتَالُوج
Catholicism	كَثْلَكَة	linen, hemp, flax	كَتَّان
catholic	كُثُوْلِيْكِي	elementary books	كُتُب الْمَبَادِئ
much, many, plentiful, abundant	كَثِير	book seller	كُتُبِي
eventful	كَثِير الحَوَادث	shoulder, shoulder blade	كَتِف/كَتْف
talkative, garrulous	كَثِير الكَلَام		
great in quantity	كَثِير المِقْدَار	lump, block, mass, joist	كُتْلَة (كُتَل)
frequent	كَثِير الوُقُوع		
much, to a great degree	كَثِيراً	concealing, hiding, secrecy	كَتْم

bite, bruise	كَدْمَة	thick, dense, heavy	كَثِيف
hard working, industrious, laborious	كَدُود	eye-powder, antimony	كِحَال
thus, so	كَذَا	eye doctor, oculist	كَحّال
swindler, liar, deceitful	كَذّاب	cough	كُحّة
lie, falsehood	كِذْب/كَذِب	hacking or dry cough	كَحْكَحَة
April fool's joke	كَذْبَة إِبْرِيل	kohl, powder of antimony	كُحْل (أَكْحَال)
a white lie	كَذْبَة بَسِيطَة		
lie, untruth, falsehood	كِذْبَة/كَذْبَة	blackened with kohl	كَحِل/كَحِيْل
thus, likewise	كَذَلِك	alcohol, rectified spirit	كُحُول
liar, deceitful	كَذُوب	alcoholic, spirituous	كُحُولِي
charge, attack	كَرّ	labour, hard work, toil	كَدّ
rent, hire, wages	كِرَاء	pile, stack	كَدَاسَة
notebook, exercise book	كُرّاسَة (كُرّاسَات)	exertion, labour, toilsome effort, pains	كَدْح
foot, trotter	كُرَاع	turbidness, trouble, grief, affliction, duskiness	كَدَر
generosity, dignity, honour, nobility	كَرَامة	muddy, dusky, dingy, troubled	كَدِر/كَدِيْر
caramel candy	كَرَامِل	muddiness, turbidness, dinginess	كُدْرَة
hate, dislike, aversion, disgust	كَرَاهَة/كَرَاهِيّة		
grief, sorrow, distress, agony, anguish	كَرْب (كُرُوب)	pile, heap, stack	كُدْس (أَكْدَاس)

armchair	كُرْسِي بِمَسَاند
rocking chair	كُرْسِي هَزَّاز
craw, paunch, belly	كِرْش (أَكْرَاش)
sip, sipping	كَرْعَة
confusion, disorder, rumbling	كَرْكَبَة
rhinocerous	كَرْكَدَم/كَرْكَدَّن
laud laughter	كَرْكَرَة
tumeric	كُرْكُم
lobster	كَرْكَنْد
kindness, favour, generosity, munificence	كَرَم
grapes, grapevines, garden	كَرْم (كُرُوم)
grapevines	كَرْم العِنَب
noble-mindedness, magnanimity	كَرَم الأَخْلاَق
noble birth, noble descent	كَرَم المَحْتِد
vine, grapevine	كَرْمَة
caramel	كَرَمَلاًّ
cabbage	كُرُنْب
quarantine	كُرُنْتِينَة
crank, crank shaft	كَرَنْك

worry, distress, anxiety, anguish	كُرْبَة (كُرَب)
coal, carbon	كَرْبُون
attack, charge, comeback, round	كَرَّة
sphere, globe	كُرَة (كُرًى/كُرَات)
a second time	كَرَّة أُخْرَى
globe, terrestrial globe	كُرَة الأَرْض
snowball	كُرَة الثَّلْج
basketball	كُرَة السَّلَّة
table tennis	كُرَة الطَّاوِلَة
football, soccer	كُرَة القَدَم
celestial sphere	كُرَة الكَوَاكِب
carton, cardboard	كَرْثُون (كَرَاتِين)
cardon, lace	كَرْدُون
sanitary cardon	كَرْدُون صِحِّي
preaching, sermon	كَرْز
cherry	كَرَز/كَرَزَة
chair, seat, throne	كُرْسِي (كَرَاسِي)
judgement seat	كُرْسِي القَضَاء
royal throne	كُرْسِي المَلِك

two eyes	كَرِيْمَتَان	dislike, hatred, abhorrence, detestation	كُرْه/كَرْه
bad smelling	كَرِيْه الرَّائِحَة	hateful, detestable, repugnant	كَرِه/كَرِيْه
distasteful, unsavaoury	كَرِيْهُ الطَّعْم	unwillingly, reluctantly	كُرْهًا
adversity, misfortune	كَرِيْهَة (كَرَائِه)	digging, excavation	كَرْو
rigid, dried, shrivelled	كَزّ	globular, spherical	كُرَوِي/كُرِيّ
tetanus	كُزَاز/كُزَّاز	sleep, slumber	كَرًى
dryness, stiffness, niggardliness	كَزَازَة	globule	كُرَّيَة
niggardliness, stinginess	كَزَز	depressed, worried, distressed	كَرِيْث
garment, dress	كِسَاء (أَكْسِيَة)	cream	كَرِيْم
sweepings, rubbish, sewage	كُسَاحَة	shaving cream	كَرِيْم الحِلَاقَة
slump, dullness of the market	كَسَاد	noble, kind, generous, beneficent	كَرِيْم (كُرَمَاء/كَرَام)
gaining, earning, gain, profit	كَسْب	noble-hearted, noble-minded	كَرِيْم الأَخْلَاق
oil cake	كُسْب	high born, of noble descent	كَرِيْم الأَصْل
chestnut	كَسْتَنَة	well-born, of noble origin, high born	كَرِيْم المَحْتِد
breaking, fracturing, infringement	كَسْر	noble-minded	كَرِيْم النَّحِيْزَة
fracture, fraction	كَسْر (كُسُور)	valuable, things of value	كَرِيْمَة (كَرَائِم)
common fraction	كَسْر اعْتِيَادي		

uncovering, disclose, كَشْف exposure, discovery, examination	decimal fraction كَسْر عُشْرِي
	complex fraction كَسْر مُرَكَّب
statement, (كُشُوف) كَشْف report, discovery	defeat, rout, كَسْرَة breakdown
bill, invoice كَشْف الحِسَاب	fragment, piece, (كِسَر) كِسْرَة slice
medical كَشْف طِبِّي examination	occultation, eclipse كَسْف
booth, stall, (أَكْشَاك) كُشْك pavilion	laziness, idleness, كَسَل inactiveness
signal cabin كُشْك الإشَارَات	lazy, idle, inactive كَسِل
call-box كُشْك التِّلفُون	lazy, inactive, كَسْلَان sluggish
sentry box كُشْك الدِّيدَبان	shape, form, style كَسْم
beggar's wallet or كَشْكُول bag	dress, (كُسَى/كِسَى) كِسْوَة garment, clothes, apparel
cloying, overeating, كِظّة surfeit	occultation, solar كُسُوف eclipse
overfilled, surfeited, كَظِيظ cloyed	lazy, inactive كَسُول
filled with anger كَظِيم	lame, paralyzed كَسِيح
ankle, joint, (كُعُوب) كَعْب heel	broken, (كَسْرَى) كَسِير shattered
cube, cubic structure كَعْبَة	rancour, grudge كُشَاحَة
cake كَعْك/كَعْكَة	discoverer, explorer, كَشَّاف scout
abstaining, refraining كَفّ	thimble كُشْتْبَان
palm of the (كُفُوف) كَفّ hand, paw, scale	lumbar region, (كُشُوح) كَشْح haunch

hamlet, small village كَفْر (كُفُور)	equal, alike كَفْء/كِفْء (أَكْفَاء)
disbelief, ingratitude كُفْرَان	equal, comparable كُفُوْ/كُفُوْء
guarantee, warranty كَفْل	equivalent كَفَاء
rump, buttocks كَفَل (أَكْفَال)	equality, likeness, competence كَفَاء
shroud, grave clothes كَفَن (أَكْفَان)	efficiency, capability, suitability, competence كَفَاءَة
sufficient, enough, satisfying كَفِي	struggle, strife, fight, combat كِفَاح
blind, stoneblind كَفِيْف/كَفِيْف البَصَر	infidel, unbeliever كَفَّار
sponsor, protector, guarantor, responsible كَفِيْل (كُفَلَاء)	expiation, atonement كَفَّارَة
	sufficiency, pittance كَفَاف
	border, hem, edge كِفَاف
all, entire, whole, each one, everyone كُلّ	bail, security, guarantee, custody كَفَالَة
fatigue, weariness, tiredness كَلّ /كَلَل	caution money كَفَالَة مَالِيّة
everybody كُلّ إِنْسَان	sufficiency, capability, suitability كِفَايَة
everything كُلّ شَيْء	cooking pot كِفْت
everywhere كُلّ مَكَان	border, edge, hem كُفَّة (كُفَف)
each one كُلّ وَاحِد	
everyday, daily كُلّ يَوْم	palm, scale كَفَّة/كِفَّة (كِفَف)
grass, pasture كَلَأ (أَكْلَاء)	fried or roasted meat balls كُفْتَة
both كِلَا	disbelief, infidelity, atheism كُفْر
no, never, not at all كَلَّا	

chest, thorax	كَلْكَل (كَلَاكِل)	hook, tongs	كُلَّاب
wound, cut, injury	كَلْم (كُلُوم/كَلَام)	classical	كَلَاسِكي
word, speech, saying	كَلِمَة (كَلِمَات)	weariness, tiredness, dullness	كَلَال/كَلَالَة
password	كَلِمَة السِّرّ	speech, talk, utterance, discussion	كَلَام
password	كَلِمَةَ المُرُور	fluent language	كَلَام سَلِس
foreign word	كَلِمَة دَخِيلَة	nonsense, guff	كَلَام فَارِغ
word by word, literally	كَلِمَة فَكَلِمَة	honeyed words	كَلَام مَعْسُول
all of them	كُلُّهُم	verbal, oral, scholastic	كَلَامِي
renal, nephritic	كُلْوِي	rabies, hydrophobia, strong thirst	كَلَب
total, entire, absolute, complete	كُلِّي	dog	كَلْبَ (كِلَاب)
absolutely, entirely, completely	كُلِّيَّةً	shark	كَلْب البَحْر
kidney	كُلْيَة (كُلًى)	rabid, affected with rabies	كَلِب/كَلِيْب
college, faculty, school	كُلِّيَّة (كُلِّيَّات)	bitch, female dog	كَلْبَة
college of arts	كُلِّيَّة الآداب	mien, facial expression	كَلْحَة
commerce college	كُلِّيَّة التِّجَارَة	lime, calcium	كِلْس
faculty of law	كُلِّيَّة الحُقُوق	limy, calcic	كِلْسِي
medical college	كُلِّيَّة الطِّبّ	calcium	كَلْسِيوم
military academy	كُلِّيَّة حَرْبِيَّة	trouble, pains, inconvenience, affectation, cost	كُلْفَة (كُلَف)

girder, beam كَمَرَة	tired, weary, dull, كَلِيْل exhausted
customs, كُمْرُك (كَمَارِك) custom house	speaker, كَلِيْم (كُلَمَاء) spokesman
conductor, ticket كُمْسَارِي collector	wounded, كَلِيْم (كَلْمَى) injured
grip, grasp كَمَش	how many, how much كَمْ
skilful, adroit كَمِش	amount, quantity كَمّ
handful كَمْشَة	sleeve كُمّ (أَكْمَام)
violin, fiddle كَمَنْجَا/كَمَنْجَة	as, likewise كَمَا
blindness كَمَه	disdain, haughtiness, كُمَاخ self-conceit
quantitative كَمِّي	pincers كَمَّاشَة
reddish brown كُمَيْت	completion, كَمَال perfection, maturity
magnitude, كَمِّيَّة (كَمِّيَّات) quantity	supplement, addition كَمَالَة
bedfellow كَمِيْع	violin, fiddle كَمَان
hidden, كَمِيْن (كُمَنَاء) concealed, ambush, ambushcade	cambrio كَمْبَرِيت
shelter, كَنّ/كِنّ (أَكْنَان) refuge, dwelling place	bill of exchange, كَمْبِيَالة draft
sweeper, cleaner كَنَّاس	exchange كَمْبِيُو
sweepings, offal كُنَاسَة	pear كُمَّثْرَى
quiver كِنَانَة (كَنَائِن)	morbidness, gloom, كَمْد/كَمَد swarthiness
allusion, metonymy كِنَايَة	gloomy, grieved, كَمِد/كَمِيد sad
shelter, covering كَنّة	

divination, fortune-telling	كِهَانَة	shed roof	كُنّة (كِنَان)
electron	كَهْرَب (كَهَارِب)	kangaroo	كَنْجَرُو
electricity	كَهْرَبَاء	magpie	كُنْدُش
electric, electrician	كَهْرَبَائي	firm, compact	كَنز
electrification, electricity	كَهْرَبَة	treasure	كَنْز (كُنُوز)
amber	كَهْرَمَان	sweeping, cleaning	كَنْس
cave, cavern, hollow	كَهْف (كُهُوف)	ecclesiastic, clerical	كَنْسِي/كَنَائِسِي
middle aged, of middle age	كَهْل (كُهُول)	console	كُنْصُول
priesthood	كَهْنُوت/كَهَنُوت	cangaroo	كَنْغَر
priestly, clerical	كَهْنُوتي	side, wing, shade, shelter, embrace	كَنَف (أَكْنَاف)
maturity of age	كُهُولَة	canvas	كَنْفَاش
electron	كُهَيْرِب	substance, essence, entity, quantity	كُنْه
electronic	كُهَيْرِبي	ingratitude, thanklessness	كُنُود
ironer, presser	كَوَّاء	nickname, surname, agnomen	كُنْيَة (كُنَى)
tumbler, drinking glass	كُوب (أَكْوَاب)	church, synagogue	كَنِيسَة (كَنَائِس)
drinking glass, tumbler	كُوبَة	enclosure, fold, water closet	كَنِيف (كُنُف)
bridge, deck	كُوبْري	concealed, hidden	كَنِين
small window, aperture	كُوَّة (كُوًى)	prophecy, prediction	كَهَانَة
abundant, copious, plentiful	كَوْثَر		

cocktail	كُوكْتيل	name of a river in	كَوْثر
cholera	كُولِيْرَا	Paradise	
side scene,	كُوليس (كَوَاليس)	hut, hovel	كُوخ (أَكْوَاخ)
back drop		heap, pile	كَوْدَة (أَكْوَاد)
pile, heap	كُوم (أَكْوَام)	camel	كُور (أَكْوَار/كِيْرَان)
pile, heap	كُوْمَة/كَوْمَة (كُوَم)	saddle	
comedy	كُومِيْديا	furnace, forge	كُور الحَدَّاد
the universe, the	كَوْن	district, small	كُوْرَة (كُوَر)
cosmos		town	
being, existence,	كَوْن (أَكْوَان)	cordon, ribbon	كُوردون
occurrence, entity, state		sanitary	كُوردون صِحِّي
contract, agreement	كُوْنْتَرَاتُو	cordon	
universal, cosmic	كَوْني	chorus	كُوْرَس
fine, well, nice	كُوَيِّس	mug, tankard	كُوز (أَكْوَاز)
ironing, cauterization	كَيّ	small drum	كُوْس
cleverness, dexterity,	كِيَاسَة	elbow, bend	كُوع (أَكْوَاع)
intelligence, elegance		head wrapper, head	كُوْفِيَّة
essence, existence,	كِيَان	dress	
being, entity		coke	كُوك
burn, brand	كَيَّة	star, planet	كَوْكَب (كَوَاكِب)
deception, deceit,	كَيْد (كِيَاد)	lustrous star	كَوْكَب دُرِّي
trick, treachery		film star	كَوْكَب سِيْنمائي
bellows	كِيْر (أَكْيَار)	star, constellation,	كَوْكَبَة
keronsene	كِيْرُوسِيْن	group	
intelligence, elegance,	كَيْس	stellar, astral, starlike	كَوْكَبِي
sagacity, cleverness			

Saturn	كَيْوَان	subtle, shrewd, intelligent, skilful	كَيِّس
cupid	كِيوبيد	small bag, purse, case	كِيس (أَكْيَاس)
ل		pillowcase	كِيس الوِسَادَة
glitter, shine, glow	لَأْلَاءِ	how	كَيْفَ
pearls	لُؤْلُؤ (لَآلِي)	condition, wish, discretion, pleasure	كَيْف
shine, glitter, twinkling, brightness	لَأْلَأَة	however, howsoever	كَيْفَمَا
pearly, pearl coloured	لُؤْلُؤِي	discretionary, optional	كَيْفِي
joining, connecting, repair	لَأْم	state, condition, mode, kind	كَيْفِيَّة
meanness, vileness, baseness	لُؤْم	directions for use or application	كَيْفِيَّة الاسْتِعْمَال
peace, harmony, concord	لِئْم	measure, corn measure	كَيْل (أَكْيَال)
because, for	لأَنَّ	kilowatt	كِيلُو وَاط
base, baseborn, vile, sordid, low	لَئِيْم (لِئَام)	kilogram	كِيلُو/كِيْلُو جرام
not, no	لَا	kilometer	كِيْلُومتْر
it doesn't matter	لابَأْس	chemical, chemist	كِيْمَاوِي/كِيْمِيائِي
inevitably, by all means	لَابُدَّ	chemicals	كِيْمَاوِيات
prospect, project, programme, rule	لَائِحَة (لَوَائِح)	chemistry, alchemy	كِيْمِيَاء
railroad guide	لَائِحَة السَّفَر	quinine	كِيْنا
		quinine	كِيْنِيْن

wireless, radio	لاسلْكي	menu, bill of rate	لَائِحَة الطَّعَام
especially, particularly, chiefly	لاسِيَّمَا	bill, draft law	لَائِحَة القَانُون
no doubt	لَاشَكَّ	refugee, one who seeks shelter	لَائِذ
nothing	لاشَيْء	involuntary	لَاإِرَادِي
nothingness, nihility	لاشَيْئِيَّة	worthy, fit, suitable, proper	لَائِق
player, athlete	لَاعب	censurer, accuser (لُوَّم)	لَائِم
gymnast, athlete	لَاعَب الجُنْبَار	censure, reproach, rebuke	لَائِمَة (لَوَائِم)
cancelled, annulled, invalid	لَاغٍ	refugee, emigrant	لَاجِئ
weary, fatigued, exhausted	لاغَب	surely, certainly	لَاجَرَمَ
faulty language	لاغْيَة	sexless, asexual	لَاجِنْسِي
gleaner, gatherer	لاقط	added, affixed, attached, following	لَاحق
indifference, carelessness	لَامُبَالَاة	appendage, appurtenance (لَوَاحق)	لَاحِقَة
decentralization	لَامَرْكَزِيَّة	irreligious, godless	لَادِيْني
shining, lustrous, shimmering	لَامِع	godlessness, irreligion	لَادِيْنِيَّة
launch, small steamer	لَانْش	very hot, biting, pungent, burning	لاذع
infinite, unending	لانِهَائي	firmly fixed, sticking	لَازب
inadvertent, inattentive, oblivious	لَاه	inevitable, necessary, indispensable, obligatory	لَازِم
worried, sad, sorrowful, grieved	لَاهف	biting, sharp, pungent	لَاسِع

deity, godhead	لَاهُوت
theological, theologian	لَاهُوتِي
intellect, heart, mind	لُبّ (أَلْبَاب)
core, essence, kernels, marrow	لُبّ (لُبُوب)
lioness	لَبُؤَة
core, quintessence, essence, marrow	لُبَاب
felt maker	لَبَّاد
clothes, dress, garments	لِبَاس (أَلْبِسَة)
modesty, decency	لِبَاس التَّقْوَى
evening dress	لِبَاس السَّهْرَة
swimming suit	لِبَاس العَوْم
uniform	لِبَاس رَسْمِي
intelligency, skill, adroitness, slyness	لَبَاقَة
breast	لَبَان
sucking, nursing	لَبَان
milkman	لَبَّان
business of producing milk	لِبَانَة
wish, desire, object	لُبَانَة

upper part of the chest	لَبَب (أَلْبَاب)
front part of the neck	لَبَّة
gold necklace	لَبَّة
stay, staying, tarrying	لَبْث/لُبْث
pause, temporary stay	لُبْثَة
matted, tangled, clouded	لَبِد
matted wool, felt	لِبْد/لَبَد
felt cap or hat	لَبْدَة
clothing, dress, apparel	لِبْس (لُبُوس)
confusion, muddle, obscurity	لَبْس/لُبْس
confusion, muddle, obscurity	لُبْسَة
costume, style of dressing	لِبْسَة
cleverness, adroitness, skill, seemliness	لَبَق
clever, adroit, skilled, fit, sly	لَبِق/لَبِيق
confusion, medley, mixture	لَبْك/لَبْكَة
milk	لَبَن (أَلْبَان)
butter milk	لَبَن الحَضّ

bridle, rein لِجَام (لُجُم)	curdled milk لَبَن زَبَادي
tumult, uproar, noise, لَجَب clamour	sundried bricks لِبْن/لَبِن
noisy, clamorous, لَجِب uproaring	storax tree لُبْنَى
tumult, uproar, hubhub لَجَّة	milky, lacteous لَبَنِي
stammerer, stutterer لَجْلَاج	lioness لَبْوَة
stammering, لَجْلَجَة stuttering	giving milk لَبُون
committee, لَجْنَة (لِجَان/لِجَن) council, board	intelligent, لَبِيب (أَلِبَّاء) sagacious, sensible
examination لَجْنَة الامْتِحَان board	corpulent, fleshy لَبِيخ
disciplinary لَجْنَة الانْضِبَاط board	worn, worn clothes لَبِيس
investigating لَجْنَة التَّحْقِيق committee	I'm at your service لَبَّيْك
jury لَجْنَة التَّحْلِيف	prattle, idle talk لَتَّ
board of directors لَجْنَة المُرَاقَبَة	talkative, chatterbox, لَتَات prattler
board of لَجْنَة تَحْكِيمِيَّة arbitration	litre لِتْر
executive لَجْنَة تَنْفِيذِيَّة committee	litmus لِتْمُوس
subcommittee لَجْنَة فَرْعِيَّة	veil, cover لِثَام
standing committee لَجْنَة قَارَّة	gums لِثَّة (لِثَى)
standing لَجْنَة مُسْتَدِيمَة committee	lisp, lisping لُثْغَة
	kiss لَثْمَة
	gingival, pertaining to لِثَوِي gums
	depth, depth of لُجّ/لُجَّة (لُجَج) the sea
	sticking, insistence لَجَاجَة

beard	لِحْيَة (لِحًى)	persistent, insistent, importunate	لَجُوج
plastics	لَدَائِن	fathomless, tumultuous	لُجِّي
pliability, flexibility, softness	لَدَانَة	silver	لُجَيْن
contemporary, coetaneous	لِدَة (لِدَات)	gravedigger	لَحّاد
violent dispute	لَدَد	quilt, wrapper, cover, blanket	لِحَاف (لُحُف)
sting, bite	لَدْغَة	joining, enrolment, entrance	لِحَاق
near, close to, at	لَدُن	welding, soldering	لِحَام
pliant, soft, supple, flexible	لَدْن (لُدُن/لِدَان)	butcher, welder	لَحّام
fierce, bitter, mortal	لَدُود	fleshiness, corpulence	لَحَامَة
pliability, flexibility, suppleness	لُدُونَة	grave, tomb	لَحْد (لُحُود)
with, at, by	لَدَى	look, glance	لَحْظ (أَلْحَاظ)
bitten, stung	لَدِيغ (لَدْغَى)	moment, glance, glimpse	لَحْظَة (لَحَظَات)
sweetness, rapture, delectation	لَذَاذَة	present moment	لَحْظَة رَاهِنَة
burning, pungent, scorching	لَذَّاع	meat, flesh	لَحْم (لُحُوم/لِحَام)
rapture, pleasure, sensual delight	لَذَّة (لَذَّات)	chopped meat, minced meat	لَحْم مَفْرُوم
burning, combustion	لَذْع	fleshy, corpulent	لَحِم/لَحِيم
hence, therefore	لِذَلِك	piece of meat or flesh	لَحْمَة
sweet, delicious, pleasant	لَذِيْذ	relationship, kinship	لُحْمَة
		tune, melody	لَحْن (أَلْحَان)
		insistent, obstinate, obtrusive	لَحُوح

robbery, theft	لَصُوصِيَّة
plaster	لَصُوق
thinness, loveliness, gracefulness, fineness	لَطَافة
stain, smear, spot	لَطْخَة
mildness, politeness, gracefulness, kindness	لُطْف
slap on the face, jolt	لَطْمَة
delicate, fine, mild, amicable, kind	لَطِيْف
witticism, a witty saying, joke	لَطِيْفَة (لَطَائف)
orphan, parentless	لَطِيْم
blaze, flame, fire	لَظَى
saliva, spittle	لُعَاب
salivary, mucilaginous	لُعَابِي
amusing, funny	لَعِب
game, sport, amusement, joke	لَعْب/لَعِب
game, trick	لَعْبَة
toy, plaything, laughing stock	لُعْبَة (لُعَب)
hesitation, stammer, stutter	لَعْثَمَة
cosuming or burning love	لَعِج

cramp, bolt	لَزّ/لَزَّة
glue, cement, adhesive	لِزَاق
requisite, necessity, obligation	لِزَام
little, small	لَزِب (لِزَاب)
sticky, adhesive, viscous	لَزِج
sticky, viscid, gluey, adhesive	لَزِق
viscidity, stickiness	لُزُوْجَة
plaster, adhesive plaster	لَزُوق
necessity, need, requirement, use	لُزُوم
tongue, language	لِسَان (أَلْسِنَة)
voluble or facile tongue	لِسَان طَلِق
candied tongue	لِسَان مَعْسُول
lingual, oral, verbal	لِسَانِي
bite, sting	لَسْعَة
bitten, stung	لَسِيع
thief, robber	لِصّ (لُصُوص)
adhesive, sticky, gluey	لَصِق
adjacent, clinging, near, close to	لَصْق/لَصِيْق

literary language لُغَة كِتَابيّة	pain, grief لَعْجَة
colloquial language لُغَة مُتَدَاوَلة	spoonful لُعْقَة
national language لُغَة وَطَنيّة	garnet لَعْل
riddle, enigma, puzzle لُغْز (أَلْغَاز)	cursing, execration لَعْن
لُغْز الكَلِمَات المُتَقَاطِعَة	curse, execration, malediction لَعْنَة (لِعَان)
crossword puzzle	playful, sportive, flirtatious لَعُوب
noise, clamour, din لَغَط (أَلْغَاط)	
nonsense, meaningless talk, garrulity لَغْو	lambative, electuary لَعُوق
exhaustion, weariness, fatigue لُغُوب	damned, cursed, detested لَعِين
linguistic, lexicographic, lexicographer لُغَوِي	froth, foam لُغَام
	language, tongue, dialect, expression لُغَة (لُغَات)
folding, wrapping, rolling لَفّ	dead language لُغَة أَثَرِيّة
thicket, scrub لفّ (أَلْفَاف)	foreign language لُغَة أَجْنَبِيّة
muffler لَفَاع	colloquial language لُغَة المُحَادَثَة
envelope, wrapper, cover لِفَافَة (لَفَائِف)	professional jargon لُغَة المِهْنَة
scroll, package, roll, coil لَفّة (لَفَّات)	mother tongue, native language لُغَة المَوْلِد
postal package لَفّة بَرِيْدِيّة	colloquial language لُغَة دَارِجَة
heat, fire, burn لَفْحَة (لَفَحَات)	
word, wording, expression لَفْظ (أَلْفَاظ)	colloquial language لُغَة عَامِّيّة
	popular language لُغَة عَامِيَة

a find, anything found	لُقْيَة/لُقْيَّة	foreign word	لَفْظ دَخِيْل
foundling, waif, picked up	لَقِيْط	verbally	لَفْظًا
dilatory, slow, tardy	لُكَأَة	word, expression, utterance	لَفْظَة
vileness, meanness, wickedness	لَكَاعَة	verbal, literal	لَفْظِي
stingy, niggardly, miserly	لَكِز	burning, scorching	لَفُوح
blow, punch, buffet	لَكْمَة	collected, gathered, crowded, group	لَفِيْف
but, however	لَكِن	packet, bundle	لَفِيْفَة
stammer, stutter	لُكْنَة	meeting, encounter	لِقَاء/لِقَابَة
so that, in order to	لِكَيْ	sperm, vaccine, virus	لِقَاح
mean, base, vile	لَكِيْع	gleanings, offal	لُقَاط/لُقَاطَة
why, for what reason	لِمَا	sagacity, quick grasp	لَقَانَة
when, as	لَمَّا	surname, family name, epithet	لَقَب (أَلْقَاب)
why	لِمَاذ	impregnation, fecundation	لَقْح
carper, caviller, faultfinder	لَمَّاز	gleanings, picked up things	لَقَط/لُقْطَة
lustrous, shining, bright, brilliant	لَمَّاع	morsel, little bite of food	لُقْمَة
lamp	لَمْبَة	delicious morsel	لُقْمَة سَائِغَة
collection, gathering, mental derangement	لَمَّة	offal, refuse, discard	لَقًى (أَلْقَاء)
ringlet, curl	لِمَّة	meeting, encounter	لُقْيا/لُقْيَان
		meeting, encounter	لُقْيَة

hence, therefore	لِهَذا	fellow-travellers, group	لُمَّة
regret, sorrow, grief	لَهْف	glance, quick look	لَمْح
sad, grieved, regretful	لَهْفَان	glance of the eye, a flash	لَمْحُ البَصَر
desire, longing, concern, grief	لَهْفَة	wink, quick look, glance	لَمْحَة (لَمَحَات)
covetous, greedy, glutton	لَهِم	carper, caviller	لُمَزَة
amusement, pastime, entertainment, sport	لَهْو	touching, feeling	لَمْس
greedy, voracious, glutton	لَهُوم	a touch, contact	لَمْسَة (لَمْسَات)
sorrowful, regretful, grieved	لَهِيف	tactile, tactual	لَمْسِي
flag, standard, brigade	لِوَاء (أَلْوِية)	shine, glow, luster, brightness, glitter	لَمْع/لَمَعَان
brigadier	لِوَاء مَحَلِّي	glitter, glow, radiance, shimmer, shine	لَمْعَة
government regulations	لَوَائِح الحُكُومة	mental derangement, touch of insanity	لَمَم
necessities, accessories	لَوَازِم	soft to touch, smooth	لَمِيْس
sodomy, pederasty	لِوَاطَة	small steamer, launch	لَنْش
pains of love	لَوَاعِج الحُبّ	flare, flame	لُهَاب
bean	لُوبيا	gasp, pant	لُهَاث
stain, spot	لَوْثَة	agony of death	لُهَاث المَوْت
board, pane, sheet, tablet, slate	لَوْح (أَلْوَاح)	flames, blazes	لَهَب/لَهِيْب
blackboard	لَوْح الكِتَابَة	panting, out of breath	لَهْثَان
		dialect, tone, language	لَهْجَة

censure, reproach, reproof	لَوْم/لَوْمَة	window pane	لَوْح النَّافذَة
colour, hue, tint, sort	لَوْن (أَلْوَان)	sheet iron	لَوْح حَدِيْد
bright colour	لَوْن زَاهٍ	pane of glass, sheet of glass	لَوْح زُجَاج
light colour	لَوْن فَاتِح	bed-board	لَوْح سَرِيْر
deep colour	لَوْن قَاتِم	metal sheet	لَوْح مَعْدني
rose colour, roseate	لَوْن وَرْدي	board, tablet, plate, sheet	لَوْحَة (لَوْحَات)
attendant, housekeeper	لَوِنْجي	chessboard	لَوْحَة الشَّطْرَنج
twisting, bending	لَيّ	blackboard, slate	لَوْحَة الكتَابَة
efficiency, capability, ability, worthiness, fitness	لِيَاقَة	blackboard	لَوْحَة سَوْدَاء
bend, fold, twist, curve	لَيَّة (لوًى)	acute, ingenious, sagacious	لَوْذَع
lion	لَيْث (لُيُوث)	almond	لَوْز/لَوْزَة
pond	لِيَرَا/لِيْرَة	tonsils	لَوْزَتان
no, not	لَيْس	almond shaped	لَوْزي
fibre	لِيْف/لِيْفَة (أَلْيَاف)	sodomite, homosexual, pederast	لُوطي
fibrous, fibred	لِيْفي	pain, torture, anguish	لَوْعَة
silk threads, putty	لِيْقَة (لِيَق)	lovesickness, ardour of love	لَوْعَة الحُبّ
night	لَيْل	screw, spring, spiral spring	لَوْلَب (لَوَالب)
day and night	لَيْل نَهَار	extension spring	لَوْلَب مَطَّاط
at night	لَيْلاً	spiral, screw-shaped	لَوْلَبي

support, backing, aid	مُؤَازَرَة	night	لَيْلَة (لَيَال)
conference, conspiracy, plot	مُؤَامَرَة	wedding night	لَيْلَة الدُّخْلَة
friendliness, familiarity, geniality	مُؤَائَسَة	wedding night	لَيْلَة الزِّفَاف
place to return to, resort	مَآب	Night of Ascension	لَيْلَة المِعْرَاج
endless, eternal, life long	مُؤَبَّد	evening dance	لَيْلَة رَاقِصَة
needlecase, needlebox	مِئْبَر	moonlit night	لَيْلَة مُقْمِرَة/قَمِرَة
catamite, sodomite	مَأْبُون	lilac	لَيْلَك
funeral ceremony, funeral meeting	مَأْتَم	nightly, nocturnal	لَيْلِي
convention, conference	مُؤْتَمَر (مُؤْتَمَرَات)	lemon	لَيْمُون
peace conference	مُؤْتَمَر الصُّلْح	tenderness, softness, gentleness, flexibility	لِين
press conference	مُؤْتَمَر صُحُفِي	soft, tender, flexible, pliable	لَيِّن
conspirators, plotters	مُؤْتَمِرون	gentle, mild, amiable	لَيِّن الجَانِب
entrusted, confidant	مُؤْتَمَن	gentle-hearted	لَيِّن العَرِيْكَة
source, origin, place of origin	مَأْتَى (مآتٍ)	tractable, docile	لَيِّن القِيَاد
furnished	مُؤَثَّث	softness, tenderness, flexibility	لُيُونَة
effective, impressive, touching	مُؤَثِّر		

favourable, suitable, propitious	مُؤَاتٍ
censure, punishment, objection	مُؤَاخَذة

مُؤَدِّي leading, conducting to	مَأْثُرة/مَأْثُرة (مَآثِر) exploit, feat, memorable deed
مُؤْذٍ injurious, harmful, painful, detrimental	مَأْثَم (مَآثِم) sin, crime, vice
مُؤَذِّن muezzin, one who calls to prayers	مَأْثُور transmitted by tradition, handed down
مَأْذَنة/مِئْذنة minaret	مُؤَجِّر lessor, landlord
مَأْرَب (مَآرِب) aim, object, goal, desire	مُؤَجَّر hired, rented, let
مُؤَرِّخ historian, biographer	مُؤَجَّل postponed, delayed, deferred
مُؤَرَّخ dated	مَأْجُور hired, salaried, employed
مِئْزاب/مِيْزاب gutter, drain	مَأْخَذ (مَآخِذ) source, manner, approach, sense, way
مِئْزر (مَآزِر) apron, cover, wrapper	مُؤَخَّر posterior, hinder part, end, stern
مَأْزِق (مَآزِق) narrow pass, predicament, fix	مُؤَخَّر السَّفِينة stern of ship
مَأْزِق حَرِج fix, predicament, critical situation	مُؤَخَّرًا lately, finally, at last
مَأْساة tragedy	مُؤَخَّرة rear, rear guard
مُؤَسِّس founder, promoter	مَأْخُوذ taken, seized, trapped
مُؤَسَّسة (مُؤَسَّسات) foundation, organization, firm, establishment	مَأْخُوذات takings, receipts
	مُؤَدِّب disciplinarian, educator
مُؤَسَّل pointed, tipped, tapered	مُؤَدَّب well-bred, polite, refined
مَأْسُور captivated, fascinated	مَأْدُبة (مَآدِب) banquet, entertainment
مِنْشار saw	

traffic manager	مَأْمُور الحَرَكة	indicator	مُؤَشِّر
order, mission, commission, errand, assignment	مَأْمُورية	sob, sobbing	مَأْقة
		confirmed, certain, emphasized	مُؤَكَّد
expected, hoped for	مَأْمُول	eatable, edible	مَأْكُول
safe, secure, trustworthy	مَأْمُون	eatables, foodstuffs	مَأْكُول (مَأكولات)
war material	مُؤَن حَرْبِيَّة	canned good, conserves	مَأْكُولات مَحْفُوظة
umbilicus	مَأْنة (مَثَنَات)		
provision, food	مُؤْنة/مَؤُوْنة (مُؤَن)	eatables and drinkables	مَأْكُولات ومَشْروبات
feminine	مُؤَنَّث	result, outcome, consequence	مَآل
familiar, accustomed	مَأْنُوس		
qualifications, aptitudes	مُؤَهِّلات	author, writer, compiler	مُؤَلِّف
percentile, percentual	مئَوي	grievous, painful, distressing	مُؤْلِم
retreat, refuge, shelter, abode	مَأْوَى (مَآوٍ)	familiar, accustomed, common	مَأْلُوف
what	مَا	hopeful, full of hope	مُؤَمِّل
except, with the exception of	ما خَلاَ	hope, prospect	مَأْمَل (مَآمِل)
water, fluid	مَاء (مِيَاه/أَمْوَاه)	place of safety	مَأْمَن
salt water, bitter water	مَاء أُجَاج	officer, representative, commissioned	مَأْمُور
stagnant water	مَاء آسِن	commissioner of police	مَأْمُور البُوليس
lime water	مَاء الجِير		

lamp, chandelier مَاثِلة	bloom of youth مَاء الشَّبَاب
events, happening, occurrences مَاجَرَى (مَاجَرَيَات)	rose water مَاء الوَرْد
master, master's degree مَاجِسْتِير	fresh or sweet water مَاء عَذْب
cistern مَاجِل (مَوَاجِل)	hard water مَاء عَسِر
insolent, impudent, shameless مَاجِن	sweet water مَاء فُرَات
quarrelsome, contentious, disputatious مَاحِك	mineral water مَاء مَعْدِني
barren, sterile مَاحِل	holy water مَاء مُكَرَّس
eraser, rubber مَاحِية	dying, moribund, near death مَائِت
ship مَاخِرَة (مَوَاخِر)	hundred مَائَة/مِئَة (مِئُون/مِئَات)
brothel, bawdy house مَاخُور (مَوَاخِير)	waving, surging, rising, high مَائِج
spreading, stretching, expanding مَادّ	giddy, dizzy مَائِد
matter, substance, material, stuff مَادَّة (مَوَادّ)	table, dining table مَائِدَة (مَائِدَات/مَوَائِد)
eulogist, panegyrist مَادِح	dining table مَائِدَة الأَكْل/السُّفْرَة
materialist, substantial, materialistic مَادِّي	operating table مَائِدَة التَّشْرِيح
materialism مَادِّيَّة	dressing table مَائِدَة الزِّينَة
what مَاذَا	writing desk مَائِدَة الكِتَابَة
passing, transient, passer-by مَارّ	liquid, fluid, liquescent مَائِع
	inclined, bent, leaning مَائِل
	watery, aquatic, liquid مَائِي
	emerging, arising, standing مَاثِل

past, last, keen, sharp, effective	مَاضٍ	defiant, rebel, refractory	مَارِد (مَرَدَة)
determined, resolute, firm	مَاضِي العَزِيْمَة	March	مَارْس
rainy, showery	مَاطِر	marshal	مَارْشال
a goat	مَاعِز	air marshal	مَارْشال جَوِّي
utensil, vessel	مَاعُون (مَوَاعِيْن)	renegade, apostate	مَارِق (مَرَقَة/مُرَّاق)
crafty, cunning, sly	مَاكِر (مَكَرَة)	mark, sign	مَارْك (مَارْكات)
shuttle, drinking cup	مَاكُوك	mark, token, sign	مَارْكَة (مَارْكات)
make-up	مَاكِيَاج	trade mark	مَارْكَة تِجَارِيَّة
machine	مَاكِيْنَة (مَاكِيْنات)	Marxist	مَارْكسِي
property, money, goods, assets	مَال (أَمْوَال)	Marxism	مَارْكسِيَّة
reserve fund	مال احْتِيَاطِي	touching, contiguous	مَاسّ
real property	مَال ثَابِت	diamond	مَاس/مَاسَة
movable property	مَال مَنْقُول	shoeshine, shoeblack	مَاسِح
hard money	مَال نَاضّ	pipe, water pipe, hose	مَاسُوْرَة (مَوَاسِيْر)
trowel	مَالَج (مَوَالِج)	pedestrian, walking	مَاشٍ (مُشَاة)
salty, briny	مَالِح	hairdresser, barber	مَاشِط
owner, proprietor, possessor	مَالِك	woman hairdresser	مَاشِطَة
		on foot	مَاشِيًا
what is the matter with you?	مَالَك؟	cattle, live-stock	مَاشِيَة (مَوَاشٍ)

undertaking, enterprise	مُبَادَرَة	melancholia	مَالِنْخُولِيَا/مَالِيْخُولِيَا
commercial exchange	مُبَادَلات تِجَارِيّة	monetary, fiscal, financial	مَالِي
exchange reciprocity	مُبَادَلَة	finance, financial affairs	مَالِيَّة
tournament, match, contest	مُبَارَاة (مُبارايَات)	mango, mango tree	مَانْجُو
final match	مُبَارَاة فَاصِلَة	grantor, donor	مَانِح
final match	مُبَارَاة نِهَائِيَّة	hindering, prohibitive, preventive	مَانِع
combatant, fighter, competitor	مُبَارِز	obstacle, impediment, hindrance	مَانِع (مَوَانِع)
duel, combat, contest, competition	مُبَارَزَة	manifest	مَانِيْفِسْتُو
blessed, auspicious, fortunate	مُبَارَك	expert, skilful, dexterous	مَاهِر (مَهَرَة)
direct, immediate, pursuer	مُبَاشِر	quality, nature, salary	مَاهِيَّة (مَاهِيَّات)
practice, sexual intercourse	مُبَاشَرة	watery, aquatic, liquid	مَاوِي
directly, immediately	مُبَاشَرةً	May	مَايُو
heedful, careful, mindful	مُبَالٍ	abode, dwelling, residence	مَبَاءة
consideration, carefulness, attention	مُبَالاة	licit, lawful, permitted, permissible	مُبَاح
exaggeration	مُبَالَغة	discussion, debate, negotiation	مُبَاحَثَة
boastfulness, self-exaltation, pride	مُبَاهاة	rudiments of learning	مَبَادِئ العِلْم

initial, principal, basic, original	مَبْدَئي	purchaser, buyer	مُبْتَاع
originally, initially, principally	مَبْدَئيًّا	beginning, subject of a sentence	مُبْتَدَأ
wastrel, scatterer, squanderer	مُبَدِّد	beginner, beginning	مُبْتَدئ
creator, fashioning, unique	مُبْدِع	innovator, creator, originator	مُبْتَدِع
squanderer, spendthrift, prodigal	مُبَذِّر	debased, trite, band, common place, ill-used	مُبْتَذَل
penknife, pocketknife	مِبْرَاة	smiling	مُبْتَسِم
severe, intense, excruciating	مُبَرِّح	inventor, creator, creative	مُبْتَكِر
afflicted, stricken	مُبَرَّح به	moist, wet, damp, saturated	مُبْتَلّ
cooling, refreshing	مُبَرِّد	afflicted, suffering from	مُبْتَلىً
file, rasp	مِبْرَد	delighted, happy, joyous	مُبْتَهِج
refreshments	مُبَرِّدات	cut off, broken, incomplete	مَبْتُور
assured, affirmed	مُبْرَم	venerable, revered, respected, honourable	مُبَجَّل
proven, proved, demonstrated	مُبَرْهَن	subject, research work, study	مَبْحَث (مَبَاحث)
blessed, accepted	مَبْرُور		
twisted, wound	مَبْرُوم	fumigator, censer	مِبْخَرَة
spittoon, cuspidor	مِبْزَقَة (مَبَازِق)	starting point, principle, basis	مَبْدَأ (مَبَادئ)
spigot, faucet, tap	مِبْزَل (مَبَازِل)	general principle	مَبْدَأ عَامّ

based, founded, built, مَبْنِي erected	high, lofty, towering مُبْسِق
building, edifice, (مَبَان) مَبْنًى structure, foundation	expanded, dilated, مَبْسُوط extended, elaborated, cheerful, well off
pleasing, delightful, مُبْهِج pleasant	announcer of good مُبَشِّر news, preacher
showy, ostentatious, مُبَهْرَج gaudy	spittoon, cuspidor مِبْصَقَة
ambiguous, obscure, مُبْهَم vague, hazy	dissecting مِبْضَع (مَبَاضِع) knife
amazed, startled, مَبْهُوت astonished	scattered, strewn, مُبَعْثَر widespread
panting, breathless مَبْهُور	sent, envoy, delegate, مَبْعُوث deputy
classified, divided into مُبَوَّب chapters	hateful, detested, مَبْغُوض loathsome
urinal, diuretic مَبْوَلَة	brothel مَبْغًى
night's lodging, مَبِيت overnight stay	early, doing early مُبَكِّر
annihilating, ruinous, مُبِيد destructive	early, early in the مُبَكِّراً morning
ovary مَبِيض	confused, anxious, مُبَلْبَل solicitous, perturbed
whitewasher, tinner مُبَيِّض	tiled, paved مُبَلَّط
sold, sale, selling مَبِيع	amount, extent, range, مَبْلَغ limit
sales مَبِيعات	messenger, informant, مُبَلِّغ denouncer
clear, obvious, evident مُبِين	
affected, impressed مُتَأَثِّر	

pursuance, chasing, following	مُتَابَعَة	blazing, flaming, glowing	مُتَأَجِّج
neighbouring, bordering	مُتَاخِم	late, delayed, behind hand, in arrears	مُتَأَخِّر
effect, goods, chattels, object of pleasure	مَتَاع (أَمْتِعَة)	arrears	مُتَأَخِّرات
delight of the eyes	مَتَاع العَيْن	the later, modern	مُتَأَخِّرون
troubles, difficulties, inconveniences	مَتَاعِب	swinging, fluctuating	مُتَأَرْجِح
firmness, solidity, strength	مَتَانَة	regretful, sorry, repentant	مُتَأَسِّف
different, dissimilar, unlike, incongruous, differing	مُتَبَائِن	deep-rooted, chronic	مُتَأَصِّل
		convinced, confirmed	مُتَأَكِّد
reciprocal, mutual, common	مُتَبَادِل	harmonious, in concord	مُتَآلِف
		shining, bright, radiant, glittering	مُتَأَلِّق
separate, isolated	مُتَبَاعِد	painful, aching, suffering	مُتَأَلِّم
braggart, boastful	مُتَبَجِّح		
profound, erudite, profoundly learned	مُتَبَحِّر	conspirators, plotters	مُتَآمِرون
donor, contributor, free giver	مُتَبَرِّع	meditative, contemplative	مُتَأَمِّل
vexed, restless, annoyed	مُتَبَرِّم	slow, deliberate, careful	مُتَأَنٍّ
unemployed	مُتَبَطِّل	meticulous, elegant, chic, nice	مُتَأَنِّق
followed, observed, adhered to	مُتَّبَع	ready, prepared, alert	مُتَأَهِّب

allied, confederate مُتَحَالِف	مُتَبَقٍّ remnant, rest, residue, leftover
petrified, changed into stone مُتَحَجِّر	spiced, flavoured مُتَبَّل
challenger, provoker مُتَحَدٍّ	dull, stupid, besotted مُتَبَلِّد
united, unanimous, combined مُتَّحِد	straw-stack (مَتَابِن) مَتْبَن
descending, sloping, slanting مُتَحَدِّر	followed, succeeded by مَتْبُوع
moving, movable مُتَحَرِّك	successive, consecutive مُتَتَابِع
biased, partial مُتَحَزِّب	successive, subsequent, consecutive مُتَتَالٍ
shabby, sloven مُتَحَشِّف	
civilized, urbane مُتَحَضِّر	similar, like, homogeneous مُتَجَانِس
museum (مَتَاحِف) مَتْحَف	adjoining, adjacent, contiguous مُتَجَاوِر
sure, convinced, confident مُتَحَقِّق	business, (مَتَاجِر) مَتْجَر merchandise, transaction
enthusiastic, zealous, excited مُتَحَمِّس	curled, wrinkled, frizzed مُتَجَعِّد
cautious, careful, prudent مُتَحَوِّط	manifest, evident, patent مُتَجَلٍّ
changeable, variable مُتَحَوِّل	directed, tending, bound to مُتَّجِه
bewildered, perplexed, dismayed مُتَحَيِّر	roving, travelling, itinerant مُتَجَوِّل
biased, partial, prejudiced مُتَحَيِّز	loving, one another مُتَحَابّ
graduate from a college or university مُتَخَرِّج	belligerent, warring مُتَحَارِب

wide, vast, extensive	مُتَرَامٍ	stiff, rigid, hard	مُتَخَشِّب
dusty, earthy, dust-covered	مُتْرِب	specialist, specialized in	مُتَخَصِّص
destitution, poverty, indigence	مَتْرَبَة	backward, waste, left over	مُتَخَلِّف
lurking, candidate	مُتَرَبِّص	afflicted with dyspepsia	مَتْخُوم
translator, interpreter	مُتَرْجِم	threatened with fall, ready to fall, declining	مُتَدَاعٍ
dressed, clothed in	مُتَرَدٍّ	current, popular, common, in circulation	مُتَدَاوَل
reluctant, hesitant	مُتَرَدِّد		
irresolute, undecided	مُتَرَدِّدُ الفكْر	tubercled, affected with tubercules	مُتَدَرِّن
bolt, rampart, barricade	مَتْرَس/مِتْرَس (مَتَارِس)	gushing, impulsive, effusive, erupting	مُتَدَفِّق
luxurious, given to luxury	مُتْرَف	hanging, pedent, suspended	مُتَدَلٍّ
haughty, disdainful, arrogant	مُتَرَفِّع	pious, devout, godly	مُتَدَيِّن
flabby, flaccid	مُتَرَهِّل	oscillating, swinging	مُتَذَبْذِب
left out, abandoned, neglected	مَتْرُوك	metre	مِتْر (أَمْتَار)
heritage, legacy	مَتْرُوك (مَتْرُوكات)	cubic metre	مِتْر مُكَعَّب
metrical	مِتْرِي	languid, slack, flabby, slothful	مُتَرَاخٍ
gradually increasing	مُتَزَائِد	synonymous, synonym	مُتَرَادِف
unsteady, precarious, shaky	مُتَزَعْزِع	synonyms	مُتَرَادِفات

haughty, proud, supercilious, lofty	مُتَشَامِخ	sycophant, flatterer, toady	مُتَزَلِّف
tenacious, obstinate	مُتَشَبِّث	staid, sedate, grave, prim	مُتَزَمِّت
garbed, clad	مُتَّشِح	well-balanced, evenly poised	مُتَّزِن
zealot, bigot	مُتَشَدِّد	married	مُتَزَوِّج
boaster, braggart	مُتَشَدِّق	forbearing, tolerant	مُتَسَامِح
vagrant, vagabond, wanderer	مُتَشَرِّد	lenient, indulgent	مُتَسَاهِل
legislator, law-giver	مُتَشَرِّع	equal, similar, alike	مُتَسَاوٍ
rising, going up, ascending	مُتَصَاعِد	equidistant	مُتَسَاوِي الأَبْعَاد
characterized	مُتَّصِف	equiangular	مُتَسَاوِى الزَّوَايَا
incessant, continual, adjoining	مُتَّصِل	dressed, clothed, blessed	مُتَسَرْبِل
relentless, rigid, unyielding	مُتَصَلِّب	prompt, rapid, fast, rash	مُتَسَرِّع
opposite, contrary	مُتَضَادّ	wide, spacious, extensive	مُتَّسِع
clear, obvious, plain, evident	مُتَّضِح	well-arranged, in good order	مُتَّسِق
expert, skilled, experienced	مُتَضَلِّع	consecutive, serial	مُتَسَلْسِل
quack	مُتَطَبِّب	beggar, mendicant	مُتَسَوِّل
extreme, utmost, extremist, radical	مُتَطَرِّف	pessimist	مُتَشَائِم
uninvited guest, sponger, intruder	مُتَطَفِّل	interlaced, entwined	مُتَشَابِك
		obscure, dubious, not clear	مُتَشَابِه

polygon	مُتَعَدِّد الأَضْلَاع	requirements	مُتَطَلَّبَات
multi-coloured	مُتَعَدِّد الأَلْوَان	curious, eager	مُتَطَلِّع
multicellular	مُتَعَدِّد الخَلَايَا	volunteer	مُتَطَوِّع
multangular	مُتَعَدِّد الزَّوَايَا	even, balanced	مُتَعَادِل
multifarious, variegated, many-sided	مُتَعَدِّد النَّوَاحِي	commonplace, usual, common	مُتَعَارَف
impracticable, impossible	مُتَعَذِّر	arrogant, proud, haughty	مُتَعَاظِم
zealous, bigot, enthusiast,	مُتَعَصِّب	successive, continuous	مُتَعَاقِب
virtuous, upright, chaste, modest	مُتَعَفِّف	contrasting, conflicting	مُتَعَاكِس
putrid, rotten, spoiled, musty	مُتَعَفِّن	high, elevated, lofty	مُتَعَالٍ
related, attached, connected	مُتَعَلِّق	tired, weary, exhausted	مُتْعَب
educated, schooled	مُتَعَلِّم	tiresome, troublesome, tedious	مُتْعِب
premeditated, deliberate	مُتَعَمِّد	pious, devout, worshipper	مُتَعَبِّد
stubborn, obstinate, stickler	مُتَعَنِّت	pleasure, enjoyment, recreation	مُتْعَة (مُتَع)
contractor, purveyor	مُتَعَهِّد	astonished, surprised	مُتَعَجِّب
habituated, used to, accustomed	مُتَعَوِّد	hasty, rash	مُتَعَجِّل
wretched, miserable	مَتْعُوس	aggressor, transitive	مُتَعَدٍّ
irate, furious, enraged	مُتَغَاظ	numerous, many, various	مُتَعَدِّد

مُتَقَارِب	close together, successive	مُتَغَايِر	heterogeneous
مُتَقَاضٍ	litigant	مُتَغَطْرِس	arrogant, conceited, self-important
مُتَقَاعِد	retired, pensioner	مُتَغَلْغِل	deeply embedded, widely extended
مُتَقَاعِس	careless, neglectful, hesitant		
مُتَّقِد	burning, blazing, flaming	مُتَغَيِّر	changeable, variable
		مُتَغَيِّم	cloudy, clouded
مُتَقَدِّم	advanced, advancing, improving	مُتَفَائِل	optimist, optimistic
		مُتَفَاوِت	different, disharmonious
مُتَقَرِّح	ulcerated, ulcerous		
مُتَقَطِّع	interrupted, disrupted, intermittent	مُتَفَتِّر	intermitted
		مُتَفَجِّر	explosive, blasting, eruptive
مُتَقَلِّب	changing, variable, changeable		
		مُتَفَرِّج	onlooker, observer, viewer
مُتَقَلِّب الأَطْوَار	fickle, versatile, capricious	مُتَفَرِّق	scattered, dispersed
مُتْقَن	precise, perfect, firm, solid	مُتَفَرِّقَات	miscellany, miscellaneous items
مُتَقَيِّح	suppurative, purulent	مُتَّفَق عَلَيْه	agreed upon, accepted
مُتَّكَأ	support, prop, staff, sofa	مِتْفَلَة	spittoon, cuspidor
		مُتَفَنِّن	multifarious, versatile
مُتَكَاثِر	numerous, multifarious	مُتَفَوِّق	surpassing, proficient, excellent, superior
مُتَكَاسِل	slugghish, lazy, indolent	مُتَّقٍ	devout, pious, godly

مُتْلِف destructive, ruinous, injurious	مُتَكَافِئ alike, commensurate, corresponding
مَتْلُوف spoiled, ruined, broken	مُتَكَامِل integral, integrative
مُتَلَوِّن multicoloured, changeable, inconstant	مُتَكَبِّر haughty, proud, arrogant, supercilious
مُتَمَاثِل homogeneous, assimilative, homologous	مُتَكَتِّل lumpy, massed, agglomerated
مُتَمَاسِك holding together, cohesive, interlocked	مُتَكَرِّر recurrent, frequent
مُتَمَدِّن civilized, educated	مُتَكَلِّف formal, ceremonial, artificial
مُتَمَرِّد rebellious, insurgent, insubordinate	مُتَكَلِّم speaker, one who speaks
مُتَمَرِّن experienced, seasoned, trained	مُتَكَهِّن fortune teller, soothsayer
مُتَمَسِّك adhering, holding fast, firm	مُتَلَأْلِئ shining, glittering, sparkling
مُتَمَغِّط elastic, tenacious, viscous	مُتَلَاشٍ evanescent, fading away, ephemeral
مُتَمَكِّن strengthened, firmly fixed, deep rooted	مُتَلَبِّد matted, tangled, clouded
مُتَمَهِّل slow, leisurely, deliberate	مُتَلَثِّم veiled, covered
مُتَمَوِّج waving, surging, rising, high	مُتَلَدِّد obstinate, headstrong, stubborn
مُتَمَوِّل wealthy, rich, well-to-do	مُتَلَذِّذ epicure
	مُتَلَعْثِم stuttering, stammering
	مُتْلَف ruined, deteriorated, damaged

illuminated, lighted مُتَنَوِّر	back, main part, مَتْن (مُتُون) body, text
negligent, careless, مُتَهَاوِن remiss	deck of the ship مَتْن السَّفِينَة
shameless, impudent, مُتَهَتِّك cheeky	middle of the road مَتْن الطَّرِيق
well-educated, مُتَهَذِّب refined, well cultured	text of a book مَتْن الكِتَاب
ironical, mocking, مُتَهَكِّم derisive	conflicting, clashing مُتَنَازِع
rejoicing, jubilant مُتَهَلِّل	disputed, litigated مُتَنَازَع فِيه
accuser, prosecutor مُتَّهِم	proportionate, مُتَنَاسِب proportional, analogous
accused, suspected, مُتَّهَم indicted	commensurate مُتَنَاسِب القِيَاس
hasty, rash, مُتَهَوِّر thoughtless	well-arranged, مُتَنَاسِق symmetrical
excited, agitated, مُتَهَيِّج infuriated	incongruous, مُتَنَافِر discordant
successive, following مُتَوَاتِر in succession	contradictory, مُتَنَاقِض conflicting, incompatible
parallel, equivalent, مُتَوَازٍ similar	contrasts, مُتَنَاقِضَات contradictions
balanced, in مُتَوَازِن equilibrium	bounded, limited, مُتَنَاهٍ extreme
continuous, مُتَوَاصِل continued, unceasing	alternative, مُتَنَاوِب successive
humble, lowly, مُتَوَاضِع insignificant, inferior	available, within مُتَنَاوَل reach
	wakeful, alert, awake مُتَنَبِّه
	movable, portable, مُتَنَقِّل roving

when, at what time	مَتَى	successive, incessant, consecutive	مُتَوَالٍ
alert, watchful, vigilant, awake	مُتَيَقِّظ	slack, remiss, slow	مُتَوَانٍ
convinced, sure	مُتَيَقِّن	tense, strained, highly strung	مُتَوَتِّر
enslaved, enthralled	مُتَيَّم	solitary, isolated, alone	مُتَوَحِّد
firm, strong, solid	مَتِين	rosy, ruddy	مُتَوَرِّد
persevering, persistent, assiduous	مُثَابِر	middle, medial, central, average	مُتَوَسِّط
persistence, perseverance, assiduousness	مُثَابَرة	middle-sized	مُتَوَسِّط الحَجْم
example, model, simile, allegory	مِثال (أَمْثِلَة)	middle-aged	مُتَوَسِّط العُمْر
ideal, exemplary, typical	مِثالي	of medium stature	مُتَوَسِّط القَامَة
bladder	مَثَانة	of medium quality	مُتَوَسِّط النَّوْع
confirmed, established	مُثْبِت	unwell, indisposed	مُتَوَعِّك
well-fixed, established	مُثَبَّت	ample, abundant, profuse	مُتَوَفِّر
discouraging, disheartening	مُثَبِّط العَزْم	dead, deceased	مُتَوَفَّى
rich, wealthy	مُثْرٍ	burning, blazing, flaming	مُتَوَقِّد
drain, trap	مَثْعَب (مَثَاعِب)	expected, anticipated, presumable	مُتَوَقَّع
weight, miskal	مِثقَال	certain, sure, positive	مُتَوَكِّد
a whit, a mote, a tiny amount, a little bit	مِثقَال ذَرَّة	in charge, entrusted	مُتَوَلٍّ

dwelling, abode, (مَثَاوٍ) مَثْوًى hostel	wimble, drill, drilling machine مِثْقَب
exciting, agitating, provocative مُثِير	cultured, refined, educated مُثَقَّف
pathetic, moving مُثِير الشُّجُون	weighted, overloaded, overburdened مُثقَّل
cushion, blanket (مَوَاثِر) مَثِيرَة	similar, similarity, (أَمْثَال) مِثْل likeness
similar, like, equal (مُثُل) مَثِيل	example, adage, (أَمْثَال) مَثَل proverb
spittle, saliva (مُجَاجَة) مُجَاج	
honey مُجَاج النَّحْل	for example مَثَلاً
disputant, quarrelsome مُجَادِل	threefold, tripled مُثَلَّث
dispute, quarrel, argument مُجَادَلَة	triangular مُثَلَّث الزَّوَايا
drainage, sewerage مَجَارِير	ice-cold, icy مُثَلَّج
passage, corridor, figure of speech مَجَاز	refrigerator, icebox مَثْلَجة
	as, as well as مِثْلَمَا
requital, repayment مُجَازاة	iced, icy مَثْلُوج
adventurous, reckless, temerarious مُجَازِف	ice beverages مَثْلُوجات
adventure, rashness, recklessness, temerity مُجَازَفة	fruitful, productive, profitable مُثْمِر
metaphorical, figuratively مَجَازِي	valuable, precious مُثَمَّن
	costly, precious مُثْمِن
famine, dearth مَجَاعَة	folded, doubled, plaited مَثْنِي
field, sphere, (مَجَالات) مَجَال scope	recompense, reward مَثُوبة
	appearance, presentation مُثُول

diligent, assiduous, industrious	مُجْتَهد
unjust, biased, unfair	مُجْحف
glory, grandeur, honour	مَجْد (أَمْجَاد)
oar	مجْدَاف
barren, unfertile, unprofitable	مُجْدِب
reformer, renewer	مُجَدِّد
lucky, fortunate	مَجْدُود
infected with small pox	مَجْدُور
twisted, braided, plaited	مَجْدُول
oar	مجْذاف (مَجَاذيف)
lunatic, insane	مَجْذُوب (مَجَاذِيب)
leper, leprous	مَجْذُوم
tester, examiner, tempter	مُجَرِّب
experienced, tested, practiced	مُجَرَّب
scraper	مجْرَد
dismantled, deprived, naked, bare, abstract	مُجَرَّد
toothbrush	مجْرَد الأسْنان

gladiator	مُجَالد
fight, duel, contest	مُجَالَدَة
social intercourse	مُجَالَسة
courtesy, civility	مُجَامَلة
impudent, shameless, jester, free	مَجّان
free of charge	مَجّانًا
similar, like, homogeneous	مُجَانس
similarity, affinity, resemblance	مُجَانَسة
free, gratuitous	مَجّاني
holy fighter, warrior	مُجَاهد
strife, struggle, fight	مُجَاهَدَة
neighbouring, next, adjacent, near	مُجَاور
proximity, nearness	مُجَاوَرة
crossing, exceeding, going beyond	مُجَاوَزة
compelled, coerced, forced	مَجْبُور
tax, impost	مَجْبَى (مَجَاب)
bold, forward, daring	مُجْتَرِئ
society, community, assembly, gathering, meeting	مُجْتَمَع

مُجَفَّف	dried, desiccated, dehydrated
مُجَفَّفَات	dehydrated foods
مَجْلَبَة (مَجَالِب)	cause, motive, incentive
مَجَلَّة (مَجَلَّات)	magazine, periodical
مَجَلَّة أُسْبُوعِيّة	weekly magazine
مُجَلْجِل	resounding, shrill, resonant
مُجَلَّد	bound, (book) frozen
مُجَلِّد الكُتُب	bookbinder
مَجْلَدَة	scourge, lash, whip
مَجْلِس	seat, gathering, board, meeting, assembly, council, session
مَجْلِس إِقْلِيمِي	regional court, council
مَجْلِس الإِدَارة	board of directors, administrative board
مَجْلِس الأَعْيَان	House of Lords, senate
مَجْلِس الأَمْن	security council
مَجْلِس التَّأْدِيب	disciplinary court

مَجْرَف (مَجَارِف)	torrent
مِجْرَفَة الزُّبَالَة	dustpan
مِجْرَفَة/مِجْراف	shovel, scoop, ladle
مُجْرِم	criminal, culprit, guilty
مَجْرُوح	wounded, hurt, injured
مَجْرُور	pulled, drawned, hauled
مَجْرًى (مَجَارٍ)	course, stream, revulet
مَجْرَى البَوْل	urethra
مَجْرَى الحَيَاة	trend of life
مَجْرَى المَاء	watercourse, channel
مَجْرَى الهَوَاء	current of air
مَجْزَرة	carnage, butchery
مُجَزَّع	variegated, marbled
مَجْزُوم	decided upon, settled
مِجَسّ	probe, sound
مُجَسَّد	embodied, corporified
مُجَسَّم	concrete, material, bodily
مُجَعَّد	curled, wrinkled

academic, academician	مَجْمَعِي	defence council	مَجْلِس الدِّفَاع
summary, abstract, compendium, synopsis	مُجْمَل	council	مَجْلِس الشُّورَى
wholesaler, wholesale dealer	مُجْمِل	senate	مَجْلِس الشُّيُوخ
total, collected, mown	مَجْمُوع	House of commons	مَجْلِس العُمُوم
shield, shelter	مِجَنّ (مَجَانّ)	lower house	مَجْلِس النَّوَّاب
foolishness, insanity, madness	مَجَنَّة	council of ministers, cabinet	مَجْلِس الوُزَرَاء
recruit	مُجَنَّد	local council, municipal council	مَجْلِس بَلَدِي
insane, crazy, foolish, obsessed	مَجْنُون (مَجَانِين)	disciplinary board	مَجْلِس تَأْدِيبِي
resource, crop	مَجْنَى (مَجَانٍ)	constituent assembly	مَجْلِس تَأْسِيسِي
loud-speaker	مِجْهَار	legislative council	مَجْلِس شُورَى القَوَانِين
microscope	مِجْهَر (مَجَاهِر)	court martial	مَجْلِس عَسْكَرِي
equipped, furnished, armed	مُجَهَّز	national assembly	مَجْلِس قَوْمِي
effort, endeavour, exertion	مَجْهُود	brazier, censer, thurible	مِجْمَرَة
unknown, anonymous	مَجْهُول	collector, accumulator	مُجَمِّع
jewels, jewellery	مُجَوْهَرات	assembly, convention, academy, meeting	مَجْمَع (مَجَامِع)
respondent, answering	مُجِيب	scientific academy	مَجْمَع عِلْمِي

مُحَاضَرة (مُحَاضَرات) lecture, discourse	efficient, excellent, proficient	مُجيد
مُحَافِظ custodian, observer, guardian, protector	glorious, glorified, exalted	مَجيْد
مُحَافَظَة preservation, defense, protection, guarding	protector, defender	مُجيْر
مُحَافَظَة على النَّفْس self-preservation	the choicest part, the best part	مُحّ
مُحَاق/مَحَاق wanning (of the moon)	partial, onesided	مُحَاب
مُحَاكاة imitation, similitude	partiality, favouritism, onesidedness	مُحَاباة
مَحَاكِم شَرْعِيّة religious court	conversation, discourse, discussion	مُحَادَثَة
مُحَاكَمَة trial, hearing of case	opposite to, facing	مُحَاذ
مُحَال impossible, unattainable, beyond reach	parallel to, opposite	مُحَاذاة
محَال cunning, craft, slyness	selfish, oystracea	مَحَار
مُحَامٍ defending, protecting, layer, advocate	warrior, fighter, belligerent	مُحَارِب
مُحَاماة defence, practicing of law	fight, battle, combat	مُحَارَبَة
مُحَاوَرَة conversation, talk, dialogue	accountant, auditor	مُحَاسِب
مُحَاوَلة attempt, trial, evasion	chartered accountant	مُحَاسِب قَانُوني
مَحَّايَة eraser, rubber	accounting, clearing	مُحَاسَبَة
مُحَايد neutral	blockade, blockage, siege	مُحَاصَرَة
مُحَايَدة neutrality	lecturer, speaker	مُحَاضِر

interwoven	مُحْتَبِك	lover, amateur, fan	مُحبّ
protester, remonstrant	مُحْتَجّ	self-loving, selfish	مُحبُّ الذَّات
origin, lineage	مَحْتِد	selfish, egoist	مُحب لذَاتِه
angry, irritated, furious	مُحْتَدّ	lovable, desirable, likable	مُحَبَّب
flaming, fuming, furious	مُحْتَدِم	love, affection, attachment	مَحَبّة
cautious, careful	مُحْتَرِس	self-love, selfishness	مَحَبّة الذَّات
professional, employed	مُحْتَرِف	self-love, selfishness	مَحَبّة النَّفْس
respectable, reverend, respected	مُحْتَرَم	inkpot, inkwell	مِحْبَرة/مَحْبَرة
modest, bashful, shy	مَحْتَشِم	prison, jail	مَحْبِس/مَحْبَس
gathering place	مُحْتَفَل	hermitage	مَحْبَسَة
contemptible, despicable, scorned	مُحْتَقَر	beloved, sweetheart, dear, popular	مَحْبُوب
red, flushed	مُحْتَقِن	sweetheart, beloved, darling	مَحْبُوبة
pubescent, adult	مُحْتَلِم	confined, locked up, imprisoned, prisoner	مَحْبُوس
tolerable, bearable, endurable, probable	مُحْتَمَل	tight, tightly drawn	مَحْبُوك
definite, decided, determined	مَحْتُوم	needy, necessitous, indigent	مُحْتَاج
contents, inclosures	مُحْتَوَيات	treacherous, artful, cunning, crafty	مُحْتَال
destination, goal	مَحَجّة		
quarantine	مَحْجَر صِحِّي		

مُحَرِّر liberator, emancipator, editor	مُحَجَّل whitefooted, bright, shining
مُحْرِز winner, gainer, obtainer	مِحْجَم cupping glass
مُحَرِّض instigator, agitator, provocator	مِحْجَن hooked stick, crosier
مُحَرَّف corrupted, distorted	مَحْجُوب veiled, hidden
مُحْرِق burning, scorching	مَحْجُور minor, ward
مَحْرَق (مَحَارِق) focus	مُحَدَّب convex, embossed
مَحَرِّك exciting, instigator, stirring	مُحَدِّث narrator, relator, spokesman
مُحَرِّك (مُحَرِّكات) motive, incentive, impulse	مُحْدَث new, upstart, modern
مُحَرِّك الشَّهِيّة appatizer	مُحَدَّد appointed, fixed, sharpened
مُحَرِّك كَهْرَبَائي electromotor	مُحْدِق encompassing, surrounding
مُحَرِّك مِيكانِيكِي motor	مِحْدَلة roller, stone roller
مُحَرَّم prohibited, forbidden, name of first month of Islamic calendar	مَحْدُود limited, confined, bounded, determined
مَحْرَم (مَحَارِم) sacrosanct, unmarriageable relations	مَحْدُود الضَّمَان limited liability
مَحْرُوم deprived, bereaved, debarred	مَحْدُود المَعْنَى unambiguous
مَحْزَرة guess, conjecture, appraisal	مَحْذُور object of caution, danger
مُحْزِن grievous, sorrowful, mournful, pathetic	مِحْراب (مَحَارِيب) mihrab, prayer niche
	مِحْراث plough

sheer, pure, unmixed, مَحْض mere	tragic-comic مُحْزِن مُضْحِك
presence, appearance مَحْضَر	grieved, sad, saddened مَحْزُون
producer, manufacturer مُحَضِّر	beautifier, improver مُحَسِّن
children's home مَحْضَن	beneficent, benevolent, charitable مُحْسِن
possessed, demoniac مَحْضُور	cosmetics مُحَسِّنات
halt, stop, stopping place مَحَطّ	excellent مَحْسَنة (مَحَاسِن) traits, good qualities
centre of attraction مَحَطّ الأَنْظار	favourite, subservient مَحْسُوب
stop, station مَحَطّة	felt, palapable, perceptible مَحْسُوس
radio station, broadcasting station مَحَطّة الإِذاعة	scythe, poker مِحَشّ
signal post مَحَطّة الإِشَارَات	stuffed, filled, loaded مَحْشُوّ
transformer station مَحَطّة تَحْوِيل التَّيّار	stuffed, filled مَحْشِي
railway station مَحَطّة سِكّة الحَدِيد	sickle مِحْصَد
airport مَحَطّة طَيَران	mowing machine مِحْصَدة
power plant مَحَطّة كَهْرَبائِيّة	tax collector, cashier مُحَصِّل
breaking, crashing, thundering مُحَطِّم	fortified, immunized مُحَصَّن
prohibited, interdicted مَحْظُور	protected, chaste مُحْصَنة
	harvested, mown مَحْصُود
prohibited things, restrictions مَحْظُورات	besieged, blocked, restricted, confined, close مَحْصُور
	product, produce, yield, outcome مَحْصُول (مَحَاصِيل)

curry comb	مِحَكّة	lucky, fortunate, glad	مَحْظُوظ
precise, perfect, exact, firm	مُحْكَم	paramour, mistress, favourite	مَحْظِيّة
well contrived	مُحْكُم التَّدْبِير	spade	مِحْفَر (مَحَافِر)
firmly bolted	مُحْكَمُ الرِّتَاج	bag, briefcase	مِحْفَظَة/مَحْفَظَة
well-made	مُحْكَم الصُّنْع	portfolio, satchel	مِحْفَظَة أَوْرَاق
court, tribunal, bar	مَحْكَمَة (مَحَاكِم)	wallet	مِحْفَظَة الجَيْب
indigenous court	مَحْكَمَة أَهْلِيّة	meeting, party, assembly	مَحْفِل (مَحَافِل)
court of first instance	مَحْكَمَة ابْتِدَائِيّة	preserved, secured, safeguarded	مَحْفُوظ
appellate court	مَحْكَمَة اسْتِئْنَافِيّة	conserves, archives	مَحْفُوظَات
court of appeal	مَحْكَمَة الاسْتِئْنَاف	destruction, obliteration	مَحْق
criminal court	مَحْكَمَة الجِنَايَات	examiner, investigator, inquirer	مُحَقِّق
court of misdemeanour	مَحْكَمَة الجُنَح	established, accepted	مُحَقَّق
summary court	مَحْكَمَة جُزْئِيّة	syringe	مِحْقَنة (مَحَاقِن)
criminal court	مَحْكَمَة جِنَائِيّة	deserving, worthy, fit	مَحْقُوق
canonical court	مَحْكَمَة شَرْعِيّة		
court martial	مَحْكَمَة عَسْكَرِيّة	touchstone, test, trial	مِحَكّ
mixed tribunal	مَحْكَمَة مُخْتَلطة	disputatious,	مَحِك
civil court	مَحْكَمَة مَدَنِيّة		
native tribunal	مَحْكَمَة وَطَنِيّة	contentious, quarrelsome	

local, parochial	مَحَلّي	place, site, spot, location	مَحَلّ
praised, commendable	مُحَمَّد		
roasted, fried	مُحَمَّر	dearth, aridity, sterility, barrenness	مَحْل
loaded, burdened, freighted	مُحَمَّل	scene of the accident	مَحَلّ الإصَابَة
laudable, praised, commendable	مَحْمُود	residence, dwelling place	مَحَل الإقَامَة
borne, bearable, load capacity, tonnage, cargo	مَحْمُول	dwelling place	مَحَلّ السُّكْنَى
feverish, fevered, hectic	مَحْمُوم	place of work	مَحَلّ العَمَل
protected, protectorate	مَحْمِي	clothe store	مَحَلّ المَلابِس
		amusement centre	مَحَلّ المَلاهِي
tribulation, trial, affliction	مِحْنَة (مِحَن)	commercial house	مَحَلّ تِجَارِي
mummified	مُحَنَّط	object of controversy	مَحَلّ نِزاع
enraged, infuriated	مُحْنَق		
bend, curve, curvature	مَحْنِى	deserving attention	مَحَلّ نَظَر
obliteration, effacement	مَحْو	camp, stopover	مَحَلّة (مَحَلّات)
pivot, axis, centre	مِحْوَر (مَحَاوِر)	cotton gin	مِحْلَج
		sworn, juror	مُحَلَّف
endorser, transformer	مُحَوِّل	analyzer	مُحَلِّل
escape, avoidance, evasion	مَحِيص	dissolved, loose, unravelled, solution	مَحْلُول
surroundings, environment	مُحيط	ornamented, decorated, sweetened	مُحَلَّى

مُخَاطَبَة تِلِفونِيّة telephone conversation	مُحيْط اَطْلَنْطي the Atlantic Ocean
مَخَاطِر dangers, perils	مُحيْط هادِئ the Pacific Ocean
مُخَاطِر venturesome, daring, bettor	مُخّ (مِخَاخ) essence, core, brain
مُخَاطَرَة venture, risk, hazard	مُخَابَرَة information, negotiation, correspondence
مَخَاطي mucous, snotty, ropy	
مَخَافة fear, dread, fright	
مَخَالِب المَوْت claws of death	مُخَابَرَة تِلِفونِيّة telephone conversation
مُخَالَة association, intercourse	مُخَابَرَة سِرِّيّة secret communiqué
مُخَالِف contrary, contrasting, contradictory, divergent	مُخَاتِل deceitful, crafty, double-dealer
مُخَالَفة disagreement, disobedience, contradiction, contravention	مُخَادِع imposter, cheat, swindler, deceiver
مُخَاوٍ brotherly, fraternal	مُخَاصِم opponent, adversary, litigant
مَخَاوِف fears, apprehensions	مَخَاض childbirth, labour pains
مَخْبَأ (مَخَابِئ) hideout, hiding place, shelter	مَخَاضة ford
مُخْبِر reporter, detective	مَخَاضة النَّهْر ford of a river
مَخْبَز bakery	مَخَاط snot, mucus
مُخَبَّل muddled, confused, baffled, confounded	مُخَاطَب addressed, spoken to
مَخْبُول insane, crazy, confounded	مُخَاطَبة conversation, talk, speech, public address

multicoloured, مُخْتَلِف الأَلْوَان	chosen, selected مُخْتَار
variegated		selection, مُخْتَارات
inventor, contriver, مُخْتَلِق	anthropology
fabricator		conceited, proud, مُخْتال
fabricated, invented مُخْتَلَق	arrogant
smothered, strangled, مُخْتَنِق	hiding, concealed مُخْتَبِئ
crammed		laboratory مُخْتَبَر
sealed, stamped مَخْتُوم	inventor, contriver مُخْتَرِع
condensed, coagulated, مُخَثَّر	invention, discovery مُخْتَرَع
curdled		stenographer مُخْتَزِل
shameful, shocking, مُخْجِل	pertinent, relevant, مُخْتَصّ
disgraceful		concerned
ashamed, abashed, مَخْجُول	short, abridged, مُخْتَصَر
pillow, cushion (مَخَادّ) مِخَد	concise, epitomized
anaesthetic, narcotic مُخَدِّر	hidden, secret, مُخْتَفٍ
numb, insensible, مُخَدَّر	concealed
intoxicated, fuddled		hide-out, hiding place مُخْتَفًى
drugs, narcotics مُخَدِّرات	insane, demented مُخْتَلّ العَقْل
destroyer, saboteur مُخَرِّب	embezzler, مُخْتَلِس
destructive, destroyer مُخْرِب	defalcator
director, producer مُخْرِج	mixed, mingled, مُخْتَلِط
excerpt, extract مُخْرَج	confused
wayout, (مَخَارِج) مَخْرَج	different, divergent, مُخْتَلِف
outlet, exit, egress		diverse, unlike
punch, awl مِخْرَز/مِخْرَاز	controversial, مُخْتَلَف
		disputed

meadow, sod, verdant land	مَخْضَرَة	lathe, turning lathe	مخْرَطَة (مَخَارِط)
wrong, incorrect, erroneous	مُخْطِئ	perforated, in holes	مُخَرَّم
dangerous, risky, hazardous	مُخْطِر	cone	مَخْرُوط
designated, marked, striped	مُخَطَّط	conic	مَخْرُوطِي
fiancée	مَخْطُوبة	conic-al	مَخْرُوطِي الشَّكْل
manuscript	مَخْطُوط (مخطوطات)	shameful, disgraceful, infamous	مُخْزٍ
guardroom, control room	مَخْفَر (مَخَافِر)	store, storehouse, warehouse, depot	مَخْزَن (مَخَازِن)
police station	مَخْفَر الشُّرْطَة	left luggage office	مَخْزَن الأمانات
deluted, reduced, thin	مُخَفَّف		
hidden, concealed	مَخْفِي	stored, deposited, treasured	مَخْزون
shameful, disgraceful	مُخِلّ	abashed, ashamed	مَخْزِي
lever, crowbar	مُخْل (مُخُول)	disadvantageous, injurious, detrimental	مُخَسِّر
claw, paw	مِخْلَب (مَخَالِب)	fertile, productive	مُخْصِب
escape, wayout, rescue	مَخْلَص	wand, stick	مخْصَرَة (مَخَاصِر)
liberator, rescuer, Redeemer	مُخَلِّص	specified, allotted designated	مُخَصَّص
sincere, devoted, loyal, honest	مُخْلِص	special, particular	مَخْصُوص
left over, left behind	مُخَلَّف	castrated, emasculated	مَخْصِي
salted, pickled	مُخَلَّل		

prolongation, lengthening	مَدّ الأَجَل	blend, mixture	مَخْلُوط
range of vision	مَدّ البَصَر	reckless, unruly, wanton	مَخْلُوع
ebb and flow, tide	مَدّ وَجَزْر	creature, created	مَخْلُوق
sycophancy, servile flattery	مُدَاجاة	putrid, rotten, mouldy	مُخِمّ
intervention, interference	مُدَاخَلة	velvet	مُخْمَل
ink, manure	مِداد	assessor, appraiser	مُخَمِّن
orbit, axis, pivot, circuit	مَدَار (مَدَارات)	drunk, intoxicated	مَخْمُور
affability, sociability, flattery	مُدَارَاة	effeminate, important	مُخَنَّث
capacities, mental faculties	مَدَارِك	neck, throat	مَخْنَق
crushed, trodden	مُدَاس	strangled, suffocated	مَخْنُوق
joking, frolicsome, fun-maker	مُدَاعِب	butter milk	مَخِيض
jesting, fun-making, dalliance	مُدَاعَبة	needle	مِخْيَط
defender, defendant	مُدَافِع	frightful, dreadful, fearful, terrible	مُخِيف
long-range guns	مَدَافِع بَعِيدة المَرْمَى	confusing, perplexing, dubious	مُخِيل
heavy artillery	مَدَافِع ضَخْمَة	conceit, haughtiness, arrogance	مَخِيلَة
anti-aircraft guns	مَدَافِع مُضَادّة لِلطَّائِرَات	imagination, phantasy	مُخَيِّلَة
		camp, encampment	مُخَيَّم
		expansion, extension, stretching, rising	مَدّ
		a dry measure	مُدّ

praise, laudation, مَدْح/مَدِيْح eulogy	defence, pleading مُدَافَعَة
egotism مَدْح الذَّات	medal مَدَالِيَة
invalid, refutable مِدْحَاض	medallion مَدَالِيون
defeated, vanquished, مَدْحُور rooted	wine مُدَام/مُدَامة
entrance, door, (مَدَاخِل) مَدْخَل hallway, way in	convicted, guilty, مُدَان culpable
drive-way مَدْخَل للسَّيَّارات	sycophan, servile مُدَاهِن flatterer, adulator
smoker مُدَخِّن	flattery, sycophancy, مُدَاهَنَة fawning
chimney, (مَدَاخِن) مِدْخَنَة funnel	treatment, cure مُدَاوَاة
income, (مَدَاخِيْل) مَدْخُول returns, receipts	negotiation, مُدَاوَلة discussion
help, assistance, (أَمْدَاد) مَدَد support, aid	continuation, مُدَاوَمَة persistence
diurectic-al مُدِرّ لِلْبَوْل	embellished, richly مُدَبَّج decorated
lactiferous, مُدِرّ لِلْحَلِيْب producing milk	manager, arranger, مُدَبِّر disposer, thrifty
producing مُدِرّ للطَّمْث menstrual discharge	plotter, intriguer مُدَبِّر المَكَايِد
diaphoretic, مُدِرّ لِلْعَرَق sudorific	tannery مَدْبَغَة
mud, slime مَدَر/مَدَرَة	duration, period, (مُدَد) مُدَّة term
flowing copiously, مِدْرار spouting	long time مُدَّة مَدِيْدَة
	armed to the مُدَجَّج بِالسِّلَاح teeth

scholastic, pertaining to school	مَدْرَسِي	trainer, instructor, coach	مُدَرِّب
armoured	مُدَرَّع	trained, drilled, experienced	مُدَرَّب
armoured cruiser	مُدَرَّعَة	entered, inserted, recorded	مُدْرَج
rational, endowed with reason	مُدْرِك	way, route, coarse, path	مَدْرَج (مَدَارِج)
claimant, prosecutor, plaintiff	مُدَّعٍ	open staircase, grand stand	مُدَرَّج (مُدَرَّجات)
invited one, called	مَدْعُو	runway	مَدْرَج الطَّائِرات
claimed	مُدَّعَى	teacher, coach	مُدَرِّس
defendant	مُدَّعَى عليه	assistant teacher	مُدَرِّس مُسَاعِد
public prosecutor	مُدَّعِي عُمُومِي	school, university	مَدْرَسَة (مَدَارِس)
bushy, perfidious, false	مُدْغِل	elementary school	مَدْرَسَة أَوَّلِيّة
stove, fire place	مِدْفَأ/مِدْفَأَة	primary school	مَدْرَسَة اِبْتِدَائِيّة
gun, cannon	مِدْفَع (مَدَافِع)	commercial college	مَدْرَسَة تِجَارِيّة
machine gun	مِدْفَع رَشّاش	secondary school	مَدْرَسَة ثَانَوِيّة
artillery, artilleryman	مِدْفَعِي		
artillery, ordnance	مِدْفَعِيّة	military academy, military school	مَدْرَسَة حَرْبِيّة
heavy artillery	مِدْفَعِيّة ضَخْمَة		
burial ground, cemetery	مَدْفَن (مَدَافِن)	boarding school	مَدْرَسَة دَاخِلِيّة
pounder, clapper	مِدَقَّة	college	مَدْرَسَة عَالِيَة
abject, wretched, miserable	مُدْقِع		

record, note, writings	مُدَوَّنة (مُدَوَّنات)	accurate, meticulous	مُدَقِّق
extent, extension, range, degree, limit	مَدَى	precise, accurate, exact	مُدَقَّق
range of vision, eyeshot, seeing, distance	مَدَى البَصَر	counterfeit, forged	مُدَلَّس
lifetime	مَدَى الحَيَاة	masseuse, masseur	مُدَلِّكة
range of one's voice	مَدَى الصَّوْت	pampered, coddled	مُدَلَّل
extent of life, lifetime	مَدَى العُمْر	proven	مَدْلُول
knife	مُدْية/مَدْية	meaning, sense	مَدْلُولات
praise, laudation, eulogy	مَدِيح	compact, tight	مُدْمَج
streched, extended, prolonged	مَدِيد	destroyer	مُدَمِّرة
far-sighted	مَدِيد البَصَر	tear duct	مَدْمَع (مَدَامِع)
director, manager, administrator, head, principal	مُدِير	addicted, given	مُدْمِن
chief of protocol	مُدِير التَّشْرِيفات	addicted, drunkard	مُدْمِن خَمْر
steersman	مُدِير الدَّقة	stamped, bearing a stamp	مَدْمُوغ
chief of protocol	مُدِير المَرَاسِيم	urban, civil, civilian	مَدَني
director, general manager	مُدِير عَامّ	civilization, refinement	مَدَنِيّة
		surprising, amazing, striking, astonishing	مُدْهِش
		oily, greasy, fatty	مُدْهِن
administress, directress	مُدِيرة	amazed, startled, surprised	مَدْهُوش
		round, circular	مُدَوَّر
		trodden, crushed	مَدُوس

notebook, reminder, مُذَكِّرة memorandum	administration, مُدِيرية direction
mentioned, cited مَذْكُور	province, مُدِيرية (مُدِيرِيّات) district
above- مَذْكُور أَعْلاه mentioned	creditor, money lender مُدِين
forementioned مَذْكُور آنِفاً	debtor, indebted مَدِين/مَدْيُون
forementioned, مَذْكُور سَابِقًا foresaid	town, city مَدِينَة (مُدُن/مَدَائِن)
obsequiousness, مَذَلّة humiliation, humbleness	taste, savour, relish, مَذَاق flavour
blame, censure مَذَمَّة	deliberation, مُذَاكَرة conference, study
blamed, blameworthy, مَذْمُوم reprehensible	slaughter مَذْبَح (مَذَابِح) house, abattoir
tailed, comet مُذَنَّب	massacre, butchery, مَذْبَحة slaughter
guilty, criminal, مُذْنِب sinner, sinful	swinging, hesitant, مُذَبْذَب unsteady
gilded, coted with مُذَهَّب gold	rotten, spoiled مَذِر
doctrine, creed, مَذْهَب (مَذَاهِب) belief, ideology, school	pitch fork, مِذْرَى/مِذْراة winnowing fork
sectarian, مَذْهَبِي denominational	obedient, pliable, مِذْعان tractable, docile
astonishing, amazing, مُذْهِل startling	obedient, compliant, مُذْعِن submissive
confused, dismayed, مَذْهُول perplexed	masculine مُذَكَّر
manger, trough مِذْوَد (مَذَاوِد)	reminiscent, recalling مُذَكِّر to mind

repetition, revision, examination	مُرَاجَعَة	dissolvent, solvent	مُذِيب
purpose, intention, desire	مُرَاد	promulgator, spreader, announcer	مُذِيع
synonym, synonymous	مُرَادِف	woman announcer (fem. of مُذِيع)	مُذِيعَة
several times, often, repeatedly	مِرَارًا	passing, corssing, transition	مَرّ
repeatedly, time and again	مِرَارًا وَتَكْرَارًا	bitter, sharp, severe	مُرّ
gall, bitterness	مَرَارَة	man, person	مَرْء
strength, vigour, stamina	مِرَاس	manly, virile, valorous	مَرِئ
correspondent, reporter	مُرَاسِل	garage, repairing shop	مِرْأَب (مَرَائِب)
special correspondent	مُرَاسِل خَاصّ	mirror, looking glass	مِرْآة (مَرَايا)
sports reporter	مُرَاسِل رِيَاضِي	subordinate, subject	مَرْؤُوس
correspondence, communication	مُرَاسَلَة	sight, vision, view	مَرْأَى
ceremonies, rituals, customs	مَرَاسِم	visible, seen	مَرْئِي
coronation, ceremonies	مَرَاسِم التَّتْوِيج	hypocrite, dissembler	مُرَاء
consideration, regard, charge, care	مُرَاعَاة	dispute, quarrel, wrangle	مِرَاء
plaintiff	مُرَافِع	hypocrisy, eyeservice, dissimulation	مُرَاءَاة
		usurer, loan sharker	مُرَاب
		reviser, checker, inspector	مُرَاجِع
		auditor, comptroller	مُرَاجِع الحِسَابَات

educator, tutor, pedagogue مُرَبٍّ	convenience, appurtenances مَرَافِق
gainful, profitable, advantageous مُرْبِح	accompanist, companion مُرَافِق
clouded, gloomy مُرَبَّد	conveniences, ease and comfort مَرَافِق الحَيَاة
sheep-fold, pen مَرْبِض (مَرَابِض)	public utilities مَرَافِق عَامَّة
stable, stall مَرْبِط (مَرَابِط)	association, accompaniment مُرَافَقَة
quadruple, square, fourfold مُرَبَّع	supervisor, observer, inspector, invigilator مُرَاقِب
meadow مَرْبَع (مَرَابِع)	supervision, observation, inspection مُرَاقَبَة
bewildering, confusing, cumbersome مُرَبِّك	vital centers مَرَاكِزْ حَيَوِيَّة
connected, bound, tied, fixed مَرْبُوط	purpose, wish, desire, aspiration مَرَام
jam, murabba مُرَبَّى	training, exercise, practice مِرَان
well-bred, brought up مُرَبَّى	pliability, flexibility, elasticity مَرَائَة
tutoress, nursemaid مُرَبِّيَة	adolescent مُرَاهِق
nursemaid مُرَبِّيَة الأَطْفَال	puberty, adolescence مُرَاهَقَة
once, at one time مَرَّةً	wagering, betting, wager, bet مُرَاهَنَة
turn, time مَرَّة (مَرَّات/مِرَار)	trickery, cunning, artifice مُرَاوَغَة
gall, bile مُرَّة (مِرَر)	
once more, once again مَرَّة أُخْرَى	
time and again مَرَّة بَعْدَ مَرَّة	

support, stay, water closet, toilet مُرْتَفَق	at once, at one time مَرَّة وَاحِدة
advanced, educated, refined مُرْتَقٍ	doubtful, suspicious مُرْتَاب
perpetrator مُرْتَكِب	at ease, comfortable, satisfied مُرْتَاح
singer, chanter, choirboy مُرَتِّل	relaxed, peaceful, tranquil مُرْتَاح البَال
pledgee, mortagagee مُرْتَهِن	arranged, regular, in proper order مُرَتَّب
twice مَرَّتَيْن	salary, emolument مُرَتَّب (مُرَتَّبَات)
elegy, dirge, monody مَرْثَاة	mattress, rank, grade, step مَرْتَبَة (مَرَاتِب)
dirge, elegy مَرْثِيَة	
confusion, disturbance مَرَج	engaged, connected, bound مُرْتَبِط
pasture, grassland, meadow مَرْج (مُرُوج)	entangled, confused, disconcerted مُرْتَبِك
hope, request مَرْجَاة	shaken, agitated مُرْتَجّ
coral, seed pearls مَرْجَان	extempory, off-hand مُرْتَجَل
preponderant, preferable, predominant مُرَجَّح	apostate, renegade, retreating مُرْتَدّ
source, reference, return, resort مَرْجَع (مَرَاجِع)	bribee مُرْتَشٍ
boiler, cauldron مِرْجَل (مَرَاجِل)	pasture, hotbed مَرْتَع (مَرَاتِع)
	hotbed of vice مَرْتَعُ الشَّرّ
expected, hoped for مَرْجُوّ	
joy, mirth, exultation, cheerfulness مَرَح	high, elevated, lofty مُرْتَفِع

transmitter	مُرْسِلة	مَرِح (مَرْحَى) cheerful, joyful,	merry, exuberant
studio	مَرْسَم		
film studio	مَرْسَم السِّينما	lavatory, مِرْحَاض (مَرَاحِيْض)	toilet, water closet
sketched, designed, drawn, ordained	مَرْسُوم	welcome! hail!	مَرْحَبًا
ordinance, decree	مَرْسُوم (مَرَاسِيْم)	pity, sympathy, mercy	مَرْحَمَة
anchorage, landing place	مَرْسَى (مَرَاسٍ)	deceased, defunct	مَرْحُوم
marshal	مَرْشَال	bravo, well done	مَرْحَى
watering can	مِرَشَّة	soft, sloppy, slack	مَرِخ
filter, percolator	مُرَشَّح	repulsion, averting	مَرَدّ
nominee, candidate	مُرَشَّح	spindle	مِرْدَن (مَرَادِن)
guide, spiritual guide, leader, preceptor	مُرْشِد	refutable, returns	مَرْدُود
ambush, look out	مِرْصَاد	spout, gargoyle	مِرْزَاب (مَرَازِيب)
telescope	مَرْصَد	vicegerent	مَرْزُبَان
observatory, observation post	مَرْصَد (مَرَاصِد)	blessed, lucky, fortunate, prosperous	مَرْزُوق
paved, laid with stone	مَرْصُوف	experienced, seasoned, veteran	مَرِس (أَمْرَاس)
satisfying, gratifying, pleasant	مُرْضٍ	anchor	مِرْسَاة (مَرَاسٍ)
disease, illness, ailment	مَرَض (أَمْرَاض)	cable, hawser	مَرَسَة
		sender, consignor	مُرْسِل
		delegated, missionary	مُرْسَل
diabetes	مَرَض السُّكَّر	consignee, addressee	مُرْسَل إِلَيْه

compulsion, force, aversion	مَرْغَمَة	internal disease	مَرَض بَاطِنِي
desirable, sought after, wished for	مَرْغُوب فِيه	venereal disease	مَرَض تَنَاسُلِي
port, harbour, quay	مَرْفَأ (مَرَافِئ)	skin disease	مَرَض جِلْدِي
carnival	مَرْفَع	venereal disease	مَرَض سِرِّي
crane	مِرْفَعَة (مَرَافِع)	nervous disease	مَرَض عَصَبِي
elbow	مِرْفَق (مَرَافِق)	mental disease	مَرَض عَقْلِي
attached, attachments	مُرْفَق بِه	infectious disease	مَرَض مُعْدٍ
enclosures, attachments	مُرْفَقَات	fatal disease	مَرَض مُمِيت
elevated, raised, lifted up	مَرْفُوع	epidemic disease	مَرَض وَبَائِي
morphine	مُرْفِين	satisfaction, pleasure, delight	مَرْضَاة
broth, thin soup	مَرَق	wet nurse, nurse	مُرْضِع (مُرْضِعَة)
stair, staircase, step ladder	مِرْقَاة (مَرَاقٍ)	soft drinks, refreshments	مُرَطِّبَات
telescope	مِرْقَب	pasture, pasturage	مَرْع
look out, ambush, observation post	مَرْقَب/مَرْقَبَة	frightful, dreadful, horrible	مُرْعِب
bed, couch	مَرْقَد (مَرَاقِد)	frightened, afraid	مَرْعُوب
dance, ball, dance hall	مَرْقَص (مَرَاقِص)	observed, regarded	مَرْعِي
		pasture, grass land, pasturage	مَرْعًى (مَرَاعٍ)
		lures, attractions	مُرَغِّبَات
patched	مُرَقَّع	margarine	مَرْغَرِين

starting point, basis	مَرْكَز أَسَاسِي	rags, tatters	مَرْقَعَة
administration centre, headquarters	مَرْكَز الإدَارة	crayon, numbering machine	مِرْقَم (مَرَاقِم)
broadcasting station	مَرْكَز الإذَاعَة	compound, composite, composed, complex	مُرَكَّب
police station	مَرْكَز البُولِيْس	chemical compound	مُرَكَّب كِيْميائي
power station	مَرْكَز التَّوْلِيد	inferiority complex	مُرَكَّب النَّقْص
centre of gravity	مَرْكَزُ الثِقَل	boat, ship	مَرْكَب (مَرَاكِب)
centre of attraction	مَرْكَز الجَذْب	freighter, transport	مَرْكَب النَّقْل
police station	مَرْكَز الشُّرْطَة	steam ship, steam boat	مَرْكَب بُخَارِي
main office, headquarters	مَرْكَز رَئِيْسِي	warship	مَرْكَب حَرْبِي
central	مَرْكَزِي	patrol boat	مَرْكَب دَوْرِي
centrality, central position	مَرْكَزِيّة	sailboat	مَرْكَب شِرَاعِي
ridden, riding animal, mount	مَرْكُوب	ingredients, components	مُرَكِّبات
repair, overhauling	مَرَمَّة (مَرَمَّات)	carriage, cab, vehicle	مَرْكَبَة (مَرْكَبَات)
marble	مَرْمَر	tram-car	مَرْكَبَة تَرَام
sandbox, pouncebox	مِرْمَلَة	concentrated, condensed	مُرَكَّز
noted, notable	مَرْمُوق	centre, post, position, situation	مَرْكَز (مَرَاكِز)
aim, goal, extent, purpose, design	مَرْمَى (مَرَامٍ)		

range of vision	مَرْمَى النَّظَر	reported, narrated	مَرْوي
rhinoceros	مِرْمِيس	suspicious, suspect	مُرِيْب
pliant, flexible, ductile, supple	مَرِن	comfortable, commodious	مُرِيْح
thin, sharpened	مُرْهَف	gay, cheerful, jolly, jovial	مَرِّيح
oppressive, overburdening	مُرْهِق	Mars	مِرِّيْخ
ointment, liniment, cream	مَرْهَم (مَرَاهِم)	disciple, adherent	مُرِيْد
dreaded, feared	مَرْهُوب الجَانِب	firm, robust, rigorous	مَرِيْر (مَرَائِر)
pledged, pawned, mortgaged	مَرْهُون	robustness, doggedness, firmness, vigour	مَرِيْرَة (مَرَائِر)
manhood, manliness, virility	مُرُوْءَة/مُرُوَّة	sick, ill, diseased	مَرِيْض (مَرْضَى)
fan, propeller	مِرْوَحَة (مَرَاوِح)	love-sick	مَرِيض الحُبّ
liniment, embrocation, unguent	مَرُوخ	hairless, scanty haired	مَرِيط
passing, passage, transition	مُرُور	frightful, dreadful, horrible	مُرِيْع
expiration of the deadline	مُرُور الزَّمَان	fertile, productive	مَرِيْع
course of time	مُرُور الوَقْت	acidulous, tart	مُزّ
dreadful, frightful	مُرَوِّع	disposition, temper, nature, mixture	مِزَاج
awe-struck, frightened	مُرَوَّع	phlegmatic temperament	مِزَاج بَلْغَمِي
deviation, straying	مُرُوق	sanguine temperament	مِزَاج دَمَوِي

crowded, packed	مُزْدَحِم	melancholic temperament	مِزَاج سَوْدَاوِي
disdainful, contemptuous	مُزْدَرٍ	bilious temperament	مِزَاج صَفْرَاوِي
double, twofold	مُزْدَوِج	phlegmatic temperament	مِزَاج لِمْفَاوِي
derogatory, despicable	مُزْرٍ	jester, joker	مَزَّاح
gargoyle, spout	مِزْرَب (مَزَارِيب)	joke, jest	مُزَاح/مُزَاحَة
iron rod	مِزْرَبَة (مَزَارِب)	competitor, rival	مُزَاحِم
throat, gullet	مَزْرَد	auction, public sale	مَزَاد
arable land	مَزْرَع	shrine, monument	مَزَار
farm, field	مَزْرَعَة (مَزَارِع)	peasant, husbandman	مُزَارِع
brocaded, embellished, embroidered	مُزَرْكَش	share cropping contract	مُزَارَعَة
piece, slice, bit	مُزْعَة/مِزْعَة	practice, pursuit	مُزَاوَلَة
disturbing, troublesome, inconvenient	مُزْعِج	bidder, outbidder	مُزَايِد
convulsed, shocked, shaky	مُزَعْزَع	public sale, auction	مُزَايَدة
alleged, so-called	مَزْعُوم	dunghill	مَزْبَلَة (مَزَابِل)
tearing, tear, rent	مَزْق	mixing, blending	مَزْج
shred, torn piece	مِزْقَة (مِزَق)	joke, jest, fun	مَزْج
sliding bold	مِزْلَاج (مَزَالِيج)	glazed, enameled	مُزَجَّج
skate, roller skate	مِزْلَج (مَزَالِج)	paltry, scanty	مُزْجًى
skate	مِزْلَق	interior decorator	مُزَخْرِف
		decorated, embellished	مُزَخْرَف

chemical composition	مَزِيج كِيْمَاوِي	slide, slippery ground	مَزْلَق/مَزْلَقَة
increased, additional, excess	مَزِيد	sledge, sleigh	مِزْلَقَة (مَزَالِق)
false, forged, counterfeited	مُزَيَّف	pipe, flute	مِزْمَار
counterfeiter, forger	مُزَيِّف	determined, resolved	مُزْمِع
counterfeiter	مُزَيِّف العُمْلَة	chronic, deep-rooted, long-continued	مُزْمِن
hairdresser, barber	مُزَيِّن	shining, blooming	مُزْهِر
decorated, adorned	مُزَيَّن	flower pot	مَزْهَرِيَّة
touch, contact, frenzy, attack	مَسّ	haughty, vainglorious	مَزْهُوّ
attack of fever	مَسّ الحُمَّى	supplier, purveyor, caterer	مُزَوِّد
problem, issue, affair	مَسْأَلة/مَسْئَلَة (مَسَائِل)	furnished, equipped, provided	مُزَوَّد
responsible, accountable	مَسْؤُول	knapsack, provision sack	مِزْوَد (مَزَاوِد)
responsibility, liability	مَسْؤُوْلِيّة	forged, spurious, counterfeit	مُزَوَّر
evening	مَسَاء	embellished, ornamented, decorated	مُزَوَّق
in the evening	مَسَاءً	sundial	مِزْوَلَة
good evening	مَسَاء الخَيْر	oiled	مُزَيَّت
evil deed, offence	مَسَاءَة (مَسَاوِئ)	merit, excellence, advantage	مَزِيَّة (مَزَايَا)
pending questions	مَسَائِل مُعَلَّقَة	mixture, blend, combination	مَزِيج

مَسَائِي	evening
مُسَابِق	contestant, competitor
مُسَابَقَة	contest, competition
مُسَاجَلَة	competition, contest
مُسَاجَلَة كَلَامِيّة	debate, discussion
مِسَاحَة	surface, area, survey
مِسَاحَة مَائِيّة	area of water
مُسَاحَقَة	lesbianism
مُسَاحِقَة	lesbian
مِسَاس	touching, feeling
مُسَاعِد	assistant, helper, supporter
مُسَاعَدَة	support, assistance, backing, maintenance
مَسَاغ	easy access
مَسَافة (مَسَاوِف)	distance, space, stretch
مُسَافِر	passenger, traveller
مُسَالَمَة	pacification, conciliation
مَسَامّ (مَسَامَّات)	pores
مُسَامَحَة	forgiveness, pardon
مَسَامِر	nightly entertainment
مُسَامِر	companion in nightly conversation
مُسَامَرَة	nightly chat or entertainment
مَسَامِي	porous
مُسَاهِم	shareholder, stockholder
مُسَاهَمَة	participation, taking part
مُسَاوٍ	equal, similar, equivalent
مُسَاوَاة	equality, evenness
مُسَاوَاة اِجْتِماعِيّة	social equality
مُسَاوَمَة	bargaining, chaffering
مِسْبار (مَسَابِير)	probe, sound
مُسَبِّب	originator, causer, occasioner
مُسَبَّب	caused, effect
مَسَبَّة	abuse, vilification
مَسْبَح (مَسَابِح)	swimming pool
مِسْبَر (مَسَابِر)	probe, sound
مُسَبَّقًا	in advance
مَسْبَك (مَسَابِك)	foundry
مَسّة	a touch

emulsion, milk	مُستَحلَب	lessee, leaseholder, tenant	مُستَأجِر
impossible, preposterous, ridiculous	مُستَحِيل	appellant	مُستَأنِف
employer, master	مُستَخدِم	appellee	مُستَأنَف عليه
submissive, subservient	مُستَخذِ	deserving, worthy	مُستَأهِل
excerpt, extract	مُستَخرَج	vexed, displeased, offended, disgusted	مُستَاء
petitioner, applicant	مُستَدعٍ	arbitrary, tyrant, despot	مُستَبِدّ
round, circular	مُستَدِير	optimist, cheerful, happy	مُستَبشِر
relaxed, at rest	مُستَرِيح	impossible, improbable	مُستَبعَد
advisor, consultant, counsellor	مُستَشار	hidden, concealed	مُستَتِر
orientalist	مُستَشرِق	excepted, excluded	مُستَثنَى
hospital (مُستَشفَيات)	مُستَشفَى	answering, responding, resonating	مُستَجِيب
scattered, widely spread, pessimist	مُستَطِير	desirable, preferable, recommendable	مُستَحَبّ
long, elongated	مُستَطِيل	agreeable, desirable, acceptable	مُستَحسَن
oblong	مُستَطِيل الشَّكل	مُستَحضَر (مُستَحضَرات) preparation	
borrowed, artificial	مُستَعار	deserving, worthy of, entitled	مُستَحِقّ
hurried, in a hury	مُستَعجِل		
urgent, pressing, speedy	مُستَعجَل	consolidated, strengthened, strong	مُستَحكَم
ready, prepared	مُستَعِدّ		
beggar, mendicant	مُستَعطٍ		
colonist, colonial	مُستَعمِر		

مُسْتَلِم	recipient, receiver, consignee	مُسْتَعْمَرَة (مُسْتَعْمَرَات)	colony, settlement
مُسْتَمِرّ	continual, unceasing, lasting	مُسْتَعْمِل	user
مُسْتَمِع	hearer, listener	مُسْتَعْمَل	used, applied
مُسْتَمِعُون	audience, listeners	مُسْتَعِير	borrower
مُسْتَنْبِط	discoverer, inventor	مُسْتَغْرِب	westernized
مُسْتَنْتِج	producer, manufacturer	مُسْتَغْرَب	strange, peculiar, unusual
مُسْتَنِد	relying, trusting	مُسْتَغْرِق	absorbed, engrossed, engaged
مُسْتَنَد (مُسْتَنَدات)	documents, papers, records	مُسْتَغِلّ	utilizer, exploiter
مُسْتَنْقَع	swamp, marsh	مُسْتَغَلّ	products, returns
مُسْتَنْكَر	reprehensible, odd	مُسْتَقْبِل	future
مُسْتَنِير	enlightened, illuminated	مُسْتَقْبَل	front, front part
مُسْتَهْتِر	reckless, rash, thoughtless, wanton	مُسْتَقِرّ	settled, firm, sedentary
مُسْتَهْتَر	infatuated, foolishly fond of	مُسْتَقَرّ	abode, dwelling
مُسْتَهْلِك	shameless, insolent, cheeky	مُسْتَقِلّ	independent, autonomous
مُسْتَهْدَف	exposed, open to	مُسْتَقِيم	upright, straight, correct, right
مُسْتَهْزِئ	scorner, mocker, scoffer	مُسْتَلْزَمات	requirements, requisites
مُسْتَهَلّ	beginning, opening, outset, start	مُسْتَلْقٍ	recumbent, lying down

prisoner, captive	مَسْجُون	consumer	مُسْتَهْلك
wiping, cleaning, rubbing	مَسْح	consumption	مُسْتَهْلَك
shovel	مِسْحَاة	straight, even, upright, level	مُسْتَوٍ
unction, touch, rub, trace	مَسْحَة	depositor, lodger	مُسْتَوْدِع
file, plane	مِسْحَل	deposited, lodged	مُسْتَوْدَع
pestle, triturator	مِسْحَنَة (مَسَاحِن)	depository, depot	مُسْتَوْدَع (مُسْتَوْدَعَات)
drawee	مَسْحُوب إِلَيْه	hidden, chaste	مَسْتُور
crushed, pounded, pulverized	مَسْحُوق	imports, imported goods	مُسْتَوْرَدَات
transformation, disfigurement, defacement	مَسْخ	clinic, dispensary	مُسْتَوْصَف
disfigured, misshapen, freak	مَسْخ (مُسُوخ)	dweller, inhabitant, deep-rooted	مُسْتَوْطِن
buffoon, clown	مُسْخَة	level, plane, standard	مُسْتَوًى
oppressor, exploitator	مُسَخِّر	living standard, standard of living	مُسْتَوَى الحَيَاة
object of ridicule, masquerade	مَسْخَرَة	living standard	مُسْتَوَى العَيْش
outrageous deed	مَسْخَطَة	water level	مُسْتَوَى المَاء
hexagonal	مُسَدَّس	awake, wary, watchful	مُسْتَيْقِظ
tommy gun	مُسَدَّس رَشَّاش	mosque, masjid	مَسْجِد (مَسَاجِد)
pistol, revolver, spray-gun	مُسَدَّسَة	notary public, registrar, recorder	مُسَجِّل
closed, blocked	مَسْدُود	registered, recorded	مُسَجَّل

مَسْقَط الرَّأْس	birthplace, hometown	مَسْرَب (مَسَارِب)	drain, sewer
مَسْقَط/مَسْقِط	falling place	مَسَرَّة (مَسَرَّات)	pleasure, happiness, delight, mirth
مَسْقُوف	roofed, covered, coated	مَسْرَح (مَسَارِح) -	theatre, play-house
مَسْك	holding, grasping, catching	مَسْرَحِي	theatrical, dramatic
مِسْك	musk	مَسْرَحِيّة	play
مَسْك الحِسَابَات	accountancy	مَسْرَد	index of a book
مَسْك الدَّفَاتِر	bookkeeping	مُسْرِف	extravagant, prodigal
مُسْكِت	silencing, inebriety	مَسْرُور	glad, delighted, happy
مَسْكَة	grip, grasp, hold	مَسْرُوق	stolen
مَسْكَة (مَسَكَات)	grip, hold, seizure	مِسْطَار	trowel
مُسْكِر	intoxicating liquor	مُسَطَّح	flat, level, surface
مُسَكِّن	tranquilizer, soother, calmative	مُسَطَّر	document, piece of writing
مَسْكِن/مَسْكَن (مَسَاكِن) residence, dwelling place, habitation		مِسْطَرَة (مَسَاطِير)	ruler, sample, pattern
مَسْكَنَة	poverty, indigence, wretchedness, servility	مِسْطَرَة الحِسَاب	slide rule
مَسْكُون	inhabited, tenanted, populous, haunted	مَسْعُود (مَسَاعِيد)	happy, fortunate
		مَسْعُور	mad, frenzied, rabid
مِسْكِين (مَسَاكِين)	poor, indigent, miserable	مَسْعَى (مَسَاعِي)	endeavour, effort, attempt
		مَسْغَبَة	famine

stethoscope, hearing	مِسْمَع	entertaining, amusing, consoling	مُسَلٍّ
fat, fattened	مُسَمَّن	consolation, amusement, fun	مَسْلاة (مَسَالٍ)
permissible, allowed	مَسْموح به	slough, shake skin	مِسْلاخ
audible	مَسْموع	armourer	مُسَلِّح
poisoned, envenomed	مَسْموم	armed, armoured, equipped	مُسَلَّح
called, named	مُسَمَّى	slaughter house, abattoir	مَسْلَخ (مَسَالِخ)
aged, elderly	مُسِنّ	chained, continuous	مُسَلْسَل
support, stay, cushion	مِسْنَد/مَسْنَد (مَسَانيد)	way, method, course of action	مَسْلَك (مَسَالِك)
arched, vaulted	مُسَنَّم	vocational, professional	مَسْلَكي
elaborated, lengthy, detailed	مُسْهِب/مُسْهَب	accepted, admitted, indisputable	مُسَلَّم
night club	مَسْهَر (مَسَاهِر)	Muslim, believer	مُسْلِم
purgative, laxative	مُسْهِل	boiled	مَسْلوق
draft, day book	مُسَوَّدَة	practicable, passable	مَسْلوك
stick, lash	مِسْوَط	consumptive, drawn	مَسْلول
good reason	مُسَوِّغ	poisonous, venomous	مُسِمّ
displeasing, offending, harmful	مُسيء	peg, tack, nail	مِسْمَار (مَسَامير)
wiped, cleaned, anointed	مَسيح	screw-nail	مِسْمَار بُرْغي
misfigured, defamed, defaced	مَسيخ	fertilizers, manures	مُسَمِّدات

disturbances, disorders	مَشَاغِب	travel, tour, march	مَسِير
riotous, subverter troublemaker	مُشَاغِب	distance, departure	مَسِيرَة
intestine broils	مُشَاغَبَات دَاخِلِيّة	touching, touch	مَسِيس
trouble, uproar, disturbance, discord	مُشَاغَبَة	sovereign, ruler	مُسَيْطِر
orally, verbally	مُشَافَهَةً	stingy, miser, tenacious	مَسِيك
dispute, quarrel, surliness, querulousness	مُشَاكَسَة (مُشَاكَسَات)	sir	مِسْيو
likeness, similarity	مُشَاكَلَة	ominous, ill-omened, inauspicious	مَشْؤُوم
carriage, porterage	مَشَال	walker, good walker	مَشَّاء
spectator, onlooker	مُشَاهِد	partisan, partial	مُشَائِع
visible, perceptible	مُشَاهَد	similar, resembling	مُشَابِه
sights, visible things	مُشَاهَد (مُشَاهَدَات)	similarity, resemblance, likeness	مُشَابَهَة
seeing, witnessing, viewing	مُشَاهَدَة	armoured infantry	مُشَاة مُدَرَّعون
sight, spectacle, view, scenery	مُشَاهَدَة (مُشَاهَدَات)	dispute, argument, quarrel	مُشَاجَرَة
monthly salary or allowances	مُشَاهَرَة (مُشَاهَرَات)	dispute, altercation, feud	مُشَاحَنَة
advisor, counsellor	مُشَاوَر	argument, exchange of words, controversy	مُشَادَّة
consultation, deliberation	مُشَاوَرَة	partnership, participation, communion	مُشَارَكَة
		wide spread, circulated	مُشَاع

containing, including, comprising مُشْتَمِل	long carpet, walker (for baby) مَشَّايَة
contents مُشْتَمَلَات	satisfied, satiated, filled مُشْبَع
craving, desirous, lustful مُشْتَهٍ	clasp, hook, pin, fastener مِشْبَك (مَشَابِك)
desirable, pleasant مُشْتَهَى	desirous, longing, yearning, covetous مُشْتَاق
abused, insulted, vituperated مَشْتُوم	intricate, entangled مُشْتَبِك
touching, moving, pathetic مُشَجٍّ	suspect, suspected مُشْتَبَه
encourager, supporter مُشَجِّع	dispersed, scattered مُشَتَّت
extreme unction مَشْحَة	buyer, seller مُشْتَرٍ
whet stone مِشْحَذ	participant, subscriber مُشْتَرِك
fatty, greasy مُشَحَّم	combined, joint, mutual, common مُشْتَرَك
charged, loaded مَشْحُون	Jupiter مُشْتَرِي
load, freight, cargo مَشْحُون (مَشْحُونات)	ablaze, on fire مُشْتَعِل
actor, stage player مُشَخِّص	busy, occupied مُشْتَغِل
actress, player مُشَخِّصَة	derivative مُشْتَقّ (مُشْتَقّات)
tight, tense, tautened مَشْدُود	complainant, plaintiff مُشْتَكٍ
baffled, perplexed مَشْدُوه	accused, defendant مُشْتَكَّى عَلَيْه
drinking place, bar مَشْرَب/مَشْرَبَة (مَشَارِب)	nursery, plant nursery مَشْتَل (مَشَاتِل)
drinking fountain, water hole مَشْرَعَة (مَشَارِع)	

cracked, crazy مَشْعُور	superintendent, مُشْرِف
cracked, crack-brained مَشْعُور العَقْل	supervisor, overseer
	radiant, shining مُشْرِق
workshop, workhouse مَشْغَل (مَشَاغِل)	east, place of rise مَشْرِق (مَشَارِق)
occupation, job, work, business, concern مَشْغَلَة (مَشَاغِل)	polytheist مُشْرِك
infatuated, enamoured مَشْغُوف	drink, drinkable, beverage مَشْرُوب (مَشْرُوبات)
occupied, busy, distracted مَشْغُول	alcoholic beverages or liquors مَشْرُوبات رُوْحِيّة
uneasy, anxious, concerned, worried مَشْغُول البال	soft drinks مَشْرُوبات مُرَطِّبة
anxiety, concern, worry مَشْغُولِيّة	legal, rightful, permissible مَشْرُوع
model, pattern مَشْق (أَمْشاق)	project, scheme, plan, interprise مَشْرُوع (مَشَاريع)
slender, slim مشْق/مَشِيق	legitimacy, legality مَشْرُوعِيّة
trouble, hardship, difficulty مَشَقَّة (مَشاقّ/مَشَقَّات)	comb, rake مُشْط (أَمْشاط)
lamp, niche مِشْكَاة (مَشَاك)	radiative, radiant مُشِعّ
variegated, diverse, different مُشَكَّل	torch, flambeau مِشْعَال
obscure, vague, difficult, problem مُشْكِل	sense, sensations مَشْعَر (مَشَاعِر)
	half-drunk, diluted مُشَعْشَع
problem, difficulty, predicament مُشْكِلَة (مَشَاكِل)	torch, flambeau مَشْعَل/مِشْعَلَة (مَشَاعِل)
	conjurer, juggler, magician مُشَعْوِذ

mixed, adulterated مَشُوب	praiseworthy, مَشْكُور worthy of thanks
counsel, مَشْوَرَة (مَشْوَرات) suggestion, advice	doubtful, dubious مَشْكُوك فيه
bewildered, confused, مُشَوَّش disturbed, muddled	dressing-box مُشْلَح
bewildered, مُشَوَّش الفِكْر confused, muddled, baffled	paralyzed, lame مَشْلُول
stimulating, exciting, مُشَوِّق attractive	loathing, disgusted, مُشْمَئِزّ nauseated
deformed, defaced, مُشَوَّه disfigured, mutilated	sunny, exposed to مُشْمِس sun
walking, walk مَشْي	apricot مِشْمِش
will, wish, desire مَشِيئَة	waxed, water proof مُشَمَّع
pace, manner of مِشْيَة walking	contained, included مَشْمُول
constructed, erected, مُشَيَّد lofty	scaffold, مِشْنَقَة (مَشَانِق) gallows
consultant, counselor, مُشِير advisor	stimulating the appetite مُشَهّ
disgraceful, مُشَيِّن scandalous	spectacle, مَشْهَد (مَشَاهِد) sight, scenery, assembly, procession
sucking, sipping, مَصّ absorption	renowned, well- مُشَهَّر known, infamous
afflicted, struck, مُصَاب injured, victim	memorable, attended مَشْهُود
endurance, مُصَابَرَة perseverance	renowned, مَشْهُور (مَشَاهِير) famous, notorious, celebrated
	grill, gridiron مِشْوَاة (مَشَاوٍ)
	errand مِشْوَار

relationship by marriage, affinity	مُصَاهَرَة	accompanying	مُصَاحَبَة
outlet, drain, funnel	مَصَبّ (مَصَابّ)	confiscation, seizure	مُصَادَرة
mouth of a river	مَصَبُّ النَّهْر	coincident, corresponding	مُصَادِف
lamp, light	مِصْبَاح (مَصَابِيْح)	chance, coincidence, haphazard	مُصَادَفَة
searchlight	مِصْبَاح كَشَّاف	by chance, by coincidence	مُصَادَفَةً
electric light, electric lamp, bulb	مِصْبَاح كَهْرَبائي	confirmation, approval, authentication	مُصَادَقَة
oil lamp	مِصْبَاح نَفْطي	clash, collision	مُصَادَمَة
dye-house, dye works	مَصْبَغَة	wrestler, fighter	مُصَارِع
cast metal goods	مَصْبُوب (مَصْبُوبات)	wrestling, fighting	مُصَارَعَة
dyed, tinted, coloured	مَصْبُوغ	estrangement, hostility	مُصَارَمَة
suck, sip	مَصَّة	secret funds	مَصَارِيف سرِّيَّة
health station, sanatorium	مَصَحَّة (مَصَحَّات)	petty expenses	مَصَارِيْف نَثْرِيَّة
vernier, proof reader	مُصَحِّح	sucker, blood sucker, cupper	مَصّاص
book, volume	مَصْحَف/مُصْحَف (مَصَاحِف)	jewellery, jewels	مَصَاغ
accompanied, associated	مَصْحُوب	peace-maker, conciliator	مُصَالِح
pounded, ground	مَصْحُون	composition, reconciliation, peace	مُصَالَحَة
rusty, rust-covered	مُصْدَأ	ironworks	مَصَانِع الحَدِيد

summer resort, summer visitor	مُصْطاف	substantiation, corroboration	مِصْداق
selected, chosen	مُصْطَفَى	exporter	مُصَدِّر
technical terms	مُصْطَلَح (مُصْطَلَحات)	source, origin	مَصْدَر (مَصادِر)
fireplace	مُصْطَلَى	reliable, trustworthy, credible	مُصَدَّق
artificial, affected, forged	مُصْطَنَع	certification, certificate	مُصَدِّقَة
anode, point of ascent	مَصْعَد	consumptive, tubercular	مَصْدُور
lift, elevator	مِصْعَد		
listener, attentive	مُصْغٍ	insistent, persistent, tenacious	مُصِرّ
diminished, reduced	مُصَغَّر	big city, metropolis	مِصْر (أَمْصار)
clarifier, trustee	مُصَفٍّ		
position, row, line	مَصَفّ (مَصافّ)	leaf of a door	مِصْراع (مَصاريع)
refinery, filter, strainer	مِصْفاة	battle ground, death	مَصْرَع (مَصارِع)
covered with plates, foliated, armoured	مُصَفَّح	bank, drain, ditch	مَصْرِف (مَصارِف)
yellow-coloured, pale	مُصَفَّر	thrown to the ground, epileptic, rabid	مَصْرُوع
refinery	مَصْفًى		
purified, pure, sheer	مُصَفًّى	expenses, expenditure	مَصْرُوف (مَصاريف)
burnisher	مِصْقَلَة	postage	مَصْرُوف البَرِيد
burnished, glazed, polished	مَصْقُول	pocket money	مَصْرُوف الجَيْب

مَصْنُوعات وَطنِيَّة	domestic products, home manufactures	مُصَلٍّ	one who prays, prayer
مصْوات	microphone	مَصْل	whey, serum
مُصَوِّت	voter, franchised	مَصْل اللَّبن	whey
مُصَوِّر	shaper, illustrator, painter, photographer	مُصْلِح	reformer, conciliator
مُصَوَّر	illustrated, painted	مَصْلَحَة (مَصَالِح)	welfare, interest, advantage, authority
مُصَوِّر الكَائنات	the Creator of the universe	مَصْلَحَة عَامَّة	public welfare
مُصَوَّرَة	camera	مَصْلَحي	administrational, official
مَصُوغَات	jewellery, jewels	مُصَلَّى	place of prayer
مُصَوَّن	kept, preserved, protected	مُصَمِّم	determined
مُصِيب	right, suited, appropriate	مُصَمِّم الأَزْياء	designer, fashion creator
مُصِيبَة (مَصَائب)	misfortune, calamity, affliction	مَصْنَع (مَصَانِع)	factory, firm, plant
مِصْيَدَة (مَصَايد)	snare, trap	مَصْنَع البارود	powder mill
مَصِير	fate, destiny, upshot	مَصْنَع الغَزْل	spinning mill
مَصِير (أَمْصِرَة)	guts, bowels	مُصَنِّف	compiler, writer, author
مَصِيص	damp, moist, humid	مُصَنَّف	literary work, compilation
مَصِيف (مَصَايف)	summer resort	مَصْنُوع (مَصْنُوعات)	products, produce
مَضّ	pain, agony, torment	مصْنُوع باليَد	handmade

embarrassment, trouble, distress, vexation مُضَايَقَة	sharpness, sagacity, discernment مَضَاء
protocol, minutes مَضْبَطَة	firmness of resolution مَضَاء العَزِيْمَة
accurate, precise, correct مَضْبُوط	bedfellow مُضَاجِع
irksome, tedious, wearisome, harassing مُضْجِر	opposite, contrary, opposed مُضَادّ
bed, bedroom مَضْجَع (مَضَاجِع)	antidotes مُضَادّ (مُضَادّات)
laughable, ludicrous, funny مُضْحِك	contraceptives مُضَادّات للْحَبْل
laughingstock, object of ridicule مَضْحَكَة	contradiction, contrast مُضَادّة
pump, squirt مِضَخّة	similar, alike مُضَارِع
suction pump مِضَخّة جَذّابَة	resemblance, similarity مُضَارَعَة
suction pump مِضَخّة رَافِعَة	pain, agony, torment مَضَاضَة
amplifier مُضَخِّم	double, multiplied مُضَاعَف
loud-speaker مُضَخِّم الصَّوْت	doubling, multiplying مُضَاعَفَة
injurious, detrimental, harmful مُضِرّ	added, apposed مُضَاف
bat, racket مِضْراب	inn, guest room مَضَافَة
bat, racket, pavilion مِضْرَب (مَضَارِب)	similar, corresponding مُضَاه
racket مِضْرَب التِّنِس	resemblance, correspondence, comparision مُضَاهَاة
damage, loss, disadvantage مَضَرَّة (مَضَارّ/مَضَرّات)	troublesome, inconvenient, disturbing مُضَايِق

tight, compressed, closed مَضْمُوم	distress, pain, torment, agony مَضَض
warranted, ensured, guaranteed, reliable مَضْمُون	bed, couch مُضْطَجَع
meaning, content مَضْمُون (مَضَامِين)	compelled, obliged, needy مُضْطَرّ
exhausted, very tired مُضْنك	confused, disordered, disturbed مُضْطَرِب
exhausted, worn out, emaciated مُضْنًى	burning, flaming مُضْطَرِم
going, passing, departure, lapse مُضِي	oppressor, persecutor مُضْطَهِد
lapse of time مُضِي المُدَّة	twofold, multiplied مُضَعَّف
luminous, shining, bright مُضِيء	chewing, mastication مَضْغ
wasteful, squanderer مِضْيَاع	chewing gum, morsel, bite مُضْغَة
hospitable, host مِضْيَاف	titbit, choice morsel مُضْغَة طَيِّبَة
wasteful, spendthrift, prodigal مُضَيِّع	misleading, delusive, deceptive مُضِلّ
host مُضِيف	misguiding, delusive, misleading مُضَلِّل
hostess, air hostess مُضِيفَة	racecourse, racetrack مِضْمَار (مَضَامِير)
guesthouse, guestroom مَضِيفَة	fading, evanescent, vanishing مُضْمَحِلّ
extension, stretching مَطّ	hidden, secret, concealed مُضْمَر
compatible, congruous, conformable مُطَابِق	
conformity, compatibility, congruence مُطَابَقَة	

printed, imprinted مَطْبُوع	airport, aerodrome مَطَار
printed material مَطْبُوعات	pursuer, hunter, مُطَارِد chaser
periodical مَطْبُوعَة دَوْرِية	expulsion, banishment, مُطَارَدَة chase
grinder مطْحَنَة	
rain مَطَر (أَمْطَار)	rubber, extensive, مَطّاط stretchable
fine rain, drizzle مَطَر خَفِيف	
heavy rain, مَطَر مِدْرار downpour	synthetic rubber مَطّاط صِنَاعِي
rainy, wet مَطِر	round trip, touring, مَطَاف travelling
metoropolitan مُطْرَان/مَطْرَان	tolerable, bearable مُطَاق
delightful, charming, مُطْرِب entertaining, singer	claimant, claimer مُطَالِب
songstress, singer مُطْرِبَة	responsible, مُطَالَب answerable
shower of (مَطَرات) مَطْرَة/مَطَرَة rain, rain drops	exorbitant مَطَالِب فَادِحَة demands
dump, place مَطْرَح	claim, demand, appeal مُطَالَبَة
successive, incessant, مُطَّرِد continual	studying, study, مُطَالَعَة reading
embroidered مُطَرَّز	obedient, compliant, مُطَاوِع pliable
hammer (مَطَارِق) مِطْرَق/مِطْرَقَة	kitchen, eating house, مَطْبَخ restaurant
thrown off, cast مَطْرُوح down	press, printing مَطْبَع/مَطْبَعَة office
trodden, beaten out, مَطْرُوق frequented	printing, مَطْبَعِي typographical
restaurant, مَطْعَم (مَطَاعِم) dining hall	

purifier, cleansing, detergent, disinfectant	مُطَهِّر
pure, purified, immaculate	مُطَهَّر
kitchen	مَطْهًى
pocket knife	مَطْوَاة
obedient, submissive, compliant	مِطْوَاع
elaborate, detailed	مُطَوَّل
tardy, procrastinator, deferring	مَطُول
folded, rolled up	مَطْوِي
penknife, pocket knife	مَطْوًى (مَطَاوٍ)
spectroscope	مِطْيَاف
mount, riding animal	مَطِيَّة (مَطَايا)
rainy, wet	مَطِير
compliant, obedient, submissive	مُطِيع
expressions, manifestations, phenomena	مَظَاهِر
manifestations of life	مَظَاهِر الحَيَاة
support, backing	مُظَاهَرَة
demonstration, manifestation rally	مُظَاهَرَة

stabbed, afflicted with plague	مَطْعُون
fire extinguisher	مِطْفَأ (مَطَافِئ)
putting off, deferring	مَطْل
quest, search	مَطْلَب
claim, request, demand	مَطْلَب (مَطَالِب)
acquainted, informed, aware of	مُطَّلِع
prelude, introduction, point of rising, rise	مَطْلَع (مَطَالِع)
absolute, unrestricted, common, complete	مُطْلَق
free, released, at large	مُطْلَق السَّرَاح
absolutely, unrestrictedly	مُطْلَقًا
sought, desired, needed, required	مَطْلُوب
quite, calm, composed, serene, safe	مُطْمَئِنّ
ambition, goal, butt, aspiration	مَطْمَح (مَطَامِح)
ambition, covetousness, coveted object	مَطْمَع (مَطَامِع)

destination, place of returning مَعَاد	envelope (مَظَارِيف) مَظْرُوف
equation, assimilation, equivalence مُعَادَلَة	victorious, triumphant مُظَفَّر
precious metals مَعَادن كَرِيْمَة	shadowy, shading مُظِلّ
refuge, taking refuge مَعَاذ	umbrella, sunshade مظَلَّة
borrowed, loaned مُعَار	parachute مظَلَّة هَابطَة
opponent, objector, opposer مُعَارِض	shadowy, shading, umbrageous مُظَلَّل
opposition, resistance مُعَارَضَة	dark, obscure, gloomy مُظْلم
fight, struggle, battle مُعَارَكَة	injustice, iniquity, grievance مَظْلمَة (مَظَالم)
goatherd, herder of goats مَعَّاز	wronged, injured, oppressed مَظْلُوم
livelihood, living, subsistence, pension مَعَاش	paratrooper مظَلِّي
pension, retiring allowance مَعَاش التَّقَاعُد	assumed, supposed, suspicious مَظْنُون
companion, associate, comrade مُعَاشر	look, aspect, appearance, exterior مَظْهَر (مَظَاهِر)
society, social intercourse, association مُعَاشَرَة	with, about مَعَ
contemporary, coetaneous مُعَاصِر	good-bye! مَعَ السَّلَامَة
aid, support, backing مُعَاضَدَة	together, simultaneously مَعًا
exempted, dispensed مُعَافًى	blemish, fault, defect, shame مَعَاب/مَعَابَة (مَعَايب)
punishment, pursuit مُعَاقَبَة	reproach, censure, rebuke مُعَاتَبَة
	hostile, antagonist مُعَاد

inspection, survey, مُعَايَنَة viewing, observation	contractor, contractant مُعَاقِد
	adverse, contrary مُعَاكِس
place of worship, مَعْبَد mosque	treatment, مُعَالَجَة management
crossing, passage (مَعَابِر) مَعْبَر	treatment, مُعَامَلَة (مُعَامَلَات)
deity, god, مَعْبُود worshipped	transaction, relation, conduct
used, accustomed, مُعْتَاد habituated	toil, efforts مُعَانَاة
	headstrong, مُعَانِد
worthy of regard, مُعْتَبَر considerable	opinionated, obstinate
	opposition, obstinacy, مُعَانَدَة
aggressor, assailant مُعْتَدٍ	pertinacity
proportionate, مُعْتَدِل moderate, straight	embrace, hug مُعَانَقَة
	treaty, pact, (مُعَاهَدَات) مُعَاهَدَة
transverse, lying مُعْتَرِض across	agreement, convention
	peace treaty مُعَاهَدَة السَّلَام
grateful, مُعْتَرِف بِالْجَمِيْل thankful	treaty of مُعَاهَدَة وَلَاء friendship
thankful, مُعْتَرِف بِالْمَعْرُوف grateful	commutative مُعَاوَضَة contract
accepted, approved مُعْتَرَف بِه of	aide, assistant, helper, مُعَاوِن supporter
powerful, proud مُعْتَزّ	assistance, help, مُعَاوَنَة
resolute, determined مُعْتَزِم	support, relief
emancipator, liberator مُعْتِق	faults, defects, vices مَعَايِر
belief, faith, (مُعْتَقَدات) مُعْتَقَد dogma	inspector, viewer, مُعَايِن observer

tooth paste مَعْجُون الأَسْنَان	detention مُعْتَقَل (مُعْتَقَلات) camp, prison camp
prepared, ready, مُعَدّ destined	ailing, weak, sickly مُعْتَلّ
infectious, catching, مُعْدٍ contagious	dark, cloudy مُعْتِم
equipments, مُعَدّات implements, appliances	authorized, reliable, مُعْتَمَد authentic
fire-fighting مُعَدّات الحَرِيْق equipments	High مُعْتَمَد سَامِي Commissioner
war materials مُعَدّات حَرْبِيّة	careful, thoughtful, مُعْتَنٍ concerned
stomach مَعِدَة/مِعْدَة	idiot, imbecile, insane مَعْتُوه
adjusted, average مُعَدَّل	moth-eaten, moth- مَعْثُوث ridden
average speed مُعَدَّل السُّرْعَة	admirable مُعْجِب
destitute, poor مُعْدِم	admirer, proud مُعْجَب
mine, mineral, مَعْدِن (مَعَادِن) metal	conceited, vain مُعْجَب بِذَاتِه
metallic, mineral مَعْدِني	miracle, miraculous مُعْجِز thing
countable, numerable مَعْدُود	miracle, مُعْجِزَة (مُعْجِزَات) wonder
lost, absent, non- مَعْدُوم existent	urgent, pressing مُعَجَّل
gastric, pertaining to مَعِدي stomach	obscure, unintelligible مُعْجَم
excuse, plea مِعْذَار (مَعَاذِيْر)	dictionary, مُعْجَم (مَعَاجِم) lexicon
excuse, pardon مَعْذِرَة (مَعَاذِر)	paste, مَعْجُون (مَعَاجِيْن)
excusable, justified مَعْذُور	electuary, cream

condoler, consoler مُعَزٍّ	Ascention of the مِعْرَاج
goat مَعْز/مَعِيْز	Prophet
piano مِعْزَف (مَعَازِف)	contentious, riotous مُعَرْبِد
mattock, hoe مِعْزَقَة (مَعَازِق)	shame, ignominy, مَعَرَّة
segregation, isolation, مَعْزِل	disgrace
seclusion	ladder, stairs مِعْرَج/مِعْرَاج
isolated, secluded, مَعْزُول	exhibition, مَعْرِض (مَعَارِض)
insulated	fair, show
difficulty, hardship, مَعْسَرة	fashion show مَعْرِض الأَزْياء
distress	press review مَعْرِض الصُّحُف
army camp, camp مُعَسْكَر	acquaintance, مَعْرِفَة (مَعَارِف)
beehive مَعْسَلَة	cognizance, knowledge,
honeyed, candied مَعْسُول	information
grassy, herbaceous مُعْشِب	shallow مَعْرِفَة سَطْحِيَّة
society, مَعْشَر (مَعَاشِر)	acquaintance
community, kinsfolk	veined, streaked مُعَرَّق
sweetheart, lover مَعْشُوق	battle, مَعْرَكَة/مَعْرُكَة (مَعَارِك)
sweetheart, beloved مَعْشُوقَة	fight, battlefield
squeezer, press مِعْصَرَة	election مَعْرَكَة اِنْتِخَابِيَّة
wrist مِعْصَم (مَعَاصِم)	campaign
impeccable, sinless, مَعْصُوم	sanguinary fight مَعْرَكَة دَمَوِيَّة
protected	petition, مَعْرُوض (مَعَارِيض)
sin, rebellion, مَعْصِيَة (مَعَاصٍ)	application
disobedience	exhibits, مَعْرُوض (مَعْرُوضَات)
supporter, assistant مُعَضِّد	proposals, offers
	well-known, famous, مَعْرُوف
	beneficence, good deed

bent, hooked, crooked	مَعْقُوف	difficult, puzzling, nonplussing	مُعْضِل
reasonable, rational, understandable	مَعْقُول	problem, difficulty, dilemma	مُعْضِلَة (مَعَاضِل)
logicality, rationality, intelligibility	مَعْقُولِيَّة	donor, giver	مُعْط
muddy, turbid, deranged	مُعَكَّر	damaged, injured	مُعَطَّب
macaroni	مَعْكَرُونَة	perfumed, scented	مُعَطَّر
inverted, reversed	مَعْكُوس	coat, overcoat	مِعْطَف (مَعَاطِف)
trough, manger	مِعْلَف (مَعَالِف)	raincoat	مِعْطَف مُشَمَّع
commentator, annotator	مُعَلِّق	jobless, unemployed, shut off, broken down	مُعَطَّل
pending, suspended, hanging	مُعَلَّق	glorious, glorified, exalted	مُعَظَّم
placard, poster	مُعَلَّقَة (مُعَلَّقَات)	majority, most	مُعْظَم
teacher, instructor	مُعَلِّم	mouldy, decayed, putrid, rotten	مُعَفِّن
taught, trained, instructed	مُعَلَّم	complicated, knotted, entangled	مُعَقَّد
sign post, landmark, spot	مَعْلَم (مَعَالِم)	curved, crooked	مُعَقْرَب
encyclopedia	مَعْلَمَة	stronghold, fortress, castle, sanctuary	مَعْقِل (مَعَاقِل)
woman teacher	مُعَلِّمَة	sterilized, disinfected	مُعَقِّم
announcer, notifier	مُعْلِن	tied, bound, knotted	مَعْقُود
stall fed	مَعْلُوف	spell-bound, tongue-tied	مَعْقُود اللِّسَان

reformatory مَعْهَد إصْلاحِي	sick, ailing مَعْلُول
well-known, familiar مَعْهُود	known, of course مَعْلُوم
accustomed, used to, مُعَوَّد habituated	knowledge, مَعْلُومَات information, news
destitute, needy, poor مُعْوِز	mason, architect, مِعْمَار builder
help, assistance, مَعُونَة support	architect, مِعْمَارِي architectural
intestinal, enteric مِعَوِي	height, climax مَعْمَعَان
intestines, bowels (أَمْعَاء) مِعًى	depth of winter مَعْمَعَان الشِّتَاء
standard, مِعْيَار (مَعَايِير) criterion, measure	turmoil, tumult, مَعْمَعَة confusion
living standard مِعْيَار العَيْش	factory, مَعْمَل (مَعَامِل) manufactory, workshop
defective, blemished, مَعِيب shameful	laboratory مَعْمَل كِيماوِي
company, attendance مَعِيَّة	baptism مَعْمُودِيَّة
demonstrator, repeator مُعِيد	inhabited, populated مَعْمُور
goat مَعِيز	inforce, in use مَعْمُول به
lender مُعِير	puzzle, riddle مُعَمَّ (مُعَمَّيات)
life, mode of life, مَعِيشَة livelihood	addressed, entitled مُعَنْوَن
rural life مَعِيشَة الرِّيف	semantic, significant, مَعْنَوِي mental, abstract
bread winner, sustainer مُعِيل	meaning, sense, مَعْنًى (مَعَان) significance, idea
helper, assistant, مُعِين supporter	institute, مَعْهَد (مَعَاهِد) institution
spring, spring water مَعِين	

grieved, distressed, worried	مُغْتَمّ	fixed, determined, appointed, specified	مَعِين
nutritious, nourishing	مُغَدٍّ	disgraceful, blemished, deficient	مَعْيُوب
copious, abundant	مُغْدق	dalliance, flirtation	مُغَازَلَة
tempting, alluring, enticing	مُغْرٍ	excess, exaggeration	مُغَالاَة
glue pot	مِغْرَاة	distortion, falsification, cheating	مُغَالَطَة
west, occident, place or time of sunset	مَغْرِب	fallacy, sophistry	مُغَالَطَة مَنْطِقِيّة
singing, twittering	مُغَرِّد	adventurer, reckless, speculator	مُغَامِر
large spoon, scoop	مِغْرَفَة	adventure, hazard, speculation	مُغَامَرَة
immersed, engrossed, sunk	مُغْرق	effect, outcome, result, upshot	مَغَبَّة
infatuated, in love with, fond of	مُغْرَم	happy, blessed, felicitous	مَغْبُوط
loss, damage, debt, fine	مَغْرَم (مَغَارِم)	wronged, deceived, defrauded	مَغْبُون
tempted, deluded, deceived, conceited	مَغْرُور	delightful, satisfied, felicitous, exultant	مُغْتَبِط
temptations, lures, incentives	مُغْرِيَات	foreigner, stranger, alien	مُغْتَرِب
military expedition, foray	مَغْزَاة (مَغَازٍ)	washroom, lavatory	مُغْتَسَل
spinning mill	مَغْزَل	brutal, usurper, violent	مُغْتَصِب
spindle	مِغْزَل (مَغَازِل)		

handcuffed, fettered, مَغْلُول parched	meaning, sense, (مَغَازٍ) مَغْزَى significance, import
shortcoming, (مَغَامِز) مَغْمَز fault, foible	washroom, lavatory مَغْسَل
	washtub, wash basin مِغْسَل
flooded, obscure, مَغْمُور unknown	wash stand, laundry مَغْسَلَة
immersed, plunged مَغْمُوس	deceived, cheated مَغْشُوش
distressed, sorrowful, مَغْمُوم grieved	gripes, colic مَغْص/مَغَص
	hepatic colic مَغْص كَبْدي
unconscious, in a مُغْمًى عليه fainting fit	renal colic مَغْص كُلَوي
singer, chanter مُغَنٍّ	forced, compelled, مَغْصُوب extorted
magnet, مَغْنَاطِيس/مِغْنَاطِيس magnetism	hated, object of hate مَغْضُوب
magnetic, مَغْنَاطِيسي/مَغْنَطِيْسي hypnotic	bathing tub مِغْطَس
	magnetism مَغْطَسَة
magnetism مَغْنَاطِيسيّة/مَغْنَطِيْسيّة	helmet مِغْفَر (مَغَافِر)
magnet مَغْنَطِيْس/مِغْنَطِيْس	forgiveness, remission مَغْفِرَة
booty, spoils, benefit, مَغْنَم gain	stupid, gullible, مُغَفَّل simpleminded, dupe
songstress, female مُغَنِّية singer	lock, padlock مِغْلاق
magnesia مَغْنِيسِيَا	captious مَغْلَطَة (مَغَالِط) question
aggressive, audacious, مِغْوَار invader	envelope, enveloped مُغَلَّف
	locked, closed, shut مُغْلَق
absence, sunsetting مَغِيب	defeated, vanquished مَغْلُوب

slanderer, calumniator مُفْتَرٍ	grass widow مُغِيب/مُغِيبَة
rapacious, ravenous, مُفْتَرِس ferocious	helper, aide مُغِيث
intersection, crossing, مُفْتَرَق junction	raider, assailant مُغِير
	opening of a مُفَائَحَة conversation
lies, calumnies مُفْتَرَيات	charms, magic powers مَفَاتِن
inspector, supervisor مُفَتِّش	sudden, unexpected, مُفَاجِئ surprising
open, opened مَفْتُوح	
ripped, unstitched, مَفْتُوق afflicted with hernia	surprises, surprising مُفَاجِئات events
twisted, plaited, مَفْتُول brawny	surprise, مُفَاجَأَة (مُفَاجَآت) wonder
enraptured, infatuated, مَفْتُون captivated	vainglorious, proud, مُفَاخِر boastful
mufti, casuist مُفْتِي	boasting, bragging, مُفَاخَرَة vainglory
glorious deed, مَفْخَرَة (مَفَاخِر) object of pride	import, meaning, مُفَاد significance
highly honoured مُفَخَّم	
flight, escape, wayout مَفَرّ	separation, partition, مُفَارَقَة departure
mincer, meat grinder مِفْرَاة	مُفَاوَضَة (مُفَاوَضَات)
cutting nippers مِفْرَاص	negotiations, talks
relief, مَفْرَج (مَفَارِج) relaxation, repose	key, switch, مِفْتَاح (مَفَاتِيح) valve
exhilarating, joyous, مُفْرِح delightful	key stone مِفْتَاح العَقْد
single, singular, lone مُفْرَد	outstanding, bragging, مُفْتَخِر boastful, proud

مُفْرَدَات words, expressions, terms	supposed, assumed, مَفْرُوض prescribed
مُفْرَدَات خَاصّة technical terms	obligations, مَفْرُوضات obligatory duties
مُفْرَزَات exudations, excretions	minced, chopped مَفْرُوم
مَفْرَزَة (مَفَارِز) detachment, group, party	terrible, terrifying, مُفْزِع dreadful
excessive, extreme مُفْرِط	terrified, frightened, مُفْزَع scared
extravagant, prodigal مُفَرِّط	corruption, مَفْسَدة (مَفَاسِد) evil acts
flat, flattened, broad مُفَرْطَح	commentator, مُفَسِّر expounder
emptying, vacuum مُفَرِّغ creator	brothel مَفْسَقَة (مَفَاسِق)
vacated, evacuated, مُفَرَّغ emptied	lancet مِفْصَد (مَفَاصِد)
point of مَفْرَق (مَفَارِق) separation, intersection	detailed, elaborate مُفَصَّل
bifurcation of مَفْرَق الطُّرُق roads	joint, knuckle مَفْصِل (مَفَاصِل) joint
explosive, blasting مُفَرْقِع	preferred, preferable مُفَضَّل
explosive, fire مُفَرْقِعَات crackers	most excellent, مِفْضَل/مِفْضَال most outstanding
mincer, mincing مِفْرَمَة machine	hideous, horrible, مُفْظِع heinous
paved, furnished, مَفْرُوش spread	full to the brim, مُفْعَم brimful, overfull
household مَفْرُوشات furnitures or effects	effect, مَفْعُول (مَفَاعِيل) impression

مَفْعُول/مَفْعُول به	object, done	مُفَوَّض سَامِي	High Commissioner
مِفْقَس (مَفَاقِس)	incubator	مُفِيْد	useful, advantageous, beneficial
مَفْقُود	missing, lost, lacking	مَفِيْض	outlet, way out, vent
مِفَكّ	screw driver	مَقَابِح	vices, ugly traits
مُفَكِّر	thinker, meditating, pensive	مُقَابِل	opposite to, facing
مُفَكِّرَات	thoughts, notions	مُقَابَلَة	encounter, interview, meeting, comparison
مُفَكِّرَة	notebook	مُقَاتِل	fighter, warrior, combatant
مُفَكِّرَة يَوْمِيَّة	diary, journal	مُقَاتَلَة	fight, combat, strife
مُفَكَّك	disintegrated, disconnected	مُقَاتَلَة	combat plane
مَفْكُوك	loose	مَقَاذِر	dirts, dirty things
مُفْلِح	successful, fortunate	مُقَارَعَة	fight, struggle
مُفْلِس	bankrupt, insolvent	مُقَارِن	comparative
مُفَلْطَح	flat, flattened	مُقَارَنَة	comparison, collation
مَفْلُوج	paralysed, paralytic	مَقَاس (مَقَاسَات)	measure, measurement, dimension
مُفَلْوِر	fluorescent	مُقَاسَاة	bearing, suffering
مَفْلُوك	unfortunate, unlucky		
مَفْلُول	dented, notched	مُقَاسَمَة	participation, partnership
مَفْهُوم	understood, known, understandable	مُقَاضَاة	hearing, trial
مفهوم (مَفَاهِيْم)	meaning, sense, notion, concept	مُقَاطَعَة	bycott, interruption, repudiation
مُفَوَّض	authorized person, mandatory		

domed, cupolaed مُقَبَّب	region, area, (مُقَاطَعَات) مُقَاطَعَة section
tomb, burial (مَقَابِر) مَقْبَر/مَقْبَرَة ground, graveyard	speech, article مَقَال
handle, haft, (مَقَابِض) مِقْبَض grip	article, treatise (مَقَالات) مَقَالَة
next, coming مُقْبِل	editorial, مَقَالَة اِفْتِتَاحِيّة leading article
arrested, under arrest مَقْبُوض	editorial, leading مَقَالَة رَئِيسِيّة article
revenue (مَقْبُوضَات) مَقْبُوض	key positions مَقَالِيد الأُمُور
popular, acceptable, مَقْبُول agreeable	place, position, مَقَام situation, rank
detestation, hatred, مَقْت abomination, aversion	place, position, مُقَام situation, set up
borrowings, loans مُقْتَبَسات	sitting, session (مَقَامَات) مَقَامَة
battle field مُقْتَتَل	gambler, player مُقَامِر
powerful, capable, مُقْتَدِر able	gambling, bet مُقَامَرَة
niggardly, tightfisted مُقْتِر	barter, exchange مُقَاوَضَة
niggardly, stingy مُقَتَّر	discussion, argument مُقَاوَلَة
proposition, (مُقْتَرَحات) مُقْتَرَح suggestion	resistant, opponent مُقَاوِم
perpetrator, one who مُقْتَرِف commits a crime	opposition, resistance مُقَاوَمَة
restricted, limited, مُقْتَصِر confined	passive مُقَاوَمَة سَلْبِيّة resistance
short, abridged, مُقْتَصَر concise	measuring, مُقَايَسَة estimation, comparision
	exchange, barter مُقَايَضَة

predestined, decreed, مُقَدَّر implicit	brief, concise, short, مُقْتَضَب improvised
estimates, destinies مُقَدَّرات	required, requisite مُقْتَضَى
military potential مَقْدُرَة حَرْبِيَّة	necessities, (مُقْتَضَيَات) مُقْتَضَى requirements
capability, مَقْدُرَة/مَقْدَرَة power, potency, aptitude	selection, (مُقْتَطَفَات) مُقْتَطَف excerpts
Christian pilgrim مُقَدِّس	murder, killing مَقْتَل
sanctified, hallowed, مُقَدَّس holy, sacred	mortal organ, (مَقَاتِل) مَقْتَل vital part of the body
coming, arrival, advent مَقْدَم	experienced, tested مُقَتَّل
offerer, donor, giver مُقَدِّم	massacre, mass مَقْتَلَة slaughter
front, front part مُقَدَّم	
applicant مُقَدِّم الطَّلَب	content, satisfied مُقْتَنِع
petitioner مُقَدِّم العَرِيضَة	acquired, possessed مُقْتَنَى
in advance, before مُقَدَّمًا hand	daring, dashing, مِقْحَام adventurous
foreward, مُقَدِّمَة/مُقَدَّمة preface, forefront	measure, (مَقَادِير) مِقْدَار extent, quantity
decreed, ordained, مَقْدُور predestined	a tiny amount, an مِقْدَار ذَرَّة iota
destiny, fate (مَقَادِير) مَقْدُور	valorous, valiant, مِقْدَام bold, interprising
ability, (مقدورات) مَقْدُور capability, faculty	fire steel, fire iron مِقْدَحَة
oar, paddle (مَقَاذِيف) مِقْذَاف	estimater, assessor, مُقَدِّر valuer
oar, paddle (مَقَاذِف) مِقْذَف	

broom, besom	مقشّة	missile, projectile	مَقْذُوف (مَقَاذِيْف)
peeled, shelled, husked	مُفَشَّر	dwelling, abode, place, residence	مَقَرّ
scissors	مقَصّ (مَقَاصّ)	place of employment	مقَر العَمَل
brocaded, trimmed with brocade	مُقَصَّب	headquarters	مَقَرّ القِيَادَة
purpose, intent, object, design, meaning	مَقْصَد (مَقَاصد)	scissors	مِقْرَاض (مَقَارِيْض)
negligent, lazy, slack, shortener	مُقَصِّر	intimate, close companion	مُقَرَّب
canteen, buffet	مَقْصَف (مَقَاصف)	nearness, proximity	مَقْرَبَة/مَقْرُبَة
intended, meant, designed	مَقْصُود	reporter, avower	مُقَرِّر
confined, restricted	مَقْصُور	money lender	مُقْرِض
compartment, cabinet, small room, closet	مَقْصُور (مَقَاصِيْر)	scourage, whip, knocker, rapper	مِقْرَعَة (مَقَارِع)
stage-box	مَقْصُورة المَلَاهِي	disgusting, loathsome	مُقْرِف
earlock, lovelock	مَقْصُوص	bedspread, bedcover	مِقْرَم (مَقَارِم)
pruning hook	مقْضَب	readable, legible	مَقْرُوء
settled, executed, accomplished	مَقْضِي	joined, connected, combined	مَقْرُون
censer	مِقْطَر (مَقَاطِر)	very hospitable	مِقْرًى
crossing, cross, section, ford	مَقْطَع (مَقَاطِع)	just, equitable, fair	مُقْسِط
		distributor, divider	مُقَسِّم
		dividend	مَقْسُوم

trimmed, pruned مُقَلَّم	cutter, cutting مِقْطَع (مَقَاطِع) instrument
pen case مِقْلَمَة	
turned over, مَقْلُوب reversed, inverted	paper cutter مِقْطَع الوَرَق
	fruit picker, مِقْطَف (مَقَاطِف) vine knife
moonlit مُقْمِر	
gambling house (مَقَامِر) مَقْمَر	large basket مَقْطَف (مَقَاطِف)
arched, vaulted مُقَنْطَر	cotton plantation مَقْطَنَة
law-maker, legislator, مُقَنِّن legislative	cut off, chopped of مَقْطُوع
	disabled, crippled مُقْعَد
regulated by law, مقَنَّن determined	seat, chair مَقْعَد (مَقَاعِد)
	arm chair مَقْعَد مُرِيح
café, cafeteria مَقْهَى/مَقْهاة	posteriors, مَقْعَدَة (مَقَاعِد) buttocks
strengthening, مُقَوٍّ fortifying, stimulant	
	deserted, uninhabited, مُقْفِر desolate
aphrodisiac مُقَوٍّ لِلْبَاه	
detested, hateful, مَقُوت abominable	unpropertied, destitute مُقِلّ
	frying pan مِقْلَاة
steering wheel مِقْوَد (مَقَاوِد)	key مِقْلَاد (مَقَالِيد)
arched, curved, bent مُقَوَّس	sling, slingshot مِقْلَاع (مَقَالِيع)
gramophone, مِقْوَل phonograph	climax, dump, مَقْلَب (مَقَالِب) plot
saying, مَقُول (مَقُولات) utterance	eyeball مُقْلَة
	troublemaker, مُقْلِق disturbing
valuer, estimator, مُقَوِّم assessor	
	unstable, unsettled, مُقَلْقَل inconstant
valued, valuable مُقَوَّم	

noble traits, مَكَارِم الأخلاق noble manners, good morals	components, basic مُقَوِّمَات elements
tax collector مَكَّاس	cosmetics مُقَوِّمَات الجَمَال
equal, equivalent, مُكَافِئ homogeneous	means of مُقَوِّمَات الحَيَاة subsistence
recompense, (مُكَافَآت) مُكَافَأَة compensation, reward	vomitive, emetic مُقَيِّئ
strife, struggle, fight, مُكَافَحَة combat	measure, (مَقَايِيس) مِقْيَاس measuring instrument, quantity
conversation, مُكَالَمَة discussion	voltmetre مِقْيَاس الجَهْد
telephone مُكَالَمَة تلفُونِيَّة conversation	thermometre مِقْيَاس الحَرَارَة
	seismometre مِقْيَاس الزَّلازِل
place, site, (أَمْكِنَة/أَمَاكِن) مَكَان locale, rank, position	rain gauge مِقْيَاس المَطَر
site of action مَكَان الحَادِث	hateful, detested, مَقِيت abominable
public place مَكَان عُمُومِي	shackled, bound, tied, مُقَيَّد restricted
place, position, مَكَانَة situation	summer residence مَقِيظ
local مَكَانِي	resting place مَقِيل
intent on, bent, مُكِبّ dedicated	staying, abiding, مُقِيم raising, resident
ball of thread, (مَكَابّ) مَكَبّ reel of thread	correspondent, مُكَاتِب reporter
brake مِكْبَح	correspondence مُكَاتَبَة
amplifier مُكَبِّر	crafty, cunning, sly, مَكَّار artful

lending library	مَكْتَبَة إِعَارِيَّة	magnified, enlarged	مُكَبَّر
subscriber	مُكْتَتِب	laud speaker	مُكَبِّر الصَّوْت
renter, lessee	مُكْتَرٍ	magnifying glass	مُكَبِّرَة
explorer, discoverer	مُكْتَشِف	press, piston	مِكْبَس (مَكَابِس)
overcrowded, overfilled, thronged	مُكْتَظّ	letter press	مَكْبَس الخِطَابَات
contented, satisfied	مُكْتَفٍ	cotton press	مَكْبَس القُطْن
large basket	مِكْتَل (مَكَاتِل)	hydraulic press	مُكْبَس مَائِي
compact, sturdy, firm	مُكْتَنِز	pressed, preserved, compressed	مَكْبُوس
enclosed, surrounded	مُكْتَنَف		
written, recorded, destined	مَكْتُوب	conserves, canned goods	مَكْبُوسات
message, note, letter	مَكْتُوب (مَكَاتِيب)	depressed, dejected, gloomy, sad	مَكْتَئِب
concealed, hidden, constipated	مَكْتُوم	office, bureau, agency, desk	مَكْتَب (مَكَاتِب)
stay, staying, remaining	مَكْث	news agency	مَكْتَبُ الأَنْبَاء
rich, wealthy	مُكْثِر	inquiry office	مَكْتَب الاسْتِعْلَامَات
condensor, capacitor	مُكَثَّف	telegraph office	مَكْتَب البَرْق
condensed, compressed	مُكَثَّف	post office	مَكْتَب البَرِيد
eye pencil, kohl stick	مِكْحَل	editorial chamber	مَكْتَب التَّحْرِير
troublesome, tiresome, annoying	مُكَدِّر	travel agency	مَكْتَب السَّفَرِيات
		library, bookshop	مَكْتَبَة (مَكَاتِب)

acquirement, gain, profit	مَكْسَب	troubled, disturbed	مُكَدَّر
profitable, lucrative	مُكْسِب	fabricated, false, refuted	مَكْذُوب
broken, fragmented, shattered	مُكَسَّر	hirer, lessor	مُكْرٍ
broken, frustrated, defeated	مَكْسُور	cunning, craftiness, artifice, trickery	مَكْر
erasing knife	مكْشَط	reel	مَكَرّ (مَكَرّات)
uncovered, exposed, unveiled, open	مَكْشُوف	trick, artifice, guile	مَكْرَة
cubic, cube-shaped	مُكَعَّب	repeated, reiterated	مُكَرَّر
inlaid, plated	مُكَفَّت	dedicated, consecrated	مُكَرَّس
blind, stoneblind	مَكْفُوف البَصَر	honourned, honourable, respectable	مُكَرَّم
guaranteed, warranted	مَكْفُول	excellent quality or trait	مَكْرَم/مَكْرَمَة (مَكَارم)
obligated, accountable, responsible	مُكَلَّف	adversities, calamities	مَكْرَه (مَكَارِه)
charge d'affaires	مُكَلَّف بالشُّؤُون	distressed, worried, anxious	مَكْرُوب
crowned, adorned with a wreath	مُكَلَّل	microbe	مكْرُوب
crazed, rabid, affected with rabies	مَكْلُوب	macaroni	مَكْرُونَة
		detested, disliked, hateful	مَكْرُوه
completed, perfected	مُكَمَّل	rented, hired	مُكْرًى
ambush, hiding place	مَكْمَن (مَكَامِن)	tax, custom, toll	مَكْس (مُكُوس)

filling, filling out مَلء	broom, مِكْنَسَة (مَكَانِس) sweeping machine
fill, filling مِلء (أَمْلاء)	vacuum مِكْنَسَة كَهْرَبَائِيّة cleaner
assembly, مَلأ (أَمْلاء) gathering, congregation	concealed, hidden مَكْنُون
fat, corpulent مَلِئ البَدَن	surnamed مُكَنَّى
handful مِلء اليَد	mechanical مَكَنِي
a cupful مِلء قَدَح	electrified, مُكَهْرَب electrically conductive
spoonful مِلء مِلْعَقَة	iron, cautery مِكْوَاة (مَكَاوٍ)
full, filled, replete مَلِئ/مَلِيئ	curling iron مِكْوَاة الشَّعْر
full, filled, replete, مَلآن plenary	remaining, staying مُكُوث
angelic, heavenly مَلائِكِي	laundryman, ironer مَكْوَجِي
suitable, fit, مُلائِم appropriate	globular, ball-shaped مُكَوَّر
	turban مِكْوَر /مِكْوَرَة
suitability, fitness, مُلاءَمَة appropriateness, concord	shattle, drinking cup مَكُوك
underwear, مَلابِس تَحْتانِيّة underclothes	creator, maker مُكَوِّن
	trick, artifice, مَكِيدة (مَكَائِد) plot, conspiracy
ready-made مَلابِس جاهِزَة clothes	air conditioner مُكَيِّفَة الهَوَاء
outer garments مَلابِس خَارِجِيّة	measurable مَكِيل
underwear, مَلابِس دَاخِلِيّة undergarments	measure, dry مِكْيَل (مِكْيال) measure
official dress, مَلابِس رَسمِيّة court dress	firm, firmly fixed, مَكِين strong, steadfast

courteous treatment, civility, friendliness	مُلاطَفة
playfellow, playmate, trickster	مُلاعَب
meeting, encounter, get-together	مُلاقَاة
essence, basis, foundation	مَلاَك/مِلاك
boxer, pugilist	مُلاكِم
boredom, weariness, ennui	مَلَال/مَلالَة
blamed, blameworthy	مُلاَم
blame, censure, admonition	مَلاَم/مَلامَة
appearance, countenance, features	مَلامِح
countenance, lineaments	مَلامِح الوَجه
touching, palpation, contact	مُلامَسَة
cunning, crafty	مُلاوِع
sheet, bedsheet	مُلاَية/مِلاَية
clothes, robe, garments	مَلْبَس (مَلابِس)
dairy	مَلْبَنة
clothes, garments, dress	مَلْبُوس (مَلْبُوسات)

intercourse, close relationship	مُلابَسَة
sailer, mariner	مَلاّح
inland navigation	مِلاَحَة
saltiness, kindliness, friendliness, grace	مَلاَحَة
navigation, shipping	مِلاَحَة
mercantile shipping	مِلاَحَة تِجَارِيَّة
aviation	مِلاَحَة جَوِّيَّة
observation, remark, notice, heed	مُلاحَظَة (مُلاحَظات)
pursuit, chase	مُلاحَقَة
navigational, nautical	مِلاَحِي
refuge, shelter, asylum	مَلاَذ
malaria	مَلاَريا
accompanying, adhering, follower, inseparable	مُلازِم
attachment, adhesion, accompanying, pursuance	مُلازَمَة
smoothness, glossiness	مَلاسَة
adjacent, adjoining, adherent	مُلاصِق
mortar	مِلاَط (مُلُط)

asylum, shelter, refuge	مَلْجَأ (مَلَاجِئ)
orphanage	مَلْجَأ الأَيْتَام
infirmary	مَلْجَأ العَجَزَة
bridled, harnessed	مُلْجَم
bridled, harnessed	مَلْجُوم
insistent, overpressing, urgent, obtrusive	مُلِحّ
salt, wit	مِلْح (أَمْلَاح)
gunpowder	مِلْح البَارُود
insistent, obstinate, importunate	مِلْحَاح
apostate, heretic	مُلْحِد
blanket, cover, wrap	مِلْحَف (مَلَاحِف)
added, affixed, annexed, adjacent, attaché	مُلْحَق
appendix, addition, supplement	مُلْحَق (مُلْحَقَات)
naval attaché	مُلْحَق بَحْري
commercial attaché	مُلْحَق تِجَاري
cultural attaché	مُلْحَق ثَقَافي
air attaché	مُلْحَق جَوّي
military attaché	مُلْحَق حَرْبي

religion, religious community	مِلَّة
ambiguous, intricate, obscure	مُلْتَبِس
refugee, seeking refuge or shelter	مُلْتَجِئ
bearded	مُلْتَح
covered, wrapped	مُلْتَحِف
contractor, concessionary	مُلْتَزِم
requirements, requisites	مُلْتَزَم (مُلْتَزَمات)
adjacent, attached, contiguous, sticking	مُلْتَصِق
rolled up, wound, coiled	مُلْتَفّ
attentive, mindful, heedful	مُلْتَفِت
meeting place, rendezvous, junction	مُلْتَقَى
request, application, petition	مُلْتَمَس
flaming, blazing, on fire, inflamed	مُلْتَهِب
curve, curvature, turn	مُلْتَوَى
twisted, bent, curved	مُلْتَوِي
veiled, covered	مُلَثَّم

plaything, toy	مَلْعَبَة	press attaché	مُلْحَق صُحُفِي
spoon	مِلْعَقَة (مَلاَعِق)	massacre, butchery, bloody fight	مَلْحَمَة (مَلاَحِم)
tea spoon	مِلْعَقَة شَاي		
damned, cursed, detestable	مَلْعُون	remarkable, noteworthy	مَلْحُوظ
abolished, abrogated, cancelled	مُلْغًى	remarks, observations	مَلْحُوظ (مَلْحُوظَات)
file, folder, reel, envelope, wrapper, covering	مِلَفّ (مِلَفَّات)	salty, saline	مِلْحِي
		summarized, abridged	مُلَخَّص
fabricated, embellished by falsehood	مُلَفَّق	extract, summary, gist	مُلَخَّص (مُلَخَّصَات)
pronounced, uttered	مَلْفُوظ	delight, pleasure, joy, delectation	مَلَذّ (مَلَذَّات/مَلاَذّ)
wrapped, rolled, twisted	مَلْفُوف		
adulator, servile flatterer	مَلِق	compact, firmly united	مُلَزَّز
		smooth, glossy, lubricous	مَلِس
surnamed, called by	مُلَقَّب		
vaccinated, pollinated	مُلَقَّح	smooth, sleek, lubricous	مَلِص/مَلِيص
tongs, pincers	مِلْقَط	attached, stuck, pasted	مُلْصَق
fire tongs	مِلْقَط النَّار	star naked, completely naked	مَلْط
prompter, instructor	مُلَقِّن		
thrown, cast away	مُلْقًى	playground, stadium, playhouse	مَلْعَب (مَلاَعِب)
meeting place, rendezvous	مَلْقًى (مَلاَق)		
		tennis court	مَلْعَب التِّنِس
reign, power, rule, kingdom, royalty	مُلْك	playhouse, theatre	مَلْعَب تَمْثِيلِي

calamity, disaster, misfortune	مُلِمّة (مُلِمّات)	property, possession, estate	مِلك
contact, touch, place of touch	مَلْمَس	angel, messenger	مَلَك (مَلائكة)
tactile, tactual	مَلْمَسي	king, sovereign, monarch	مَلِك (مُلُوك)
restlessness, fidgetiness	مَلْمَلَة	real estate, real property	مِلك ثابِت
tangible, palpable, perceptible to touch	مَلْمُوس	joint property	مِلك شائِع
		landed property	مِلك عَقاري
tangible things	مَلْمُوسات	personal property, movables	مِلك مَنْقُول
melancholia	مَلَنْخُوليا		
amusing, entertaining, distracting	مُلْهٍ	trait, faculty, characteristic feature	مَلَكَة
farce, comedy	مَلْهاة	queen, queen consort	مَلِكَة (مَلِكات)
popular farce	مَلْهاة عامِيَة	beauty queen	مَلِكَة الجَمال
inspired	مُلْهَم	kingdom, empire, kingship	مَلَكُوت
concerned, worried, yearning	مَلْهُوف	divine, heavenly	مَلَكُوتي
amusement, diversion, place of entertainment	مَلْهًى (ملاه)	royal, regal, monarchic, angelic	مَلَكي
		royalty, kingship	مَلَكِيّة
stained, blotted, soiled	مُلَوَّث	property, ownership	مِلْكِيّة
signal, semaphore	مُلَوِّحَة	weariness, tiredness, boredom, disgust	مَلَل
saltiness, saltness	مُلُوحَة	well-acquinted with, conversant	مُلِمّ
royal, regal, kingly	مُلُوكي		

million	مَلْيُون (مَلْيُونَات/مَلايِين)	kingship, royalty, monarchism	مُلُوكِيّة
death, decease	مَمَات	weary, tired, disgusted	مَلُول
antiquated, obsolete, out of date	مُمَات	blamed, blamable, blameworthy	مَلُوم
similar, resembling, analogous	مُمَاثِل	coloured, colourful	مُلَوَّن
similarity, resemblance, likeness	مُمَاثَلَة	curved, bent, twisted, crooked	مَلْوِي
quarrelsome, disputatious, contentious	مُمَاحِك	a long space of time	مَلِي
dispute, quarrel, wrangle	مُمَاحَكَة	full, filled, replete	مَلِيئ
practice, exercise, experience	مُمَارَسَة	for a long time	مَلِيّا
impudent, insolent, shameless	مُمَارِق	milliard	مِلْيَار
touch, contiguity, contact	مُمَاسَّة	milligram	مِلِّيجَرَام
resistence, denial, opposition	مُمَانَعَة	salty, salted, graceful, beautiful	مَلِيح
distinguished, excellent, outstanding	مُمْتَاز	tasteless, insipid	مَلِيخ
obedient, yielding, submissive	مُمْتَثِل	smooth, sleek, lubricous	مَلِيص
examiner, one who examines	مُمْتَحِن	king, sovereign, proprietor	مَلِيْك (مُلَكَاء)
examinee, examined, tested	مُمْتَحَن	queen	مَلِيْكَة
		blamable, blameworthy	مَلِيم
		millimetre	مِلِّيمِتْر
		softening, laxative	مُلَيِّن
		laxatives	مُلَيِّنَات

passage, aisle, corridor مَمَرّ (مَمَرّات)	extensive, extended, outstretched مُمْتَدّ
underpass مَمَر سُفْلي	absorbent, soaking up مُمْتَصّ
nurse, sicknurse مُمَرِّض	pleasant, delightful, enjoyable مُمْتِع
nurse, sicknurse مُمَرِّضَة	pleasant, enjoyable, delightful مُمَتَّع
trainer, coach مُمَرِّن	indignant, upset, vexed مُمْتَعِض
seasoned, trained, practiced مُمَرَّن	pale, wan, ghastly مُمْتَقَع
torn off, rent مُمَزَّق	full, filled, replete مُمْتَلِئ
dust cloth, cloth for cleaning مِمْسَحَة	fat, corpulent, stout مُمْتَلِئ الجِسْم
door-scraper مِمْسَحَة الأَحْذِيَة	owned, in possession, possessed مُمْتَلَك
door mat مِمْسَحَة الأَرْجُل	possessions, property, estates مُمْتَلَكات
mop, floor rag مِمْسَحَة الأَرْض	
restraining, holding, closefisted مُمْسِك	prevented, disallowed مُمْتَنِع
wiped off, rubbed off مَمْسُوح	representative, deputy, actor مُمَثِّل
defaced, marred, deformed مَمْسُوخ	eraser, rubber مِمْحاة
touched, tangible, mentally deranged مَمْسُوس	barren, sterile مُمْحِل
slim, slender مَمْشُوق	extended, expansive, outstretched مَمْدُود
passage, corridor مَمْشَى (مَمَاشٍ)	passing, crossing, going by مَمَرّ
sucking tube, siphon مِمَصّ	

indebted, grateful, obliged	مَمْنُون	soaked up, sucked, emaciated	مَمْصُوص
paved, levelled, even, prepared	مُمَهَّد	painful, agonizing	مُمِضّ
propertied, wealthy	مُمَوَّل	signer, signatory	مُمْضٍ
deadly, mortal, fatal	مُمِيت	signed, undersigned	مُمْضًى
distinguishing, discriminating, distinctive	مُمَيِّز	rainy, wet, showery	مُمْطِر
		rain coat	مِمْطَر
distinguished, privileged	مُمَيَّز	possible, potential, probable	مُمْكِن
who, whosoever	مَنْ	attainable, within reach	مُمْكِن المَنَال
from, of, out of	مِنْ		
gift, benefit, favour, blessing	مَنّ	possibilities	مُمْكِنَات
because of, for	من أَجْل	irksome, tiresome, wearisome, tedious	مُمِلّ
where from, whence	مِنْ أَيْنَ	saltern, salina (مَمَالِح)	مَمْلَحَة
distance, remoteness	مَنْأَى	kingdom, empire	مَمْلَكَة
substitution, substitute	مَنَاب	filled up, imbued	مَمْلُوء
secret or confidential talk	مُنَاجَاة	salted, salty	مَمْلُوح
strife, struggle, fight	مُنَاجَزَة	owned, possessed	مَمْلُوك
wailing, loud weeping	مَنَاح/مَنَاحَة	purchased slave, slave	مَمْلُوك (مَمَالِيْك)
walks of life	مَنَاحِي الحَيَاة	forbidden, prohibited	مَمْنُوع
adobe, dwelling, habitation	مُنَاخ (مُنَاخَات)	no smoking	مَمْنُوع التَّدْخِيْن
		no entry	مَمْنُوع الدُّخُول

help, support, backing	مُنَاصَرَة	climate	مُنَاخ/مَنَاخ
		climatic	مُنَاخي
combatant, fighter	مُنَاضِل	announcer, caller, herald	مُنَادٍ
struggle, contest, fight, dispute	مُنَاضَلَة	shouting, calling, announcement	مُنَادَاة
bullfight	مُنَاطَحَة		
like, similar, opponent, rival	مُنَاظِر	drinking companion, pot companion	مُنَادِم
scenic views, landscapes	مَنَاظِر طَبِيْعِيَّة	lighthouse, minaret	مَنَار/مَنَارَة (مَنَائِر)
debate, argument, discussion, supervision	مُنَاظَرة	disputed, contested	مُنَازَع فِيْه
impregnability, immunity, invincibility	مَنَاعَة	dispute, controversy, fight	مُنَازَعَة
incompatible	مُنَاف	amusement centers	مَنَازِل اللَّهْو
contradiction, opposition	مُنَافَاة	appropriate, adequate, fit	مُنَاسِب
competitor, rival	مُنَافِس	suitability, adequacy, fitness, affinity, occasion	مُنَاسَبَة
competition, rivalry, contest	مُنَافَسَة	rituals of hajj (Islamic pilgrimage)	مَنَاسِك الحَجّ
commercial competition	مُنَافَسَة تجَارِيَّة		
hypocrite, dissembler	مُنَافِق	adjuration, earnest appeal	مُنَاشَدَة
argument, discussion, interlocution	مُنَاقَشَة	escape, wayout, avoidance	مَنَاص
heated discussion	مُنَاقَشَة حَادّة	supporter, helper, protector	مُنَاصِر

handing over, delivering, delivery	مُنَاوَلَة	contrary, contradictory	مُنَاقِض
nursery plantation, source, origin	مَنْبَت/مَنْبِت (مَنَابِت)	self-contradictory	مُنَاقِض ذَاتِه
emanating, proceeding	مُنْبَثِق	contrast, opposition, contradiction	مُنَاقَضَة
pulpit, mimbar, dais	مِنْبَر (مَنَابِر)	obtainment, attainment, achievement	مَنَال
cheerful, extending, extensive	مُنْبَسِط	sleep, dream, bedroom	مَنَام
prostrate, flat, supine	مُنْبَطِح	nightwear, nightdress	مَنَامَة
spring, fountain head, source	مَنْبَع (مَنَابِع)	kind, gracious, benign	مَنَّان
oil well	مَنْبَع بِتْرُول	research methodology	مَنَاهِج البَحْث
warning, awakening, stimulant	مُنَبِّه	resistance, opposition	مُنَاهَضَة
cast off, discarded, abandoned	مَنْبُوذ	hostile, unfriendly	مُنَاوٍ
grace, favour, blessing, kindness	مِنَّة (مِنَن)	resistance, opposition	مُنَاوَأَة
		alternation, rotation	مُنَاوَبَة
alert, attentive, careful	مُنْتَبِه	alternatively, successively	مُنَاوَبَةً
producing, bearing, producer, fertile	مُنْتِج	monoeuvre, trick	مُنَاوَرَة
yields, products, production	مُنْتَجَات	air manoeuvre	مُنَاوَرَة جَوِّيَّة
resort, retreat, sanatorium	مُنْتَجَع	diplomatic manoeuvre	مُنَاوَرَة دِبْلُومَاسِيّة
		skirmish, bickering, clash	مُنَاوَشَة
		armed clash	مُنَاوَشَة حَرْبِيّة

critic	مُنْتَقِد	suicide, one who commits suicide	مُنْتَحِر
objectionable, criticized	مُنْتَقَد	plagiarist	مُنْتَحِل
movable, ambulatory, contagious	مُنْتَقِل	elector, voter	مُنْتَخِب
vindictive, revengeful	مُنْتَقِم	chosen, selected, elected	مُنْتَخَب
selected, select	مُنْتَقَى	assigned, delegated, commissioned	مُنْتَدَب
belonging, pertaining, relating	مُنْتَمٍ	regretful, remorseful	مُنْتَدِم
origin, relationship, affiliation	مُنْتَمَى	club, gathering place	مُنْتَدَى (مُنْتَدَيَات)
rotten, putrid, decayed, malodorous	مُنْتِن	taken away, drawn	مُنْتَزَع
finished, done, ended, terminated	مُنْتَهٍ	park, recreation ground	مُنْتَزَه (مُنْتَزَهَات)
end, extreme, extremity, utmost	مُنْتَهَى	spread, widespread	مُنْتَشِر
product, production	مَنْتُوج (مَنْتُوجَات)	raised, erect, planted	مُنْتَصِب
		victorious, triumphant	مُنْتَصِر
menthol	مِنْثُول	middle,	مُنْتَصَف
scattered, dispersed	مَنْثُور	midway	مُنْتَصَف الطَّرِيق
rescuer, saviour, deliverer	مُنَجٍّ	midnight	مُنْتَصَف اللَّيْل
		midday, noon	مُنْتَصَف النَّهَار
inclined, attracted, drawn	مُنْجَذِب	regular, systematic, uniform	مُنْتَظِم
scythe, sickle	مِنْجَل (مَنَاجِل)	blown up, puffed up, swollen	مُنْتَفِخ

مُنْحَطّ low, base, degraded, inferior	مُنَجِّم astrologer
مُنْحَلّ dissolved, broken up, decomposed	مَنْجَم (مَنَاجِم) mine, source, origin
مَنْحَل (مَنَاحِل) beehive, apiary	مُنْجَمِد icy, frozen, frosted
مُنْحَنٍ twisted, curved, bent, crooked, inclined	مَنْجَنِيق mangonel, ballista
مَنْحُور slaughtered, killed	مَنْجُو mango
مَنْحُوس luckless, ill-fated, inauspicious, sinister	مَنْجًى safety, security
مَنْحُوف slim, thin, slender	مَنْح granting, conferring, bestowal
مَنْحًى (مَنَاحٍ) purpose, object, goal, realm, field	مُنْحاز isolated, secluded, retired
مِنْخَار (مَنَاخِير) nostril, nose	مِنْحَة (مِنَح) gift, benefaction, bounty, grant, allowance
مِنْخَاس (مَنَاخِيس) spur, goad	مِنْحَة الإِقَامَة living allowance
مَنْخَر/مَنْخِر (مَنَاخِر) nostril, nose	مِنْحَة السُّكْنَى housing allowance
مِنْخَس (مَنَاخِس) spur, goad	مِنْحَة دِرَاسِيَّة scholarship
مُنْخَفِض low, faint, soft, subdued	مِنْحَة مَلَكِيَّة royal bounty
مَنْدَم remorse, regret	مُنْحَدِر slopping, declining, slanting
مُنْدَمِج incorporated, tight, compact	مُنْحَدَر slope, declivity
	مَنْحَر throat, neck
مُنْدَهِش startled, amazed, surprised	مُنْحَرِف oblique, slanted, deviating
	مُنْحَرِف المِزَاج indisposed, out of sorts

rank, status, position مَنْزِلة	delegate, deputy, مَنْدُوب
sliding, slippery مُنْزَلِق	representative, bewailed
domestic, household مَنْزِلي	insurance agent مَنْدُوب التَّأمِين
infallible, unerring مُنَزَّه	special envoy مَنْدُوب خَاصّ
garden, park, (مَنَازِه) مَنْزَهَة	High مَنْدُوب سَامٍ
entertainment	Commissioner
retired, secluded مُنْزَوٍ	authorized مَنْدُوب مُفَوَّض
	agent
taken away, removed مَنْزُوع	carded, combed مَنْدُوف
exhausted by loss of مَنْزُوف	kerchief, (مَنَادِيل) مِنْدِيل
blood	handkerchief
loom, handloom مِنْسَج	since, for مُنْذ
harmonious, fluent مُنْسَجِم	from now on مُنْذ الآن
absent-minded, مُنْسَرِحُ الفِكْر	from the beginning مُنْذُ البَدْء
distracted	from this day on مُنْذ اليَوْم
winnow (مَنَاسِف) مِنْسَف	warner, one who مُنْذِر
well-ordered, in good مُنَسَّق	cautions
order	distracted, baffled, مُنْذَهِل
hermitage, (مَنَاسِك) مَنْسِك	confused
hermit, cell, rituals	pledged, vowed, مَنْذُور
attributed, ascribed, مَنْسُوب	dedicated to God
related	house, apartment, (مَنَازِل) مَنْزِل
woven, woven fabric مَنْسُوج	dwelling place
textiles, (مَنْسُوجَات) مَنْسُوج	rest house مَنْزِل الاسْتِرَاحَة
textures, woven goods	sent down, مُنْزَل/مُنَزَّل
abrogated, abolished مَنْسُوخ	revealed

مَنْصُوص	defined, determined, fixed	مَنْسيّ	forgotten, omitted
مَنْصُون	monsoon	مَنْشَأ	origin, source, growth, genesis, birth, birth place
مِنْضَح	shower bath	مُنْشِئ	writer, originator, establisher, founder
مِنْضَحَة (مَنَاضِح)	sprinkler, watering pot, douche	مِنْشَار	saw
مُنَضِّد	typesetter, compositor	مُنْشِط	incentive, stimulus
مِنْضَدَة (مَنَاضِد)	desk, table	مِنْشَفَة (مَنَاشِف)	towel, napkin
مُنْضَمّ	connected with, close	مَنْشُود	aspired, desired
مُنْطاد	balloon, aerostat	مَنْشُور	spread, published
مُنْطاد مُسَيَّر	dirigible balloon	مَنْشُور (مَنَاشِير)	proclamation, circular
مُنْطاد مُقَيَّد	kite balloon		
مَنْطِق	logic, faculty of speech	مَنْشُور تِجَاري	prospectus
مِنْطَقَة (مَنَاطِق)	zone, region, territory	مَنْصِب (مَنَاصِب)	position, post
مِنْطَقَة اسْتِوَائِيّة	tropical zone	مِنَصَّة (مَنَاصّ)	dais, raised platform
مِنْطَقَة الحَرْب	war zone	مِنَصَّة الخَطَابَة	rostrum, tribune
مِنْطَقَة النَّجاة	life buoy	مُنْصَرَف	going away, departure
مِنْطَقَة حَارَّة	torrid zone	مُنْصَرِم	past, bygone
مِنْطَقَة حُرَّة	free zone	مُنْصِف	just, fair, upright, righteous
مِنْطَقَة صِناعِيّة	industrial area	مَنْصُوب	fixed, installed, raised, set up
مِنْطَقَة مَمْنُوعَة	prohibited area		
مَنْطِقي	logical, logician	مَنْصُور	supported, victorious

مَنْعَة resistance, strength, power, force	مِنْطَقِي zonal
مُنْعَرِج curved, crooked, twisting	مُنْطَوٍ depressed, low-spirited
مُنْعَرَج twist, turn, curve	مَنْطُوق uttered, pronounced, spoken
مُنْعَزِل sporadic, solitary, isolated	مَنْظَر (مَنَاظِر) sight, view, aspect, scenery
مُنْعِش reviving, animating, refreshing	مَنْظَر عَامّ landscape, panorama
مُنْعَطَف turn, curve, twist, alley	مِنْظَر/مِنْظَار telescope, eyeglass, spyglass
مُنْعَكِس reflected, reversed	مَنْظَرَة (مَنَاظِر) views, landscape, scenery
مُنْعِم benefactor, donor	مُنَظِّم organizer, sponsor, arranger
مَنْعُوت person or thing qualified	مُنَظَّم well-arranged, in good order, regular
مَنْعَى news of death	مُنَظَّمَة (مُنَظَّمَات) organization, association
مُنْغَاظ irate, furious	
مُنَغِّص exciting, stimulating	مَنْظُور seen, visible, expected
مَنْغَنِيس manganese	مَنْظُوم in good order, well-arranged, metrical
مِنْفَاق spendthrift, profligate, extravagant	مَنْع prevention, prohibition, hindering
مُنْفَجِر explosive, blasting, eruptive	مَنْع التَّجَوُّل curfew
مُنَفِّذ executant, executor	
مَنْفَذ (مَنَافِذ) opening, way-out, escape, passage, exit	مِنْعَام munificent, graceful, benefactor

depressed, distressed, مُنْقَبِض low-spirited	flood gate مَنْفَذ المِيَاه
depressed, low-spirited مُنْقَبِض الصَّدْر	repulsive, repellent مُنَفِّر
down cast, in poor spirit, depressed مُنْقَبِض القَلْب	divergent, wide-open, مُنَفَّرِج relaxed
low-spirited, dejected مُنْقَبِض النَّفْس	alone, solitary, isolated مُنْفَرِد
saviour, rescuer, deliverer مُنْقِذ	breathing hole, (مَنَافِس) مَنْفَس air hole
chisel مِنْقَش/مِنْقَاش	separate, detached, dissociated مُنْفَصِل
dappled, spotted, dotted مُنَقَّط	ashtray, (مَنَافِض) مِنْفَضَة feather duster
interrupted, detached, مُنْقَطِع disconnected, discontinued	blistering, vesicant مُنَفِّط
unequal, unique, مُنْقَطِع النَّظِير matchless, incomparable, peerless	use, advantage, benefit, profit مَنْفَعَة
tropic, resort, final destiny مُنْقَلَب	excited, enraged مُنْفَعِل
tropic of capricorn مُنْقَلَب شَتَوِي	blown up, inflated مَنْفُوخ
tropic of cancer مُنْقَلَب صَيْفِي	fluffy, puffed up مَنْفُوش
painted, engraved, sculptured, inscribed مَنْقُوش	exile, banishment, expulsion مَنْفَى
incomplete, deficient, lacking مَنْقُوص	negative, negated, denied, exiled مَنْفِي
	beak, bill مِنْقَاد
	beak, bill مِنْقَار
	explorer, examiner مُنَقِّب
	punch, drill مِنْقَب/مِنْقَبَة

procedure, manner, method, course مَنْهَج (مَنَاهِج)	broken, demolished, violated, refuted مَنْقُوض
curriculum مَنْهَج التَّعْلِيم	dotted, spotted, pointed, dappled مَنْقُوط
gruelling, exhausting, consuming مُنْهِك	soaked, macerated مَنْقُوع
watering place, fountain مَنْهَل (مَنَاهِل)	trasnfered, carried, transcribed, portable مَنْقُول
absorbed, engrossed, given up مُنْهَمِك	movable properties مَنْقُولات
consumed, exhausted مَنْهُوك	bent, intent, devoted مُنْكَبّ
worn out, exhausted, spent مَنْهُوك القُوَى	shoulder, flank, side مَنْكِب (مَنَاكِب)
prohibited, forbidden مَنْهِي	disowned, detestable مُنْكَر
way, manner, method مِنْوَال	reversed, inverted مُنَكَّس
illuminated, shining, brilliant مُنَوَّر	shrunk, absorbed مُنْكَمِش
dependent on, conditional مَنُوط	afflicted with disaster مَنْكُوب
loom, handloom مِنْوَل	unfortunate, unhappy مَنْكُود
monologue مُنُولُوج	unfortunate, ill-starred مَنْكُود الحَظّ
somniferous, soporific مُنَوِّم	reversed, inverted مَنْكُوس
fate, destiny, death مَنُون	striped, spotted مُنَمَّر
semen, sperm مَنًى/مَنِيّ	embellished, adorned, decorated مُنَمَّق
fate, destiny, death مَنًى/مَنِيّة (مَنَايا)	way, method, clear road مِنْهَاج (مَنَاهِيج)
repentant مُنِيب	

blowing of (مَهَابّ) مَهَبّ wind, direction of wind, windward	wish, desire, (مُنَى) مُنْيَة longing
fall, falling, (مَهَابط) مَهْبط landing, landing place	luminous, illuminative, مُنِير radiant
cradle of Islam مَهْبطُ الوَحْي	strong, powerful, مَنِيع invincible, impregnable
vagina (مَهَابِل) مَهْبِل/مَهْبَل	high, lofty, imposing, مُنِيف stately
vaginal مَهْبَلِي	
dolt, stupid, fool مَهْبُول	object of reverence مَهَاب
rightly guided مُهْتَد	revrence, dignity مَهَابَة
trembling, quivering, مُهْتَزّ vibrating	emigrant, refugee مُهَاجِر
mindful, interested, مُهْتَمّ concerned	emigration, مُهَاجَرَة migration
soul, life, (مُهَج/مُهَجَات) مُهْجَة breath of life, lifeblood	attacker, assailant مُهَاجِم
place of (مَهَاجِر) مَهْجَر emigration, colony	attack, assault, مُهَاجَمَة charge
bedchamber (مَهَاجِع) مَهْجَع	bed, resting place مِهَاد
deserted, forsaken, مَهْجُور abandoned	skill, dexterity, مَهَارَة cleverness, proficiency
cradle, crib, bed (مُهُود) مَهْد	important matters مَهَامّ الأُمُور
threatening, menacing مُهَدِّد	dispised, disdained مُهَان
threatened, menaced مُهَدَّد	humiliation, disgrace, مَهَانَة contempt
demolished, مَهْدُود destroyed, razed	complaisance, مُهَاوَدَة consideration

comedy مَهْزَلَة (مَهَازِل)	demolished, مَهْدُوم destroyed, razed down
smashed, broken into مُهَشَّم pieces	rightly guided, مَهْدِي presented
digested, digestible مَهْضُوم	well-mannered, well- مُهَذَّب bred, cultured, polite
slim, slender, مُهَفْهَف floating in the air	educator, instructor مُهَذِّب
bewildered, مَهْفُوت perplexed	seal, signet, foal مُهْر (أَمْهَار)
whiffler, fickle, مَهْفُوف light-headed	dower, bridal مَهْر (مُهُور) ransom
bloom of youth مُهْكَة/مَهْكَة	mortar مِهْرَاس (مَهَارِيس)
ease, convenience, مَهْل/مَهَل slowness, leisure	poured out, spilled, مُهْرَاق shed
slowly, gently مَهْلاً	smuggler, trafficker مُهَرِّب
respite, delay مُهْلَة	flight, escape, مَهْرَب (مَهَارِب) outlet, retreat
pernicious, lethal, مُهْلِك deadly, destructive, ruinous	jester, buffoon مُهَرِّج
danger, مَهْلَكَة/مَهْلُكَة (مَهَالِك) peril, perilous place	festival, gala, مَهْرَجَان/مِهْرَجَان celebration
important, significant, مُهِمّ momentous	in a disorderly state مُهَرْجَل
whenever, whatever مَهْمَا	poured out, shed, مُهْرَق effused
important matter مَهَمَّة (مَهَامّ)	beach, coast مُهْرَقَان
mission, مُهِمَّة (مُهِمَّات) errand, important matters	in a hurry, hasty مُهَرْوِل
	derision, mockery, مَهْزَأَة disdain

crazy, mad, blind	مُهَوَّس	goad, spur, prod	مهْمَز/مهْمَاز
instigating, exciting, agitating	مُهَوِّش	neglectful, careless, remiss	مُهْمِل
terrible, terrifying, dreadful	مُهَوِّل	neglected, antiquated, unobserved, omitted	مُهْمَل
prepared, made ready	مُهَيَّأ	unsigned, without signature	مُهْمَل الإمْضَاء
awful, dreadful, fearful	مَهِيب	undated	مُهْمَل التَّارِيخ
awesome, grave, impressing	مُهِيب	unsigned, anonymous	مُهْمَل التَّوْقِيع
stimulating, exciting, inciting	مُهَيِّج	worried, concerned	مَهْمُوم
broken, disabled, helpless	مَهِيض	congratulator, well-wisher	مُهَنِّئ
controller, overseer, supervisor	مُهَيْمِن	profession, occupation, job	مِهْنَة (مِهَن)
insulting, humiliating, disgraceful	مُهِين	engineer, architect	مُهَنْدِس
despised, despicable	مَهِين (مُهَنَاء)	agricultural engineer	مُهَنْدِس زِرَاعِي
refuge, asylum	مَوْئِل	architect, builder	مُهَنْدِس مِعْمَارِي
mewing (of cat)	مُوَاء	mechanical engineer	مُهَنْدِس مِيكَانِيْكِي
harmony, unity, agreement	مُوَاءَمَة	well-arranged, well-ordered, trim	مُهَنْدَم
favourable, suitable, propitious	مُوَاتٍ	vocational, professional	مِهْنِي
		ventilator, fan	مِهْوَاة

inflammable things	مَوَادّ مُلْتَهِبَة
lifelessness, lifeless or inanimate things	مَوَات
equivocation, ambiguity	مُوَارَبَة
pleasant, agreeable, favourable	مُوَاتٍ
parallel, equivalent, similar	مُوَازٍ
confrontation, confrontment, facing	مُوَاجَهَة
parallelism, equivalence	مُوَازَاة
face to face, person to person	مُوَاجَهَةً
comparison, counter balance, equipoise	مُوَازَنَة
raw materials, elementary materials	مَوَادّ أَوَّلِيّة
consolation, assistance	مُوَاساة
explosives	مَوَادّ الِانْفِجَار
rainy seasons	مَوَاسِم مُمْطِرَة
cosmetics	مَوَادّ التَّجْمِيل
connection, continuation, communication	مُوَاصَلَة
medicaments, drugs	مَوَادّ التَّطْيِيب
dyestuffs, dyes	مَوَادّ الصِّبَاغَة
collusion, secret agreement	مُوَاطَأَة
foodstuffs	مَوَادّ القُوت
countryman, citizen	مُوَاطِن
vocabulary of a language	مَوَادّ اللُّغَة
persevering, assiduous, regular attendant	مُوَاظِب
commodities, articles of commerce	مَوَادّ تجارِيّة
perseverance, assiduity, regularity	مُوَاظَبَة
war materials	مَوَادّ حَرْبِيّة
raw materials	مَوَادّ خَام
accordant, agreeable, fit, congruous	مُوَافِق
food, foodstuffs	مَوَادّ غِذَائِيّة
manufactured goods	مَوَادّ مَصْنُوعَة
agreement, accordance, conformity, fitness	مُوَافَقَة
antibiotics	مَوَادّ مُضَادَّة لِلْحَيَوِيّات

necessary, obligatory, affirmative	مُوجَب	capitalist, financier	مَوّال
cause, reason, necessity	مُوجِب (مُوجِبَات)	supporter, helper, adherent	مُوَالٍ
cause, motive, reason	مُوجِبَة	friendship, incessancy	مُوَالَاة
billow, surge, wave	مَوْجَة	deception, fraud, double dealing	مُوَالَسَة
bloom of youth	مَوْجَة الشَّبَاب	place of perdition	مَوْبِق
creator, originator	مُوجِد	grave, offence, atrocity, abomination	مُوبِقَة (مُوبِقَات)
concise, short, summary	مُوجَز		
existent, available, present	مَوْجُود	infected, infested with pestilence	مَوْبُوء
existing things, creations	مَوْجُودَات	death, demise	مَوْت/مَوْتَة
revealing, inspiring	مُوحٍ	sudden death	مَوْت الغَفْلَة
unifier, monotheist	مُوَحِّد	sudden death	مَوْت ذُعاف
unified, consolidated, combined	مُوَحَّد	pact, contract, agreement	مَوْثِق (مَوَاثِق)
dreary, desolate, dismal, gloomy	مُوحِش	trustworthy, reliable	مَوْثُوق
muddy, miry, dirty	مُوَحَّل	waves, surges	مَوْج (أَمْواج)
inspiration, revelation	مُوحَى	long wave	مَوْج طَوِيل
		short wave	مَوْج قَصِير
love, affection, friendship	مَوَدَّة	medium wave	مَوْج مُتَوَسِّط
depositor, consigner, mild, meek	مُودِع	medium waves	مَوْجَات مُتَوَسِّطَة
		causing, necessitating	مُوجِب

summer season	مَوْسِم الاصْطِيَاف
harvest season	مَوْسِم الحَصَاد
suspicious, anxious, obsessed with delusions	مُوَسْوَس
encyclopedia, thesaurus	مَوْسُوْعَة
encyclopedic	مَوْسُوْعِي
branded, marked	مَوْسُوم
safety razor	مُوْسَى (مَوَاسٍ)
musician	مُوسِيقَار
music	مُوْسِيقَى
music, musical	مُوْسِيقِي
dance music	مُوْسِيقِي رَاقِصَة
testator, mandatory, recommender	مُوَصٍّ/مُوْصٍ
conductor	مُوَصِّل
described, portrayed, explained	مَوْصُوف
bound, tied, joined, connected	مَوْصُول
bequeathed, decreed, recommended	مُوْصَى
place, site, position, locality	مَوْضِع (مَوَاضِع)

model, pattern	مُوْدِل/مُوْدِيل
legator, testator, ancestor	مُوَرِّث
legator, testator	مُوْرِث
supplier, contractor	مُوَرِّد
resource, origin, income, source of income	مَوْرِد (مَوَارِد)
watering place	مَوْرِدَة
in a dilemma	مُوَرَّط
morphine	مُورفِين
swollen, tumefacient	مُوَرَّم
oblique, twisted, diagonal	مَوْرُوب
inherited, hereditary	مَوْرُوث
banana	مَوْز
distributor	مُوَزِّع
postman, mailman	مُوَزِّع البَرِيد
balanced, evenly poised, weighed, metrical	مَوْزُون
paved, smooth	مُوَسَّد
well-to-do, rich, wealthy, prosperous	مُوْسِر
rich, wealthy	مُوْسِع
season, time	مَوْسِم (مَوَاسِم)

exhortation, sermon, preaching	مَوْعِظَة (مَوَاعِظ)	object of admiration	مَوْضِع الإعْجَاب
fixed, appointed, promised	مَوْعُوْد	object of sympathy	مَوْضِع الحَنَان
indisposed, ill, unwell	مَوْعُوك	local	مَوْضِعِي
plentiful, abundant, ample	مَوْفُور	put, placed, laid down	مَوْضُوع
timetaker, timekeeper, punctual	مُوَقِّت	subject, topic, issue, article	مَوْضُوع (مَوَاضِيْع)
appointed, temporary, for a time only	مُوَقَّت	objective, concerning the subject	مَوْضُوْعِي
fixed or appointed time	مَوْقِت (مَوَاقِت)	footing, foothold	مَوْطَأ (مَوَاطِئ)
fireplace, hearth, stove	مَوْقِد (مَوَاقِد)	firm, strong, solid, stable	مُوَطَّد
respected, venerable, worthy of reverence	مُوَقَّر	place, locality, region, home, dwelling place	مَوْطِن (مَوَاطِن)
signed, registered	مُوَقَّع	employee, employed, appointed	مُوَظَّف
place, locality, location, site, position	مَوْقِع (مَوَاقِع)	government official	مُوَظَّف الحُكُومة
battle, battle field	مَوْقَعَة (مَوَاقِع)	public functionary	مُوَظَّف عُمُومِي
attitude, stand, stop, position, place	مَوْقِف (مَوَاقِف)	clerical worker	مُوَظَّف كِتَابِي
		civil servant	مُوَظَّف مُلْكِي
strategic situation	مَوْقِف حَرْبِي	appointment, appointed time, promise	مَوْعِد (مَوَاعِد)

new born baby, infant	مَوْلُود (مَوَالِيْد)
lord, protector, benefactor, friend	مَوْلًى (مَوَال)
max	مُوم
prostitute, whore	مُوْمِس/مُوْمِسَة
mummy	مُوْمِياء/مُوْمِيَه
provision	مُوْئَة
gift, talent, parts	مَوْهِبَة (مَوَاهِب)
granted, given, bestowed, gifted	مَوْهُوب
imaginary, imagined	مَوْهُوم
desperate, hopeless	مَيْؤُوس
supplier, provider	مَيّار
inclined, disposed to	مَيّال
liar, deceitful	مَيّان
territorial waters	مِيَاه إِقْلِيْمِيَّة
rain waters	مِيَاه الأَمْطَار
coastal waters	مِيَاه سَاحِليَّة
carbonated water	مِيَاه غَازِية
dead, deceased, lifeless	مَيْت/مَيِّت (أَمْوَات)
corpse, dead animal	مَيْتَة
manner of death	مِيْتَة

political situation	مَوْقِف سِيَاسِي
hostile attitude	مَوْقِف عِدَائِي
certain, convinced, confident	مُوْقِن
appointed time	مَوْقُوت
kindled, lit	مَوْقُود
stopped, arrested, suspended, dependent	مَوْقُوف
procession, parade	مَوْكِب (مَوَاكِب)
funeral procession	مَوْكِب الجَنَازَة
emphasized, sure, certain	مُؤَكَّد
mandatory, constituent	مُؤَكَّل
procreator, procreative, generative	مُوَلِّد
generator, dynamo	مُوَلِّد (مُوَلِّدات)
begotten, generated, produced	مُوَلَّد
birthplace, birthday	مَوْلِد (مَوَالد)
midwife	مُوَلِّدَة
passionately in love, crazy	مُوْلَع

ease, affluence, luxury, comfort	مَيْسَرَة	orphanage	مَيْتَم (مَيَاتِم)
left wing, left side	مَيْسَرَة (مَيَاسِر)	agreement, convenant, pact, contract	مِيْثَاق (مَوَاثِيق)
easy, easy to carryout, lucky	مَيْسُور	length, distance	مِيْدَاء
lavatory, place for ablution	مِيْضَأَة	field, square, open space	مَيْدَان (مَيَادِين)
liquidity, fluidity, flow	مَيْع	training centre	مَيْدَان التَّدْرِيب
appointment, appointed time, promise	مِيْعَاد (مَوَاعِيْد)	theatre of war	مَيْدَان الحَرْب
date of delivery	مِيْعَاد التَّسْلِيْم	skating rink	مَيْدَان الزَّحْلَقَة
period, menses	مِيْعَاد المَرْأَة	race-course	مَيْدَان السِّبَاق
time, appointed time, date	مِيْقَات (مَوَاقِيْت)	field of activity	مَيْدَان العَمَل
mechanics	مِيْكَانِيْكَا	battle field	مَيْدَان القِتَال
mechanic, mechanical	مِيْكَانِيْكِي	inheritance, heritage	مِيْرَاث (مَوَارِيْث)
microbe	مِيْكُرُوب	provisions, supplies	مِيْرَة (مِيَر)
microphone	مِيْكُرُوفُون	brigadier general	مِيْرلِوَاء
mile	مَيْل (أَمْيَال)	drain, gutter, spout	مِيْزَاب (مَيَازِيْب)
inclination, tendency, attachment, deviation	مَيْل (مُيُول/أَمْيَال)	scales, balance, measure	مِيْزَان (مَوَازِين)
birth, birthday	مِيْلَاد (مَوَالِيْد)	balance, balance sheet, budget	مِيْزَانِيّة
After Christ (AC)	مِيْلَادِي	characteristic, property, quality, distinguishing trait	مِيْزَة
		within easy reach, prosperous, well off	مُيَسَّر

calamity, misfortune	نَائِبَة (نَوَائِب)	right side, right flank	مَيْمَنَة
hired mourner (female)	نَائِحَة (نَوَائِح)	blessed, auspicious, fortunate	مَيْمُون
obtainer, gainer, acquirer	نَائِل	lie, falsehood	مَيْن (مُيُون)
sleeping, asleep	نَائِم (نِيَام)	enamel, glaze	مِيْنَا/مِيْنَاء
eyetooth, canine tooth	نَاب (أَنْيَاب)	dial (of a watch)	مِيْنَا/مِيْنَاء (مَوَانِئ)
palpitating, beating	نَابِض	harbour, port	مِيْنَاء (مَوَان/مِيَن)
vibrant with life	نَابِض بالحَيَاة	airport	مِيْنَاء جَوِّيَّة
distinguished, outstanding, brilliant	نَابِغ	liquidity, unsteadiness	مُيُوعَة

swelling, swollen, bulging	نَاتِئ	sound asleep, slumberer	نَؤُوْم
protuberance, protrusion, elevation	نَاتِئَة (نَوَاتِئ)	remoteness, isolatedness	نَأْي
resulting, ensuing, consequent, result, consequence	نَاتِج	trench, dry mot, fosse	نُؤَّى
		ditch, trench	نَأْي (آنَاء)
maker, producer, manufacturer	نَاتِج (نَاتِجُون)	remote, distant, far away	نَاء
		share, portion, quota	نَائِب
successful, prosperous	نَاجِح	deputy, substitute, representative	نَائِب (نُوَّاب)
molar	نَاجِذ (نَوَاجِذ)	vice president	نَائِب الرَّئِيْس
full, entire, complete	نَاجِز	vice-consul	نَائِب القُنْصُل
beneficial, useful, effective, salubrious	نَاجِع	viceroy	نَائِب المَلِك

explosive, dynamite ناسِف	direction, side, (نَواح) ناحِيَة
ascetic, pious, (نُسَّاك) ناسِك	corner, aspect, area, field
hermit	elector, voter ناخِب
humanity, human ناسُوت	decayed, decaying ناخِر
nature	club, (أَنْدِيَة/نَوَاد) نادٍ
sinus, fistula (نَوَاسِير) ناسُور	association, union
anal fistula ناسُور شَرَجِي	rare, uncommon, نادِر
growing, developing, ناشِئ	strange
resulting from	unique, peerless نادِر المِثَال
publisher ناشِر	seldom, rarely نادِرًا
elevated, raised, high ناشِز	rarity, rare (نَوَادِر) نادِرة
lively, brisk, active, ناشِط	things
agile	waiter (نُدُل) نادِل
dry, stiff ناشِف	repentant, regretful, نادِم
sincere adviser, (نُصَّح) ناصِح	remorseful
counsellor	fire, conflagration (نِيرَان) نار
helper, (أَنْصَار) ناصِر	coconut نَارْجِيل/نَارْجِيْلَة
supporter, protector	fiery, burning نارِي
clean, pure, manifest ناصِع	emigrant, faraway نازِح
fistula, tumour ناصور	inclination, (نَوَازِع) نازِعَة
forelock, (نَوَاص) ناصِيَة	tendency
forepart of the head	calamity, (نَوَازِل) نازِلَة
dry, arid, (نُضَّب) ناضِب	mishap, blow, catastrophe
unproductive	men, people ناس
mature, ripe, well- ناضِج	one who abolishes, ناسِخ
cooked	transcriber

نَافِعَة public works	نَاضِر fresh, beautiful, flourishing
نَافِلَة (نَوَافِل) supererogatory services, booty, gift	نَاطِر guard, keeper
نَافُورَة (نَوَافِيْر) fountain	نَاطِق speaking, rational
نَاقَة (نِيَاق/نُوْق) she camel	نَاظِر (نُظَّار) observer, overseer, supervisor, onlooker
نَاقِد (نَقَدَة) critic	
نَاقِص incomplete, effective, insufficient, missing, short of	نَاظِر المَدْرَسَة head master, principal
	نَاظِر الوَقْف trustee, curator
نَاقِل (نَقَلَة) bearer, carrier, copyist, transmitter	نَاظِرَة (نَوَاظِر) eye, look
نَاقِلَة (نَاقِلَات) transport, transport vessel	نَاظِم organizer, arranger, poet
نَاقِلَة البِتْرُول oil tanker	نَاعِس drowsy, dozing
نَاقِلَة الطَّائِرَات aircraft carrier	نَاعِم soft, smooth, powdery
نَاقِم indignant, hostile, revengeful	نَاعِم اللِّسَان tender mouthed
نَاقُور (نَوَاقِيْر) ١ a wind instrument	نَاعُوظ aphrodisiac, stimulating
	نَاف yoke
نَاقُوس (نَوَاقِيْس) bell, bell jar, gong	نَافِخ flatulent, blowing
نَاكِث faithless, perfidious	نَافِدَة void, vacuum
نَاكِر disavowing, hostile	نَافِذ in force, effective, operative
نَاكِر الجَمِيْل ungrateful, thankless	نَافِذَة (نَوَافِذ) window, air hole
	نَافِر (نُفَّار) shy, timid, fleeing
نَاكِر المَعْرُوف ungrateful, thankless	نَافِع useful, advantageous, beneficial

nobility, magnanimity, نُبَالَة generosity	motion, movement, stir نَامَّة
nobility, intelligence, نَبَاهَة vigilence, renown	honour, (نَوَامِيْس) نَامُوس dignity, rule, cunning, crafty, shrewed, slanderer
sprout, plant, نَبْت germination, growth	mosquito net نَامُوْسِيّة
sprout, shoot نَبْتَة	growth, property of نَامِيَة growth
bark, barking, نَبْح/نَبِيْح baying	prohibitory, inhibitory, ناهٍ interdicting
discarding, throwing نَبْذ away, rejection	full, well-developed, نَاهِد swelling
portion, section, (نُبَذ) نُبْذَة note, treatise, article	rising, standing, نَاهِض active
accent, accentuation نَبْر	news, information (أَنْبَاء) نَبَأ
granary, barn, (أَنْبَار) نِبْر storehouse	plants, vegetations, نَبَات herbs
accent, stress, (نَبَرَات) نَبْرَة tone, swelling	economic plant نَبَات اقْتِصَادِي
nickname (أَنْبَاز) نَبَز	ornamental plant نَبَات الزِّيْنَة
digging, excavation, نَبْش disclosure	medicinal plant نَبَات طِبِّي
	herbivorous, vegetarian نَبَاتِي
desecration of نَبْش القُبُور graves	barkerer, animal that نَبَّاح barks
pulse, pulsation, (أَنْبَاض) نَبْض pulpitation	barking, baying نُبَاح/نِبَاح
	gravedigger نَبَّاش
pulse, beat, pulsation نَبْضَة	bowman, archer نَبَّال

produce, production, yield, brood	نِتَاج	depth, profundity	نَبَط
nitrogen	نِتْرُوجِين	gushing out, rising	نَبْع
a pinch, bit	نُتْفَة (نُتَف)	spring, source	نَبْع (نُبُوع)
putrid, stinking, decayed	نَتِن	nobility, gentleness, generosity	نُبْل
putrefaction, stench, bad smell	نَتْن/نَتَانَة	arrows	نَبْل (نِبَال/أَبَال)
swelling, protuberance, tumour, elevation	نُتُوء	noble, highborn, generous	نَبْل/نَبِيْل (نِبَال/نُبَلاَء)
result, outcome, effect	نَتِيْجَة (نَتَائِج)	perception, vigilence, attention	نُبْه
fragments, small pieces	نُثَار	outstanding, eminent, noble, highborn	نَبِه/نَبِيْه
scattering, dispersion, prose	نَثْر	prophecy	نُبُوْءَة
prosaic, petty	نَثْرِي	prophethood, prophecy	نُبُوَّة
high land, elevation	نِجَاء	excelling, eminence, genius, exceptional aptitude	نُبُوغ
nobility, generosity, superiority	نَجَابَة	prophetic	نَبَوِي
rescue, salvation, deliverance	نَجَاة	prophet, messenger	نَبِي (أَنْبِيَاء)
success, progress	نَجَاح	discarded, repudiated, cast off	نَبِيْذ
brilliant success	نَجَاح بَاهِر	wine, alcohol	نَبِيْذ (أَنْبِذَة)
swordbelt	نِجَاد	bark, barking, baying	نَبِيْح
carpenter, joiner	نَجَّار	hill, hillock	نَثْأَة
origin, stock	نُجَار		

astral, starlike	نَجْمِي	carpentry, joinery	نِجَارَة
excrement, faeces	نَجْو	wood shavings	نُجَارَة
plateau, tableland	نَجْوَة	execution, accomplishment, achievement	نَجَاز/نَجْز
film stars	نُجُوم السِّينما		
in instalments	نُجُوْمًا	filth, uncleanliness, impurity	نَجَاسَة
secret conversation	نَجْوَى (نَجَاوَى)	astrologer	نَجّام
close friend, bosom friend	نَجِيّ (أَنْجِيَة)	noble, generous, highborn	نَجْب
noble, highbred, excellent, intelligent	نَجِيْب (نُجُب/نُجَبَاء)	progress, success	نُجْح
		plateau, highland	نَجْد (نِجَاد)
beneficial, useful, effective, healthful	نَجِيع	help, aid, relief, succour, bravery	نَجْدَة (نَجْدَات)
sculptor, stone mason	نَحّات	uncleanliness, impurity, filth	نَجَس
splinters, slivers	نُحَاتَة		
coppersmith	نَحَّاس	filthy, unclean, impure, defile	نَجِس
copper	نُحَاس	small village, hamlet	نَجْع (نُجُوع)
brass, bronze	نُحَاس أَصْفَر		
slenderness, slimness, emaciation	نَحَافَة	hill, chandelier	نَجَف/نَجَفَة
		son, offspring, progeny	نَجْل (أَنْجَال)
flamingo	نُحَام		
carving, sculpturing, sculpture, stonework	نَحْت	star, instalment	نَجْم (نُجُوم)
		comet	نَجْم ذُوْ ذَنَب
killing, slaughtering	نَحْر	star, asterisk	نَجْمَة

throat, lower front protion of the neck	نَحْر (نُحُور)
misfortune, calamity, bad luck	نَحْس (نُحُوس)
unlucky, unfortunate, ill-starred, inauspicious	نَحْس/نَحِس
bee	نَحْل
present, gift, sect, creed	نِحْلَة (نِحَل)
toward, approximately, about, like	نَحْوَ
direction, side, manner, way, course	نَحْو (أَنْحَاء)
thinness, slimness, leanness, emaciation	نُحُول
crying, wailing, lamentation	نَحِيب
slaughtered, killed	نَحِير
nature, disposition	نَحِيزَة
thin, lean, slim	نَحِيف
slim, slender, lean, emaciated	نَحِيل
slave trader, cattle merchant	نَخّاس
cattle trade, slave trade	نِخَاسَة

spinal cord, medulla	نُخَاع/نِخَاع (نُخُع)
spinal cord	نُخَاع شَوْكِي
phlegm, mucus	نُخَاعَة
phlegm, mucus	نُخَامَة
toast, selection, choice	نَخْب
selected items, choice, pick	نُخْبَة (نُخَب)
snoring, snuffling, decay, rottenness	نَخْر
rotting, decaying, carious	نَخِر
palm trees, date palms	نَخْل/نَخْلَة
pride, arrogance, haughtiness	نَخْوَة
snoring, snuffling	نَخِير
palm, date palm	نَخِيل
equal, alike, rival, partner	نِدّ (أَنْدَاد)
call, proclamation, announcement	نِدَاء
repentance, remorse, regret	نَدَامَة،نَدَم
dampness, moisture	نَدَاوَة
lament, lamenting, wailing	نَدْب

vow, solemn pledge	نَذر (نُذُور)	lament, lamentation, dirge	نُدْبَة
base, low, mean	نَذْل/نَذِيْل	heart attack	نَدْبَة قَلْبِيَّة
warner, harbinger	نَذِير (نُذُر)	rare, scare, strange	نَدْر
narcissus	نَرْجِس/نِرْجِس	rarity, scarcity, rareness	نَدْرَة/نُدْرَة
backgammon, dice	نَرْد		
nervousness	نَرْفَزَة	carding, combing	نَدْف
leakage, seepage	نَزّ/نَزَازَة	repentance, remorse, regret	نَدَم
tending, leaning, having an inclination	نَزَّاع	regretful, remorseful, repentant	نَدْمَان (نَدَامَى)
fight, struggle, dispute, controversy	نِزَاع	council, association, club	نَدْوَة
purity, probity, uprightness	نَزَاهة	literary club	نَدْوَة عِلْمِيّة
sensuality, passion, lust	نَزّة/نِزّة	night club	نَدْوَة لَيْلِيّة
draining, drainage	نَزْح	scarcity, rarity	نُدُورَة
muddy water	نَزَح	moist, damp, wet	نَدِي
little, scant, small quantity	نَزْر/نَزِير	dew, moistness, wetness	نَدَّى (أَنْدَاء)
removal, taking away, withdrawal	نَزْع	open-handed, generous	نَدِي الكَفّ
disarmament	نَزْع السِّلَاح	equal, alike, rival	نَدِيد
expropriation	نَزْع المِلْكِيّة	companion, friend, favourite	نَدِيم (نُدَمَاء)
tendency, inclination, stand	نَزْعَة (نَزَعَات)	baseness, meanness, rascality	نَذَالَة

getting off, descending, alighting, falling	نُزُول	satanic inspiraton	نَزْغ الشَّيْطَان
rainfall	نُزُول المَطَر	incitement, dissension	نَزْغ/نَزْغَة (نَزَغَات)
falling, recessive	نُزُولِي	exhaustion, draining	نَزْف
faraway, remote, distant	نَزِيح	haemorrhage, loss of blood	نَزْف الدَّم
passionate, sensual, inconstant	نَزِيز	rashness, recklessness, thoughtlessness	نَزَق
exhausted by loss of blood	نَزِيف	rash, hasty, reckless, thoughtless	نَزِق
guest, inmate, lodger	نَزِيل (نُزَلَاء)	food served to a guest	نُزْل (أَنْزَال)
pure, honest, upright, virtuous	نَزِيه (نُزَهَاء)	inn, hotel, hostel, lodging	نَزْل (نُزُول/نُزُل)
women	نِساء	cold, catarrh	نَزْلَة (نَزَلَات)
feminine, womanly	نِسَائِي	purity, probity, uprightness	نَزَه
weaver	نَسَّاج	pure, honest, upright, virtuous	نَزِه)
weaving, weaver's trade	نِسَاجَة	excursion, outing, trip, entertainment, picnic	نُزْهَة (نُزَه/نُزْهَات)
transcriber, copyist	نَسَّاخ		
chaff	نُسَافَة	sally, surge, eruption, leap	نَزْوَة
lineage, relationship, affinity	نَسَب (أَنْسَاب)	migration, emigration	نُزُوح
ascription, relationship, affinity, proportion, ratio	نِسْبَة	faraway, distant	نَزُوح

forgetfulness, oblivion	نَسْي/نِسْيَان	death rate	نِسْبَة المَوْت
forgetful, oblivious	نَسِيّ/نَسْيَان	percentage	نِسْبَة مِئَوِيّة
texture, textile, woven fabric	نَسِيج (نُسُج/أَنْسِجَة)	relative, proportional, percentile	نِسْبِي
spider web, cobweb	نَسِيج العَنْكَبُوت	weaving	نَسْج
vascular tissue	نَسِيج وِعَائِي	abolition, abrogation	نَسْخ
well-arranged, in good order, symmetrical	نَسِيق	copy, transcript, recipe	نُسْخَة (نُسَخ)
fresh air, gentle breeze	نَسِيم (نِسَام)	eagle, vulture	نَسْر (نُسُور)
sea-breeze	نَسِيم البَحْر	destruction, dissipation	نَسْف
arising, evolution, generation	نَشْء	arranging, putting in order	نَسْق
new or young generation	نَشْء جَدِيد	order, arrangement, system	نَسَق
growth, genesis, birth	نَشْأَة	devoutness, piety, sacrifice	نُسْك/نُسُك
rebirth, renaissance	نَشْأَة مُسْتَأْنِفَة	progeny, issue, offspring, generation	نَسْل (أَنْسَال)
aroma, scent, perfume	نَشَاً	breath of life	نَسَم (أَنْسَام)
arrows	نُشَّاب	soul, person, creature	نَسَمَة (نَسَمَات)
sawyer	نَشَّار	breath of air	نَسَمَة هَوَاء
sawdust	نُشَارَة	women	نِسْوَة
liveliness, activeness, activity, agility, zeal, vigour	نَشَاط	feminine, womanly	نِسْوِي

intoxicated, drunk	نَشْوَان	atomic energy	نَشَاط ذَرِّي
intoxication, inebriety	نَشْوَة	blotting paper	نَشَاف
ecstasy, elation, rapture	نَشْوَة الطَّرَب	pickpocket	نَشَّال
resurrection	نُشُور	mark, target, goal, medal	نِشَان
discord, animosity, disobedience	نُشُوز	property, possession	نَشَب
snuff	نُشُوق	spreading, publication, promulgation	نَشْر
starchy	نَشَوِي	propaganda	نَشْر الدَّعْوَة
anthem, hymn (نَشَائِد)	نَشِيد	publication, publishing	نَشْر الكُتُب
serenade	نَشِيد لَيْلِي	advertisement, (نَشَرَات) publication, notice	نَشْرَة
royal anthem	نَشِيد مَلَكِي	weekly publication	نَشْرَة أُسْبُوْعِيَّة
national anthem	نَشِيد وَطَنِي/قَوْمِي	periodical publication	نَشْرَة دَوْرِيَّة
active, lively, agile, spirited	نَشِيط	elevated place (أَنْشَاز)	نَشَز
text, phrase, expression, term (نُصُوص)	نَصّ	active, lively, agile, spirited	نَشِط/نَشِيط
swindler, imposter	نَصَّاب	seepage, infiltration water	نَشْع
handle, hilt, halt (نُصُب)	نِصَاب	inhaling, inhalation	نَشْق
obviousness, cleanliness, purity	نَصَاعَة	pocket picking	نُشْل
installation, erection, settin up	نَصْب	growth, development, evolution	نُشُوء
fatigue, toil, drudgery	نَصَب		

نَصْل (نُصُوْل/نِصَال) spearhead, arrowhead, blade	نَصَب (أَنْصَاب) planted flag, a raised flag
نَصُوح sincere, true	نُصُب تَذْكَارِي monument
نَصِيْب (نُصُب/أَنْصِبَاء) share, portion, lot	نُصُب/نُصْب idol, statue
نَصِيْحَة (نَصَائِح) good advice, counsel	نُصْبَة signpost, post, guidepost
نَصِيْر (نُصَرَاء) helper, protector, follower	نَصْبَة (نَصْبَات) plant
نَصِيْع clean, pure, obvious	نَصْح/نُصْح advice, council
نَصِيْف veil	نَصْر victory, triumph, help
نَضّ cash, hard money	نَصْرَانِي Christian
نَضَّاحَة sprinkler	نُصْرَة help, assistance, aid
نَضَارَة freshness, bloom, gracefulness	نِصْف الدَّائِرَة semicircle
نِضَال struggle, fight, contest, despute	نِصْف/نُصْف (أَنْصَاف) half, middle
نَضْج/نُضْج ripeness, maturity	نِصْف الْكُرَة hemisphere
نَضْح sprinkling, watering, exudation	نِصْف اللَّيْل midnight
نُضُد tables	نِصْف النَّهَار midday, noon
نَضَد (أَنْضَاد) bedstead	نِصْف سَاعَة half an hour
نَضِر/نَضِيْر fresh, beautiful, bloomy	نِصْف سَنَوِي half yearly
نَضْرَة freshness, bloom, splendour	نِصْف شَهْرِي biweekly, fortnightly, semimonthly
	نَصَف/نَصَفَة justice, uprightness
	نِصْفِي half, semi (adj)

speech, utterance, power of speaking نُطْق	dirty, unclean, soiled نَضف/نَضِيف
medical fomentation نَطُول	ripeness, maturity نُضُوج
butted, struck by horns نَطِيح	ripe, mature, well-cooked نَضِيج
optician نَظَّاراتي	in order, in rows نَضِيد
management, supervision, inspection نِظَارَة	mattress, pillow, cushion نَضِيدَة (نَضائد)
eyeglasses, spectacles نَظَّارَة (نَظَّارَات)	fresh, beautiful, bloomy نَضِير
magnifying glass نَظَّارَة مُكَبِّرَة	dirty, unclean, soiled نَضِيف
neatness, cleanliness نَظَافَة	leap, jump, jumping نَطّ
order, discipline, arrangement, poetical composition نِظَام (نُظُم)	skipping the rope نَطّ الحَبْل
constitutional law نِظَام أَسَاسِي	girdle, girth, belt, limit, zone نِطَاق (نُطُق)
the existing order of society نِظَام اجْتِمَاعِي	jump, leap نَطّة
economic system نِظَام اقْتِصَادِي	thrusting, butting نَطْح
quota system نِظَام الحِصَص	thrust, butt نَطْحَة
way of life نِظَام الحَيَاة	watch, guard نَطْر
traffic regulations or laws نِظَام المُرُور	skilled, erudite, experienced, well-informed نَطْس
solar system نِظَام شَمْسِي	a rug of skin نَطْع
military discipline نِظَام عَسْكَري	drop, sperm, semen نُطْفَة (نُطَف)

description, qualification	نَعْت	cosmic system	نِظَام كَوْنِي
		regular, systematic	نِظَامِي
attribute, quality, characteristic, qualifier	نَعْت (نُعُوت)	equal, similar	نَظْر
descriptive, qualifying	نَعْتِي	eyesight, vision, look, insight, view, speculation	نَظَر (أَنْظَار)
female sheep, ewe	نَعْجَة (نِعَاج)	glance, look, view	نَظْرَة (نَظَرَات)
noise, clamour, din	نَعْرَة	general view	نَظْرَة إِجْمَالِيَّة
gadfly, horsefly	نُعَرَة	farewell look	نَظْرَة الوَدَاع
sleepy, drowsy	نَعْسَان	visual, theoretical	نَظَرِي
slumber, doze	نَعْسَة	theory, theorem	نَظَرِيَّة
bier, coffin	نَعْش	atomic theory	نَظَرِيَّة ذَرِّيَّة
death song	نَعْشَة المَوْت	individualism, individuality	نَظَرِيَّة فَرْدِيَّة
shoe, boot	نَعْل (نِعَال)	order, arrangement, system, system of regulations	نَظْم
yes, yea, surely	نَعَم		
live stock, stock of cattle or sheep, etc.	نَعَم (أَنْعَام)	versification	نَظْم الأَشْعَار
blessing, favour, grace, boon	نَعْمَاء	similar, parallel, equal	نَظِير (نُظَرَاء/نَظَائِر)
ease, comfort, prosperity	نَعْمَة	neat, clean	نَظِيف
		croaking, cawing	نُعَاب
boon, blessing, grace	نِعْمَة (نِعَم)	sleepiness, drowsiness, slumber	نُعَاس
happiness, prosperity	نُعْمَى	ostrich	نَعَام (نَعَائِم)

childbed, childbirth, confinement نِفَاس	tenderness, delicacy, smoothness نُعُوْمَة
rivalry, competition, contest نِفَاس	who announces a death نَعِيّ
hypocrisy, dissimulation نِفَاق	news of death نَعْيَة
falls off نُفَاضَة	noise, din, roar, clamour نَعِير
refuse, offal, throw out نُفَايَة	ease, comfort, happiness, felicity نَعِيْم
pinch of snuff نَفَّة	flirtation, dallying, teasing نَغَاشَة
expectoration نَفْث	illegitimate child, bastard نَغْل/نَغِيْل
erotic poetry نَفْث الشَّيْطَان	
expectoration, saliva نَفْثَة (نَفَثَات)	symphony, consonance of sound نَغْم/نَغَم
boasting, bragging نَفْج	tone, melody, sound نَغْمَة/نَغَمَة
puff of wind, fragrance نَفْحَة (نَفَحَات)	
blowing, inflating نَفْخ	bastardy, illegitimacy نُغُوْلَة
puff, blow, gust نَفْخَة	refuse, waste matter نَفَاة
orifice, hole, outlet, wayout نَفَذ (أَنْفَاد)	sorceress نَفَّاثَة
troop, band, party, individual نَفَر (أَنْفَار)	braggart, boastful نَفَّاج
dislike, aversion نَفْرَة	windy, flatulent نَفَّاخ
breath, puff نَفَس (أَنْفَاس)	exhaustion, consumption نَفَاد
soul, spirit, life, person نَفْس (نُفُوس/أَنْفُس)	penetration, execution, effectuation نَفَاذ

aversion, dislike, flight, estrangement	نُفُور	instigating self of a man	نَفْس أَمَّارة
shy, timid, reticent, self-conscious	نَفُور	confined, in childbed	نَفْسَاء
very useful	نَفُوع	psychic, mental	نَفْسَانِي
denial, negation, rejection, banishment	نَفْي	psychological, spiritual, mental	نَفْسِي
denied, discarded, rejected	نَفِي	psyche, mentality	نَفْسِيَّة
netative	نَفْيٌ نَفْيِيّ	wool	نَفَش
party, group, band	نَفِير	shaken off	نَفَض
precious, costly	نَفِيس	petroleum	نَفْط
gem, object of value	نَفِيسَة (نَفَائِس)	blister, vesicle	نُفْطَة
scouting party	نَفِيضَة (نَفَائِض)	advantage, profit, use, avail, utility	نَفْع
purity, cleanness	نَقَاء/نَقَاوَة	public utility	نَفْع عَامّ
punch	نَقَّاب	tunnel, subway, passageway	نَفَق (أَنْفَاق)
veil	نِقَاب (نُقُب)	expenditure, expenses, maintainance	نَفَقَة (نَفَقَات/نِفَاق)
union, association	نِقَابَة	supererogation, supererogatory services	نَفْل
trade union	نِقَابَة العُمَّال	booty, spoil, loot, gift	نَفَل (أَنْفَال)
syndicated, corporation	نِقَابَة تِجَارِيَّة	influence, authority, effectiveness	نُفُوذ
critic, reviewer	نَقَّاد	forceful influence	نُفُوذ قَوِي
small drum	نَقَّارَة	full authority	نُفُوذ مُطْلَق
painter, sculptor	نَقَّاش		

experienced doctor, gout	نقْرِس /نقْرِيْس	debate, discussion, argument	نقَاش
jump, leap	نقْزَة	painting, sculpture	نقَاشَة
painting, engraving, inscription	نقْش (نُقُوش)	infusion	نُقَاعَة
		frog	نقَّاقة
lack, shortage, loss, decrease, deficiency	نقْص	portable, transportable	نقَّال
fault, lack, defect, deficiency, damage	نُقْصَان	stretcher, transport vehicle	نقَّالَة
breach, violation, refutation, undoing	نقْض	recovery, convalescence	نقَاهَة
rubble, rubblestone	نُقْض (أَنْقَاض)	excavation, digging, perforating	نقْب
reversal of a sentence	نقْض الحُكْم	hole, opening, perforation	نقْب (نقَاب/أَنْقَاب)
breach of peace	نقْض السَّلَام	criticism	نقْد
breach of faith, breach of promise	نقْض العَهْد	cash, ready money	نقْد (نُقُود)
		cash, ready money	نقْد حاضِر
point, full stop, spot, item, position, site	نُقْطَة (نُقَط)	monetary, pecuniary	نقْدِي
key position	نُقْطَة أَسَاسِيَّة	carving, engraving, inscribing	نقْر
point of contact, junction	نُقْطَة الاتِّصَال	angry, offended	نقِر
fortified position	نُقْطَة الارْتِكَاز	hollow, cavity, pit	نُقْرَة (نُقَر)
interrogtion mark	نقْطَة الاسْتِفْهَام	rap, blow, knock	نقْرَة (نقَرات)
		small drum	نقْرَزَان

convalescence, recovery	نَقه/نَقْهَة	starting point	نُقْطَة الائْطِلاق
hard cash	نُقود الحَجَر	police station	نقْطَة البُوْلِيْس
counterfeit money	نُقود زَائفَة	turning point	نُقْطَة التَّحَوُّل
wedding gift	نُقُوط الزَّوَاج	pivot, crucial point	نُقْطَة الدَّائرَة
dried fruit	نَقُوع	mole, beauty spot	نُقْطَة العَنْبَر
pure, clean, immaculate	نَقِي (نقَاء/أَنْقِيَاء)	combat area	نُقْطَة القتَال
chief, head, leader, captain	نَقِيْب (نُقَبَاء)	fire station	نُقْطَة المَطَافِئ
virtue, excellence, good trait	نَقِيْبَة (نَقَائب)	full stop, stop	نُقْطَة الوَقْف
tiny or worthless thing	نَقِير	custom house	نُقْطَة جُمْرُكِيَّة
defect, fault, shortcoming	نَقِيْصَة (نَقَائص)	soaking, steeping, infusion	نَقْع
contrary to, opposite, opposition, contrast	نَقِيْض	transport, carriage, conveyance, transfer, transcription, copying	نَقْل
infusion	نَقِيْع	candy, sweets, desserts	نَقْل (نُقُول)
croak, croaking	نَقِيْق	blood transfusion	نَقْل الدَّم
marriage, matrimony	نكَاح	migration	نُقْلة
morganatic marriage	نكَاح المُتْعَة	traditional, unwritten	نَقْلي
example, warning, punishment	نكَال	vengeance, revenge, grudge, spite	نقْمَة
vanquish, harm, vexation, annoyance, spite	نكَايَة	revenge, grudge, spite, affliction	نقْمَة/نَقمَة (نقَم)
		recovering, convalescent	نَقه

withdrawal, retreat نُكُوص	calamity, نَكْب (نُكُوب)
denial, disapproval نَكِير	disaster, misfortune
calmumny, slander نَمَّ	misfortune, نَكْبَة (نَكَبَات)
talebearer, نَمّ (أَنِمَّاء)	calamity, disaster
slanderer	joke, witty نُكْتَة (نُكَت/نِكَات)
growth, increase نَمَاء	saying, spot, speck
slanderer, calumniator نَمَّام	breach, violation نَكْث
luse نِمَّة	ill-tempered, peevish, نَكِد
leopard, tiger نَمِر (نُمُر)	petulant
leopardess, tigress نَمِرَة	misfortune, نَكْد (أَنْكَاد)
spot, speck نُمْرَة	trouble, adversity
cushion, pillow نُمْرُق (نَمَارِق)	denial, disavowal نُكْر
mongoose نِمْس (نُمُوس)	denial, disavowal نُكْرَان
freckled نَمِش	ingratitude, نُكْرَان الجَمِيْل
fashion, way, نَمَط(أَنْمَاط)	thanklessness
mode, manner, sort	self-denial نُكْرَان الذَّات
prickle, tickling نَمَل	infedinite noun نَكِرَة
nimble, light, creepy نَمِل	relapse, نُكْس/نَكْسَة
ant نَمْل/نَمْلَة	degeneration
growth, progress نُمُوّ	parotid gland نَكَفَة
model, نَمُوْذَج (نَمَاذج)	parotid نَكَفِي
example, specimen	nickel نِكْل
exemplary, typical, نَمُوْذَجِي	shackles, نِكْل (نُكُول/أَنْكَال)
model	fetters
	smell of the breath, نَكْهَة
	flavour, fragrance

full grown breast, نَهْد (نُهُود) rise, elevation	growth, augmentation, نَمِيّ accretion
river, large stream نَهْر (أَنْهُر/أَنْهَار)	talebearing, نَمِيْمَة (نَمَائِم) calumny
opportunity, occasion نُهْزَة	limit, end, termination نِهَاء
rising, rise, awakening نَهْض	ultimate, last, final, نِهَائِي conclusive
rise, rising, نَهْضَة (نَهْضَات) upswing, resurgence, revival	at last, finally نِهَائِيًّا
exhaustion, wasting away, consumption نَهْك	plunderer, robber, نَهَّاب spoiler
exhaustion, emaciation نَهْكَة	day, day time نَهَار
greed, avidity, gluttony نَهَم	by day and night نَهَارًا ولَيْلاً
voracious, greedy, نَهِم/نَهِيْم avid, glutton	opportunist نَهَّاز الفُرَص
rising, growth, نُهُوض promotion, advancement	biting, sharp, snappish نَهَّاش
reason, intellect, نُهَى intelligence	bray, braying نُهَاق
prohibition, inhibition, نَهْي forbidance	end, termination, نِهَايَة utmost degree
panting, rapid breathing نَهِيْج	plunder, loot, pillage, نَهْب robbery
rivulet, streamlet نُهَيْر	booty, spoils, loot نُهْبَة/نُهْبَى
bray, braying نَهِيق	manner, method, نَهْج (نُهُوج) main road
voracious, greedy, نَهِيْم avid, glutton	the right way, نَهْج قَوِيْم proper manner
	panting, rapid breathing نَهَج/نَهِيْج

gas light	نُور الغَاز	prohibitive,	نَهْيِي
searchlight	نُور كَشَّاف	prohibitory, inhibitory	
electric light	نُوْر كَهْرَبَائِي	hurricane,	نَوْء (أَنْوَاء)
luminous, shining	نُورَانِي	tempest, storm	
luminous, lighting	نُوْرِي	pits, kernel,	نَوَاة (نَوَيَات)
kind, type, sort,	نَوْع (أَنْوَاع)	nucleus	
quality, nature		atomic nucleus	نَوَاة الذَّرَّة
human race	نَوْع إِنْسَانِي	mourner, wailer	نَوَّاح
specific, peculiar	نَوْعِي	wailing,	نُوَاح/نَوْح
excess, surplus	نَوْف (أَنْوَاف)	lamentation, mourning	
fountain	نَوْفَرَة (نَوَافِر)	hired mourner	نَوَّاحة
November	نُوْفمْبِر	(female)	
giving, granting,	نَوْل (أَنْوَال)	swinging, dangling	نَوَّاس
gift, freight		sleeper, slumberer	نَوَّام
freightage, freight	نَوْلُون	turn, shift,	نَوْبَة (نُوَب)
sleep, slumber	نَوْم	occasion, rotation	
sleep, nap	نَوْمَة	fit, paroxysm	نَوْبَة (نَوْبَات)
nuclear, nucleal	نَوَوِي	nervous criss	نَوْبَة عَصَبِيَّة
distance, remoteness	نَوًى	misfortune,	نُوْبَة (نُوَب)
representation,	نِيَابَة	calamity	
substitution, delegation		seaman, sailor, mariner	نُوْتِي
wailing, loud	نِيَاح/نِيَاحَة	wailing,	نَوْح
weeping		lamentation, mourning	
intention, purpose,	نِيَّة (نِيَّات)	light, lamp,	نُوْر (أَنْوَار)
resolution		brightness, glow	
		search light	نُوْر كَاشِف

bring me, give me	هَات	nitrogen	نِيتُرُوجِين
these (dual f.)	هَاتَان	shining, luminous, bright	نَيِّر
shouting, making loud outcry	هَاتِف	meteor, shooting star	نَيْزَك
telephone	هَاتِف (هَوَاتِف)	small lance, shooting star	نَيْزَك (نَيَازِك)
mobile phone	هَاتِف جَوَّال	April	نِيسَان
telephonic	هَاتِفِي	surplus, overplus	نَيِّف
defamer, slanderer, satirist	هَاجٍ	fastidious, dainty, hard to please	نَيِّق
notion, idea, anxiety, apprehension	هَاجِس (هَوَاجِس)	nicle	نِيكِل
guide, leader, leading	هَادٍ (هُدَاة)	getting, obtainment, attainment	نَيْل
quiet, calm, tranquil	هَادِئ	indigo	نِيلَح
composed, at ease, peaceful	هَادِئ البَال	white water lily	نِيلُوفَر
calm, quiet, confident	هَادِئ القَلْب	nylon	نَيْلُون

destructive, destroyer, demolisher	هَادِم	these (plu. m/f)	هَؤُلَاء
raving, delirious, crazy	هَاذ	excited, agitated, stirring, enraged	هَائِج
fugitive, runaway	هَارِب	frightful, terrible, dreadful, formidable	هَائِل
scorner, mocker, scoffer	هَازِئ	madly in love, confused, baffled	هَائِم (هُيَّم)
cheerful, gay, blithe, crisp	هَاشّ	falling, descending	هَابِط

soot, smut	هِبَاب	famished, faint with hunger	هَافّ
gust, sudden blast of wind	هَبَّة	mirage	هَال
gift, grant, donation, bounty	هِبَة (هِبَات)	halo of the moon	هَالَة
meat, flesh	هَبْر	perishing, mortal, doomed to perdition	هَالِك
lowering, reducing, diminution	هَبْط	important, serious, momentous	هَامّ
descent, fall, pit	هَبْطَة	top, summit, head	هَامَة
mirage, swift, nimble	هَبْهَاب	vermin, pests	هَامَّة (هَوَامّ)
strong wind, dust-laden wind	هَبُوب	extinct, quiescent, quiet, still	هَامِد
blowing of wind	هُبُوب	margin	هَامِش
fall, descent, landing, sinking, reduction	هُبُوط	marginal	هَامِشِي
slope, declivity	هَبُوط	happy, delighted, pleased	هَانِئ
emergency landing	هُبُوط اِضْطِرَارِي	here	هَاهُنَا
cowardly, dolt, booby	هَبِيْت	amateur, in love, falling	هَاوٍ (هُوَاة)
hyena	هُبَيْرَة	mortar	هَاوُن/هَاوُوْن
cry, crying, shouting, exclamation	هُتَاف	abyss, hell, bottomless pit	هَاوِيَة
acclamation, shout of applause	هُتَاف الاِسْتِحْسَان	fine dust	هَبَاء
war cry	هُتَاف الحَرْب	scattered atoms of dust	هَبَاء مَنْثُور
		fine dust	هَبَاب

attack, onset, (هَجَمَات) هَجْمَة	chip, fragment, breakage هُتَامَة
counterattack هَجْمَة مُعَاكَسَة	drivel, twaddle, lie (أَهْتَار) هِتْر
defect, fault, blemish هُجْنَة	cry, shout هَتْفَة
defamation, ridiculing, satire, mockery هَجْو	tearing, rending, disgracing هَتْك
slumber, sleep, lul, quiescence هُجُوع	disclosure, uncovering هَتْك الأَسْتَار
flank attack هُجُوم جَانِبِي	rape, ravishment هَتْك العِرْض
air attack هُجُوم جَوِّي	disgrace, infamy, scandal هَتِيكَة
aggressive, violent هُجُومِي	defamation, derision, satire هِجَاء
defamatory, satiric, disparaging هَجْوِي	satiric, defamatory هِجَائِي
midday, midday heat هَجِير/هَجِيرَة	quack, braggard, vain boaster هَجَّاس
low, of low birth, base (هُجُن) هَجِين	leaving, abandonment, desertion هَجْر
racing camel (هَجَائِن) هَجِينَة	obscene language هُجْر/هَجْرَاء
demolition, breaking, pulling down هَدّ	exodus, emigration, departure هِجْرَة
quietness, calmness, tranquillity هَدْأ	nonsense, foolish talk, thought, notion هَجْس
fringe, edging هُدَّاب	notion, (هَجَسَات) هَجْسَة thought, idea, anxiety
raging, roaring, surging هَدَّار	slumber, sleep هَجْعَة
waterfall هَدَّارَة	

way, direction, method, manner	هَدْية/هِدْيَة	marksman, good shot	هَدّاف
roar, uproar, surge, rumbling	هَدِير	destructive, ruinous	هَدّام
this (mas.)	هَذَا	guidance, right way	هِدَايَة
delirium, raving, drivels	هُذَاء	having long eyelashes	هَدِب
these (dual mas.)	هَذَان	eyelashes	هُدْب (أَهْدَاب)
idle talk, prattle	هَذْر	thud, crash	هَدَّة
prattler, babbler	هَذِر	tumble, spill, heavy fall	هُدْر
this (fem.)	هذه	uselessly, in vain	هَدْرًا
this time, on this occasion	هذه المَرَّة	target, objective, aim, goal	هَدَف (أَهْدَاف)
raving, delirium, craze	هَذَيَان	demolition, destruction, pulling down	هَدْم
cat, tom cat	هِرّ (هِرَرَة)	quietness, stillness, tranquillity	هُدْنة (هُدْنَات)
nonsense, prattle, idle talk	هُرَاء	hoopoe	هُدْهُدْ
quarrel, fight, wrangle	هِرَاش	quietness, calmness, tranquillity	هُدُوْء
hurry, haste	هُرَاع	quietness, stillness, tranquillity	هُدُون
stick, cudgel	هَرَاوَة	guidance, right way	هُدَى
flight, get away, escape	هَرَب	way, path, manner	هَدْي
runaway, fugitive	هَرْبَان	gift, present, offering	هَدِيَّة (هَدَايَا)
cat	هِرَّة (هِرَر)	wedding present	هَدِيَّة الزَّوَاج

object of ridicule, laughing stock	هُزْأَة	commotion, disorder, disturbance, confusion	هَرْج
derisive, mocking	هُزْئِي	confusion, hubhub, tumult, agitation, turmoil	هَرْج ومَرْج
jesting, joking	هِزَار		
shaking, rocking, moving	هَزَّاز	confusion, muddle, disturbance, disorder	هَرْجَلَة
leanness, thinness, emaciation	هُزَال	scratching, wear & tear	هَرْش
joker, jester	هَزَّال	heresy	هَرْطَقَة
shake, trembling, stir, agitation, shock	هَزَّة (هَزَّات)	heretic	هَرْطُوقِي
earthquake	هَزَّة أَرْضِيّة	haste, rush	هَرَع
orgasm	هَزَّة الجِمَاع	senility, old age	هَرَم
rapture, excitement	هَزَّة السُّرُور	decrepit, senile, old	هَرِم
rapture, ecstasy	هَزَّة الطَّرَب	Pyramid	هَرَم (أَهْرَام)
joking, jesting, fun making	هَزْل	hormone	هَرْمُون
jocker, jester	هَزِل	flight, escape	هُرُوب
humorous, funny, jocular	هَزْلِي	quick pace, hasty walk	هَرْوَلَة
defeating, vanquishing	هَزْم	growling, yelping	هَرِير
convulsion, commotion, agitation	هَزْهَزَة	kitten	هُرَيْرَة
		a meat dish	هَرِيْسَة
emaciated, very lean	هَزِيل	shaking, moving, stirring	هَزَّ
thunder, rumble	هَزِيْم	derision, ridicule, mockery	هُزْء/هَزْء

shining, flashing, sparkling هَفَّاف	defeat, rout, discomfiture هَزِيْمَة (هَزَائِم)
exhausted, faint with hunger هَفْتَان	whisper, soliloquy هَسّ
slender, thin, slim هَفْهَاف	hush! silence! هُسّ/هُشّ
whispering of the wind هَفْهَفَة	hysteria هِسْتِيْرِيا
lapse, slip, fault هَفْوَة (هَفَوَات)	whisper, susurration هَسِيْس
thus, in this way هَكَذَا	brittle, fragile, crisp, cheerful هَشّ
particle of interrogation هَل	hush! silence! هُشّ
why not? هَلَّا	soft, friable, easily crumbled, cheerful هَشَّاش
perdition, total loss, ruin هَلَاك	cheerfulness, gaiety هَشَاشَة
new moon, crescent, parethesis هِلَال (أَهِلَّة)	soft, fragile هَشِيْش
lunar, crescent-shaped هِلَالِي	fragile, frail, feeble هَشِيْم
jelly, gelatin هُلَام	hill, elevation, mound هَضْبَة (هِضَاب)
jelly-like, gelatinous هُلَامِي	digestion, process of digesting هَضْم
hairy, hirsute, shaggy هَلِب	digestive, digestant هَضُوم
bristles, hair هُلَب	digestigble, digested هَضِيْم
anchor, grapnel, hook هِلْب (أَهْلَاب)	pouring down هُطُول
debauchery, derilium, nonsense, consumption هَلْس	downpour, continuous rainfall هُطُول الأَمْطار
impatience, dismay, restlessness هَلَع	light, light-headed, fickle هِفّ

savagery, barbarism هَمَجِيّة	impatient, restless, appalled هَلِع
downpour, heavy shower هَمْرَة	death, destruction, perdition هُلْك
spurring, goading, pressing, backbiting هَمْز	perdition, ruin, destruction هَلْكَة/هَلَكَة
backbiter, slanderer هُمَزَة	fright, consternation هَلَل
whisper, mumble, susurration هَمْس	come! come on! هَلُمَّ
whisper, mumble هَمْسَة (هَمَسَات)	hallucination, vision, delirium هَلْوَسَة
extinction, quiescence, lull هُمُود	restless, uneasy, dismayed, impatient هَلُوع
they (fem.) هُنَّ	helicopter هَلِيْكُوبتر
here, in this place هُنَا	they (mas.) هُمْ
happiness, bliss, felicitation, prosperity هَنَاء/هَنَاءَة	sorrow, grief, anxiety, care هَمّ (هُمُوم)
there, in that place هُنَاك	backbiter, slanderer هَمَّاز
trifles, unimportant matters هَنَة (هَنَوَات)	energetic, active, vigorous, solicitous هَمَّام
trimness, orderliness, harmony هِنْدَام	brave, gallant, magnanimous, valiant هُمَام
engineering, architecture هَنْدَسَة	ardour, zeal, ambition, vigour هِمَّة (هِمَم)
irrigation engineering هَنْدَسَة الرِّيّ	starvation, savage, gnats هَمَج
architecture هَنْدَسَة العمَارَة	savage, barbaric, uncivilized هَمَجِي

airy, aerial, antenna هَوَائِي	agronomy هَنْدَسَة زِرَاعِيّة
clemency, indulgence, هَوَادَة complaisance	electrical هَنْدَسَة كَهْرَبَائِيَّة engineering
fan, ventilator هَوَّايَة	civil engineering هَنْدَسَة مَدَنِيَّة
pit, hole, cavern (هُوًى) هُوَّة	architecture هَنْدَسَة مِعْمَارِيّة
thoughtlessness, هَوْج rashness	mechanical هَنْدَسَة مِيْكَانِيْكِيَّة engineering
tornado, hurricane هَوْجَاء	geometrical, هَنْدَسِي technical
howdah, litter (هَوَادِج) هَوْدَج	
camel litter هَوْدَج الجِمَال	orderliness, trimness, هَنْدَمَة adjustment
lagoon, lake (أَهْوَار) هَوْر	time هِنْو
peril, danger, jeopardy هَوْرَة	delicious, pleasant, هَنِيّ wholesome
hormone هُورمون	
craze, frenzy, raving, هَوَس infatuation	pleasant, agreeable, هَنِيء comfortable
commotion, هَوْشَة disturbance, tumult, riot	a little while هُنَيْهَة
	for a little while هُنَيْهَةً
hockey هُوكِي	here, in this place, now هَهُنا
terror, horror, (أَهْوَال) هَوْل fright, dread	he, it هو
monster, grotesque هَوْلَة figure	air, wind, (أَهْوَاء/أَهْوِيَة) هَوَاء atmosphere, climate
easiness, comfort, هَوْن convenience	atmospheric air هَوَاء جَوِّي
	open air, fresh air هَوَاء طَلْق
disgrace, disdain هُوْن	compressed air هَوَاء مَضْغُوط

هَيْئَة دِبْلُومَاسِيَّة diplomatic corps	هَوْنًا gently, slowly, unhurriedly
هَيَّا come! come on!	هَوًى (أَهْوَاء) passion, craving, inclination, caprice
هَيَّاب timid, diffident, awful	
هِيَاج agitation, excitement, outbreak, disturbance, fury	هَوًى أَحْمَر sexual intercourse, coition
هِيَام passionate or inordinate love, insatiable thirst	هُوِيّة identity, essence
هَيْبَة dread, awe, dignity, apprehension, respect	هُوَيْنَا slowness, gentleness, leisureliness
	هِيَ she
هَيْتَ لَكَ come here	هَيِّئ good looking, beautiful, handsome
هَيْج excitement, turmoil, commotion	هَيْئَة (هَيْئَات) shape, situation, appearance, association, society, board, organization
هَيْجَا/هَيْجَاء combat, fight, battle	
هَيَجَان excitement, agitation, turmoil	هَيْئَة اجْتِمَاعِيّة human society
هِيْدُروجين hydrogen	هَيْئَة التَّحْكِيم board of arbitration, jury
هِيرُوين heroin	هَيْئَة التَّدْرِيس teaching staff
هَيْشَة turmoil, commotion	هَيْئَة المُحَلَّفِين jury
هَيْضَة cholera, diarrhoea	هَيْئَة المُحَلَّفِين الاتِّهَامِيّة grand jury
هَيْط/هِيَاط shouting, uproar, clamour	هَيْئَة المُحَلَّفِين القَاضِيَة petty jury
هَيْف parching wind	هَيْئَة تَعَاوُنِيّة cooperative corporation
هَيَفَان parched, very thirsty	

heavy downpour, heavy shower	وَابِل
locomotive, engine, railroad train	وَابُور
express train	وَابُور اكْبرِيْس
goods train	وَابُور البضَاعَة
passenger train	وَابُور الرُّكَّاب
steam roller	وَابُور الزَّلَط
steam engine, steamer, steamship	وَابُور بُخَارِي
watt	وَات
confident, sure, certain	وَاثِق
obligatory, necessary, inevitable, essential	وَاجِب
duty, task, obligation, assignment	وَاجِب (وَاجَبَات)
home work	وَاجِب مَنْزِلِي
finder, upset, angry	وَاجِد
disturbing thought, evil premonition	وَاجِس
beating, throbbing, tremulous	وَاجِف
silent, dumfounded, sullen	وَاجِم
oasis	وَاحَة

temple, frame, skeleton	هَيْكَل (هَيَاكِل)
madly in love, lost in love	هَيْمَان
supremacy, control, superintendence	هَيْمَنَة
easy, simple, facile, insignificant, worthless	هَيِّن
ease, easiness, leisure	هِيْنَة
far from…	هَيْهَات
timid, fearful, diffident, awful	هَيُوب
matter, primordial matter	هَيُولَى
pertaining to matter, material	هَيُولِي/هَيُولاَنِي

agreement, concord, harmony	وِئَام
burying daughters alive	وَأْد
deliberate, slow	وَئِيْد
slowly, deliberately	وَئِيْدًا
oh grief! alas! what a pity!	وَا أَسْفَاه

وَاسِع الصَّدْر	generous, forbearing	وَاحِد	one, someone, single, unique
وَاسِع النِّطَاق	extensive, far-reaching	واحَسْرتاه	what a pity
وَاشٍ (وُشَاة)	calumniator, slanderer, backbiter	وَاخِز	stinging, pricking, sharp, pungent
وَاصِب	lasting, permanent	وَادٍ (أَوْدِيَة)	valley, dale
وَاضِح	obvious, clear, manifest, apparent, conspicuous	وَادِع	depositor, consignor, mild
وَاضِح بِذَاته	self-evident, self-explanatory	وَارِث (وَرَثَة)	heir, inheritor
وَاضِع	creator, writer, originator	وَارِث شَرْعِي	legal heir
		وَارِد (وَارِدَات)	imports, receipts
وَاضِعُ القَانُون	legislator, lawmaker	وَارِد (وُرَّاد)	coming, arriving, newcomer
وَاضِع اليَد	occupier, possessor	وَارِدَات وَصَادِرَات	imports and exports
واط	watt	وَارِش	intruder
وَاطٍ	slow, inferior, soft	وَارِق	leafy, verdant
وَاطِئ	low, subdued	وَارِم	swollen, tumefacient
وَاعٍ	attentive, cautious, careful, alert	وَازِن	weighty, of full weight
		وَاسِطَة (وَسَائط)	mediator, mediacy, medium
وَاعِظ	preacher, religious teacher	وَاسِع	broad, wide, large, vast
وَاغِل	intruder, parasite, deep-rooted	وَاسِع الأَرْجاء	vast in extent
		وَاسِع الانْتِشَار	widespread

faint, weak, feeble, exhausted	وَانٍ	faithful, complete, sufficient, enough	وَافٍ
faint, weak, flimsy, frivolous	وَاهٍ (وهاة)	coming, arriving, envoy	وَافِد (وُفُود)
donor, giver	وَاهِب	epidemic	وَافِدَة
phantasy, imagination	وَاهِمَة	abundant, plentiful	وَافِر
weak, feeble, faint	وَاهِن	protective, protector, guardian	وَاقٍ
epidemic, pestilence	وَبَأ/وَبَاء	situated, actual, factual, event, taking palce, occurring	وَاقِع
infected, infested with pestilence	وَبِئ/وَبِيْء		
epidemic, pestilential, infectious	وَبَائي	factual evidence	وَاقِع الحَال
hairy, hirsute	وَبِر	incident, accident, event, fact	وَاقِعَة
fur, soft hair	وَبَر (أَوْبَار)	actual, real, factual	وَاقِعي
rubbish, trash, nonsense	وَبَش	reality, actuality	وَاقِعيَّة
ruffian, riffraff, rabble	وَبَش (أَوْبَاش)	standing, erect, staying	وَاقِف (وُقُوف)
downpour, heavy shower of rain	وَبْل	ruler, governor, administrator	وَالٍ (وُلاَة)
infected, infested with pestilence	وَبِىئ	progenitor, father	وَالِد
		father and mother, parents	وَالِدَان
unhealthy, of evil result	وَبِيْل	mother, woman in childbed	وَالِدَة
peg, stake, pole	وَتَد/وَتِد (أَوْتَاد)	giddy, confused, distracted	وَالِه

idolatory, paganism	وَثَنِيَّة	string, cord, sinew (أَوْثَار)	وَثَر
soft, cozy, smooth, comfortable	وَثِير	vocal cord	وَثَر صَوْتِي
firm, solid, strong	وَثِيق (وِثَاق)	uneven, odd	وَثْر/وِثْر
document, record, voucher, certificate	وَثِيقَة (وَثَائِق)	stringed	وَثَرِي
warrant of attorney	وَثِيقَة التَّفْوِيْض	manner, way, method	وَتِيرَة (وَتَائِر)
marriage certificate	وَثِيقَة الزَّوَاج	bruise, contusion	وَثْء
rope of hemp	وَثِيل	bruise, contusion, wrench	وَثَاءَة
den, lair	وِجَار	leaping, saltant, bouncy, clashing	وَثَّاب
prestige, notability, rank	وَجَاهَة	soft bed	وِثَار
meal, repast	وَجْبَة (وَجَبَات)	bond, tie, fetter	وَثَاق/وِثَاق (وُثُق)
emotion, passion, joy, ecstasy of love	وَجْد	jumping, leaping	وَثْب
ecstasy, intuition, inner consciousness	وِجْدَان	broad jump	وَثْب طَوِيْل
emotional, sentimental	وِجْدَانِي	high jump	وَثْب عَالٍ
cave, cavern	وَجْر (أَوْجَار)	jump, spring, leap	وَثْبَة
pitfall	وَجْرَة/وَجَرَة	soft, cozy, smooth, comfortable	وَثِر
concise, brief, short, summary	وَجْز	rope of hemp	وَثَل
		idol, graven image	وَثَن (أَوْثَان)
		idolator, pagan, idolatrous	وَثَنِي

existence, presence, being, entity	وُجُود	apprehension, anxiety, misgivings	وَجْس
existential, existentialist	وُجُودِي	pain, ache, ailment	وَجْع (أَوْجَاع)
silence, speechlessness	وُجُوم	earache	وَجْع الأُذُن
concise, brief, short, summary	وَجِيز	headache	وَجْع الرَّأْس
painful, grievous	وَجِيع	toothache	وَجْع السِّنّ
throbbing, beating	وَجِيف	afraid, fearful, apprehensive	وَجِل
notable, noted, distinguished	وَجِيه	apprehension, fear, dead	وَجَل (أَوْجَال)
lady of high social standing	وَجِيهَة	gloom, sullenness	وَجْم
strange craving, special appetite	وَحَام/وِحَام	silent, sullen, dumfounded	وَجِم
single, alone, sole, solitary, unequalled	وَحْدَانِي	cheek	وَجْنَة (وَجَنَات)
oneness, unity of God, singleness, loneliness	وَحْدَانِيّة	face, countenance, appearance, surface, manner, reason, objective	وَجْه (وُجُوه)
oneness, loneliness, unity	وَحْدَة	approximately	وَجْه التَّقْرِيب
alone, by himself	وَحْدَه	handsome face	وَجْه كَرِيم
unit, crew, branch office	وَحْدَة (وَحْدَات)	direction, side, intention, objective, regard	وِجْهَة/وُجْهَة
time unit	وَحْدَة الزَّمَن	view point, point of view	وِجْهَة النَّظَر
		facial, of the face	وَجْهِي

stinging, pungent, pricking	وَخَّاز	monogamy	وَحْدَة الزَّوَاج
unhealthiness, unwholesomeness	وَخَامَة	Arab Unity	وَحْدَة عَرَبِيّة
pricking, piercing, stinging	وَخْز	deserted, desolate, wild (animal)	وَحْش
compunctions, remose	وَخْز الضَّمِير	wild animal, wild beast, monster	وَحْش (وُحُوش)
prick, sting	وَخْزَة	desolation, dreariness, alienation, gloom	وَحْشَة
heaviness, dullness, squalor	وَخَم	wild, savage, uncivilized, brutal	وَحْشِي
unwholesome, heavy, squalid	وَخِم	savagery, brutality, wildness	وَحْشِيَّة
intention, design, plan, goal	وَخْي	miry, muddy, covered with mud	وَحِل
unhealthy, bad, unwholesome, heavy	وَخِيم	mire, slime, slough	وَحْل/وَحَل (أَوْحال/وُحُول)
love, affection, amity	وَدّ/وُدّ	longing, craving, appetite	وَحَم
affectionate, loving, sociable	وَدّ/وُدّ (أَوْدَاد)	craving for certain food	وَحْمَى (وِحَام)
jugular vein	وِدَاج	predatory animals	وُحُوش ضَارِية
love, friendship, amity	وَدَاد/وِدَاد	revelation, divine inspiratioin	وَحْي
friendly, amicable	وَدَادِي	alone, solitary, isolated, unique	وَحِيد
farewell, valediction	وَدَاع		
last farewell	وَدَاع أَخِير		

hereditary	وِرَاثي	farewell, adieu!	وَدَاعا
paper manufacturer, stationer	وَرَّاق	mildness, meekness, gentle-heartedness	وَدَاعَة
paper manufacturing	وِرَاقَة	valedictory	وَدَاعي
obliquity, oblique direction	وَرْب (أَوْرَاب)	jogular vein	وَدَج (أَوْدَاج)
inheritance, legacy	وِرْث	depositing, lodging	وَدْع
watering place	وِرْد	fat, grease	وَدَك
supplementary worship	وِرْد (أَوْرَاد)	greasy, fat	وَدِك
rose, flower	وَرْد/وَرْدَة	friendly, attached, devoted	وَدُود
rosy, pink	وَرْدي	friendly, amicable, sociable	وَدِّي/وُدِّي
brisk, lively, frolicsome	وَرِش	fond, friendly, attached	وَدِيد
workshop	وَرْشَة (وَرْشَات)	meek, mild, gentle	وَدِيع
laundry	وَرْشَة غَسِيل	trust, charge	وَدِيعَة (وَدَائِع)
plight, difficult situation, predicament, fix	وَرْطَة (وَرَطَات)	deposit, deposited amount	وَدِيعَة مَالِيّة
piety, piousness, godliness	وَرَع	meadow, lawn	وَدِيقَة (وَدَائِق)
pious, god fearing, godly	وَرِع	greasy, fat	وَدِيك
leafy, verdant	وَرِق	behind, beyond	وَرَاء
paper, leaves, sheet	وَرَق (أَوْرَاق)	behind the scene	وَرَاء الكَوَالِيس
stamped paper	وَرَق الدَّمْغَة	back, rear	وَرَائي
		heredity, inheritance, legacy	وِرَاثَة

swelling, tumour, rising	وَرَم (أَوْرَام)	drawing paper	وَرَق الرَّسْم
varnish, shoepolish	وَرْنِيش	printing paper	وَرَق الطَّبْع
arrival, advent, coming	وُرُود	writing paper	وَرَق الكِتَابَة
mankind	وَرَى	playing card	وَرَق اللَّعِب
heir, inheritor	وَرِيث (وُرَثَاء)	wrapping paper	وَرَق اللَّفّ
vein, jugular vein	وَرِيد (أَوْرِدَة)	banknotes, paper money	وَرَق النَّقْد
goose, geese	وَزّ	tracing paper	وَرَق شَفَّاف
ministry, cabinet	وِزَارَة (وِزَارات)	carbon paper	وَرَق كَرْبُون
ministry of religious endowments, wakf ministry	وِزَارَة الأَوْقَاف	marble paper	وَرَق مُجَزَّع
		wallpaper	وَرَقُ مَزَرْكَش
ministry of information	وِزَارَة الاسْتِعْلاَمَات	stamped paper	وَرَق مَطْبُوع
		blotting paper	وَرَق نَشّاش
ministry of commerce	وِزَارَة التِّجَارَة	blotting paper	وَرَق نَشّاف
ministry of education	وِزَارَة التَّرْبِيَة	paper money	وَرَق نَقْدِي
		leaf, sheet of paper	وَرَقَة
ministry of supply	وِزَارَة التَّمْوِين	bill of indictment	وَرَقَة الاتِّهَام
foreign ministry	وِزَارَة الخَارِجِيَّة	post card	وَرَقَة البَرِيد
home ministry	وِزَارَة الدَّاخِلِيَّة	banknote	وَرَقَة البَنْك
		playing card	وَرَقَة لَعِب
ministry of defence	وِزَارَة الدِّفَاع	banknote	وَرَقَة مَالِيَّة
		stamped sheet	وَرَقَة مَدْمُوغَة
		hip, haunch	وَرْك/وَرِك (أَوْرَاك)

share, portion (وَزَائِع) وَزِيعَة	ministry of وِزَارَة الزِّرَاعَة agriculture
precautionary measures وَسَائِل الاحْتِيَاط	وِزَارَة الشُّؤُون الاجْتِمَاعِيّة ministry of social affairs
educational aids وَسَائِل التَّعْلِيم	وِزَارَة الشُّؤُون الخَارجِيّة ministry of foreign affairs
means of وَسَائِل المُوَاصَلَات communications	وِزَارَة الصِّحَّة العُمُومِيَّة ministry of public health
transportation, وَسَائِل النَّقْل conveyance, means of transportation	aviation وِزَارَة الطَّيَرَان ministry
dirtiness, filthiness وَسَاخَة	ministry of وِزَارَة العَدْل justice
pillow, وَسَاد/وِسَاد (وُسُد) cushion	finance ministry وِزَارَة المَالِيّة
pillow, وِسَادَة (وَسَائِد) cushion	ministry of وِزَارَة المُوَاصَلَات communication
mediation, وِسَاطَة intercession	ministerial وِزَارِي
decoration, وِسَام (أَوْسِمَة) medal	sin, crime, heavy (أَوْزَار) وِزْر burden
beauty, grace, وَسَامَة comliness	loincloth وِزْرَة
dirty, filthy, unclean, وَسِخ soiled	weight, metre, (أَوْزَان) وَزْن measure
dirt, filth (أَوْسَاخ) وَسَخ	minister, وَزِير (وُزَرَاء) secretary
middle, وَسْط/وَسَط (أَوْسَاط) centre, heart, central point	foreign minister وَزِيرُ الخَارجِيّة
	home minister وَزِير الدَّاخِلِيّة
midsummer وَسَط الصَّيْف	minister of وَزِير الطَّيَرَان aviation

wide, spacious, vast وَسِيع		midway, middle وَسَط الطَّرِيْق of the way
means, medium, (وَسَائل) وَسِيْلَة instrument, measure		medial, central, وَسْطَانِي intermediate
beautiful, (وُسَمَاء/وسَام) وَسِيْم comely, graceful		of environment وَسْطِي/وَسَطِي
scarf, (أَوْشِحَة/وَشَائح) وِشَاح band, tie, swordbelt		capability, capacity, وُسْع ability
sword وِشَاحَة		wideness, roominess, وُسْعَة extent
defamation, وِشَايَة calumniation		load, cargo, (وُسُوق) وَسْق charge
quickness, وَشْك/وُشْك swiftness		cargo, shipment وَسْق المَرْكَب
swiftness, وَشْكَان/وُشْكَان quickness		whiskey وِسْكِي
tattoo, tattoo (وِشَام) وَشْم mark		brand, mark (وُسُوم) وَسْم
		slumber, doze وَسَن
whisper, whispering وَشْوَشَة		drowsy, sleepy وَسِن
close tie (وَشَائج) وَشِيْجَة		sleepy, drowsy وَسْنَان
hedge وَشِيْع		temptation, (وَسَاوِس) وَسْوَاس evil suggestion, misgiving
reel, shuttle وَشِيْعَة		
imminent, impending وَشِيْك		temptation, (وَسَاوِس) وَسْوَسَة evil suggestion, rustle, suspicion
hostility, malice وَشِيْمَة		
instruction, وَصَاة/وَصَايَة counsel, direction		middle, medial, وَسِيْط intermediary
depicter, artist, وَصَّاف painter		means, (وَسَائط) وَسِيْطَة medium

testament, وَصِيَّة (وَصَايا) advice, counsel, injunction	communication, وِصَال connection, communion
threshold, وَصِيْد (وُصُد) doorstep	guardianship, وِصَايَة executorship
servant, lad وَصِيْف	lasting وَصَب (أَوْصَاب) illness, suffering
maid servant, (وَصَائِف) وَصِيْفَة lass	description, depiction وَصْف
intimate friend, chum وَصِيْل	quality, وَصْف (أَوْصَاف) attribute, characteristic
bright, brilliant, pure وُضَّاء	portrayal, description, وَصْفَة prescription
purity, cleanliness, وَضَاءَة brightness	depictive, qualitative, وَصْفِي descriptive
bright, shining, وَضَّاح radiant, luminous	connecting, relation, وَصْل connection, junction, link
humbleness,lowliness, وَضَاعَة baseness	limb, part وُصْل/وِصل (أَوْصَال) of body
brightness, وَضَح (أَوْضَاح) radiance, brilliance	وُصْلَة (وُصْلَات/وُصَل)
putting, placing, pose, وَضْع posture	connection, link, joint, attachment
condition, وَضْع (أَوْضَاع) position, situation, usage, circumstance	stigma, disgrace, وَصْم/وَصْمَة blemish
present situation وَضْع حَالي	arrival, reaching, وُصُول attainment, receipt
situation, وَضْعَة/وِضْعَة position, posture	receipt, وُصُول (وُصُولَات) voucher
situational, positional, وَضْعِي positive	testator, legal وَصِيّ (أَوْصِيَاء) guardian, executor, trustee

functional	وَظِيْفِي	ablution, cleanliness	وُضُوْء
vessel, receptacle	وِعَاء (أَوْعِيَة)	water for ablution	وَضُوْء
blood vessel	وِعَاء دَمَوِي	clarity, clearness	وُضُوْح
vascular	وِعَائِي	pure, clean, bright	وَضِيْء
hard, difficult, tiresome	وَعْث/وَعِث	mean, base, low, humble	وَضِيْع (وُضَعَاء)
hardship, difficulty, toils	وَعْثَاء	deposit, trust	وَضِيْعَة (وَضَائِع)
promise	وَعْد	treading, sexual intercourse	وَطْء
parole	وَعْد شَرَف	low, flat	وَطِئ
rugged, rough, hard, riven	وَعْر/وَعِير	pressure, constraint, coercion	وَطْأَة
sermon, lesson, admonition, preaching	وَعْظ	desire, wish, aim, object	وَطَر (أَوْطَار)
indisposed, ill, unwell	وَعْك	home, homeland, native place	وَطَن (أَوْطَان)
indisposition, sultriness	وَعْكَة	national, native, domestic, patriotic	وَطَنِي
roughness, unevenness	وُعُوْرَة	nationalism, patriotism	وَطَنِيّة
attention, care, consciousness, advertence	وَعْي	steadfast, firm, fixed, strong	وَطِيْد
threats, promises	وَعِيْد	furnace	وَطِيْس
rugged, rough, hard, riven	وَعِيْر	function, work, post, duty, assignment, salary	وَظِيْفَة (وَظَائِف)
servile, mean, scoundrel	وَغْد (أَوْغَاد)		

preventive, protective وِقَائِي	intruder, parasite وَغْل
impudence, وَقَاحَة shamelessness, sauciness	clamour, tumult, وَغِي/وَغًى uproar, conflict
fuel وِقَاد	accomplishment, وَفَاء fulfilment, faithfulness
burning, flaming, وَقَّاد heated	payment of debt وَفَاء الدَّيْن
veneration, sedateness, وَقَار sobriety	execution of a وَفَاء الوَعْد promise
talebearer, instigator وَقَّاع	demise, death وَفَاة (وَفَيَات)
protection, وِقَايَة/وِقَايَة prevention, shelter	concord, harmony, وِفَاق conformity
cavity, hole, وَقْب (أَوْقَاب) socket	coming, arrival وَفْد
cavity, hollow وَقْبَة	delegation, وَفْد (وُفُود) deputation
time, period وَقْت (أَوْقَات)	wealth, abundance, وَفْر affluence
overtime وَقْت إِضَافِي	surplus, excess وَفْر (وُفُور)
meal time وَقْت الأَكْل	abundance, profusion وَفْرَة
freetime, leisure وَقْت الفَرَاغ	agreement, harmony, وَفْق accordance
critical time وَقْت عَصِيب	true or exact copy وَفْق الأَصْل
temporary, transient, وَقْتِي provisional	arrival, coming وُفُود
shameless, saucy, وَقِح/وَقِيح impudent	loyal, faithful, وَفِي (أَوْفِيَاء) full, complete, sufficient
burning, fuel وَقْد/وَقَد	abundant, ample, in وَفِير profusion
fire, blaze وَقْدَة	

protection, safeguard	وِقْي	heavy burden or load	وِقْر (أوْقَار)
protector, guardian	وَقِي	cavity, hollow, pit	وَقْر/وَقْرَة
fuel	وَقِيد	occurring, happening, falling, fall, thud	وَقْع
shameless, saucy, impudent	وَقِيح	footsteps, footfall	وَقْع الأقْدَام
event, incident, happening, combat	وَقِيعَة (وَقَائِع)	impression, effect	وَقْع الكَلَام
agency, proxy, representation	وَكَالَة	fall, occurrence, blow, assault	وَقْعَة
news agency	وَكَالة الأخْبار	stopping, standing, stop, halt, pause	وَقْف
advertising agency	وَكَالَة الإشْهَار	wakf, religious endowment	وَقْف (أوْقَاف)
news agency	وَكَالَة الأنْبَاء	cease-fire	وَقْف إطْلَاق النَّار
aspiration, intention, strenuous effort	وَكْد	stay of execution	وَقْف التَّنْفِيذ
nest of bird	وَكْر (وُكُور)	stand, stop, pause, posture	وَقْفَة (وَقْفَات)
nest of a bird	وَكْرَة (وُكَر)	shamelessness, cheek impudence, insolence	وُقُوحَة
thrusting, hitting	وَكْز	fuel	وَقُود/وَقِيد
detraction, decline, loss	وَكْس	venerable, sedate, grave	وَقُور
leakage, leak	وَكْف	occurance, fall, happening	وُقُوع
nest, eyrie	وَكْن (وُكُون)	stopping, halting, halt, stand	وُقُوف
nest, eyrie	وُكْنَة/وَكْنَة (وُكُنَات)		
sure, certain, positive	وَكِيْد		

passion, craving, وَلَع inordinate desire or love	agent, deputy, وَكِيْل (وُكَلاَء) substitue, lawer
madly in love, very وَلِع fond of	undersecretary وَكِيْل الوِزَارَة of state
but, however وَلَكِنْ/وَلَكِنَّ	vice-consul وَكِيْل قُنْصُل
confusion, enthralment, وَلَه fascination,	deputy director وَكِيْل مُدِيْر
utterly confused, وَلْهَان giddy, bewildered	friendship, loyalty, وَلاَء devotion, proximity
entering, penetration وُلُوْج	succession, sequence وِلاَء
prolific, fertile, fecund وَلُود	in succession, وِلاَءً successively
childishness, puerility وُلُودِيَّة	birth, childbirth, وِلاَدَة delivery
overhead and ears in وُلُوع love	the United وِلاَيَات مُتَّحِدَة States
passion, craving, وُلُوع passionate love	power, sovereignty, وِلاَيَة government
wails, mournful (وَلاَوِل) وَلْوَلَة outcry	province, state (وِلاَيَات) وِلاَيَة
patron, friend, وَلِي (أَوْلِيَاء) supporter, guardian, saint	boy, child, وَلَد (أَوْلاَد) offspring, issue
heir apparent, وَلِي العَهْد successor, crown prince	bastard, illegitimate وَلَد الزِّنا child
chum, bosom, وَلِيْجَة intimate friend	birth, childbirth وَلْدَة
baby, newborn (وِلْدَان) وَلِيْد	deception, fraud, وَلْس duplicity
girl child, girl وَلِيْدَة	volt وَلْط

whisky	وِيْسكي	banquet, feast, party	وَلِيْمَة
woe, grief, sorrow	وَيْل	glow, gleam, blink, sparkle	وَمْض/وَمْضَة
woe unto you	وَيْلَك	glow, gleam, blink	وَمِيْض

despair, desperation, utter hopelessness	يَأْس	winch, crane	وِنْش
		derrick crane	وِنْش دَوَّار
desperate, hopeless	يَؤُوس	floating crane	وِنْش عَائِم
o, oh	يا	glowing, incandescent, blazing	وَهَّاج
alas! what a pity!	يا أَسَفاه	glow, incadenscence, blaze	وَهَج
oh, my misfortune	يا حَسْرَتي	blaze, flame, glow	وَهَجَان
good heavens	يا سَلاَم	low or depressed ground	وَهْد
unfortunately	يا لَلْأَسَف	terror, dismay, fright	وَهْرَة
alas!	يَا لَلْحَسْرة	terror, dismay, fright	وَهَل
alas! oh	يا لَهْفَ	terror, fright, dismay	وَهْلَة
persistent, habituated, assiduous	يَائِب	illusion, delusion, (أَوْهَام) imagination, suspicion, apprehension	وَهْم
dry, dried, arid	يَابِس	imaginary, fanciful, presumed	وَهْمِي
yard	يَارْدَه	weakness, feebleness, faintness	وَهْن
astrology	يَازَرْجَة/يَزَرْجَة	glow, glare, incandescence	وَهِيْج
astrologer	يَازَرْجِي/يَزَرْجِي		
jasmine	يَاسْمِيْن/يَسْمِيْن		
signboard, plaque	يَافِطة		

ease, comfort, affluence, left hand	يَسَار	adult, adolescent, pubescent	يَافِع
to the left	يَسَارًا	collar	يَاقَة (يَاقَات)
left-wing, leftist	يَسَارِي	sapphire	يَاقُوت
ease, comfort, luxury, prosperity, wealth	يُسْر	ruby	يَاقُوت أَحْمَر
left side, left hand	يُسْرَى	ripe, mellow, well-matured	يَانِع
Jesus	يَسُوع	dryness, aridity	يَبْس/يُبْس
little, slight, small, shoot	يَسِير	dry, dried, arid	يَبْس/يَبَس
jasper	يَشْب	dryness, rigidity	يُبُوسَة
jade	يَشْم	orphanage, orphanhood	يَتْم/يُتْم
hill, high land	يَفَاع	orphan, parentless, unique	يَتِيم (أَيْتَام/يَتَامَى)
signboard, plaque	يَفْطَة	fatherless	يَتِيم الأَب
adolescence, puberty	يَفْع	motherless	يَتِيم الأُمّ
hill, high land	يَفَع	yacht	يَخْت (يُخُوت)
winter squash	يَقْطِين	ragout	يَخْنَة /يَخْنِي
awake, wakeful, watchful	يَقِظ (أَيْقَاظ)	hand, arm, foreleg, power	يَد (أَيْدٍ/أَيَادٍ)
awake, watchful, circumspect	يَقْظَان	blistered hand	يَد نَافِطَة
wakefulness, watchfulness, vigilance	يَقْظَة/يَقَظَة	manual, made by hand	يَدَوِي
		glowworm, reed pen	يَرَاع/يَرَاعَة
certainty, certitude, assurance	يَقْن/يَقَن	jaundice, mildew	يَرَقَان

uranium	يُورَانِيوم	certainly, surely, assuredly	يَقِينًا
July	يُولِيو	positive, absolute	يَقِينِي
day, time	يَوْم (أَيَّام)	sea, ocean	يَمّ (يُمُوم)
Sunday	يَوْم الأَحَد	pigeon, dove (يَمَائِم) يَمَام/يَمَامَة	
Wednesday	يَوْم الأَرْبِعاء	prosperity, good fortune	يُمْن
Monday	يَوْمُ الاثْنَيْن	right hand, right side	يُمْنَى
the Day of Resurrection	يَوْم البَعْث/التَّغَابُن	right hand, right (أَيْمَان) side	يَمِين
Tuesday	يَوْم الثُّلَاثاء	oath	يَمِين (أَيْمُن/أَيْمَان)
Friday	يَوْم الجُمْعَة	oath of allegiance	يَمِين الوَلَاء
the Judgment Day	يَوْم الحِسَاب	to the right	يَمِينًا
the Day of Resurrection	يَوْم الحَشْر	to the right and left	يَمِينًا وَشِمَالاً
Thursday	يَوْم الخَمِيس	right, right side	يَمِينِي
the Day of Judgment	يَوْم الدِّين	January	يَنَائِر/يَنَايِر
Saturday	يَوْم السَّبْت	spring, source, origin	يَنْبُوع (يَنَابِيع)
the Day of Judgement	يَوْم العَرْض	sulfur spring	يَنْبُوع كِبْرِيتِي
holiday	يَوْم العُطْلَة	ripe, mellow, well-matured	يَنِيع
Doomsday, the Day of Judgment	يَوْم الفَصْل	Jews	يَهُود
the Resurrection Day	يَوْم القِيَامَة	Jew, Jewish	يَهُودي
		Judaism	يَهُودِيَّة
Day of Immolation	يَوْم النَّحْر	iodine	يُود

day after day	يَوْمًا فَيَوْمًا	the Day of resurrection	يَوْم النُّشُور
someday	يَوْمًا ما	very hot day	يَوْم عَصِيْب
daily, everyday	يَوْمِي	memorable day, red-letter day	يَوْم مَشْهُود
diary, day book, daily wages	يَوْمِيّة	Doomsday	يوم مَشْهُود
June	يَوْنِيو	that day, then	يَوْمَئِذٍ